MAY 17 2013

[redacted]

D0857704

DISCARDED

Islam and the Fate of Others

Islam and the Fate of Others

The Salvation Question

ORANGEBURG LIBRARY
20 S. GREENBUSH RD
ORANGEBURG, NY 10962

MOHAMMAD HASSAN KHALIL

OXFORD
UNIVERSITY PRESS

OXFORD
UNIVERSITY PRESS

Oxford University Press, Inc., publishes works that further
Oxford University's objective of excellence
in research, scholarship, and education.

Oxford New York
Auckland Cape Town Dar es Salaam Hong Kong Karachi
Kuala Lumpur Madrid Melbourne Mexico City Nairobi
New Delhi Shanghai Taipei Toronto

With offices in
Argentina Austria Brazil Chile Czech Republic France Greece
Guatemala Hungary Italy Japan Poland Portugal Singapore
South Korea Switzerland Thailand Turkey Ukraine Vietnam

Copyright © 2012 by Oxford University Press, Inc.

Published by Oxford University Press, Inc.
198 Madison Avenue, New York, New York 10016

www.oup.com

Oxford is a registered trademark of Oxford University Press

All rights reserved. No part of this publication may be reproduced,
stored in a retrieval system, or transmitted, in any form or by any means,
electronic, mechanical, photocopying, recording, or otherwise,
without the prior permission of Oxford University Press.

Library of Congress Cataloging-in-Publication Data
Khalil, Mohammad Hassan.
Islam and the fate of others : the salvation question / Mohammad Hassan Khalil.
p. cm.
ISBN 978-0-19-979666-3 (hardcover : alk. paper) — ISBN 978-0-19-979673-1 (ebook)
1. Salvation—Islam. 2. Islam—Doctrines—History. I. Title.
BP166.77.K43 2012
297.2′2—dc23
2011028848

3 5 7 9 8 6 4 2

Printed in the United States of America
on acid-free paper

To my family, near and far

Contents

Acknowledgments

I DO NOT for a moment take for granted the generosity of my mentors, colleagues, and peers. I am grateful to the following professors and scholars for taking the time to review and comment on certain portions of earlier drafts of this book: Sherman Jackson, Robert McKim, Mohammed Rustom, Frank Griffel, Michael Bonner, Alexander Knysh, Juan Cole, Ovamir Anjum, Muhammad Hozien, Faruq Nelson, Aisha Sobh, and the anonymous reviewers. Words cannot begin to express my debt to Professor Sherman Jackson for being an exceptional and phenomenal teacher and mentor, Professors Robert McKim and Mohammed Rustom for their devoted support and their always thoughtful suggestions, and Professors Raji Rammuny and Michael Bonner for providing me with the tools and assistance I needed to devote my energy to this project. I must also thank the following individuals for directing me to or providing me with resources that proved invaluable: Yasir Qadhi, Jon Hoover, Umar Ryad, A. Kevin Reinhart, Lejla Demiri, Mohammad Fadel, Arafat Razzaque, al-Husein Madhany, Jonathan Rodgers, Ahmed K. S. Salem, Suheil Laher, Abdul-Aleem Somers, Joseph Lumbard, and my brother, Omar Khalil. For their helpful suggestions, I would like to express my appreciation to William Chittick, Marcia Hermansen, Edward Curtis, Edward Renollet, Khuram Siddiqui, Mucahit Bilici, Youshaa Patel, Gernot Windfuhr, Jakob Wirén, David Freidenreich, Ozgen Felek, Sara Pursley, Muhammad al-Faruque, Matthew Niemi, Jeffrey Peyton, Anas Mahafzah, Steve Tamari, Robert Haug, Kristina Richardson, Hasan Shanawani, and David Hughes. Needless to say, any shortcomings in this book are mine alone.

I must express my deepest gratitude to Cynthia Read of Oxford University Press for believing in this project from day one. I am also indebted to her assistant, Charlotte Steinhardt; the entire production staff at Oxford University Press, especially Jaimee Biggins; and the affiliated production team at Newgen North America, particularly Peter Mavrikis and Molly Morrison. I am also extremely thankful to the exceptional Valerie Turner of Joy of Editing for her always helpful advice and careful copyediting.

For their warm support, I sincerely thank the faculty, staff, and students of my alma mater, the University of Michigan (Ann Arbor), and my colleagues, coworkers, and students at the University of Illinois (Urbana-Champaign) and Michigan State University. Here I must mention my wonderful colleagues at the University of Illinois Department of Religion and the Michigan State University Department of Religious Studies: Valerie Hoffman, Jonathan Ebel, Richard Layton, Alexander Mayer, Rajeshwari Pandharipande, Wayne Pitard, David Price, Bruce Rosenstock, Brian Ruppert, James Treat, Arthur Versluis, Amy DeRogatis, Diana Dimitrova, Christopher Frilingos, Robert McKinley, Benjamin Pollock, David Stowe, and Gretel Van Wieren. Much credit is due to the superb staff of these universities, especially Richard Partin, Margaret Casazza, Beth Creek, Deborah Ray, Yvonne Knight, Joyce Roberts, Sabrina Sawyer, Jessica Hale, Angela Radjewski, Marita Romine, Deborah Kraybill, and Cody Mayfield.

I dedicate this book to my family, immediate and extended, near and far. Here I must single out my supportive and sagacious parents, Amina and Hassan, and the four people most affected by this project: my wife, Suzanne; our daughters, Maryam and Aya (both of whom were born during the writing of this book); and my youngest brother, Yousuf. I am indescribably grateful to them all for their patience and understanding. This is especially true for my better half, Suzanne—an exquisite and inspiring human being who has taught me much about life. Finally, I must apologize to Maryam for deleting her beautiful contribution to chapter 4: "ggggg."

Conventions

I USE THE expressions “the Prophet” and “the Messenger” to refer to the Arabian prophet Muḥammad ibn ʿAbd Allāh, the central figure in Islam. Unless I specify otherwise, the terms *eternal, eternality,* and *infinite* denote that which is without end, and not necessarily that which is without beginning; *temporal, temporality,* and *finite* denote that which ceases. Furthermore, I freely use modern terminology to describe premodern entities and realities (an example being Ghazālī's “endowed chair”).

Premodern dates are generally written according to the Islamic (*hijrī*) calendar, followed by the Gregorian (Common Era) date. For instance, 11/632 refers to the eleventh lunar year after the Hijra (the Prophet's emigration to the city now known as Medina) and 632 CE. Qur'anic passages are cited numerically, for example, Q. 7:156 refers to chapter (or sura) 7, verse (or *āya*) 156. Qur'anic verses are numbered according to the standard Royal Egyptian edition. My translation of the Qur'an often follows that of M. A. S. Abdel Haleem in *The Qur'an: A New Translation* (2008). Italicized words in Qur'anic verses represent my own emphasis, as the typesetting of Qur'anic Arabic does not include any typographical indications of emphasis. In works translated from Arabic, an asterisk (*) represents the blessings that typically follow references to the Prophet, such as “God's blessings and salutations be upon him” (*ṣallā Allāhu ʿalayhi wa-sallama*).

For the sake of accessibility, I avoid certain abbreviations common among scholars of Islamic studies (for example, b. for ibn). Arabic names are transliterated in full, except when referring to individuals living after 1950 whose names are commonly written in English or who have published works in English. In this case, names are written in accordance with common English conventions, without diacritics (for instance, Yusuf al-Qaradawi, instead of Yūsuf al-Qaraḍāwī). Additionally, Arabic names are often simplified by removing the definite article (for example, Ghazālī for al-Ghazālī, Ibn ʿArabī for Ibn al-ʿArabī, and so forth). When discussing Arabic primary sources, I typically provide a transliteration of the title followed by an English translation in parentheses; if the translation matches an already published title, it appears italicized. After introducing works, I normally refer to them by a single significant word in the title (for example, *Futūḥāt* for *al-Futūḥāt al-makkiyya*).

In general, I follow the transliteration system utilized by the *International Journal of Middle East Studies*. Certain Arabic words that now commonly appear in English dictionaries (for example, *Allah, Qur'an, sura, hadith, Shi'ite, Wahhabi, Salafi*) are typically written without diacritics. A glossary is provided to clarify these and other terms.

Islam and the Fate of Others

Introduction: Rethinking Our Assumptions

The Question

"WHAT DOES ISLAM say about the fate of non-Muslims?" This ubiquitous question has clear and profound theological and practical implications. It also tends to evoke one-dimensional responses. And with academics, pundits, and politicians debating whether we are approaching, or even already engaged in, a "clash of civilizations," there has been a recent proliferation of discourses that present the matter in black and white.

One popular sentiment is that Islam condemns non-Muslims to everlasting damnation. "In this light, the people who died on September 11 were nothing more than fuel for the eternal fires of God's justice," Sam Harris proclaims in his *New York Times* best seller, *The End of Faith*.[1] An entirely different response, less common but gaining currency, is that Islam, at its core, is ecumenical: it recognizes other traditions as divinely ordained paths to Paradise. In his celebrated book, *No god but God*, Reza Aslan makes precisely this point, depicting Jews and Christians as "spiritual cousins" to Muslims.[2]

Further complicating matters for the serious inquirer is the fact that there is a lacuna in the Western study of Islam on the topic of soteriology—a term derived from the Greek *sōtēria* (deliverance, salvation) and *logos* (discourse, reasoning), thus denoting theological discussions and doctrines of salvation. Yet nearly fourteen centuries since Islam's inception, this remains a subject on which Muslim scholars write extensively. And rightfully so: salvation is arguably *the* major theme of the Qur'an.

In point of fact, the question at hand is not a simple one, regardless of whether by "Islam" one means the sacred texts of the faith or the theological positions presumed to be grounded in those texts. There has always been a general agreement among Muslim scholars that, according to Islamic scripture, some will rejoice in Heaven while others will suffer in Hell. But who, exactly, will rejoice, and who will suffer? And what is the duration and nature of the rejoicing and the suffering? These have long been contentious issues—issues that ultimately involve working out the precise implications of God being both merciful and just.

In what follows, I examine the writings of some of the most prominent medieval and modern Muslim scholars on this controversial topic, demonstrating, among other things, just how multifaceted these discussions can be. The four individuals I have selected for my analysis are Abū Ḥāmid al-Ghazālī (d. 505/1111), Muḥyī al-Dīn Ibn al-ʿArabī (d. 638/1240), Taqī al-Dīn Ibn Taymiyya (d. 728/1328), and Muḥammad Rashīd Riḍā (d. 1935). These scholarly giants, whose names and legacies are familiar to any student of Islamic studies, continue to influence countless Muslims, from Jakarta to Jeddah to Juneau. But before attempting to elucidate their thought and assess their place in the Islamic soteriological narrative, we must first explore the nature of salvation in Islam and the attendant notions of Heaven and Hell.

A Brief Introduction to Salvation in Islam

Whether it takes the form of a soft whisper in prayer or a piercing chant before a crowd, the Qur'an's most often recited sura (chapter) is its first, "al-Fātiḥa" (The Opening). In reciting it, believers highlight the role of God as "Master of the Day of Judgment" (Q. 1:4) and beseech His guidance to "the straight path: the path of those You have blessed, not of those who incur anger, nor of those who go astray" (1:6–7). There is a sense of urgency in this appeal. Toward the end of the Qur'an, we read: "By the declining day, humanity is [deep] in loss, except for those who believe, do good deeds, urge one another to the truth, and urge one another to steadfastness" (Q. 103:1–3). The message is unambiguous: people must choose their life paths wisely.

It is God's messengers who bring this reality to light. The Qur'an frequently portrays the Prophet Muḥammad (d. 11/632) (as well as the messengers before him) as a "bearer of good news" (*bashīr, mubashshir*) and a "warner" (*nadhīr, mundhir*) (2:119) to those whom he commands to "worship God and shun false gods" (16:36).[3] Good news of continuous paradisiacal pleasure is given to "those who have faith and do good works" (Q. 2:25), while warnings of continuous anguish in the flames of Hell are given to "those who reject faith and deny [God's] revelations" (2:39). Thus, although both outcomes come to fruition *only* through God's will,[4] the dichotomy between salvation and damnation is closely associated with the distinction between obedience and disobedience and what Toshihiko Izutsu describes as the Qur'an's "essential opposition" of *īmān* (belief, faith, assent, sincerity, fidelity) and *kufr* (unbelief, rejection, dissent, concealment of the truth, ingratitude).[5]

These themes are captured in the following plea to Pharaoh's people by an unidentified "believer":

> My people, follow me! I will guide you to the right path. My people, the life of this world is only a brief enjoyment; it is the hereafter that is the lasting home. Whoever does evil will be repaid with its like; whoever does good and believes, be it a man or a woman, will enter Paradise and be provided for without measure. My people, why do I call you to salvation [*al-najāh*] when you call me to the Fire? You call me to disbelieve in God and to associate with Him things of which I have no knowledge; I call you to the Mighty, the Forgiving... our return is to God alone, and it will be the rebels who will inhabit the Fire. [One Day] you will remember what I am saying to you now, so I commit my case to God: God is well aware of His servants. (Q. 40:38–44)[6]

While there is a notion of salvation in this world (*al-dunyā*), the Qur'anic emphasis is undoubtedly on the next (*al-ākhira*).[7] Indeed, the Qur'an has much to say about Judgment Day, which is referred to as, among other names, the Last Day (*al-yawm al-ākhir*) (2:8), the Hour (*al-sāʿa*) (6:31), the Day of Resurrection (*yawm al-qiyāma*) (21:47), and the Day of Reckoning (*yawm al-ḥisāb*) (38:16). It is on this "day" that "whoever has done an iota of good will see it, but whoever has done an iota of evil will see that" (Q. 99:6–8), for all souls, none of which are born tainted with sin, are responsible for their own actions (6:164). Because humanity is generally prone to err, however, its deliverance, and indeed triumph, is predicated on self-rectification and, above all, divine forgiveness. Thus, the frequent claim that Islam has no concept of salvation because it has no doctrine of original sin is true only if we assume a narrow definition of salvation.[8] When discussing eschatological reward and punishment, it is customary for Muslim theologians, including those examined here, to employ the Qur'anic term *najāh*, which appears in the plea to Pharaoh's people in the passage quoted above and is typically—and for good reason—translated as "salvation" or "deliverance."

Looking to prophetic traditions, or hadiths, we learn that individuals on the Last Day will be required to cross a bridge.[9] Those believers (*mu'minūn*, sing. *mu'min*) who successfully traverse it will make their way into Heaven, which the Qur'an calls the Home of Peace (*dār al-salām*) (6:127), the Lasting Home (*dār al-qarār*) (40:39), Paradise (*al-firdaws*) (18:107), the Garden (*al-janna*) (81:13), and its plural, Gardens (*jannāt*) (4:13). Hell is described by names such as Gehenna (*jahannam*) (3:12), the Fire (*al-nār*) (2:39), the Crusher (*al-ḥuṭama*) (104:4), and the Bottomless Pit (*al-hāwiya*) (101:9), and it awaits sinners and unbelievers (*kāfirūn* or *kuffār*, sing. *kāfir*) who fall.

Underscoring the consequentiality of decisions made in this life, the Qur'an depicts both multileveled, multigated afterlife abodes in great detail.[10] As Sachiko Murata and William Chittick observe, "No scripture devotes as much attention as the Koran to describing the torments of hell and the delights of paradise."[11] While some of these descriptions parallel features of the afterlife according to older traditions, including ancient Egyptian religion, Zoroastrianism, Judaism, and Christianity, we also observe certain characteristics representative of the Arabian environment in which Islam arose. Apart from enjoying the peaceful presence of God (Q. 6:127), Heaven's inhabitants will find, among other things, rich gardens (42:22), rivers (2:25), shade (56:30), green cushions (55:76), superb rugs (55:76), meat (56:21), fruits (77:42), youths who serve them cups overflowing with pure drink (56:17–18, 78:34), and companions with beautiful eyes (44:54)[12]—a clear contrast to the pangs and burning agonies of Hell (22:19–22, 88:4–7), where the wretched will be veiled from God (83:15).

When considering Qur'anic references to the hereafter it is important to keep in mind that many such references are, to quote Michael Sells, "placed in an elusive literary frame that gives them a depth far beyond any simple-minded notion of heavenly reward and hellish punishment";[13] there "is an openness as to what the warning or promise actually means."[14] At the heart of these descriptions—interpreted literally or metaphorically—is the spur to transform and rectify the audience.

But it is precisely the Qur'an's openness that helps to explain some of the more heated debates in Islamic intellectual history. Consider, for instance, that while the Qur'an declares that God "guides whomever He wills" and "leads astray whomever He wills" (14:4), it also states that those who disregard God's message "have squandered their own selves" (7:53) and that their punishment is "on account of what [they] stored up for [themselves] with [their] own hands, and God is never unjust to His servants" (3:182). It is perhaps not astonishing, then, that Muslim theologians have long debated the role of human agency. Without attempting to resolve the matter, it should suffice to note that the vast majority of Muslim scholars have affirmed in varying degrees *some* form of human responsibility, and it is generally presumed that the admonition of messengers can induce a bona fide moral response.[15]

A righteous response is that which is in tune with the pure natural disposition (*fiṭra*) God instilled in humankind (Q. 30:30). According to a traditional reading of the Qur'an, at some point in the mysterious, primordial past, God brought forth all of Adam's descendants and asked, "Am I not your Lord?" to which they replied, "Yes, we bear witness" (7:172).[16] As Seyyed Hossein Nasr explains:

> Men and women still bear the echo of this "yes" deep down within their souls, and the call of Islam is precisely to this primordial nature, which uttered the "yes" even before the creation of the heavens and the earth. The call of Islam therefore concerns, above all, the remembrance of a knowledge deeply embedded in our being, a confirmation of a knowledge that saves, hence the soteriological function of knowledge in Islam.... The great sin in Islam is forgetfulness and the resulting inability of the intelligence to function in the way that God created it as the means to know the One. That is why the greatest sin in Islam and the only one God does not forgive is *shirk*, or taking a partner unto God, which means denying the Oneness of God.[17]

Accordingly, "every community has been sent a warner" (Q. 35:24), a "guide" (13:7), and a "messenger" (10:47), with Muḥammad being the "seal of the prophets" (33:40) sent to all of humanity (25:1).[18] While it is clear that messengers warn of impending doom for the wicked, Muslim scholars continue to dispute over what awaits individuals who never receive this warning, that is, the "unreached." (The verse "every community has been sent a warner" need not mean that each and every person has received the divinely inspired message or that all communities have "adequately" preserved it.) According to the Qur'an, it is *because* of messengers that people will "have no excuse before God" (4:165); "every group that is thrown in" Hell will confess that it received a "warner" (67:6–11); and in a passage that we shall revisit often, God, speaking in the plural, announces, "We do not punish until We have sent a messenger" (17:15). Nevertheless, the Qur'an also states that Pharaoh transgressed *before* receiving the warning of Moses (79:17). Can one "transgress" and still be saved solely on the grounds that one never encountered the message? Or, perhaps more controversially, should we broaden our understanding of "warners" and "messengers"? For instance, some theologians hold that these terms often connote "reason."[19] But assuming that the statement "We do not punish until We have sent a messenger" (Q. 17:15) refers to messengers as traditionally understood (that is, select humans who convey God's message), and assuming that it represents a general principle applicable both to this life and to the next,[20] we are left without an answer to the question of how exactly God will deal with the unreached in the life to come. Similarly unclear is the qualification(s) for being counted among the "reached" in the first place. Is mere exposure to the message all that matters? Or is there more to it?

The Qur'an, through its openness, undoubtedly allows for a wide variety of soteriological interpretations. Although it foretells the ominous destiny awaiting specific figures, such as Satan (Iblīs) (17:61–63), Pharaoh (Firʿawn) (79:15–25),[21] and the Prophet's callous uncle Abū Lahab and his similarly heartless wife (111:1–5), the fact that its warnings are typically general in nature allows for an array of viewpoints regarding the fate of those whose destiny has not been revealed. The question of the status of those innumerable individuals who do not fit, or at least appear not to fit, the Qur'anic categories of righteous believers and unrighteous unbelievers is vexing. The Qur'an refers in passing to those who are in between the two groups (35:32) but never explicitly mentions their fate. It also provides a tantalizingly brief reference to the "people of the heights" (*al-aʿrāf*) standing between Heaven and Hell (7:46–49) but leaves us wondering whether they are outstanding on account of their elevation (on "the heights") or in a state of limbo on account of their being in between Heaven and Hell.[22] It is, therefore, not surprising that Muslim scholars have failed to reach a consensus on questions such as, What awaits unrepentant, sinning believers, particularly those who seem to reflect the rebellious (Q. 72:23), evildoing (37:63), oppressive (78:22) nature of Hell-bound unbelievers? What about "sincere" monotheists who are not part of the Muslim community? Or even "earnest" polytheists, deists, agnostics, and atheists? What *exactly* constitutes salvific belief and damnatory unbelief?

Salvation for Whom?

Like other faiths, Islam has developed its own unique currents of soteriological intra- and, more relevant for our purposes, interreligious exclusivism, inclusivism, and pluralism. I define these terms as follows: "exclusivists" maintain that only their particular religious tradition or interpretation is salvific and that adherents of all other beliefs will be punished in Hell. "Inclusivists" similarly affirm that theirs is the path of Heaven but hold that sincere outsiders who could not have recognized it as such will be saved. "Pluralists" assert that, regardless of the circumstances, there are several religious traditions or interpretations that are equally effective salvifically. This terminology would seem alien to premodern and many modern Muslim scholars, but this tripartite classification—versions of which are commonly employed by many contemporary philosophers of religion[23]—allows us to develop a clearer conception of the Islamic soteriological spectrum. Needless to say, these categories are not monolithic, and I shall examine various subcategories, particularly in those cases where further distinctions are necessary.

Soteriological pluralists often point to Qur'anic passages such as 5:48, which indicates that God never intended for humanity to remain a single community with a single law:

> We have revealed to you [Muḥammad] the scripture in truth, confirming the scriptures that came before it and as a guardian [*muhaymin*] over them: so judge between them according to what God has sent down. Do not follow their whims, which deviate from the truth that has come to you. We have assigned a law [*shir'a*] and a path [*minhāj*] to each of you. If God had so willed, He would have made you one community, but He wanted to test you through that which He has given you, so race to do good: you will all return to God and He will make clear to you the matters about which you differed.

In this light, it is notable that while the Qur'an presents itself as "the criterion" (*al-furqān*) (25:1), it also states that it is only one in a line of divinely revealed books that includes the Torah (*tawrāh*) (3:3), Psalms (*zabūr*) (4:163), and Gospel (*injīl*) (3:3).[24] This is why Jews and Christians are designated as People of the Book (*ahl al-kitāb*), and it is this proximity to Muslims that best explains why the latter may intermarry and share meals with the former (Q. 5:5). And while many Muslims argue as a matter of faith that the scriptures on which contemporary Jews and Christians rely have been corrupted, one pluralist position is that a careful reading of the Qur'an (particularly 2:75–79, 3:78, 4:46, and 5:13) leads only to the conclusion that *certain groups* among the People of the Book "distorted" scripture by misrepresenting its message and supplementing it with falsehoods.[25] An apparent example of this distortion would be the Jewish and Christian exclusivist claim, "No one will enter Paradise unless he [or she] is a Jew or Christian" (Q. 2:111). The Qur'an rejects this claim and promises heavenly reward to "any who direct themselves wholly to God and do good" (2:112). Even more poignant are Q. 2:62 and 5:69, passages that portend the salvation of righteous, faithful Jews and Christians and a mysterious group called the Sabians:[26]

> The believers, the Jews, the Christians, and the Sabians—all those who believe in God and the Last Day and do good—will have their rewards with their Lord. No fear for them, nor will they grieve. (2:62)

> For the believers, the Jews, the Sabians, and the Christians—all those who believe in God and the Last Day and do good—there is no fear: they will not grieve. (5:69)

Reflecting on Q. 2:62, which is probably the most often cited passage in pluralist discourse, Mahmoud Ayoub laments the fact that exegetes have generally restricted its message in several ways, such as declaring it abrogated (meaning that it was revoked and replaced by Qur'anic statements revealed later in time) or accepting "the universality of the verse until the coming of Islam, but thereafter [limiting] its applicability only to those who hold the faith of Islam."[27] Another restrictive interpretation maintains that the reference to Jews, Christians, and Sabians is based on origins, affiliations, or even ethnicity, rather than religion.[28] In a similar vein, many theologians hold that the reference in Q. 5:48 to the divisions within humanity is not a vindication of this diversity, especially in a context in which Muḥammad's corrective message (a "guardian" over the previous scriptures) is made available: Islam alone is the "straight path" to God. This particular interpretation allows for declarations like that made by the famed scholar of hadith and jurisprudence Yaḥyā ibn Sharaf al-Nawawī (d. 676/1277) that anyone who follows a religion other than Islam is an unbeliever and the same applies to any self-professing Muslim who doubts this or considers other religions valid.[29]

Along these lines, soteriological exclusivists often cite the Qur'an's condemnation of the unforgivable sin of *shirk* (associating partners with God) (4:116), as well as its censure of various beliefs and practices of Jews and Christians. Well known is Q. 9:29, which calls for war against those People of the Book "who do not believe in God and the Last Day, who do not forbid what God and His Messenger have forbidden, who do not follow the religion [*dīn*] of truth" until they surrender and pay a tax called the *jizya*.[30] (Needless to say, the precise meaning and implications of this command are issues of debate among Muslims.)[31] The next two verses (Q. 9:30–31) rebuke Jews for taking their rabbis as lords and saying, "Ezra [ʿUzayr] is the son of God" (an ostensibly Arabian phenomenon),[32] and Christians for taking Jesus and their monks as lords and saying, "The Messiah is the son of God." Two verses later, we find the pronouncement that it is God "who has sent His messenger with guidance and the religion [*dīn*] of truth, to show that it is above all [other] religions" (9:33). As such, the Qur'an characterizes those People of the Book who accept what was revealed to them (for example, the Torah) but reject "what came afterward" as "unbelievers" (2:90–91).[33] We are also informed that "any revelation" God causes "to be superseded or forgotten," He replaces "with something better or similar" (Q. 2:106). Accordingly, Q. 5:3—believed by many to have been the last verse revealed—states, "Today I have perfected your religion [*dīn*] for you, completed My blessing upon you, and chosen *islām* as your religion." Most significant in exclusivist discourse, however, are Q. 3:19 and 3:85, which speak of *islām* being the only acceptable religion, or *dīn*:

> True religion [*al-dīn*], in God's eyes, is *islām*. Those who were given the Book disagreed out of rivalry, only after they had been given knowledge—if anyone denies God's revelations, God is swift to take account. (3:19)

> If anyone seeks a religion [*dīn*] other than *islām*, it will not be accepted from him [or her]: he [or she] will be one of the losers in the hereafter. (3:85)

One may object, however, that the Qur'anic conception of *dīn* may not be as rigid as later interpreters have made it out to be.[34] And *islām* (to be precise, *al-islām*) may be understood literally and broadly as "submission" to God (or "the submission"), rather than simply reified Islam. In the words of one modern translator of the Qur'an, the "exclusive application" of *islām* to followers of Muḥammad "represents a definitely post-Qur'anic development."[35] The Qur'an itself uses the term *muslim*—the active participle of the verb *aslama* (to submit) from which *islām* is derived—in a manner that is undoubtedly general in nature. To quote Mahmut Aydin,

> When Joseph demanded to die as a "muslim" in his prayer [Q. 12:101] and Abraham described himself as a "muslim" [Q. 3:67], they did not mean that they were members of the institutionalized religion of the Prophet Muhammad. Rather, they meant to submit to God/Allah and to obey God's orders.[36]

There is in fact more to be said about the role of semantics in this debate. As I indicated earlier, the Qur'an presents *īmān* and *kufr* as opposing orientations with contrasting soteriological consequences. While *īmān* is usually translated as "belief," it also denotes faith, assent, sincerity, and fidelity; while *kufr* is usually translated as "unbelief," it also denotes rejection, dissent, concealment of the truth, and ingratitude. In this light, although the Qur'an rejects certain Jewish and Christian truth claims, one could argue that it only condemns "wicked" People of the Book living in the Prophet's context who recognized the truth of his message yet deliberately denied it (3:70–86), ridiculed it (5:57–59), and rebelled against it—a rebellion that would explain the Qur'anic call to arms. Although "most" People of the Book in contact with Muḥammad are described as being "wrongdoers" (Q. 3:110), what are we to think of the remaining Jews and Christians? Similarly, the scriptural censure of "associationists" (*mushrikūn*), that is, those guilty of *shirk*, could be contextualized in light of the injustices and antagonism that Arab pagans and others engendered in their defiance of the Prophet. In other words, rather than being entirely a doctrinal matter, *shirk* might also connote hubris and insolence against those seeking to devote themselves to God alone. It is perhaps no coincidence, then, that the Qur'an characterizes certain People of the Book—all or some of whom would qualify as monotheists by modern designations—as "associationists" in Q. 9:33, immediately after informing us that they "try to extinguish God's light with their mouths" (9:32) and immediately before noting that "many rabbis and monks wrongfully consume people's possessions and turn people away from God's path" (9:34).

Soteriological pluralists need not maintain that the various, equally salvific religious paths are equally true ontologically. Many pluralists, for example, argue that although Islam and Christianity are just as effective salvifically, the truth claims of the former are superior to those of the latter. Some, however, are willing to go a step further. To quote the Iranian thinker Abdolkarim Soroush:

> The vast scope of insoluble religious differences compounded by the self-assurance of everyone involved gives rise to the suspicion that God may favor...pluralism and that each group partakes of an aspect of the truth.... Is the truth not one, and all the differences to paraphrase [the Persian mystic Jalāl al-Dīn Rūmī (d. 672/1273)], "differences of perspective"?[37]

For those who are not moved by the pluralist project, and also not satisfied with the exclusivist alternative, there is inclusivism. A group I classify as "limited inclusivists" maintain that, among non-Muslims, only the unreached may be saved (even if there is no consensus on how exactly they will be judged, if at all). This is based in part on a generalized reading of the scriptural pronouncement that God does "not punish until [He has] sent a messenger" (Q. 17:15), as well as the following prophetic proclamation (recorded in the *Ṣaḥīḥ Muslim* hadith collection): "By Him in whose hand is the life of Muhammad, anyone among the community of Jews or Christians *who hears about me* and does not believe in that with which I have been sent and dies (in this state), will be among the denizens of the [Fire]."[38]

Limited inclusivists reject the claim often made by exclusivists, especially in modern times, that the category of the unreached no longer exists. These inclusivists may insist that non-Muslims must encounter specific features of the final message—the message in its "true" form (however understood)—in order to be counted among the reached; should they then refuse to submit, they would be considered "insincere."

On the other end of the inclusivist spectrum, "liberal inclusivists" assert that the category of sincere non-Muslims includes individuals who have been exposed to the message in its true form yet are in no way convinced. Thus, liberal inclusivists generally read passages such as Q. 17:15 and the aforementioned "*who hears about me*" hadith—assuming they accept the authenticity of this hadith (most Sunnis do)—in much the same way limited inclusivists (not to mention pluralists) read those verses that condemn Jews and Christians, that is, they elucidate, contextualize, and/or qualify the statements in light of other scriptural passages and assumptions.[39]

The debate among inclusivists, then, revolves around the question, What qualifies as a sincere response to the Islamic message upon encountering it?

For limited inclusivists, the answer is simple: conversion to Islam. For others, the answer is either conversion or active investigation of the content of the message. For liberal inclusivists, if the message were never seen to be a possible source of divine guidance, it would make little sense to speak of a sincere response. But however one qualifies sincere non-Muslims, inclusivists generally agree that these are individuals who never actively strive to extinguish the light of God's message and never take on the rebellious, evil-doing, oppressive characteristics of the damned. The God of mercy and justice, so goes the argument, would surely save such earnest non-Muslims, if only through some form of intercession on Judgment Day.[40]

Such discussions of the fate of non-Muslims have intensified in recent decades. This discourse has fostered a unique debate, particularly evident in the context of Western scholarship, which pits pluralists against inclusivists. At the same time, however, numerous modern treatments of Islam seem to present the exclusivist paradigm in passing, as a foregone conclusion. Johannes Stöckle writes, "The impure who are not purified by Islam shall be in hell-fire,"[41] while Muhammad Abul Quasem affirms that "entry into Islam fulfills the most basic requirement of salvation."[42] Neither Stöckle nor Abul Quasem qualifies these statements, leaving the reader with the impression that salvation is reserved only for Muslims, the adherents of reified Islam. Like many earlier scholars, Abul Quasem also presents a pessimistic view of the Islamic afterlife: on the basis of a famous hadith, he states that most of humanity, 999 out of every one thousand, "will fall down into Hell";[43] however, he adds, since sinning believers will attain "salvation after damnation," it is "only infidels [who] will be suffering in Hell forever."[44] (I provide an optimistic inclusivist reassessment of the hadith on the 999 in chapter 1.) Pessimistic exclusivism is also a common theme in historical portrayals of the earliest Muslims. On the basis of historiographical writings and hadith collections, Patricia Crone argues that the common belief among those factions that evolved into the groups later referred to as Sunnis, Shi'ites, and Khārijites was that salvation could only be achieved through Islam and under the guidance of a single, "true" imam (leader):[45] "Anyone who joined the wrong caravan became an unbeliever (*kāfir*), for there was only one community of believers." Thus, all other leaders were illegitimate and led their "caravan[s] to Hell."[46] This image of a solitary, select caravan stands in sharp contrast to the conception of a faith that embraces and even promotes other religious paths. Despite occasional publications by scholars such as Fred Donner, who presents Islam as an originally ecumenical tradition embracing certain Jews and Christians,[47] this and similar visions of Islam are, seemingly, less popular. This helps to explain why, particularly in recent years, growing contingents of Muslim pluralists have been active in promoting their own paradigms, leading, in turn, to inclusivist rebuttals by their coreligionists. I survey this modern debate, particularly in its Western manifestation, later in this book.

Salvation for the Damned?

While the discourse of salvation on Judgment Day has attracted a great deal of attention, another pivotal controversy hinges on the duration of punishment: are the inhabitants of Hell doomed to be chastised in the Fire for all of eternity, despite the temporality of their evil deeds and despite God's ability to grant them an opportunity to reform themselves at some point in the hereafter?[48] Here, too, we find a plethora of responses in the history of Islamic thought, with theological discussions of the eternality of Hell (and even Heaven) beginning to proliferate from around the second/eighth century.[49] In fact, as we shall see, this may have been a divisive topic as early as the period of the first four caliphs (11–40/632–661). I refer to those who hold that everyone will be granted everlasting life in Paradise as "universalists." In contrast, "damnationists" maintain that at least some will endure everlasting chastisement. Universalists who believe that all of Hell's inhabitants will be admitted into Heaven following a significant period of time—the overwhelming majority of Muslim universalists—will occasionally be described as having interim and ultimate positions (for example, "interim inclusivism" or "ultimate universalism").

It is perhaps only fitting at this point to restate my initial observation: discussions of salvation in Islam have generally been plagued with oversimplifications. One possible explanation for why this is true of modern scholarship is an overreliance on a limited array of Muslim creedal, theological, and popular works. Many of these works present "Islam's position" as follows: while sinning believers may be punished in Hell for a finite period of time, eternal damnation awaits anyone who dies an unbeliever. This belief forms part of the Islamic creed according to theologians as prominent as Abū Jaʿfar al-Ṭaḥāwī (d. 321/933), Shaykh Ṣadūq (d. 381/991), Najm al-Dīn al-Nasafī (d. 537/1142), and ʿAḍud al-Dīn al-Ījī (d. 756/1355).[50] The famous Abū al-Ḥasan al-Ashʿarī (d. 324/935) implies it by stating that only a group of monotheists (that is, believers) will be taken out of the Fire—a Fire that he never characterizes as finite.[51] This damnationism is also presented in a number of Muslim theological works as the consensus, or *ijmāʿ*, opinion.[52] This is extremely significant given the widespread acceptance of the prophetic report that reads, "My community shall never agree on an error."[53] Even so, from an academic standpoint, conscious of the realm of influential historical orientations and textual possibilities, regarding the everlasting damnation of unbelievers as "Islam's position" is problematic. And yet the eternality of Hell is considered standard in many foundational Western academic works that describe either Muslim scholarly views or the Qur'an itself. The following examples serve to illustrate this point:

1. In *Islam: The Straight Path,* specifically in a discussion of the Qur'anic afterlife, John Esposito writes:

> The specter of the Last Judgment, with its eternal reward and punishment, remains a constant reminder of the ultimate consequences of each life. It underscores the Quran's strong and repeated emphasis on the ultimate moral responsibility and accountability of each believer.... In sharp contrast [to Heaven's inhabitants], the damned will be banished to hell, forever separated from God.[54]

2. In *Major Themes of the Qur'an* by Fazlur Rahman (d. 1988), we find a similar account of the life to come:

> The central endeavor of the Qur'an is for man to develop... "keen sight" here and now, when there is opportunity for action and progress, for at the Hour of Judgment it will be too late to remedy the state of affairs; there one will be reaping, not sowing or nurturing. Hence one can speak there only of eternal success or failure, of everlasting Fire or Garden—that is to say, for the fate of the individual.[55]

3. In *Approaching the Qur'án: The Early Revelations,* Michael Sells describes the Day of Judgment as a time when what "seems secure and solid turns out to be ephemeral, and what seems small or insignificant is revealed as one's eternal reality and destiny."[56] Accordingly, we read in Sells's translation of Q. 98:6 that unbelievers will have an "eternal" stay in the Fire.[57]

To be sure, the field of translation can be a theological battleground. As we shall see, much debate revolves around the wording the Qur'an employs in discussing the duration of punishment in Hell and the extent to which it differs from depictions of heavenly reward. Two common word types cited in these discussions are those that have the three-letter root *kh-l-d* (for example, *khālidīn* or *khulūd*) and *ʾ-b-d* (for example, *abad* or its accusative form *abadan*). An expression like *khālidīn fīhā* (Q. 9:68), used in reference to Hell, can be translated as "they will remain in it forever" or, simply, "they will remain in it"; *khālidīn fīhā abadan* (Q. 72:23) can be translated as "they will remain in it forever" or "they will remain in it for a long time." If we assume the latter translation, we are left with a series of questions: does the Qur'an contain *any* categorical affirmation of Hell's eternality? Does the fact that "transgressors" will remain in Hell "for ages" (*aḥqāban*) (Q. 78:23) mean that there is a limit to their stay after all—even if they were guilty of *shirk*? Is the Qur'anic reproval of those Jews who maintained that the punishment in the Fire would only last "a limited number of days" (3:23–24) a forewarning that chastisement is everlasting or that it is just considerably longer? When the Qur'an states that "their punishment will not be lightened, nor will they be reprieved" (2:162), and "they will have no share in the hereafter" (2:200), is it speaking of a temporal or eternal reality? If the latter, is it not possible that such statements are ultimately qualified by God's volition, as indicated by the Qur'anic pronouncement in 6:128 that Hell's inhabitants will remain in the Fire "unless God wills otherwise"? Is the Qur'anic declaration that Hell's inhabitants will remain in the Fire "for as long as the heavens and earth endure, unless your Lord wills otherwise: your Lord carries out *whatever* He wills" (11:107) significantly different from the pronouncement regarding Heaven's inhabitants: "they will be in Paradise for as long as the heavens and earth endure unless your Lord wills otherwise—*an unceasing gift*" (11:108)? (The overwhelming majority of Muslim scholars take the expression "for as long as the heavens and earth endure" to mean "forever.")[58] Leaving aside the Qur'an, what are we to make of reports attributed to the Companions of the Prophet, several of which I examine in chapter 3, which seem to foretell the eventual salvation of Hell's inhabitants? Can they be harmonized with other traditions that appear to affirm the exact opposite? And, from a theological standpoint, is salvation for *all* (including, for example, Pharaoh, Abū Lahab, Hitler) just? Conversely, is *everlasting* damnation fair and congruous with God's merciful nature?

Many modern scholars of Islam have overlooked the fact that the eternality of Hell has long been a contentious issue among Muslim thinkers. To the best of my knowledge, the earliest English academic work to focus exclusively on this controversy is James Robson's article "Is the Moslem Hell Eternal?" Published in *The Moslem World* journal in 1938, the article is a response to the twentieth-century universalist Maulana Muhammad Ali. Robson's conclusion is that the Islamic Hell must be eternal and that this has historically been the consensus view of Muslim scholars.[59] (I examine this debate between Ali and Robson in chapter 3.) Western scholarship has had little to say on the matter since 1938 besides those numerous instances in which the eternality of Hell is assumed.[60] One interesting exception is Jane Smith and Yvonne Haddad's monograph *The Islamic Understanding of Death and Resurrection* (1981). "In general," Smith and Haddad assert, "it can be said that the non-eternity of the Fire has prevailed as the understanding of the Muslim community" thanks to important scholars who took note of the careful wording of the Qur'an and certain hadiths—even though "the vast majority of reports support the understanding of the eternality of the Fire."[61] This is to be sharply contrasted with Binyamin Abrahamov's relatively recent assessment that, despite the presence of detractors, the "orthodox" position has been Hell's eternality.[62] I evaluate these conflicting statements below.

Salvation and God

One important corollary of exclusivist–inclusivist–pluralist and universalist–damnationist discourses is that they allow us to reconsider the nature of the Qur'anic God, the subject of considerable discussion in Western scholarship. Writing nearly a century ago, W. Knietschke describes Him as "an Absolute Despot" whose prevailing concern is justice rather than loving mercy.[63] Along these lines, almost half a century later, Daud Rahbar argues that the Qur'an's "central notion is God's strict justice," and that "all themes are subservient to this central theme"—a theme that is constantly reaffirmed in reference to the Day of Judgment.[64] To this he adds, "God's forgiveness, mercy and love are strictly for those who believe in Him and act aright. Wherever there is an allusion to God's mercy or forgiveness in the Qur'ān, we find that within an inch there is also an allusion to the torment He has prepared for the evil-doers."[65]

Although Johan Bouman states that he is not completely satisfied with Rahbar's study, and acknowledges the fact that the Qur'an is replete with references to mercy, he ultimately agrees with Rahbar that divine justice trumps all other characteristics in the Qur'anic universe.[66] In contrast, Sachiko Murata and William Chittick characterize mercy as "God's fundamental motive."[67] Meanwhile, Fazlur Rahman, who speaks of God's "merciful justice," writes:

> The immediate impression from a cursory reading of the Qur'ān is that of the infinite majesty of God and His equally infinite mercy, although many a Western scholar (through a combination of ignorance and prejudice) has depicted the Qur'ānic God as a concentrate of pure power, even as brute power—indeed, as a capricious tyrant. The Qur'ān, of course, speaks of God in so many different contexts and so frequently that unless all the statements are interiorized into a total mental picture—without, as far as possible, the interference of any subjective and wishful thinking—it would be extremely difficult, if not outright impossible, to do justice to the Qur'ānic concept of God.[68]

David Marshall defends Rahbar and Bouman and argues that Rahman's emphasis on divine mercy is a function of what J. M. S. Baljon describes as a modern hermeneutic strategy that features both a "blurring out of terrifying traits of the Godhead" and "the accentuation of affable aspects in Allah."[69] Marshall maintains, also in agreement with Rahbar, that the Qur'an presents the unbelievers as "utterly excluded from any experience of God's mercy" once this life ends.[70] I assess these conflicting claims below.

It is worth stressing that these discussions are informed by particular understandings of Islamic soteriology. Despite its obvious salience, however, a search for contemporary critical studies on salvation in Islam leaves much to be desired. Many of the currently available works present a particular author's reading of Islamic scripture; when Muslim soteriological discourse is examined, the analyses, with few exceptions, are relatively brief and superficial. It is my hope that the present work will demonstrate the benefits of delving further into this critically important field.

The Question Reconsidered

Each of the four chapters of this book explores the specific views of eminent Muslim scholars on the fate of non-Muslims. This is accompanied by an examination of their methodologies, specifically, how they develop their arguments, employ Islamic scripture, and situate themselves vis-à-vis the larger hegemony of Islamic thought. To be clear, my main focus is Muslim scholarly discussions of the soteriological status of adults of sound mind living in a post-Muḥammadan world who do not believe in the content of the Islamic declaration of faith, the *shahāda*, which affirms both the existence and the unity of God, as well as the messengership of Muḥammad ibn ʿAbd Allāh.[71] Other aspects of Islamic theology and even soteriology are beyond the compass of the present work. Where relevant, however, I address auxiliary topics, such as the line between belief (*īmān*) and unbelief (*kufr*), as well as the fate of those individuals who lived during the interstices between prophets, the so-called people of the gap (*ahl al-fatra*)—a category that includes Arab pagans who died just before the era of Muḥammad's prophethood and were thus not exposed to the divine message, at least in what is considered its true, unadulterated form.[72] These particular discussions become relevant when considering the soteriological status of individuals living in a post-Muḥammadan world who have not been "properly" exposed, if at all, to Islamic scripture. Because my chronological focus is on life beginning with the judgment of the Last Day, I do not examine specific deliberations on the nature of the period that immediately follows death and precedes Judgment Day, that is, the period of the *barzakh*.[73] For our purposes, such discussions generally fail to provide meaningful additional or alternative soteriological insights. I should add that although I take into consideration the environments and periods in which these authors were writing (no one writes in a vacuum), it is not my intention here to provide a comprehensive sense of these circumstances and their influences on each author. Owing to the paucity of historical evidence available, especially in the case of medieval scholars, such an enterprise would be extremely speculative.

As I noted earlier, the four central figures of this book are Ghazālī, Ibn ʿArabī, Ibn Taymiyya, and Rashīd Riḍā. Although quite diverse, this sampling is by no means exhaustive or inclusive of all the major schools of Islamic thought, such as the Shīʿite, Māturīdite, and Muʿtazilite. Nor is it even representative of the diversity of viewpoints within the schools of thought represented here. With regard to milieus, although I reference scholars of various backgrounds, my main selections tend to represent Middle Eastern, Muslim majoritarian contexts. (Even the Andalusian Ibn ʿArabī made his way to the Middle East, where he composed his most important works.) And, needless to say, all four are men. Nevertheless, the authority of these four exceptional, paradigmatic figures extends well beyond their respective schools of thought, and they have long received and will likely continue to receive extensive attention throughout the Muslim world. Their interpretations of Islam, therefore, are extremely and unusually consequential.

Given the importance of each of the four scholars, and the benefits of comparative analysis as a means of evaluating their conclusions, I explore some related discussions by later thinkers, identifying instances of influence, convergence, and divergence. While these are not intended to be comprehensive analyses of all the potential issues that arise from the writings of the four central figures, they nonetheless shed light on the significance of the soteriological claims and contentions that we shall encounter. Chapter 1 focuses on Ghazālī's optimistic inclusivism and includes a brief excursus on the comparable soteriological views of the much later twelfth/eighteenth-century Indian theologian Shāh Walī Allāh (d. 1176/1762). Chapter 2 highlights Ibn 'Arabī's distinctive mystical vision and briefly looks at its impact on Sufi thought, as seen in the works of the Persian Shī'ite philosopher Mullā Ṣadrā (d. 1050/1641). Chapter 3 is a discussion of the writings of Ibn Taymiyya, the controversy surrounding his universalist arguments for a noneternal Hell (including a dispute over whether this was really his position), a response by the Ash'arite scholar Taqī al-Dīn al-Subkī (d. 756/1355), an expanded defense of universalism by Ibn Taymiyya's disciple Ibn Qayyim al-Jawziyya (d. 751/1350), and a strikingly similar twentieth-century debate between Maulana Muhammad Ali (d. 1951) of Lahore and the Western scholar James Robson (d. 1981). Chapter 4 features Rashīd Riḍā's relatively eclectic approach and surveys some noteworthy modern trends, from the famous neorevivalist Sayyid Qutb's (d. 1966) move toward exclusivism to South African activist Farid Esack's promotion of pluralism.

Given the differences in both emphasis and audience, these discussions tend to be uneven. Compared with Ghazālī, for instance, Ibn Taymiyya devotes more of his attention to the question of whether Hell will one day cease to exist. Furthermore, the inclusion of the mystic Ibn 'Arabī might seem out of place in light of his unique esoteric approach. T. J. Winter explains why, in his work, he chose to focus only on exoteric discussions of salvation:

> Islamic mysticism has been excluded, not because it is less normatively Islamic than the [formal exoteric theology] but because of the difficulties posed by the elusive informality of much Sufi discourse, with its tropical and hyperbolic features of poetic license whose

aim is typically to interpret or arouse transformative affective states rather than to chart fixed dogmatic positions.[74]

Nevertheless, Winter rightly implies that were one to examine the esoteric, Ibn ʿArabī would be a logical selection.[75] Given his widespread influence, the inclusion of his vision provides an important additional layer of depth. And while it is true that Ibn ʿArabī's discourse is often elusive, the relevant aspects of his soteriology are sufficiently discernible.

I show that while none of the central figures of this book qualify as soteriological pluralists, neither are they exclusivists. Instead, all four represent different shades of inclusivism. While most leave the door of salvation open for sincere individuals who have encountered but not accepted the final message, Ibn Taymiyya, whom I classify as a limited inclusivist, vindicates only unreached non-Muslims. Yet this constitutes only his interim position, as he, along with Riḍā, favors ultimate universalism: both conceptualize Paradise as the final abode of every single person. Among the two nonuniversalists, Ghazālī maintains that all but a small group of people will be saved, while Ibn ʿArabī argues that Hell's inhabitants will eventually begin to enjoy their stay in the Fire despite being veiled from God—a view that I classify as "quasi-universalism." Thus, all but one anticipate the ultimate deliverance of the damned from chastisement, and in the eyes of all four, *at least* the overwhelming majority of humanity will ultimately enjoy a life of pleasure and contentment.

In demonstrating this, I explain how some of these scholars' views have been misunderstood and misrepresented in contemporary works. I also show that although they were motivated by diverse historical, sociocultural impulses (the precise identification of which is outside the scope of the present work), belonged to various schools of thought, and espoused dissimilar soteriological doctrines, their discussions of the salvation of Others emphasize the same two themes: (1) the superiority of Muḥammad's message, which is often tied to the notion of divine justice and the idea that the way God deals with His servants is related to their acceptance or rejection of His final message when its truth has become manifest, and (2) the supremacy of divine mercy (*raḥma*), which is often associated with the notion of divine nobility and the idea that God generously overlooks His right to punish those who may "deserve" it.

As we shall see, all four scholars seem to portray mercy as the Qur'anic God's *dominant* attribute. This runs counter to the conclusions of scholars such as Daud Rahbar, Johan Bouman, and David Marshall, who instead reserve that description for God's "strict" justice. This also discredits the notion that the emphasis on divine mercy is simply a *modern* hermeneutic phenomenon. What is more, like Fazlur Rahman, most of the central and peripheral figures of this book do not seem to view divine mercy and justice as being mutually opposed. Even when universalists characterize God as being overwhelmingly merciful and not bound by considerations of justice, they may nevertheless assert that it would be unjust for God to punish people in aeternum. This latter assertion is to be sharply contrasted with those of scholars, particularly Muʿtazilites, who made it a point to stress the correlation between justice and unceasing torment.[76] (In fact, the Muʿtazilites often included unrepentant sinning believers among Hell's eternal inhabitants.)[77] Common among the four scholars is the view that mercy is—in either all or most cases—the reason God punishes in the first place: to rectify those plagued with moral imperfections. According to the universalists, chastisement cures all spiritual ills; once Hell's inhabitants submit to God wholeheartedly they will find themselves in a state of happiness—a position that is incompatible with the assumption held by scholars such as Rahbar and Marshall that, according to the Qur'an, divine mercy will never be granted in the afterlife to those who reject faith.

Be that as it may, we have no reason to think that either universalism or quasi-universalism has come to represent the prevailing view among Muslims in general and Muslim scholars in particular. I suspect that Jane Smith and Yvonne Haddad arrived at the conclusion that the conception of a noneternal Hell has "prevailed as the understanding of the Muslim community" for two reasons. First, Ibn Taymiyya's student Ibn Qayyim, whose arguments for universalism Smith and Haddad briefly cite,[78] is a high-profile scholar whose writings have helped shape popular modern movements. Later in this book, however, I show that the intellectuals of these movements have responded to his universalism in radically different ways. Second, Smith and Haddad ascribe the position that punishment is of limited duration to the creeds of the major Sunni theologians Ṭaḥāwī, Ashʿarī, and Nasafī.[79] But as I noted earlier, their statements on God pardoning Hell's inhabitants are strictly in reference to believers and should be regarded as responses to the position maintained by numerous Muʿtazilites and Khārijites that sinners, Muslim or otherwise, will be eternally damned.[80] The material I present in this book corroborates Binyamin Abrahamov's assessment that the dominant stance among traditional scholars has been the eternality of Hell, specifically, damnationism. Yet I part company with Abrahamov in my assessment of the nature and degree of that dominance. Given the enduring influence of the scholars examined here (in general and in matters soteriological), it is problematic, particularly from an academic standpoint, to claim that damnationism represents orthodoxy—unless, of course, one chooses to side with a particular theological group. One would be justified to think of the matter as having been ultimately unresolved, especially since orthodoxy in Sunni Islam is generally based on *informal* authority, namely, the community of scholars.[81] Indeed, there was never a formal council that declared (or could declare) the noneternality of Hell and/or its punishment a heresy.[82] More important, while most traditional scholars have been damnationists, the proportion of those who were not is greater among the leading figures of Islamic intellectual history. Ibn ʿArabī's argument for a noneternal punishment has attracted scores of Sufis, and a wide variety of groups have adopted Ibn Taymiyya's universalism. A crucial component of the latter's argument is the notion that universalism, far from being discredited by appeals to an alleged consensus, can be traced to some of the most well-known Companions of the Prophet. If there is any truth to this claim, it would be an understatement to describe the implications as profound, and this would certainly cast a shadow of doubt over the prevailing reading of Islamic scripture. Whatever the case may be, the doctrine that every single person will one day live a life of contentment is significant enough that it cannot be placed in the same category as other minority opinions that have attracted far fewer advocates. The latter include the view that Hell's inhabitants will eventually perish, that is, ultimate annihilationism, and the rare opinion attributed to, among others, Jahm ibn Ṣafwān (d. 128/745) that both Heaven and Hell are finite in duration.[83] To claim without qualification that eternal damnation is characteristic of Islam is to mask centuries of serious scholarly debate and alternative scriptural considerations.[84]

Likewise, one must be cautious when addressing the seemingly more popular question of whether Islam promotes exclusivism, inclusivism, or pluralism. We can affirm that, while there is no one orthodox position, pluralism in Islam, as in Christianity, has historically been marginalized. The fact that, as we shall see, the inclusivists Ibn ʿArabī and Riḍā are recurring figures in contemporary pluralist works only seems to underscore this point. Indeed, it is not easy to locate *indisputable* examples of premodern Muslim pluralists. Even Rūmī, the Sufi poet invoked by the contemporary pluralist Abdolkarim Soroush in a quotation cited earlier, occasionally makes statements one would not expect from a pluralist, as when he rebukes a man named al-Jarrāḥ for adhering to Christianity rather than

Islam.[85] (If these statements represent poetic license, might not the same be true of Rūmī's seemingly ecumenical declarations?) Even so, it is also not easy to locate *indisputable* examples of premodern Muslim exclusivists. Thanks in large part to scriptural statements such as "We do not punish until We have sent a messenger" (Q. 17:15), countless Muslim scholars have regarded limited inclusivism (the view that the unreached may be saved) as a bare minimum. Even Nawawī, whose ostensibly exclusivist pronouncement I cited earlier, maintains that God will excuse non-Muslims who never "heard" of the Prophet for not adhering to his way.[86] Accordingly, when surveying classical commentaries of the Qur'an, we typically find both that pluralist interpretations are effectively ruled out and that salvation is rendered possible for the unreached.[87]

Now between exclusivists and pluralists, it is perhaps not *as* difficult to identify premodern examples of the former. There is in fact at least one prominent medieval theologian whose proclamations are unmistakably exclusivist: the fifth/eleventh-century Andalusian scholar Ibn Ḥazm (d. 456/1064). His exclusivism, developed in an Iberian context "fraught with *Reconquista* angst,"[88] is predicated on the unusual belief that mere exposure to anything having to do with the Islamic message—even if all one hears are rumors and inaccuracies—makes one culpable for not converting to Islam. Ibn Ḥazm goes so far as to make the baseless, perhaps defensive assertion that this "minimal/superficial exposure" criterion represents the consensus view.[89] What is more, he claims that all of humanity has somehow encountered the Prophet's message and—at least in the case of sane adults—can therefore be considered reached.[90] For a medieval scholar, the combination of Ibn Ḥazm's stringent soteriological stance and his assessment of the facts on the ground is nothing short of bizarre. It is telling that, as we shall see in chapter 1, when a scholar like Ghazālī argues for an inclusivist doctrine that clearly violates Ibn Ḥazm's alleged consensus, he never once bothers to mention this "consensus" view; if there really were anything near a consensus, we would have expected preemptive responses by Ghazālī to his many potential detractors. It is also revealing that Ghazālī wastes no effort to defend a claim that was surely obvious to most premodern scholars: some non-Muslims, especially those living far from Muslim lands, had never heard anything—positive or negative—about the Prophet.[91]

I would hazard that the norm in Islamic thought, even in modern times, has been to recognize the existence of at least some contemporaneous non-Muslims who do not qualify as reached, and that, accordingly, inclusivism has generally prevailed. What is less clear, however, is which form or forms of inclusivism have been dominant. But since inclusivism covers a wide spectrum of orientations, this obscurity is hardly insignificant. Consider, for instance, the case of a limited inclusivist who espouses a minimal/superficial exposure criterion to determine which non-Muslims are culpable, while also holding that, in order to be saved, the unreached must independently arrive at a specific form of monotheism, one that rejects, for instance, mainstream Christian doctrines concerning Jesus. We might consider this an extreme form of limited inclusivism: although it allows for the salvation of some non-Muslims, the line between it and exclusivism appears blurry.

It is remarkable that only one of the four central figures of this book (Ibn Taymiyya) espouses limited inclusivism, yet not an extreme form, and only as an interim position. Again, the other three advocate more liberal versions of inclusivism (of varying degrees), and all four envisage a Paradise that is one day replete with non-Muslims. To be sure, none of these scholars—living in contexts far removed from our own—would have recognized a reading of Islamic scripture that leaves room for the contemporary assertion that "the people who died on September 11 were nothing more than fuel for the eternal fires of God's justice"[92] (and not simply because some of the victims were Muslim).

More important is the following observation: all four scholars utilize most of the same texts (the exceptions being a few hadiths and other reports that usually function to supplement a particular argument), emphasize similar themes, and yet, because of differences in hermeneutic strategies and motivations, arrive at conclusions that are notably dissimilar. The dissimilarities become even more pronounced when one takes into consideration the other positions surveyed in this book. Whatever one's reading, Islamic scripture undoubtedly gives rise to the kind of polysemy that makes the often monolithic characterizations put forth by numerous writers a demonstration of apologetic misrepresentation, polemical oversimplification, or intellectual laziness. Indeed, we would do well to avoid simply echoing a single side of a particular debate, even if that side happens to represent a majority.

"What does Islam say about the fate of non-Muslims?" This question should not be taken lightly, for its implications are far-reaching: how one views the Other affects how one interacts with the Other. While it is true that Islamic law (*sharīʿa*) lays out the rules of proper conduct, its interpreters are scholars whose theological presuppositions undergird their approaches to law. And while soteriology is but one of many factors that govern intra- and interfaith relations, it is a factor nonetheless. A universalist paradigm, for instance, might promote recklessness on the assumption that all will be made well; or it might spur people to acknowledge the good—actual or latent—within every single individual on the assumption that although life's paths are many, they all somehow lead to the Garden. Exclusivists might go to great lengths to win over the hearts of non-Muslims in an attempt to save them; or they might look down upon them as the damned—and treat them as such.[93] By the same token, what "Islam says" about the salvation of Others also affects how Others regard Islam and its adherents. However one chooses to approach the question at hand, I submit that a deeper appreciation of the rich diversity of possibilities is both necessary and overdue.

I

Damnation as the Exception: The Case of Ghazālī

WHEN CONSIDERING THE intellectual heritage of Islam, it is difficult to overestimate the contributions of Abū Ḥāmid Muḥammad al-Ghazālī (d. 505/1111). He is widely regarded as Islam's "greatest theologian,"[1] and some have gone so far as to proclaim him "the greatest Muslim after Muḥammad."[2] Like the Prophet, the scholar who became known as "the proof of Islam" (*ḥujjat al-islām*) grew up as an orphan. Unlike the Prophet, there is no debate regarding whether he was lettered. Born around 448/1056 in northeast Iran,[3] Ghazālī studied in various cities in his pursuit of knowledge, finally settling in Nishapur. There he was trained by the renowned Imām al-Ḥaramayn al-Juwaynī (d. 478/1085), an Ash'arite theologian and Shāfi'ite jurist. Before long, and as a result of his own brilliance, Ghazālī quickly worked his way through the madrasa system and was given an endowed chair in 484/1091 at the legendary Niẓāmiyya college in Baghdad. The turning point of his life, however, came roughly four years later when, after reassessing his intentions, he experienced a crisis of faith. Believing that in his current state he was destined for damnation, he abandoned his prestigious position and began to travel throughout the Muslim world.[4] Having spent much time and effort establishing himself in a scholarly culture preoccupied with reputation, he came to appreciate the limits of human reason and the vitality and vivacity of Sufism's spiritual approach—an appreciation that would later be articulated in his writings and appreciated by a mainstream audience. (This was Sufism devoid of "antinomian tendencies, saint-*cultus* . . . and a total dependence upon a spiritual guide or shaykh.")[5] Having chosen to return to academic life, he eventually became a lecturer at the Niẓāmiyya college in Nishapur; following his retirement, he completed the circle of his life when he moved to Ṭābarān, the very town in which he was born.

As a scholar's scholar, Ghazālī addressed many of the controversies of his time and produced monumental works on a wide range of topics, including law, philosophy, logic, dogmatic theology, Sufism, and his own intellectual evolution. In examining his soteriological views, I shall limit myself to those relevant works that may be safely ascribed to him. As we shall see, he maintains an inclusivism that balances his belief that Muḥammad's message supersedes all other guides to salvation and his profound trust in God's generous mercy (*raḥma*).

The Nature of Belief and the Hierarchy of Humanity

Why have countless individuals rejected the Islamic faith? This was a question that troubled Ghazālī for some time; we find an account of his evolving musings on this issue in the introduction to his spiritual autobiography, *al-Munqidh min al-ḍalāl* (Deliverer from error).[6] Composed during his later years (around 500/1107),[7] it portrays a youthful, inquisitive Ghazālī whose desire for knowledge is piqued by the observation that Christian children tend to remain Christian as they grow older, Jews tend to remain Jewish, and Muslims tend to remain Muslim.[8] As he pondered the purported words of the Prophet that "each person is born with a [pure] natural disposition [*fiṭra*], and it is his [or her] parents who make him [or her] Jewish, Christian, or Zoroastrian,"[9] Ghazālī came to appreciate the extent to which people typically endow their parents and teachers with authority. This revelation led him to contemplate the essence of humanity's pure natural disposition. The fruits of these meditations may be found, among other works, in his magnum opus, *Iḥyāʾ ʿulūm al-dīn* (*Revival of the Religious Sciences*), and a similar Persian work entitled *Kīmiyā-yi saʿādat* (*The Alchemy of Happiness*), both of which he probably completed by 495/1102.[10]

All humans, he declares, have affirmed their belief in God in the depths of their consciousness:

> God states, "When your Lord took out the offspring from the loins of the Children of Adam and made them bear witness concerning themselves, He said, 'Am I not your Lord?' and they replied, 'Yes' " [Q. 7:172]. [And] God states, "If you ask them who created them, they are sure to say, 'God.' " [Q. 43:87] This means that if they consider their state, their souls, and their inner selves, they will bear witness

> about "the [pure] natural disposition God instilled in humankind." [Q. 30:30] That is to say that every human is endowed [*fuṭira*] with faith in God the Exalted.[11]

Yet just as mirrors may become rusty and begrimed, the heart may become tarnished to the extent that it is unable to reflect divine light.[12] This explains why humanity split into groups:

> those who renounced and forgo [their true faith in God], that is, the unbelievers [*al-kuffār*], and those who pondered and remembered, similar to one who has a testimony [*shahāda*] that he forgets due to negligence, and then remembers it. For this reason, the Exalted states, "So that they may remember" [Q. 2:221], "So that those with understanding may remember" [Q. 38:29], "Remember God's blessing on you and the pledge with which you were bound" [Q. 5:7]. [And] remembrance is of two sorts: one is to recall an image that once existed in one's heart but then disappeared; the other is to remember an image that was ingrained in [oneself] by way of the [pure] natural disposition [*fiṭra*]. These truths are quite apparent to those who contemplate, but are disagreeable to those [used] to following authority [*taqlīd*], rather than investigating and observing [on their own].[13]

Thus, people corrupt their pure natural disposition and "forget" their true, primordial faith when they endow false guides with authority and reject those sent by God. And the implications of this rejection are grave. In Ghazālī's theological treatise *al-Iqtiṣād fī al-iʿtiqād* (The middle path in belief), he states point-blank that whoever denies (the prophethood and messengership of) Muḥammad is an unbeliever (*kāfir*) and will remain in Hell.[14] He goes on to declare that "the Jews, the Christians, and the members of all [non-Islamic religious] communities, whether Zoroastrians, idol-worshipers, or others, are all to be considered unbelievers as is indicated by the Book [the Qur'an] and agreed upon [*mujmaʿ ʿalayh*] by the Muslim community [*al-umma*]."[15] What is more, he continues, unbelief (*kufr*) is more pronounced among deists (*barāhima*) and, especially, atheists (*dahriyya*), since both groups deny prophethood, with the latter also denying the Creator.[16] Although the *Iqtiṣād* is the earliest of his works examined here, having been composed by 489/1096,[17] Ghazālī never softens his stance toward non-Islamic faiths and, in fact, elaborates his position in later writings. In the *Iḥyā'*, Ghazālī affirms his belief in Islamic supersessionism:

> [God] sent the unlettered [*ummī*], Qurayshite prophet Muḥammad with His message to all Arabs and non-Arabs, to *jinn* and humans. And by his revealed law [*sharī'a*], He abrogated all other laws except whatever He confirmed from among them. And He preferred [Muḥammad] over all other prophets and made him master of humanity. And He made faith in the attestation [*shahāda*] of the unity of God [*tawḥīd*]—the statement "there is no god but God"—imperfect [if] the attestation of the Messenger—[the] statement "Muḥammad is the Messenger of God"—is not conjoined to it. And He obligated humanity to believe in all that [the Messenger] related regarding matters of this world and the hereafter.[18]

We acquire a better sense of Ghazālī's worldview by examining his unique delineation of humanity in *Mishkāt al-anwār* (*The Niche of Lights*). A mature work,[19] the *Mishkāt* is an esoteric commentary on the Qur'an's celebrated "light verse" (24:35)[20] and on a hadith that speaks of "seventy veils of light and darkness" between God and humanity.[21] Relevant for our purposes is Ghazālī's hierarchical categorization of those veiled from God's light[22]—a categorization that, as W. H. T. Gairdner observes, curiously omits any explicit reference to Jews or Christians.[23]

At the bottom of Ghazālī's hierarchy are those veiled by "pure darkness"—a tier that includes atheists who "believe neither in God nor in the Last Day" (Q. 4:38) and "who prefer the life of this world over the life to come" (Q. 14:3). These are of two types: those who regard Nature (as opposed to God) as the ultimate cause of the universe and those who are consumed with themselves, "living the life of beasts."[24] Ghazālī subdivides the latter into four groups: first, those for whom "sensual delight is their god";[25] second, those who believe that the objective of life is "victory, conquest, killing, and taking captives"—a paradigm that Ghazālī ascribes to certain bedouin, certain Kurds, and "many fools";[26] third, those whose main goal is to acquire "much wealth and affluence";[27] and fourth, those who suppose that happiness comes from the elevation of their standing in society and the expansion of their influence. Included among these groups are those who publicly identify themselves as Muslim while secretly disbelieving.

Above all these are Ghazālī's next category, those "veiled by a mixture of light and darkness," which encompasses three kinds of people.

First are those veiled by the "darkness of the senses." These are people who have gone beyond the "self-absorption" characteristic of the first category since they deify that which is other than the self. These include idolaters; animists, particularly some of the remote Turks who have no revealed law and worship objects of beauty, including humans, trees, and horses; and those who worship fire, stars, the sun, and light. Second are those veiled by the "darkness of imagination," who believe in one God who physically (rather than metaphorically) sits on His throne. These include Muslims on the fringes of traditionalism, a sect once prominent in Iran called the Karrāmites, and those who claim that God is physically "above" (and may descend). Third are those veiled by the "darkness of the intellect's false appraisals," namely, Muslim theologians who conceive some of God's attributes, such as speech, as being somehow comparable to ours.[28]

Even higher are those "veiled by pure light." Although not on the same level as the major prophets, these are individuals who avoid anthropomorphic conceptualizations of God and who have a relatively firm grasp of His nature and attributes. And still higher are those who are completely unveiled, such as the prophets Abraham and Muḥammad, whose understanding of the divine is superior to that of all others.[29]

This schema may appear at first blush to correspond to a continuum between unbelief and belief and, by extension, damnation and salvation. In his other writings, Ghazālī provides statements that support this link. Consider, for instance, his declaration in the *Kīmiyā* that excessive love of this world (a veil of "pure darkness") is the root cause of all punishment in the afterlife,[30] as only those who come to God "with a heart devoted to Him" will be saved (Q. 26:89).[31] But a better understanding of the nature of things (such as the transient nature of this world) need not correlate with proper faith (*īmān*) in God. Was it not Satan (Iblīs) who transgressed against a God he *knew* to exist, leading the Almighty to brand him an unbeliever (*kāfir*) (Q. 2:34)? In a recent study, Frank Griffel maintains that among those Ghazālī has in mind when referring to those "veiled by pure light"—those who are a mere step away from the unveiled—are the illustrious philosophers and polymaths al-Farābī (d. 339/950) and Ibn Sīnā (Avicenna, d. 428/1037).[32] As we shall soon see, Ghazālī regarded some of their doctrines as proof of apostasy. They, unlike the Muslim theologians "veiled by a mixture of light and darkness," could not be considered believers. The hierarchy of veils, therefore, is but a piece of the soteriological puzzle.

To be sure, Ghazālī recognized that only God knows who exactly is or is not a true believer. The designation of belief (*īmān*) made by humans is primarily legal in nature. We can assess whether people's convictions render them believers or unbelievers according to the standard God has established, but we can only know so much about each person's real status before God, let alone someone's hidden beliefs (as some openly profess the declaration of faith [*shahāda*] but completely reject it in their hearts).[33] Similarly, the designation of unbelief (*kufr*) made by humans is limited. Those whom Islamic law classifies as unbelievers may in fact be believers who are unaware of the false or faulty nature of their convictions.[34]

This notion of individuals being one thing according to Islamic law and another in the eyes of God—a nuance that is all too often overlooked in contemporary writings—is made clearer in Ghazālī's inclusivist treatise *Fayṣal al-tafriqa bayna al-Islām wa-l-zandaqa* (The decisive criterion for distinguishing Islam from masked infidelity). Composed around 500/1106,[35] this is a relatively late work by Ghazālī and one that appeared during an era of intense intra-Muslim debates over what constitutes orthodoxy and what qualifies as unbelief. Setting the stage decades earlier, the prominent theologian ʿAbd al-Qāhir al-Baghdādī (d. 429/1037) claimed that any Muslim who departs from Ashʿarite orthodoxy risks not being counted among the believers.[36] In response, Ghazālī argues that true unbelief consists in rejecting one of the three fundamental principles, that is, belief in one God, the Prophet, and the hereafter; or refusing to accept secondary doctrines derived from prophetic reports that are diffuse and congruent (*mutawātir*)—in effect, a rejection of the Prophet's veracity. According to this standard, rationalists (*mutakallimūn*) within and without Ashʿarism, traditionalists (Ḥanbalites), and Twelver Shīʿites could all be considered true Muslims, even if some of their views are problematic.[37] The same, however, could not be said of those self-professing Muslims among the *falāsifa*, the philosophers of the Islamic intellectual heritage, such as al-Farābī and Ibn Sīnā. This is because they denied essential tenets such as the creation of the universe at a particular point in time, bodily resurrection (and physical pleasure in the hereafter),[38] and God's knowledge of particulars, and because they held that the Prophet knowingly taught untruths for the greater good, to benefit the so-called masses.[39]

That Ghazālī took issue with the *conscious, informed* rejection of the Prophet's truthfulness is an aspect of his soteriology that also figures significantly in his assessment of those who do *not* profess to be Muslim. As he explains:

> Unbelief [involves] deeming anything the Messenger* brought to be an untruth. . . . Thus, the Jew and the Christian are unbelievers because they deny the truthfulness of the Messenger*. Deists are

> all the more unbelievers because, in addition to our messenger, they reject all of the messengers. Atheists are even more so unbelievers because, in addition to our messenger who was sent to us, they reject the very God who sends the prophets altogether.... Now, there are explicit texts regarding the [status of] Jews and Christians. Deists, dualists, heretics [*zanādiqa*, sing. *zindīq*], and atheists are assigned the same status on a fortiori grounds. And all of these parties are [associationists (*mushrikūn*)] inasmuch as all of them deem the Messenger* to be one who speaks untruths.[40]

This last line is striking. It is common for Muslims to label Christians "associationists" because of their trinitarian beliefs, and Ghazālī himself presents the trinity as an example of *shirk* (associating partners with God).[41] Elsewhere, however, and without contradicting himself, Ghazālī defends the monotheistic claims of Christians. As they see it, he explains, the three persons of the trinity are simply "attributes" (*ṣifāt*) of the one God. If they "refer to God as the third of the three," they generally "do not mean that God is (numerically) three."[42] What makes the trinity an example of *shirk*, then, is its accompanying rejection of the Prophet's truthfulness in general and his teachings on God and Jesus in particular. It entails attributing divine attributes to what the Prophet taught is not divine (Jesus) and possibly even divine knowledge to oneself.[43] By the same token, Jewish monotheists who repudiate the Prophet would also qualify as associationists. But what of those who know him not?

Returning to the *Fayṣal*, Ghazālī asserts that God's mercy will encompass most Byzantine Christians and Turks, "whose lands lie far beyond the lands of Islam" and whose rejection of the Prophet could hardly be described as informed.[44] This is in keeping with the "high" view of revelation, popular among the Ashʿarites, which holds that only those who have been exposed to the final message in its authentic form are culpable if they do not heed it and adhere to its law.[45] This view, which is grounded in Qur'anic statements such as "We do not punish until We have sent a messenger" (17:15), was even adopted by Baghdādī. Despite his dismal assessment of non-Ashʿarite Muslims, he maintained that those "who infer the unity and justice of God but are ignorant of revealed law" are comparable to conventional Muslims and can attain Paradise. Meanwhile, unreached non-Muslims "who die in a condition of unbelief (*kufr*) because of a failure to make this deduction may expect neither reward nor punishment, although God may admit them to Paradise" through His grace, "just as

[He] does for children who die before maturity."[46] Ghazālī takes this inclusivism a step further in the *Fayṣal* while also providing a relatively specific criterion for the salvation of non-Muslims. In the absence of either explicit scriptural support or known theological antecedents for the particulars of this criterion, it stands as a unique contribution to Islamic thought.

The Criterion

Ghazālī designates three general categories of non-Muslims: (1) those who never even heard the name Muḥammad, (2) "blasphemous unbelievers" who lived near the "lands of Islam" and were thus in contact with Muslims and knew of Muḥammad's true character, and (3) those who fall in between the first two groups:

> These people knew the name Muḥammad,* but nothing of his character and attributes. Instead, all they heard since childhood was that some arch-liar carrying the name Muḥammad claimed to be a prophet, just as our children heard that an arch-liar and deceiver called [al-Muqanna'][47] falsely claimed that God sent him [as a prophet] and then challenged people to disprove his claim.[48]

This third group, Ghazālī explains, is on an equal footing with the first since they were not given "enough incentive to compel them to investigate" Muḥammad's actual status.[49] It is one thing to be well aware of the Prophet's nature and then claim that he lied; it is quite another to make the same claim on the basis of misinformation—the kind of misinformation that may dissuade even the most "sincere." As such, both the first and third groups (those who were never "properly" exposed to the message) will be granted mercy. Otherwise, if a non-Muslim comes to know through diffuse and congruent reports (*tawātur*) about

> the Prophet, his advent, his character, his miracles that defied the laws of nature—such as his splitting the moon, his causing pebbles to celebrate the praises of God, the springing forth of water from his fingers, and the inimitable Qur'an with which he challenged the masters of eloquence, all of whom failed to match it—whoever hears all of this and then turns away from it, ignores it, fails to investigate it, refuses to ponder it, and takes no initiative to confirm it, such a person is a cynical [self-]deceiver [*kādhib*].[50]

It is only these non-Muslims who qualify as true unbelievers on account of the fact that they either lack the motivation or are too careless to investigate the reality of the Prophet.[51] As Ghazālī explains in the *Iḥyā'*, "The reason miracles attest to the veracity of messengers is that whatever is beyond human capabilities can only be the doing of God the Exalted. So whatever is associated with the prophetic* challenge is equivalent to that [regarding] which God [confirms by saying], 'You are correct.' "[52]

As such, Ghazālī asserts in the *Iqtiṣād*, it is part of the nature of the intellect to accept the message once these supernatural elements are known through diffuse and congruent reports.[53] After all, he notes, the Prophet's miracles succeeded in convincing the generality of Arabs, whose belief in Muḥammad was such that they were willing to defend his prophethood with their own possessions and, indeed, lives.[54] Nevertheless, the realization of the truthfulness of the Prophet is ultimately predicated on the purity of the soul. And if the soul is pure enough, he explains in the *Kīmiyā*, it has the ability to see the truth in the Prophet's message without the aid of miracles.[55] Furthermore, the line between prophetic miracles and sorcery is not always clear to most people. What leads to certainty, then, is the way in which the prophetic message touches the soul.[56] The function of miracles is simply to spur people to investigate and contemplate. As for those who dismiss Muḥammad's message after having been properly exposed both to it and to its accompanying miracles, in the *Iḥyā'* Ghazālī likens these individuals to a person who is told that a wild lion is immediately behind him and that his only means of survival is to flee. If at this point he insists on doing nothing until the presence of the lion can be ascertained, then he would be making a foolish mistake and could expect to be devoured.[57] For those who no longer qualify as "unreached," prophetic warnings must be taken seriously, if only for practical reasons.

Nevertheless, in the *Iqtiṣād*, Ghazālī makes it a point to articulate what he considers to be rational proofs for Muḥammad's prophethood and provides rebuttals to those who reject, on the basis of logic, the final message, its universality, and the accompanying miracles.[58] On the surface, it might seem odd that Ghazālī would bother producing arguments addressed to those attempting to debunk Muḥammad's prophethood. Based on his own criterion, they were already properly exposed to the Prophet's message and miracle narratives. One explanation appears in the *Iḥyā'*:

> The Qur'an, from beginning to end, is an argument with the unbelievers.... And the Messenger* did not cease to dispute and debate

> with the deniers. God states, "Debate with them in the best manner." [Q. 16:125] So the Companions (may God be pleased with them) also used to dispute with the deniers and debate [with them], but only when there was a need [for it]. And the need for it was low during their era.... [Disputation] has only one benefit: to protect the [Islamic creed] for the common people and to guard it from the confusions of innovators by various kinds of argumentation, for the common person is weak and is agitated by the argument of the innovator, even if it is unsound.[59]

Since the Prophet's main miracle, the Qur'an, is itself "an argument with the unbelievers" and since he "did not cease to dispute and debate" with them, Ghazālī's arguments and counterarguments signify adherence to the Prophet's example and possibly an extension of the Qur'anic miracle. They also represent an attempt to preserve the Islamic creed among the "common people," as Ghazālī's defense of Muḥammad was probably intended to assist doubting Muslims and possibly guide sincere non-Muslims. This, however, would call into question the inherent persuasiveness of the Prophet's message.

This may help us to understand why Ghazālī has more to say in the *Fayṣal* regarding non-Muslims who do not immediately (or ever) convert upon learning of the Prophet's miracles: those who are "religious and not among those who prefer the life of this world to the hereafter" and are "possessed of faith in God and the Last Day, whatever religious community they might belong to," cannot but be driven to investigate earnestly the final message. Yet even if death overtakes them "before being able to confirm [the reality of Islam]"—Ghazālī never indicates a time limit for completing this investigation and converting—God will be compassionate toward them and forgive them. And this is because of His vast, "all-encompassing mercy."[60] Ghazālī's claim here is somewhat reminiscent of the following passage from the Qur'an: "If anyone leaves his [or her] home as an emigrant in the way of God and His Messenger and is then overtaken by death, his [or her] reward from God is sure. God is most forgiving and most merciful" (4:100).

Ghazālī, in effect, introduces a "fourth category" of non-Muslims: sincere truth-seekers. These, in contrast to "blasphemous unbelievers," will be saved even though they were properly exposed to the message and remained outsiders. Such individuals, far from being unmotivated or negligent in investigating Muḥammad's prophetic claim, are quite unlike

Table 1.1 Ghazālī's Categories of Non-Muslims

First Category (excused)	Those who did not hear of the Prophet.
Second Category (damned)	Those who rejected or ignored the Islamic message after encountering it in its "true" form.
Third Category (excused)	Those who heard only negative things about the Prophet.
Fourth Category (excused)	Those who actively investigated the Islamic message after encountering it in its "true" form.

those attached to this world, who fail "to appreciate the gravity of relgion [*dīn*]."[61] This distinction is crucial to understanding Ghazālī's inclusivism. (See Table 1.1.)

Again, Ghazālī reserves his condemnation for non-Muslims who, after having been properly exposed to Islamic revelation, ignore or reject it without further consideration. This is a point he develops in *al-Mustaṣfā min ʿilm al-uṣūl* (The essentials of legal theory), which may have been composed relatively late.[62] Here Ghazālī raises the question of whether God would excuse ("reached") non-Muslims who reject Islam. The well-known Iraqi belletrist and Muʿtazilite ʿAmr ibn Baḥr al-Jāḥiẓ (d. 255/869) reportedly held that Jews, Christians, and atheists (*dahriyya*) who do not recognize the truth of the final message—as well as those who never come to realize that they should investigate the final message in the first place—will be excused. This is because God "does not burden any soul with more than it can bear" (Q. 2:286). Accordingly, the only non-Muslims who are culpable are the "stubborn" among them, those who recognize the truthfulness of the Prophet yet refuse to accept his message.[63]

Jāḥiẓ's position is not unreasonable, Ghazālī writes, but it finds no support in Islamic scripture. Instead, we read in our sources that the Prophet commanded the Jews and Christians to have faith in him and follow him; when they insisted on adhering to their respective creeds he deemed them blameworthy and even fought them. Although these condemned People of the Book include "stubborn" unbelievers who recognized yet rejected the truth of Islam, they also include many Jews and Christians who blindly adhered to the religions of their parents. These "blind" followers encountered the Prophet's message and learned of his aforementioned miracles, yet they failed to recognize his truthfulness and the miracle of Islamic revelation. According to Ghazālī, it could not be argued that the ability to recognize the truth of the final message is "a burden" that those of sound mental disposition cannot "bear," for God has provided them with intellects that allow them to appreciate the Prophet's proofs. There is, therefore, only one explanation for their failure to see: they have a "disease in their hearts" (Q. 2:10). In other words, their "mental blindness," or their inability to recognize the authenticity of the message, results from their "spiritual blindness," or their refusal to open the eyes of their hearts to the path of righteousness.[64] It is precisely for this reason, Ghazālī adds, that the Qur'an frequently rebukes the "insincere" for their faulty convictions and suppositions: "it was the thoughts you entertained about your Lord that led to your ruin" (41:23); "that may be what the unbelievers assume—how they will suffer from the Fire!" (38:27); "they rely on guesswork" (2:78); "they think they have something to stand on" (58:18); and so on.[65] Again, Ghazālī assumes that these passages are primarily in reference to sane yet "mentally blind" individuals who are unable to recognize the truthfulness of the Prophet. In opposition to this, one could posit that these verses actually refer to stubborn unbelievers who are able to recognize the authenticity of the Prophet yet choose to reject or ignore him and his teachings; consequently, they are ignorant of the nature of things, and God takes them to task for their erroneous beliefs. If, however, we assume that these passages are indeed in reference to the mentally blind, then it is easier to appreciate Ghazālī's larger point: the "earnest" among the reached would never arrive at such erroneous beliefs. They can see. But not everyone sees the same, and the earnest need not convert to Islam to establish their earnestness. While conversion demonstrates acceptance, nonconversion is not synonymous with disregard or denial.

This brings us back to the *Fayṣal*. Although Ghazālī was not a liberal inclusivist, his embrace of sincere, truth-seeking non-Muslims who have been properly exposed to the final message—his fourth category of non-Muslims—places him beyond the pale of limited inclusivism. Among the reached, conversion to Islam is not the only path to salvation; also salvific is the sincere willingness to investigate the truth claims of Islamic revelation. It is for God to determine whether the truth-seeker should arrive at the whole truth in this life.

As we shall soon see, we have reason to believe that the category of truth-seeking non-Muslims may well be numerically significant. But the manner in which Ghazālī describes them in the *Fayṣal* leaves unresolved the question of whether he conceives of God's mercy as extending to those truth-seekers who do not regard themselves as monotheists. As I noted earlier, Ghazālī asserts in passing that "religious" non-Muslims, possessing "faith in God and the Last Day," would feel obligated to investigate the final message after encountering it. But this reference to "faith in God and the Last Day" is never explicitly presented as a prerequisite for the salvation of sincere non-Muslims.

Addressing this question requires that we first determine Ghazālī's position regarding *unreached* polytheists, deists, agnostics, and atheists. That is, we have to establish whether his belief in divine mercy encompassing the first and third categories of non-Muslims is somehow restricted. By the same token, we must determine if there are exceptions to his depiction of atheists as bona fide unbelievers who have forgotten their primordial faith.

As Ghazālī indicates elsewhere, abstract proofs are not required for establishing belief in God.[66] Nevertheless, he concedes that, on occasion, some have attained faith through such proofs.[67] Ghazālī himself develops teleological arguments for the existence of God and is remembered today as a strong advocate of the cosmological argument.[68] This is in keeping with his conviction that the intellect (*ʿaql*) is capable of contemplating God and, thus, His existence.[69] We are led to believe, therefore, that one need not have recourse to revelation to recognize the reality that is God. As for the Last Day, Ghazālī devotes more lines to rebutting deniers than providing proofs. Belief in the hereafter, he proclaims, is "obligatory"; like the "first creation," "restoring life after death" is logically within God's abilities. What could possibly hinder a second creation?[70] When Ghazālī does make the case for belief in the afterlife, scripture figures prominently.[71] Yet even if a lack of faith in both God and the Last Day were deemed unnatural and illogical in the absence of revelation, this need not translate into soteriological consequences.

Delving further, we find that Ghazālī in fact leaves the door of hope open for certain nonmonotheists. This becomes evident when we examine the *Mustaṣfā*, specifically, his response to certain Muʿtazilites on the question of whether the intellect can comprehend the goodness or detestability of a particular act, independent of revelation (*al-ḥusn wa-l-qubḥ al-ʿaqliyān*). Taking the position that all moral judgments not grounded in scripture are driven by subjective biases and preferences, Ghazālī disavows the notion of intelligible moral essences.[72] Accordingly, it is unguided reason that leads to the erroneous conclusion that lying and killing, for example, are inherently evil. Yet this would mean that lying to save the Prophet's life and establishing execution as a punishment for certain crimes are morally objectionable—a conclusion that the Islamic tradition opposes, according to Ghazālī. Additionally, the very existence of widespread disagreement among intellectuals over numerous moral issues undermines the notion that people have a priori knowledge of good and evil. And even when there is widespread agreement, there typically exist multifarious interpretations of the very thing agreed upon, as moral convictions are complex and based on considerations that vary significantly from person to person. As such, revelation provides the only reliable source of moral guidance; in its absence, it is self-interest, not reason, that drives people's moral judgments.[73] By extension, it is not unguided reason that leads to salvation but, rather, the following of prophets whose authenticity is supported by miracles.[74]

Given Ghazālī's dismissal of the intellect as a reliable source of moral truths, emphasis on psychology, and recognition that people tend to maintain the core beliefs with which they are raised, it would have been curious if he had insisted that the truly unreached—those who have never been properly exposed to any form of revelation—must—as a moral responsibility—have faith in God and the Last Day. In truth, Ghazālī held that in the absence of revelation, one is under no obligation to thank God or to know Him truly—primordial faith notwithstanding.[75] In this vein, Ghazālī's reference in the *Fayṣal* to Turks "whose lands lie far beyond the lands of Islam" as an example of non-Muslims who will be saved is telling. These would likely include the remote Turkic tribes who, as he claims in the *Mishkāt*, worshiped animate objects and who, unlike the Christian monotheists of Byzantium, would qualify as pagans. They would not, however, qualify as damnable associationists, precisely because their paganism was not accompanied by knowledge of any form of the message.

This brings us back to the question of whether Ghazālī's soteriology could tolerate reached nonmonotheists, particularly those who actively investigate the message (rather than reject or ignore it). Ghazālī never provides us with an explicit answer. Perhaps he was agnostic about this matter, preferring to remain on solid ground by providing as an example of his fourth category of non-Muslims those truth-seekers who had already accepted two of the three fundamental principles, that is, belief in one God and the hereafter. He was certainly mindful of the Qur'anic promise that "the Jews, the Christians, and the Sabians—*all those who believe in God and the Last Day and do good*—will have their rewards with their Lord. No fear for them, nor will they grieve" (2:62).[76] Nevertheless, support for an *unqualified* fourth category of non-Muslims may be derived from Ghazālī's soteriological optimism, to which we now turn.

Sanguine Expectations

Everlasting pleasure will be the norm and eternal torment the exception, so argues Ghazālī in the *Fayṣal*. This may appear to be an unwarranted view of the afterlife in light of certain ostensibly pessimistic prophetic reports, such as the famous hadith on the 999: God will say to Adam on Judgment Day, "O Adam, send forth from your progeny the party of the Fire [*baʿth al-nār*]." Adam will ask, "How many, my Lord?" God will respond, "999 out of every one thousand."[77] Responding to his imaginary interlocutor, Ghazālī submits that while this hadith is authentic, the phrase "party of the Fire" should not be taken to refer to "unbelievers who will remain in the Fire [forever]."[78] Instead, it refers to those who deserve to be sentenced to the Fire because of their sins; however, because of the well-attested "magnitude of God's mercy," these individuals may be "diverted from the path to Hell by an act of intercession," as a number of hadiths indicate.[79] Another pessimistic report examined in the *Fayṣal* states that the Prophet's "community will divide into seventy-odd sects, only one of which will be saved."[80] According to Ghazālī, "saved" here means not encountering Hell, requiring intercession, or being made to account for one's deeds, for one could not be considered truly "saved" if one had to endure any form of humiliation—a view that mirrors the well-known prophetic statement, "Whoever is made to account for his [or her] deeds has [in effect] been punished."[81] What is more, Ghazālī observes, there are different, less popular versions of the hadith on the sects, one of which states that "only one of them will perish." Another declares that "all of them are in Paradise except the heretics [*zanādiqa*]," who, Ghazālī clarifies, constitute only one sect. Thus, he argues, if we take these variants into consideration, this would mean that those who "perish" are those who will continue to dwell in Hell.[82] Others will remain in it for an amount of time proportionate to the "extent of the erroneousness of their beliefs and unsanctioned innovations, as well as the plentitude or paucity of their sins."[83] The key distinction between these two groups bound for Hell is that the former (the eternally damned) affirmed the possibility that the Prophet could speak untruths "in pursuit of some [putative] common good [*maṣlaḥa*]"[84]—an implicit yet obvious jab at the philosophers (*falāsifa*).

One can imagine Ghazālī's opponents taking issue with his employment of variant reports in making his case, especially as the sounder version is ostensibly more accommodating to their (the opponents') position.

To bolster his case for soteriological optimism, Ghazālī cites the following hadith narrated by the Prophet's wife ʿĀʾisha (d. 58/678):

> One night I noticed that the Prophet* was missing. So I searched for him and found him in a vestibule, praying. Upon his head I saw three lights. When he completed his prayer he said, "Who's there?" I replied, "ʿĀʾisha, O messenger of God." "Did you see the three lights?" he asked. "Yes, messenger of God." Thereupon he said, "A visitor came to me from my Lord bearing the good news that God will cause seventy thousand people from my community to enter Paradise with no account of their deeds being taken and no punishment exacted from them. Then another visitor came in the second light and informed me that for every one of this seventy thousand God will cause seventy thousand from my community to enter Paradise with no account of their deeds being taken and no punishment exacted from them. Then another visitor from my Lord came in the third light and informed me that for every one of this seventy thousand God will cause another seventy thousand from my community to enter Paradise with no account of their deeds being taken and no punishment exacted from them." To this I replied, "O messenger of God, your community will not reach this number." To this he answered, "It will be reached by including bedouin who neither fasted nor prayed."[85]

While this report singles out Muḥammad's "community," Ghazālī deduces that "God's mercy will encompass many bygone communities as well, even if most of them may be briefly exposed to the [Fire] for a second or an hour or some period of time, by virtue of which they earn the title, 'party of the [Fire].'"[86] As Ghazālī insists, God's compassion is vast and cannot be measured "with the adumbrative scales of formal reasoning."[87] And since the afterlife is "ever so close to this world," as indicated by Q. 31:28 ("Both the creation and the resurrection of all of you are like a single being"), he introduces another reason to be optimistic:

> Just as most people in the world enjoy health and material well-being or live in enviable circumstances, inasmuch as, given the choice, they would choose life over death and annihilation, and just as it is rare for even a tormented person to wish for death, so too

> will it be rare for one to dwell in the Fire forever, compared with [the number of] those who will be saved outright and those who will ultimately be taken out of the Fire. And none of this, it should be noted, is a function of God's attribute of mercy having changed in any way due to changes in our circumstances. It is simply the fact of our being in this world or in the hereafter that changes. Otherwise, there would be no meaning to the statement of the Prophet*: "The first thing God inscribed in the First Book was, 'I am God. There is no god but Me. My mercy outstrips My wrath. Thus, whoever says, "There is no god but God and Muḥammad is His servant and messenger," for him is Heaven.'"[88]

As this passage in the *Fayṣal* indicates that everlasting damnation will be "rare," and appears almost immediately after Ghazālī's interreligious inclusivist proclamations, his goal here is simply to highlight the predominance of divine mercy, rather than use the prophetic report cited at the end of this passage as evidence for an optimism limited to those who recognize the messengership of Muḥammad.

But is there really textual support for Ghazālī's position? Leaving aside the aforementioned hadiths on the sects and the 999, we are still left with Qur'anic statements that may seem difficult to reconcile with Ghazālī's optimism. For instance, the Prophet is informed that "however eagerly you may want them to, most people will not believe" (Q. 12:103); he is instructed to say, "Travel through the land, and see how those before you met their end—most of them were associationists [*mushrikīn*]" (Q. 30:42). Nevertheless, it is not difficult to imagine how Ghazālī would approach these and similar passages:[89] when the Qur'an states that "most people will not believe" (12:103), it is referring to a particular group during a particular era, in this case, Meccans at the time of revelation. Furthermore, "those before you," most of whom were "associationists" (Q. 30:42), are specific ancient communities that received and spurned the message delivered by pre-Muḥammadan prophets and whose fate is recounted in the Qur'an. In this light, such passages need not undermine a vision of mercy for the multitudes.

Ghazālī's apparent confidence in his soteriological outlook might surprise those familiar with his other writings. For instance, in more than one place, he stresses divine omnipotence through a common Ashʿarite argument: God is not bound either to reward the obedient or to chastise the disobedient.[90] But here we must distinguish between what is possible and what is probable. The proclamations in the *Fayṣal* reflect one of Ghazālī's recognized characteristics: "He expounds the religious argument from probability."[91]

Those who have carefully examined Ghazālī's corpus might also detect what at least appear to be discrepancies between the *Fayṣal* and some of his other works. For instance, in the *Iḥyā'* Ghazālī comments that the Qur'anic passage "Every one of you will approach [Hell]" (19:71) is "almost explicit" (*ka-l-ṣarīḥ*) in declaring that punishment "definitely" awaits "all, since no believer has never committed a sin."[92] Meanwhile, in the *Fayṣal*, which is a later work, Ghazālī writes that one out of every one thousand "enjoys divine protection from committing sin altogether."[93] He goes on to explain that while such individuals are absolutely safe from chastisement, those taken to account or requiring intercession are, in effect, "punished" despite not having spent even a second in Hell. It is not impossible to harmonize these seemingly incongruous statements: it is conceivable that the quotation from the *Iḥyā'* implicitly excludes the elect (the outstanding one out of every one thousand) and accounts for all forms of punishment, physical or otherwise, continuous or brief.

Be that as it may, it is widely recognized that Ghazālī's writings occasionally appear discordant. This is because, naturally, his views evolved over time, and he wrote for different audiences and had to negotiate between competing considerations.[94] It is, therefore, important to stress that the *Fayṣal* is a mature work, its case for optimism is clearly laid out, and we have no evidence that Ghazālī ever abandoned the soteriological outlook presented therein.

Revisiting the Criterion

Returning to Ghazālī's discussion of specifically non-Muslim salvation, although one may find his inclusivist exposition in the *Fayṣal* compelling, it is not without its shortcomings. For instance, Ghazālī presents proper exposure to the message as being correlated to a person's proximity to the "lands of Islam"; however, this is questionable, as one would expect a greater intensity of polemical discourse among certain non-Muslims residing nearer to these regions. Such polemics could even flourish within the abode of Islam because of the relative isolation of certain non-Muslim communities, particularly in cities where governments could enforce segregation. To quote Albert Hourani, "there remained a gulf of ignorance and prejudice" between Muslims and non-Muslims in these regions.[95]

It is certainly possible that a sizable portion of such segregated non-Muslims habitually heard that the Prophet was an "arch-liar" and were never properly exposed to his reported miracles.

This leads to another problem: Ghazālī's framework appears to contain a troubling double standard. As I noted earlier, Ghazālī criticizes non-Muslims who reject the message out of blind adherence to authority. Yet in the *Iḥyāʾ* he states that if one were raised in a household that adhered to Islam and simply continued to adhere to the religion without any investigation or contemplation (because of blind adherence to authority), then he or she would be saved in the hereafter, for "the revealed law [*al-sharʿ*] did not obligate the uncivilized bedouin [to do] anything more than maintain firm faith in the apparent meaning of [the articles of faith]."[96] Later in the *Iḥyāʾ*, Ghazālī writes:

> The hearts of Jews and Christians are also assured by what they hear from their fathers and mothers; however, they believe in that which is erroneous [simply] because error was presented to them. Muslims [however] believe in that which is true, not because of their examination [into the matter], but because the true word was presented to them.[97]

As such, and given Ghazālī's recognition of the prevalence of blind faith, according to his framework, merely being raised in a non-Muslim household is generally disadvantageous. Along these lines, the soteriology expounded in the *Fayṣal* fails to address the question of why God would not simply direct sincere non-Muslims to the message in the first place. Since the Qur'an declares, "We shall be sure to guide to Our ways those who strive hard for Our cause" (29:69), one might suppose that the mere fact that non-Muslims were never guided to the religion of Muḥammad is an indication of their standing before God. In fact, Ghazālī himself makes statements that could be cited to confirm this supposition. He asserts, for instance, that God grants religious knowledge and guidance to those whom He loves,[98] which is significant since eternal bliss can only be attained through "knowledge and good deeds," the former being the only means of recognizing the proper manner of performing the latter.[99] He also states that those who are ignorant of God will be miserable after death.[100] Perhaps such statements were intended to be qualified; perhaps Ghazālī's notion of religious knowledge ultimately transcends any discussion of reified Islam. But consider the following: Ghazālī never explicitly describes how non-Muslims of the first and third categories (the unreached) would be tested and judged (we know that the reached are at least expected to investigate actively the reality of the message); his only claim is that they will receive mercy. Thus, for all of Ghazālī's emphasis on following the Prophet and holding beliefs that are in line with scripture, there appears to be a tension in his view of revelation: the message is at once significant and insignificant. Given that some of its significance lies in the fact that it functions as a justification for chastisement, ignorance, in this case, *is* bliss, while simple knowledge of the message is potentially dangerous.[101]

Yet even if God saves non-Muslims of the first, third, and fourth categories, does this necessarily mean that they will find themselves among the believers in Paradise? In the *Iḥyāʾ*, Ghazālī makes a distinction between "those who will attain success" (*al-fāʾizūn*) and "those who will be saved" (*al-nājūn*).[102] While the former are Heaven-bound, the latter will inhabit the limbo of "the heights" (*al-aʿrāf*) between Heaven and Hell—an understanding of "saved" that differs from what we encountered in Ghazālī's assessment of the hadith on the sects.

The notion of the limbo of the heights, popular in Islamic thought, is derived from Q. 7:46–49:

> A barrier divides [the people of Heaven and the people of Hell] with men on its heights recognizing each group by their marks: they will call out to the people of the Garden, "Peace be with you!"—they will not have entered, but they will be hoping. And when their glance falls upon the people of the Fire, they will say, "Our Lord, do not let us join the evildoers!"—and the people of the heights will call out to certain men they recognize by their marks, "What use were your great numbers and your false pride? And are these the people you swore God would never bless? [Now these people are being told], 'Enter the Garden! No fear for you, nor shall you grieve.'"[103]

The inhabitants of these heights, Ghazālī writes, include "those who never received the call" of the message, the "insane," the mentally impaired, and the deceased "children of unbelievers"—people who, given their limitations, neither obeyed nor disobeyed God during this life.[104] (Ghazālī is quick to point out that while there is some uncertainty regarding the fate of children due to conflicting evidence from the hadith corpus,[105] the same cannot be said regarding the very notion of the heights.)[106] Yet the *Fayṣal*, which was composed after the *Iḥyāʾ*, never once references the heights and never once suggests that the unreached (or anyone for that matter) will be in a state of limbo. The reader of the *Fayṣal* might just as well assume that those who are saved from torment immediately find themselves in Heaven. But assuming that Ghazālī never abandoned his belief in the limbo state, he, like many of his peers, likely held that the inhabitants of the heights will eventually join the "people of Paradise" through divine mercy or prophetic intercession—a common claim in exegetical discussions of Q. 7:46–49.[107] Based on this understanding, the heights might be regarded as a temporary location, a purgatory of sorts, where non-Muslims of the first and third (and possibly fourth) categories (as well as the other groups mentioned by Ghazālī in the *Iḥyāʾ*) would be tested and given opportunities to grow. Whatever the case may be, again, the end result, as Ghazālī explains in the *Fayṣal*, is that most people in the afterlife will ultimately be pleased.

"Those Who Will Perish"

What, then, of the minority who will not be pleased? Like other Ashʿarites, Ghazālī maintains that true unbelievers will remain in Hell "forever" (*ʿalā al-taʾbīd*).[108] (Since he gives no explicit indication otherwise, we shall assume that he uses words such as *taʾbīd*, which is derived from the three-letter root *ʾ-b-d*, to denote eternality.) Nevertheless, he occasionally makes statements one would expect from a universalist, particularly in his treatise *al-Maqṣad al-asnā fī sharḥ asmāʾ Allāh al-ḥusnā* (The noblest aim in explaining the ninety-nine most beautiful names of God), which was composed sometime between 490/1097 and 499/1106.[109] In his exposition of the two divine names recited before nearly every sura, the Compassionate (al-Raḥmān) and the Caring (al-Raḥīm),[110] Ghazālī discusses the purpose of divine punishment—a discussion incidentally not found in his teacher Juwaynī's exposition of these same two names.[111] Compassion and punishment, Ghazālī writes, may be reconciled if we consider the parable of an ill child: although the child's mother, due to her maternal compassion, may seek to prevent him from being cupped, it is actually the father's decision to have the child cupped that is more prudent and thus most compassionate.[112] Likewise, the fact that God occasionally punishes His servants and causes them to feel pain does not detract from His being most merciful. Ghazālī insists, "There is no harm [*sharr*] in existence but that it has good [*khayr*] within it," even if that good is not apparent. The amputation of a festering hand may appear to be nothing more than a harmful act, but it is in reality beneficial, and indeed necessary, for the well-being of the body.[113] One must not confuse objectives: the preservation of the body is the essential concern, while the amputation is simply the means of achieving this end. It is in this context that Ghazālī cites the aforementioned prophetic report that quotes God as saying, "My mercy outstrips My wrath." As Ghazālī explains, God's wrath is His will (*irāda*) for harm (*sharr*), while His compassion is His will for good (*khayr*). Yet He wills both good and evil for the sake of the good within each—an aspect of Ghazālī's theodicy of optimism that is derived from one of the very philosophers he criticizes most vehemently: Ibn Sīnā.[114] Thus, what is good is essential and what is evil is incidental. If the good within an evil act is indiscernible, it is because of the intellect's limitations—the same limitations that, according to Ghazālī, lead a child to see cupping as evil and an ignoramus to see retaliatory execution as "pure evil," whereas in reality, both are "pure good."[115]

If God's wrath is in fact a merciful treatment and pure good, this leaves unanswered the question, What is good about eternal damnation? If the purpose of Hell is to cleanse its inhabitants of all their moral ills, why make it everlasting? Is not everlasting chastisement futile in this case? Although one might be tempted to read Ghazālī's statements in the *Maqṣad* as implicit support for universalism, as we shall soon see, one need not assume that the only kind of good within wrath is treatment or that everyone is treatable.

Ghazālī's belief in everlasting damnation is made evident in the *Iḥyā'* in his delineation of four categories of people in the hereafter: (1) "those who will perish" (*al-hālikūn*), (2) "those who will be punished" (*al-mu'adhdhabūn*), (3) "those who will be saved" (*al-nājūn*), and (4) "those who will attain success" (*al-fā'izūn*).[116] Having already discussed the latter two, we turn our attention to the former two. The first group, "those who will perish," includes "unbelievers [*al-jāḥidūn*] and those who have turned away [from faith] and devoted themselves to this life, disbelieving in God, His prophets, and His books."[117] By "perish," Ghazālī means "be destroyed," not "cease to exist." This group will be forever deprived of divine compassion and therefore miserable, as "happiness in the afterlife is [the result of] nearness to God."[118] The evidence from the Qur'an and hadith corpus regarding their demise, Ghazālī asserts, is staggering. Although it is true that not all unbelievers are at the same level (that is, some assassinate prophets and saints and fornicate, while others live uneventful lives), in all cases, true unbelief (*kufr*) leads to everlasting destruction in the Fire.[119] In the *Fayṣal*, Ghazālī describes "those who will perish" as the eternally damned individuals "of whom there is no hope of reforming. For no good can be expected of [them] after [they perish]."[120] This is congruous with a particular reading of the Qur'anic pronouncement that if unbelievers sentenced to Hell "were brought back [to this life], they would only return to the very thing that was forbidden to them" (6:28). In contrast, "those who will be punished," a group consisting of sinners who possess a minimal level of faith, "will be taken out of the Fire after vengeance has been obtained";[121] the duration of their corrective punishment will last anywhere from a single moment to seven thousand years.[122] Hence, "by the grace of God the Exalted, no [true] monotheist will remain in Gehenna [*jahannam*]."[123] (Owing to their "false" beliefs and rejection of God's final message, Ghazālī's second category of non-Muslims would not qualify here as true monotheists, even if they were, for example, Jewish.)

Given Ghazālī's distinction between "those who will perish" and "those who will be punished," one can assume that his discussion in the *Maqṣad* of chastisement being a merciful corrective does not apply to all. Accordingly, what is "good" about everlasting punishment is that it establishes God's justice and omnipotence ("what God wills, is"),[124] and the more the inhabitants of Hell suffer, the more the inhabitants of Heaven appreciate their blessings.[125] As for "those who will perish," given their separation from the divine, they will experience "absolute suffering."[126] Thus, according to Ghazālī, the notion of God's mercy outstripping His wrath does not entail the kind of overwhelming mercy ascribed to Him by universalists.

Yet I would be remiss not to mention Ghazālī's cryptic conclusion to his exposition of the divine names, the Compassionate and the Caring:

> Never doubt that [God] is "the most merciful of the merciful" [Q. 7:151], or that "His mercy outstrips His wrath," and never doubt that the one who intends evil for the sake of evil and not for the sake of good is undeserving of the name of mercy. Beneath all this lies a secret whose divulgence the revealed law [*al-sharʿ*] prohibits, so be content with prayer and do not expect that it be divulged.[127]

Ghazālī goes on to state that this "secret" is not discernible to most people. One can only wonder what it is. Given the available evidence, however, it would be difficult to aver that this is a sign of his being a closet universalist.[128]

Excursus

Looking to the "Other Ghazālī": Shāh Walī Allāh's Alternative Inclusivism

For the purpose of comparative analysis, we now turn our attention to the soteriological views of another important scholar who, approaching the topic at hand from a different angle and much later, arrived at an alternative form of inclusivism involving the limbo of the heights. Quṭb al-Dīn Aḥmad Abū al-Fayyāḍ, more commonly known as Shāh Walī Allāh of Delhi (d. 1176/1762), was a prominent hadith expert, Sufi, and theologian associated with Ashʿarism.[129] Born in 1114/1703, he was trained in the Islamic sciences by his father, whom he eventually succeeded as principal of the well-known Raḥīmiyya madrasa at Delhi. He is remembered today for his Persian translation of the Qur'an and, perhaps more significantly, his conciliatory approach to resolving various tensions within Sunnism, including that between dogmatic theology and Sufism. For this reason and because of his wide-ranging expertise, he has been called the "Ghazālī of Islam of the Indian subcontinent."[130] Despite their commonalities, however, one should not read too much into this honorific title: Walī Allāh was influenced by numerous other scholars and was unique in his own right.[131]

Walī Allāh's magnum opus is *Ḥujjat Allāh al-bāligha* (*The Conclusive Argument from God*), a comprehensive work dealing with issues as diverse as mystical philosophy and politics. It was composed shortly after (and presumably inspired by) his pilgrimage to Mecca and Medina in 1143–1144/1731–1732. While there, he reportedly had a vision of Muḥammad's grandsons Ḥasan and Ḥusayn repairing a broken pen and presenting him with one of the robes of the Prophet, which, as Walī Allāh saw it, meant that his task was to restore the Islamic sciences.[132] This deeply embedded desire to rectify and revivify the study of Islam is indeed a similarity between Walī Allāh and Ghazālī. And the list of similarities goes on: in the *Ḥujjat*, Walī Allāh has much to say about the natural inclination to God and uses the metaphor of veils to illustrate the varying degrees in which the pure natural disposition (*fiṭra*) is manifested.[133] At the bottom of Walī Allāh's hierarchy of humanity are atheists: becoming an atheist, he declares, is a person's "greatest misfortune."[134] He also affirms Islamic supersessionism,[135] discusses the role of miracles in confirming the truthfulness of prophets,[136] and states that unbelievers will be eternally damned.[137] Meanwhile, he maintains a Ghazālī-like theodicy of optimism and attests to the abundant good already evident in this life: "God decided in pre-existence to create the world in the best way possible."[138] Yet while Walī Allāh cites and occasionally appears to mimic Ghazālī in the *Ḥujjat*, again, the differences between the two are significant. This becomes clear when we consider their respective soteriologies.

Particularly pertinent is Walī Allāh's depiction of the life to come, which appears in the *Ḥujjat* and, with some variation, in another comprehensive yet more mystical work written later in his life, *al-Budūr al-bāzigha*

(*Full Moon Appearing on the Horizon*).[139] Humanity, Walī Allāh writes, will split into three groups. One will be the inhabitants of Paradise, and they themselves are made up of three factions. Most remarkable of all are those "who are instructed" by God and the angels (*al-mufahhamūn*); these include prophets and others "whose angelic side is of the very highest" rank.[140] Following them will be "those who excel" (*al-sābiqūn*); these include the wise, martyrs, those dedicated to God consciousness, and others who have "succeeded in perfecting what they were created for." Those who have not succeeded in this regard but are virtuous nonetheless will make up the "people of the right" (*aṣḥāb al-yamīn*).[141] These inhabitants of Paradise are to be contrasted with those on the other end of the spectrum, the damned. This second group consists of people veiled by nature, convention, and/or their own (mis)conceptions of God, and includes insubordinate individuals who will be punished for a limited time, as well as unbelievers:

> the defiant, disobedient ones who refuse to say, "There is no [god] but [God]," despite the maturity of their intelligence and despite true religious information having reached them, or [who] contradict the will of God to put into effect the command of the prophets, may peace be upon them. Thus they turn (people) away from the path of God, and are satisfied with the life of [this] world, and are not attentive to what comes after it. They are cursed eternally, and are imprisoned forever, and among them are the people of the Ignorant Age [*jāhiliyya*] and some hypocrites who said they believed with their tongues while their hearts remained absolutely unbelieving, and God knows better.[142]

Residing between the Fire and the Garden are the "people of the heights" (*aṣḥāb al-aʿrāf*), who are in a state of limbo.[143] In the *Budūr*, Walī Allāh states that this third group includes

> (a) people of a wicked disposition, ignorant, performing their good deeds always perfunctorily, not purposefully; (b) people of a strong disposition, but who did not receive the opportunity either to devote themselves to God or to the present world, overcome as they were with [the sleep of] heedlessness [*ghafla*].[144]

The latter, who are the only inhabitants of the heights mentioned in the *Ḥujjat*, consist of two factions. The first includes those "whose minds are deficient, such as most children, insane people, peasants, and slaves."[145] As for the second, in the *Ḥujjat* they are described as those

> who are sound in body and disposition, but who have not been reached by the message of Islam at all; or it has reached them, but only in such a way that the proof was not established, and confusion about it did not cease. Thus they grew up neither indulging in despicable traits nor in destructive actions, nor did they turn [their] attention to the direction of God either to deny or confirm, and most of their concern is preoccupied with the immediate worldly supports of civilized life. Therefore, when they die [they] return to a state of unconsciousness, neither to punishment nor to reward. Finally their animalistic side is abolished, then some of the angelic twinkling shines on them.[146]

An alternative description of this faction appears in the *Budūr*:

> [These are] people who have not received the message of Islam at all as, for instance, dwellers of high and inaccessible mountains. They do not attribute associates to their Lord, nor do they deny Him or believe in Him. They are like animals who do not concentrate their being upon God.... They are merely interested in things by which profit is gained. And if they receive the message of Islam, they do not derive benefit from it on account of their stupidity. They are like people who neither understand the language nor the argument of Islam. Or they grow up without paying attention to reflection.... They only learn that Muslims are people whose turbans are like this and whose shirts are like that, who eat these things and consider those forbidden.... Still, if these people attack us to capture our country, we have to fight them, notwithstanding the fact that they do not associate anyone with God. They behave like animals, though they have a sound mental disposition.[147]

Owing to God's mercy and justice, Walī Allāh asserts without further elaboration that these people of the heights will all be admitted into Heaven.[148] These pronouncements leave us with many questions and few answers regarding Walī Allāh's form of inclusivism; however, it is clear that, like Ghazālī, Walī Allāh was aware that the context in which one is raised affects the probability that one will ever embrace Islam. And the dissimilar environments in which Ghazālī and Walī Allāh themselves lived seem to explain at least some of the idiosyncratic differences in their soteriologies. While Ghazālī, who lived under Muslim rule and among a Muslim majority, points to Byzantine Christians and Turks living "far beyond the lands of Islam" as examples of potential candidates for salvation, Walī Allāh, who lived among a Hindu majority during an era that witnessed the gradual decline of the Mughals and growing Sikh and Hindu threats to Muslim rule,[149] simply mentions agnostic or nonreligious "dwellers of high and inaccessible mountains"—a group that, interestingly, occupies "the heights" of this world. There are, however, much starker differences between the two. Those among the unreached who either deny God or ascribe partners to Him are blameless by Ghazālī's standard yet culpable by Walī Allāh's. (Needless to say, each takes a different stance on the question of moral obligations in the absence of revelation.) Nevertheless, while Ghazālī designates those non-Muslims who have been properly exposed to the message yet shirk from the responsibility of actively investigating its truth claims as true unbelievers destined for Hell, Walī Allāh leaves the door open for those whose lack of faith is predicated on what he characterizes as worldliness or "stupidity." In the final analysis, however, despite differences in hermeneutics and backgrounds, Walī Allāh effectively corroborates Ghazālī's inclusivist emphasis on divine mercy while providing Muslim theologians alternative considerations and points of departure.[150]

Closing Thoughts

Despite some loose ends and surface incongruities, Ghazālī's case for inclusivism offers a generally comprehensible criterion for non-Muslim salvation. Ghazālī never explicitly indicates what proportion of non-Muslims will be among "those who attain success" on the Last Day or whether certain polytheists, deists, agnostics, and atheists who have been properly exposed to the message could be counted among the sincere bound for Paradise. But he does make clear that multitudes of non-Muslims, indeed the great majority of humanity, will ultimately be saved and pleased.

It is worth stressing that Ghazālī's optimism stems largely from his understanding of divine mercy; it is not grounded in those Qur'anic passages popular among pluralists (such as 2:62, 5:48, and 5:69). In fact, on account of Ghazālī's deep faith in Islamic supersessionism, he occasionally writes as if he were on the side of exclusivism. An illustrative example of this occurs at the very conclusion of the *Iḥyāʾ*, as Ghazālī approvingly cites—without qualification—the following hadith: "Whenever a Muslim male dies, God the Exalted consigns a Jew or a Christian to Hell in his place."[151] Perhaps Ghazālī took this to refer to insincere Jews and Christians living near Muslim lands. Whatever he had in mind, it is sometimes easy to forget that Ghazālī's Paradise is populated by Others.

One can only wonder, of course, whether he would have reconsidered the particulars of his soteriology were he somehow transported to the modern world. For in some post-Enlightenment, post-Darwinian, secular societies and communities, a general apathy with regard to religion has become the norm rather than the exception. Hence, it is ostensibly challenging for modern Muslim thinkers to affirm Ghazālī's soteriological optimism while maintaining the same level of expectation that the sincere will actively investigate the message upon learning of, for example, the miracles associated with it. This is especially true in milieus in which miracles are often passed off as delusions, exaggerations, or fabrications. This is also true of communities—including electronic ones—in which polemical campaigns directed against Islam are pervasive. Is it any surprise that as we proceed through the Information Age and more people than ever before learn of Muḥammad's miracles, only a small proportion of them become Muslim? One cannot overlook the fact that Ghazālī was living in a context in which Muslims constituted the majority and represented the ascending culture—notwithstanding the fragmentation of Muslim political powers and the surprise incursion of the Crusaders. (In contrast, Walī Allāh, who held lower expectations for the conversion of certain reached non-Muslims, was in the religious minority during a period of Muslim decline.) Nevertheless, thanks in part to Ghazālī's enormous influence, his criterion for non-Muslim salvation—either as is or in modified form—continues to sway many modern figures living in radically different environments. These include, for instance, Muḥammad Rashīd Riḍā, the subject of chapter 4, and the contemporary American Muslim thinker Hamza Yusuf.[152] What seems to have allowed Ghazālī's criterion to stand the test of time is its partial ambiguity and, by extension, its malleability: moving beyond generalities, at what point *exactly* does one cease to be unreached? Who *exactly* qualifies as a sincere truth-seeker? In the next chapter, we shall examine another criterion that is at once more ambiguous and more inclusive.

2

All Paths Lead to God: The Case of Ibn ʿArabī

THE EPITHET "THE grand master" (*al-shaykh al-akbar*) belongs to Abū Bakr Muḥammad ibn ʿAlī, more commonly known as Muḥyī al-Dīn Ibn al-ʿArabī (d. 638/1240). His is "the great name" in Islamic theosophical mysticism.[1] Not only have his teachings "dominated much of Sufism,"[2] but it could be argued that, with the possible exception of Ghazālī, no intellectual figure has been more influential in the history of Islam.[3] Born into an elite family in 560/1165 in the city of Murcia in al-Andalus (Muslim Iberia) and raised from the age of eight in Seville, he had the privilege of meeting eminent scholars, including no less than the renowned philosopher Ibn Rushd (Averroes, d. 595/1198). While still young and, as he puts it, unable to grow facial hair, he experienced a mystical moment that forever changed his life. He subsequently withdrew from society and began to receive additional "illuminations" (or "openings"). What followed was an extraordinary encounter with Jesus, who instructed him to abandon his worldly possessions. Before long, he met again with Jesus, this time accompanied by Moses and Muḥammad. The three Abrahamic giants are said to have received Ibn ʿArabī under their protection.[4] Feeling impelled to journey eastward, he eventually made his way to Mecca, arriving there in 598/1202. He was so moved by his experience at the Kaaba that he began to compose what would become his magnum opus, *al-Futūḥāt al-makkiyya* (*The Meccan Openings*), a voluminous work containing an extensive exposition of his Sufi doctrine. In 620/1223, he finally settled in Syria, where he completed and revised the *Futūḥāt*. It was there that he produced another influential (albeit much shorter) work, *Fuṣūṣ al-ḥikam* (*The Bezels of Wisdom*), which, he maintains, was dictated to him by the Prophet in a dream and which expounds the wisdom in the teachings of twenty-seven prophets, beginning with Adam and concluding with Muḥammad himself.[5]

With hundreds of works on a variety of topics ascribed to him, Ibn ʿArabī is widely regarded as the most prolific of all Sufi writers.[6] Of all his writings, however, the *Futūḥāt* and the *Fuṣūṣ* often evoke the strongest reactions by both supporters and detractors, and it is the worldview expounded in these that allows us to make sense of Ibn ʿArabī's approach to the topic of salvation. While one might argue that his soteriology is either pluralistic or *indescribable*, I maintain that it would be safest to classify him as a liberal inclusivist. And, as we shall see, while he affirms the salvation of "sincere" non-Muslims, because of his belief that every single path we take is not only created by but leads to God—a God of mercy (*raḥma*) and nobility (*karam*)—he maintains that *all* of humanity, including even the most wicked, will ultimately arrive at bliss.

God Is All

Adorning the walls of countless homes worldwide are decorative lists of the ninety-nine "most beautiful names" of God.[7] These names, most of which are taken verbatim from the Qur'an, signify God's attributes. He is Allah, the Compassionate, the Caring, the Creator, the Shaper, the First, the Last, the Vast, the Victorious, the Glorious, the Great, the Light, the Living, the Loving, the Forgiving, the Finder, the Firm, the Affirming, the Avenger, the Abaser, the Exalter, the Enricher, the Rich, the Real, the Peace, the Patient, the Propitious, the Illustrious, the Incomparable, the Noble, the Holy, the One, and so on. These names, William Chittick observes, "are the single most important concept" in Ibn ʿArabī's works: "Everything divine or cosmic, is related back to them."[8]

This takes us to one of the most controversial yet crucial aspects of Ibn ʿArabī's teachings, a doctrine that eventually acquired the name "Oneness of Being" (*waḥdat al-wujūd*). According to this often misunderstood doctrine, God is "all," not in the "pantheistic sense"[9] but in the sense that all of creation "is a locus of manifestation for the divine names."[10] In other words, everything reflects God in some way and is thus a "sign" of the divine (even if the Almighty Himself remains incomparable).[11] People are exceptional in this regard because they are "created in the form of God" and are the only beings allotted every divine attribute.[12] Hence, meditation on *every* divine name is required for those seeking both a better understanding of reality and the actualization of their potential for human perfection.

It is precisely the attempt to comprehend all the properties of the divine attributes that defines the *Futūḥāt*, and it can only be an attempt given the

Almighty's limitlessness.[13] Indeed, "God is greater" than any of our conceptualizations of Him.[14] But God's vastness entails a complication. As Ibn ʿArabī explains, "Neither your heart nor your eye ever witnesses anything but the form of your own belief concerning God."[15] Thus, people "worship only what they believe" about God; "they only worship that which is created."[16] This leads to the bold proclamation that everyone is, in a sense, an "idol-worshiper,"[17] as each person's conception of the divine represents a particular "carving" of an idol, and it is only through such idols that people can recognize God.[18] Fortunately for humanity, the Compassionate pardons this form of idol worship.[19]

By the same token, Ibn ʿArabī simultaneously maintains that, because God is "all," everyone, to some extent, "knows" God, even if many are oblivious to the fact that the very objects they witness (not to mention themselves) manifest divine names.[20] What is more, because these names exist "within every conceptualization" of the human mind, *every* single belief is, in a sense, true and meaningful.[21] This, Ibn ʿArabī informs us, is a fact recognized by those attaining to perfection who actualize all the divine names latent in their pure natural disposition (*fiṭra*): they "have been given an all-inclusive overview of all religions, creeds, sects, and doctrines concerning God" and deem none of them erroneous and consider none of them vain, as it "was not without purpose that [God] created the heavens and the earth and everything in between" (Q. 38:27).[22] And because all things—including all religions and systems of thought—reflect an aspect of the divine, they also lead to the divine.[23] As the Qur'an itself affirms, "Everything is brought back to God" (57:5); "all journeys lead to Him" (5:18).

Even so, the many paths, however true and meaningful they may be, are not all the same. Some people, particularly those who fail to attain a "proper balance" of all the divine attributes contained in their pure natural disposition,[24] approach God in a state of "wretchedness"; others approach Him in a state of "felicity." "The road of felicity," Ibn ʿArabī proclaims, "is that set down by revealed religion, nothing else."[25] (This is despite the fact that the "felicitous" recognize the significance of the other roads.) Conversely, it is only "the existence of the revealed religions" that produces unbelief, "resulting in wretchedness."[26] Remarkable, therefore, are the implications:

> God gives to His servants from Himself, and also on the hands of His messengers. As for what comes to you on the hand of the Messenger, take it without employing any scale. But as for what comes to you from the hand of God, take it with a scale. For God is identical to every giver, but He has forbidden you from taking every gift.[27]

God's creation is replete with both the beneficial and the harmful. It is His revelations, however, that allow us to distinguish the one from the other and to recognize our moral responsibility: "accept whatever the Messenger gives you, and abstain from whatever he forbids you" (Q. 57:7). The ideal, therefore, is the narrow yet inclusive "straight path" of Muḥammad.

The Superiority of the Final Message

Although God has "assigned a law and a path to each" community (Q. 5:48) (such as the Torah revealed to the followers of Moses), one revelation, Ibn ʿArabī asserts, stands above the rest:

> The Muḥammadan leader chooses the path of Muḥammad and leaves aside the other paths, even though he acknowledges them and has faith in them. However, he does not make himself a servant except through the path of Muḥammad, nor does he have his followers make themselves servants except through it. He traces the attributes of all paths back to it, because Muḥammad's revealed religion is all-inclusive. Hence the property of all the revealed religions has been transferred to his revealed religion. His revealed religion embraces them, but they do not embrace it.[28]

In metaphorical terms, the "path of Muḥammad" is like sunlight, while all other divinely revealed religions are like starlight. With the appearance of the former, the latter disappear (which is not to say that they no longer exist) and, if anything, only contribute to the luminosity of the former.[29] The final message is nothing short of exceptional.

Despite Ibn ʿArabī's clear preference for his own tradition, in recent years there has been an intensifying debate over whether he leaves the door open for the kind of religious pluralism that accepts other faiths in a post-Muḥammadan context as independently valid paths to Paradise (however conceived)—paths that are not necessarily equal to Islam in all respects but are at least equally salvific. The pluralist Frithjof Schuon (d. 1998), a leading thinker of the Sophia Perennis school of thought (briefly discussed in chapter 4), maintains that he does. Schuon writes:

> [It] has been argued that [Ibn] ʿArabī denied [the universality of religion] when he wrote that Islam was the pivot of the other religions. The truth is, however, that every religious form is superior to the others in a particular respect, and it is this characteristic that in fact

> indicates the sufficient reason for the existence of that form. Anyone who speaks in the name of his religion always has this characteristic in mind; what matters, where the recognition of other religious forms is concerned, is the fact—exoterically inconceivable—of such recognition, not its mode or degree.[30]

It is easy to appreciate Schuon's contention when one considers what is reputed to be Ibn ʿArabī's most well-known lines of poetry, at least in the West:

> *My heart has become capable of every form: it is a*
> *pasture for gazelles and a convent for Christian*
> *monks.*
> *And a temple for idols and the pilgrim's [Kaaba] and*
> *the [tablets of the Torah] and the book of the Koran.*
> *I follow the religion of Love: whatever way Love's*
> *camels take, that is my religion and my faith.*[31]

Nevertheless, as T. J. Winter rightly notes, claims of Ibn ʿArabī's pluralism "need to be tempered by a survey of his less eirenic statements."[32] In the *Fuṣūṣ*, for example, Ibn ʿArabī explicitly rejects the doctrine of the divine incarnation in Christ (on the assumption that it *restricts* God) and says that its advocates are guilty of unbelief (*kufr*).[33] As we shall soon see, this charge of unbelief is in fact qualified and does not entail the damnation of all or even most Christians. Still, in other writings, Ibn ʿArabī, in passing, pejoratively refers to certain Christians as associationists (*mushrikūn*), those who ascribe partners to God.[34]

More significant, however, is the fact that within the *Futūḥāt* itself, Ibn ʿArabī avers that Muḥammad's message is not simply superior to other messages but supersedes them as well: it does not abrogate their sacred *truths*, but it does abrogate their sacred *rulings*.[35] Thus, were the previous messengers alive during Muḥammad's time, "they would have followed him, just as their laws [*sharāʾiʿuhum*] have followed his law [*sharʿahu*]."[36]

Although it would be tempting to dismiss Ibn ʿArabī's ostensibly conflicting statements concerning religious diversity as contradictions resulting from his mystical approach, I submit that we have no reason to jump to this conclusion (even if such contradictions exist in other matters). Again, Ibn ʿArabī's so-called Oneness of Being doctrine renders all beliefs, religious or otherwise, "true" in at least one sense: they are of divine origin; they are "real." From this standpoint, even "a temple for idols" can be worthy of love. But true or real is not necessarily the same as proper or salvific. It is the divine message that indicates which beliefs and practices lead to supreme contentment. In the pursuit of salvation, perfection, and satisfaction, Ibn ʿArabī points to the "path of Muḥammad." God, he writes, conveys to humanity "His actual situation on the tongue of His messengers so that He will have an argument against those who contradict His speech and who say about Him things that oppose what He has said about Himself."[37] In short, to reject Muḥammad's message is to challenge God. But it is only the "insincere" rejection of this (or any other) divine message that leads to the lowest prospects.

"*... Until We Have Sent a Messenger*"

Ibn ʿArabī writes extensively of the rewards awaiting the righteous and the punishments to be meted out to the rejecters. But what of those who do not recognize the very best of what God provides as such? What of those who are simply not convinced by the proofs of His messengers, particularly Muḥammad? Like Ghazālī, Ibn ʿArabī does not present Islamic supersessionism as grounds for the damnation of earnest non-Muslims. Instead, he invokes the familiar theme of mercy. But he goes a step further than Ghazālī, espousing a liberal form of inclusivism comparable to the doctrine ascribed to Jāḥiẓ. As we saw in the previous chapter, Ghazālī concedes that Jāḥiẓ's liberal inclusivism is rationally sound, yet he ultimately dismisses it as scripturally indefensible. Ibn ʿArabī challenges us to reread scripture. Consider his explication of the Qur'anic pronouncement "We do not punish until We have sent a messenger" (17:15):

> Note that [God] did not say, "until We send forth a person." Hence the *message* of the one who is sent must be established for the one to whom it is directed. There must be clear and manifest proofs established for each person to whom the messenger is sent, for many a sign [*āya*] has within it obscurity or equivocality such that some people do not perceive what it proves. The clarity of the proof must be such that it establishes the person's [messengership] for each person to whom he is sent. Only then, if the person refuses it, will he be taken to account. Hence, this verse has within it a tremendous mercy, because of the diversity of human dispositions that lead to a diversity of views. He who knows the all-inclusiveness of the divine mercy, which God reports, [*encompasses*] *all things* [Q. 7:156], knows that God did this only because of mercy toward His servants.[38]

By extension, non-Muslims who do not recognize Muḥammad's messengership are not culpable. Following this line of reasoning, it is noteworthy that the Qur'an speaks of unbelievers among pagans and People of the Book being damned only after having received "*clear* evidence" (*al-bayyina*) (Q. 98:1–6). The wording of this verse would suggest that the *clarity* of the final message must be established before one could be chastised for refusing to accept it. This interpretation arguably finds support in other passages such as Q. 4:115, a verse that condemns anyone who "opposes the Messenger, after guidance has been *made clear* to him [or her]."[39]

Accordingly, sincere non-Muslims for whom the Prophet's "messengership" (or "evidence" or "guidance") has not been "made clear" may qualify as true *muslims*, even if some of their beliefs are incongruous with his message, as in the case of Trinitarian Christians.[40] As Ibn ʿArabī observes, the term *islām* in the Qur'anic context (specifically, 3:19) denotes "submission" (*inqiyād*), not reified Islam.[41] Hence, owing to the wide range of human submissions to the divine and the consequent wide range of manifestations of bliss, there are—on the basis of mystical insight—*at least* 5,105 "degrees of the Garden," only twelve of which are designated specifically for "the Muḥammadan community."[42] Hell is the everlasting abode not of anyone who does not identify as a follower of Muḥammad but, rather, of those who refuse to surrender to God after the truth has been made clear to them. These are the "guilty ones" (Q. 36:59) who "deserve" their fate. Ibn ʿArabī identifies these "people of the Fire who are its [true] inhabitants"—an expression derived from a prophetic report—as the arrogant (*mutakabbirūn*), who, like Pharaoh, claim to be divine;[43] associationists (*mushrikūn*); those who divest God of His attributes (*muʿaṭṭila*); and hypocrites (*munāfiqūn*).[44] Their dismissal of the reality of the one God—a reality affirmed in the pure natural disposition[45]—constitutes a failure to recall their primordial covenant with God:

> When your Lord took out the offspring from the loins of the Children of Adam and made them bear witness concerning themselves, He said, "Am I not your Lord?" and they replied, "Yes, we bear witness." So you cannot say on the Day of Resurrection, "We were not aware of this." (Q. 7:172)

Be that as it may, the "people of the Fire who are its [true] inhabitants" can only encompass those for whom the proofs of the message are established (in the manner I described earlier). This is why, again, it is *only* "the existence of the revealed religions" that produces unbelief "resulting in wretchedness." The "people of the Fire," therefore, do not include "earnest" individuals who have never had what they could recognize to be a compelling encounter with any form of the message, particularly the message conveyed to all prophets: "There is no god but Me, so serve Me" (Q. 21:25).

Nevertheless, Ibn ʿArabī's soteriology ensures that everyone will at some point—even after death—be exposed to at least one of God's messages in a manner that is manifestly compelling prior to being consigned either to Heaven or Hell. This is implied by Ibn ʿArabī's position on the fate of deceased children, those who are mentally impaired, and those who lived during the interstices between prophets, that is, the people of the gap (*ahl al-fatra*). As reported in a hadith, and as a confirmation of divine justice, Ibn ʿArabī maintains that such individuals will be distinguished from the rest of humanity and assigned a messenger on the Day of Resurrection. This messenger-of-resurrection, whose message would presumably be unanimously regarded as genuine, will present his people with a tremendous test: he will command them to enter the Fire. Those who obey will find it cool—just as Abraham found the fire of this life when his people cast him into it (Q. 21:69)—and they will proceed to the Garden; those who refuse to enter the Fire will be thrust into its painful depths.[46] Interpreted literally or metaphorically, this is a daunting test, but one that is at least symbolically similar to those of this life.[47] (As we shall see, although Ibn ʿArabī writes about "the heights" [*al-aʿrāf*] [Q. 7:46–49], he does not identify this landmark as either the site of this test or a place of limbo.)

We may speculate, then, that non-Muslims in a post-Muḥammadan world who have never had a compelling encounter with any form of the message (that is, the Qur'an or any of the earlier revelations) will be treated in the manner of the people of the gap. As for righteous non-Muslims who, in this life, accept at least one form of the message (for example, the Torah) and do not reject other forms on account of insincerity, Ibn ʿArabī's soteriology suggests that they will be among the inhabitants of Paradise. We may suppose that the same is true of non-Muslims who earnestly investigate the final message after recognizing aspects of the truth within it yet who pass away without ever converting to Islam.

Compared with Ghazālī's form of inclusivism, Ibn ʿArabī's criterion is ostensibly simpler (albeit more vague) and seems to expand considerably the circle of *muslim* non-Muslims. It would be superfluous for Ibn ʿArabī to provide specific examples of "goodhearted" non-Muslims living "far beyond the lands of Islam"[48] or to list the specific features of the message that one must encounter to be considered "reached." Again, for Ibn ʿArabī "proper" exposure is simply that which the recipient finds compelling. (According to Ghazālī, learning about certain qualities of the Prophet and his message is presumed to be necessarily compelling—even if the recipient fails to recognize this.) Additionally, unlike the soteriology articulated by Walī Allāh centuries later, Ibn ʿArabī does not—explicitly at least—limit his inclusivism to those who fail to recognize the reality of revelation on account of their "stupidity" or obsession with worldly affairs.

As with both Ghazālī and Walī Allāh, however, Ibn ʿArabī's inclusivism is predicated on a controversial reading of scripture. To be sure, it is not immediately apparent that Q. 17:15 leaves the door wide open for the salvation of sincere non-Muslims who would normally be considered among the reached. Yet one need not be rooted in Sufism to appreciate the logic of Ibn ʿArabī's tenable, thought-provoking interpretation. What is, therefore, most unusual about his soteriology is his stance regarding the wicked: although barred from the Garden, even they will come to enjoy a life of bliss—where one would least expect it.

A Paradisiacal Hell?

Among the denizens of Ibn ʿArabī's Hell, only believers (whatever their religious affiliation)—punished in the first place because of their sins—will one day delight in the rich gardens of Paradise.[49] Those remaining behind will never leave. Yet while Ibn ʿArabī's interpretation of scripture renders Hell eternal, the same is not true of its punishment. This is borne out in his discussion of the following Qur'anic passage:

> The wretched ones will be in the Fire, sighing and groaning, there to remain for as long as the heavens and earth endure, unless your Lord wills otherwise: your Lord carries out whatever He wills. As for those who have been blessed, they will be in Paradise, there to remain as long as the heavens and earth endure, unless your Lord wills otherwise—an unceasing gift. (11:106–108)

These verses, Ibn ʿArabī explains, indicate that the "wretched" will remain forever in the Fire, but never describe "the state within which they will dwell" as "unceasing"—an adjective reserved for the "gift" awaiting the "blessed."[50] Instead, we are informed that God "carries out whatever He wills"—a statement Ibn ʿArabī highlights.[51] He also draws attention to

Q. 56:33, which states that Heaven's provisions will "neither be limited nor forbidden" (*lā maqṭūʿa wa-lā mamnūʿa*). Islamic scripture, he observes, never offers a similar proclamation concerning the torments of Hell.[52] This is notwithstanding the Qur'anic reference to the "lasting punishment" (*ʿadhāb al-khuld*) (10:52) that "will not be lightened" (*lā yukhaffaf*) (2:162). Notice, however, that the "evildoers" will merely "taste" the "lasting punishment" (10:52).[53] If "tasting" signifies a finite phenomenon, then it would only be during this "tasting" period that chastisement would "last" and "not be lightened."

Ibn ʿArabī's conviction in the temporality of punishment is derived principally from his conception of divine mercy. Citing the Qur'anic pronouncement "My mercy encompasses all things" (Q. 7:156) and a prophetic report that quotes God as saying, "My mercy outstrips My wrath," Ibn ʿArabī asks rhetorically, "How could there be everlasting wretchedness? Far be it from God that His wrath should take precedence over His mercy…or that He should make the embrace of His mercy specific after He had called it general!"[54] Because wrath in the form of punishment experienced by the inhabitants of Hell is "a thing," an ephemeral accident (in the philosophical sense), we should expect mercy to encompass it, limit it, and dominate it.[55] It is not of the essence of God, the Necessary Being, and is therefore a fleeting "deviation"; it must necessarily "dwindle and become nonexistent."[56] Reality, therefore, is circular: it begins and ends in mercy.[57] Reflecting further, Ibn ʿArabī provides us with the following rumination:

> I have found in myself—who am among those whom God has innately disposed toward mercy—that I have mercy toward all God's servants.…The possessors of this attribute are I and my peers, and we are creatures, possessors of fancy and personal desire. God has said about Himself that He is "the most merciful of the merciful" [*arḥam al-rāḥimīn*] [Q. 7:151], and we have no doubt that He is more merciful than we are toward His creatures. Yet we have known from ourselves this extravagant mercy. How could chastisement be everlasting for [the wretched], when He has this attribute of all-pervading mercy? God is more noble than that![58]

Nobility is a recurring theme in Ibn ʿArabī's soteriological expositions, as it is often paired with mercy to explain why God does what is best and forgives what is worst.[59] The Qur'an states, "Let harm be requited by an equal harm, although anyone who forgives and puts things right will have his [or her] reward from God Himself" (42:40). With this principle in mind, and given God's nobility and superiority, Ibn ʿArabī insists that He (the Forgiving) "will pardon, show forbearance, and make things well."[60] How else would He treat His creatures, all of whom are weak and dependent on Him?[61] As one hadith instructs, one should only assume the best of God.[62] Even if we suppose that scripture both promises eternal reward and threatens eternal punishment, the Qur'an only tells us that we should "not think that God will break His promise" (14:47); there is no similar affirmation of His threat.[63] And were God to limit or qualify His threat, it would allow for a deeper appreciation of His mercy. We know that God is "the best of those who are merciful" (Q. 23:109), but we have no evidence that He is "the best of those who punish."[64]

It is true that mercy, nobility, and forgiveness are not the only divine attributes. They must be considered alongside those that denote "subjugation, domination, and severity."[65] Ibn ʿArabī finds that both types figure prominently in the Qur'an. What allows him to accentuate mercy, however, is not only the aforementioned passages but also the special positioning of the divine names "the Compassionate (al-Raḥmān), the Caring (al-Raḥīm)" (Q. 1:1).[66] These names appear in the *basmala* formula ("In the name of God, the Compassionate, the Caring") with which the first sura of the Qur'an begins and which precedes all but one of the remaining suras (the exception being sura 9). What better confirmation of mercy's precedence?[67]

When, then, will mercy triumph over wrath through the cessation of chastisement? Ibn ʿArabī identifies this moment as the termination of the Day of Resurrection, a "day" that will likely last fifty thousand years.[68] At that point, all of the "people of the Fire" will finally recognize what they had affirmed in the primordial covenant: they are God's servants. It is, therefore, only when the wretched end their discord (*shiqāq*) and submit to God wholeheartedly that their wretchedness (*shaqā'*) will cease.[69] For, in the first place, their chastisement was the result of their protesting God's actions.[70] Thus, they "will pluck the fruit of their words [at the primordial covenant], 'Yes, [we bear witness]' [Q. 7:172]. They will be like those who submit to God after apostasy. The authority of 'Yes' will rule over everything and finally give rise to their felicity."[71]

This transformation will necessarily occur because the accidents of "falsehood, unbelief, and ignorance" are temporal, whereas "faith, truth, and knowledge"—attributes of the divine—endure forever.[72] All people will continue to exist on account of their connection to the Necessary Being; it is only their evil accidents that will cease.[73] What other possibility could there be? The very injunction to worship God, against which Hell's inhabitants rebelled, was itself an accident. Ibn ʿArabī classifies this kind of worship as "worship based on commands" (*ʿibādat al-amr*), meaning that it accords with the precepts of the prophets. Because "every accident comes to an end" in the afterlife, the wretched, along with everyone else, will only engage in the form of worship they had always engaged in, without necessarily realizing it: "essential worship" (*al-ʿibāda al-dhātiyya*).[74] They will recognize that their very existence is defined by submission: "There is no one in the heavens or earth who does not come to the Lord of Mercy as a servant" (Q. 19:93).[75] So while the wicked currently enjoy the freedom to sin, they will one day find true bliss in the removal of this freedom. (Although Ibn ʿArabī's God is "the only true and real actor,"[76] He has nonetheless "compelled" people "to have free choice" in matters of this life.[77] God's "will in the things is that they be what they are.")[78]

To his imaginary interlocutor who insists that Hell's denizens could never attain God's mercy because of His justice, Ibn ʿArabī invokes the Qur'anic message of hope: "My servants who have harmed themselves by their own excess, do not despair of God's mercy; God forgives *all* sins" (39:53). Accordingly,

> [God] brought forgiveness and mercy for the repentant and those who do good deeds, and He also brought it for those who are "immoderate," those who do not repent. The latter He forbids to despair, and He confirms the point with His word "all." Nothing could be greater in divine eloquence concerning the final issue of the servants at mercy.[79]

One apparent problem with this assertion, however, is that although God "forgives all sins," as the Qur'an clarifies elsewhere, He forgives everything but *shirk* (associating partners with Him) (4:48). Associationists who "choose other protectors beside Him, saying, 'We only worship them because they bring us nearer to God'" (Q. 39:3), are therefore denounced. This, Ibn ʿArabī clarifies, is not because of their *shirk* per se but because of their rejection of "worship based on commands": they "set up" for themselves "a special road of worship which was not established" for them by a revealed law.[80] Yet, like everyone else, these associationists were a party to the primordial covenant. Even they will be forgiven, Ibn ʿArabī intrepidly declares, once they come to realize that, in reality, they had only ever worshiped God, "for no worshipper worships any but God in the place to which he ascribes divinity to Him."[81] To support this claim, Ibn ʿArabī points to the Qur'anic statement "Your Lord has ordained [*qaḍā*] that you should worship none but Him" (17:23).[82] Thus, when the Qur'an states that "each party" of those who ascribe partners to God rejoices "in what is theirs" (30:32), Ibn ʿArabī interprets this as real happiness in the hereafter, as such rejoicing is "not known in this life, or rather, it occurs for many but not all."[83] Similarly, the Qur'anic statement "God is pleased with them, and they with Him" (98:8) refers to everyone, and not, as most assume, those residing in Paradise.[84]

Time and again, Ibn ʿArabī challenges his readers to think outside the proverbial box. Interestingly, he finds an additional hint of mercy toward the wretched where one might least expect it: the Qur'anic term for punishment, *ʿadhāb*. Although it is used frequently and only in the context of threats, given the common Sufi belief that scripture contains multiple layers of meaning[85] and that God's judicious selection of words contains lessons for those who reflect, Ibn ʿArabī is keen to observe that the three-letter root of *ʿadhāb* (*ʿ-dh-b*) connotes sweetness, pleasantness, and agreeableness. What this signifies is that the Qur'an's recurring use of this particular term in referring to chastisement is "good news from God," as it mysteriously suggests that the suffering in Hell will become "sweet when mercy envelops" those consigned to it.[86] Thus, the punishment of the Fire is called *ʿadhāb* "due to the sweetness [*ʿudhūba*] of its food."[87] And it is precisely the initial agonizing torments that allow one to taste of this "sweetness."

Like Ghazālī, Ibn ʿArabī conjures the image of a compassionate physician causing a patient harm for the greater good. Chastisement is therapeutic; it rectifies.[88] This is to be expected given mercy's pervasiveness and predominance; "wrath disposes itself only through mercy's ruling property. Mercy sends out wrath as it will."[89] "Sweetness," therefore, will manifest itself once the punishment serves its purpose, that is, when the wicked reform themselves, consciously submit to God, and resign themselves to their fate, surrendering any hope of leaving Hell. At that point, in a dramatic show of compassion, the nineteen angels guarding Hell (Q. 74:30–31) will stand in the way of the angels of chastisement,[90] and the Fire, like Abraham's fire, will feel cool. After this first bliss, the "damned" will never again feel pain and will actually find their perpetual "punishment" pleasant.[91] And this enjoyment will be tremendous: "There is no surprise if roses are found in rose gardens. Surprise comes from roses in the pit of the Fire."[92]

Meanwhile, the people of Paradise will find pleasure in climbing a wall separating Heaven and Hell, gazing at the latter, and appreciating their own peace and security, which they would otherwise take for granted.[93] Interestingly, this very wall, which Ibn ʿArabī conflates with "the heights" (*al-aʿrāf*),[94] is taken to be yet another sign of the noneternality of punishment on the basis of its Qur'anic description:

> On the same Day, the hypocrites, both men and women, will say to the believers, "Wait for us! Let us have some of your light!" They will be told, "Go back and look for a light." A wall with a gate will be erected between [the hypocrites and believers]: inside it lies mercy, outside lies torment. (57:13)

According to the Sufi worldview, that which is inside (*al-bāṭin*) takes precedence over that which is outside (*al-ẓāhir*). Since mercy is located inside the wall, it constitutes the essence of the wall. And given mercy's supremacy, it must eventually conquer chastisement, making it accessible to Hell's inhabitants.[95] Curiously, however, the gate within the wall will remain forever shut. But this impediment of passage is, as we shall soon see, to the benefit of people in both abodes.

The Veil

Although all will eventually attain felicity as they proceed toward God, the righteous will be spared the "deserts, perils, vicious predators, and harmful serpents" found along the way.[96] Furthermore, God will continue to distinguish heavenly reward from hellish "torment" even after the completion of the Last Day. Wrath in the form of experienced chastisement will cease to be for the reasons I noted earlier. But since the divine attributes are necessarily eternal, and since wrath is one such attribute, the Fire must be everlasting, and the "attribute of chastisement" must "remain forever" with the true inhabitants of Hell.[97] Accordingly, even though the latter will be in a state of bliss, there will always be a fear that they may once again be punished—an imagined scenario that will never actually take place.[98] Ibn ʿArabī explains:

> No chastisement will remain in the Fire except imaginal chastisement within the presence of imagination, in order that the properties of the divine names may subsist. A name necessitates only

> the manifestation of the property that its reality demands. It does not specify the presence nor the individual.... Hence, whenever the property of the Avenger becomes manifest within an imaginal body or a corporeal body or in anything else, its rights are fulfilled through the manifestation of its property and effectivity. So the divine names continue to exercise effectivity and determine properties for all eternity in the two abodes, and the inhabitants of the two abodes never leave them.[99]

In this way, although all of God's "creatures are drowned in mercy," the "property of mutual contradictoriness" of His names persists.[100]

Imagined punishment, however, is not the only distinction between the inhabitants of the two abodes. More remarkable is "the veil." According to the Qur'an and hadith corpus, Heaven has eight gates, while Hell has seven.[101] All fifteen gates will eventually open, but a mysterious "eighth gate" of Hell will remain shut. This eighth gate constitutes "the veil" concealing God.[102] While the people of Heaven will find true, euphoric pleasure in the indescribable vision (*ru'ya*) of the divine, the people of Hell will *always* be veiled (*maḥjūb*) from that vision.[103]

The Qur'an states that the inhabitants of Gehenna (*jahannam*) will neither live nor die (20:74). As Ibn ʿArabī explains, they will not "die" because they will "find relief through the removal of pain"; they will not "live" because "they will not have a bliss like the bliss of the folk of the Gardens, a bliss that would be something in addition to the fact that He has relieved them in the abode of wretchedness."[104] Yet even in the inability to behold their Lord there is mercy:

> Were God to disclose Himself to [Hell's inhabitants] in the Fire, given their precedent evildoing and their worthiness for punishment, that benevolent self-disclosure would yield nothing but shame before God for what they had done, and shame is chastisement—but chastisement's period has come to an end. Hence they will not know the joy of witnessing and vision, so they will have bliss while being veiled. The goal is bliss, and it has been achieved with the veil—but for whom? How can the bliss of the vision of God be compared to bliss with the veil![105]

Despite Hell's obvious inferiority, another reason its inhabitants will be better off barred from Paradise relates to their very nature. Because they are immoderate, Ibn ʿArabī informs us, they will have extreme "constitutions," either "hot" or "cold." Hell itself consists not only of scorching heat but also of biting cold (*zamharīr*). This is made evident in the hadith corpus; the Qur'an is less explicit, stating that Paradise has neither scorching heat nor biting cold (76:13) and referring to a fluid in Hell that, according to one interpretation, is "extremely cold" (*ghassāq*) (38:57).[106] Ibn ʿArabī holds that God, out of His wisdom, will keep "the bitter cold of Gehenna for those with hot constitutions and the Fire for those with cold constitutions.... If they were to enter the Garden with the constitutions that they have, they would suffer chastisement because of the Garden's equilibrium."[107]

As such, happiness has nothing to do with physical locations per se but everything to do with "what is accepted by the constitution and desired by the soul." Thus, wherever "agreeableness of nature and attainment of desire are found, that is the person's bliss."[108]

In the final analysis, Ibn ʿArabī cannot be described as a universalist. But considering his belief that all of humanity will ultimately attain harmony and contentment, he is what I would describe as a quasi-universalist. And yet there are instances in which he appears to contradict himself and approach something resembling universalism. In the *Fuṣūṣ*, for example, he leaves open the possibility that Hell's denizens may in fact enjoy "an additional, distinct bliss like the bliss" of the people of Paradise.[109] There are other instances in which one wonders why he does not go the extra step of affirming this "additional bliss." In his discussion of "the veil," for example, Ibn ʿArabī cites the Qur'anic statement "On that Day they will be veiled from their Lord" (83:15). Never does he point to the expression "on that Day" as a hint of temporary veiling. In contrast to his insistence that scripture never explicitly describes punishment as everlasting, it is curious that he stretches the meaning of this particular verse to reflect an eternal reality. Considering the esoteric nature of his writings, however, it is to be expected that some interpretations will seem selective.

Excursus

Corroborating Ibn ʿArabī's Quasi-Universalism: The Case of Mullā Ṣadrā

Ibn ʿArabī's quasi-universalism impressed a variety of Muslim scholars of later generations, from the Persian exegete ʿAbd al-Razzāq al-Kāshānī

(d. 736/1335) to the Yemen-based mystical writer ʿAbd al-Karīm al-Jīlī (d. 832/1428) to the Ottoman "master of Islam" (*shaykh al-Islām*) Muḥammad ibn Ḥamza al-Fanārī (d. 834/1431) to, perhaps most significant of all, the Persian Shīʿite philosopher Ṣadr al-Dīn al-Shīrāzī, more commonly known as Mullā Ṣadrā (d. 1050/1640).[110] As "one of the most profoundly original and influential thinkers in the history of Islamic philosophy,"[111] Ṣadrā has left an indelible mark on Iranian and Shīʿite history. Born in approximately 980/1571 in Safavid Iran, he lived in an era in which Twelver Shīʿism was the official state religion. Ṣadrā's own world, however, encompassed both Shīʿite and Sunni thought. In his search for "transcendent wisdom," he mastered speculative theology (*kalām*) and the philosophy of Ibn Sīnā, Shihāb al-Dīn Suhrawardī (d. 587/1191), and Ibn ʿArabī. Much of Ṣadrā's eclectic study was conducted early in his life in the city of Isfahan; however, his Sufi leanings earned him the wrath of the religious establishment, and he was eventually forced into exile. Following a familiar pattern, he withdrew from society to connect with his spiritual self. This was followed by a return late in his life to his native city of Shiraz, where he spent much of the remainder of his days teaching.[112]

The differences between Ṣadrā and Ibn ʿArabī are many, thanks to Ṣadrā's range of influences, but so too are their similarities. This becomes apparent when comparing their worldviews and soteriologies. Most relevant for our purposes are two of Ṣadrā's works: his magnum opus, *al-Asfār al-arbaʿa al-ʿaqliyya* (The four intellectual journeys), which was completed by 1038/1628, and his commentary on the Qur'an's first sura, which was composed four to six years later.[113] Like Ibn ʿArabī, Ṣadrā speaks of the human limitation in conceptualizing the divine and thus each individual's "idol-carving,"[114] God being the true object of all forms of worship,[115] God being the final destination of all human paths,[116] and essential worship.[117] Ṣadrā also affirms that Hell will become an abode of bliss, as the end decreed by "the most merciful of the merciful" will be one of joy for all of creation.[118] He even adopts the punishment-to-sweetness (*ʿadhāb*-to-*ʿudhūba*) argument and presents mercy as the "root" of chastisement.[119] Thus, all harm is in fact beneficial; divine wrath is itself a manifestation of divine mercy.[120]

Ṣadrā's quasi-universalism may surprise those familiar with some of his other works, particularly *al-Ḥikma al-ʿarshiyya* (*The Wisdom of the Throne*), which may have been his final work. In it, Ṣadrā quotes one of Ibn ʿArabī's many affirmations of bliss within Hell and then states, "Now as for myself and what I have learned from the studies and practical (spiritual) exercises to which I have devoted myself, it would appear that Hell...is not an abode of comfort." Instead, it "is only a place of pain, suffering, and endless torment; its pains are continuous and constantly renewed, without ceasing."[121] These particular statements, however, must be read in context. As Mohammed Rustom notes, given the Safavid repression of certain forms of Sufi philosophy (or theoretical Sufism), Ṣadrā occasionally conceals or minimizes his connection to Ibn ʿArabī. The *Ḥikma*, compared with most of his other writings, uses less technical language and is accessible to a broader audience. Thus, Rustom argues, in the *Ḥikma* Ṣadrā disassociates himself from his real views on Hell for the sole purpose of avoiding censure.[122] (It should be recalled that he was expelled from Isfahan precisely for his Sufi views.) This is corroborated by James Morris's observation that "Ṣadrā's suppression here in [the *Ḥikma*] of all but the faintest allusion to his agreement with Ibn Arabi is in keeping with one level of intention in his work," that is, to reach a broad audience without undermining himself.[123]

It is, therefore, telling that Ṣadrā uses the word *appears* in his statement on Hell in the *Ḥikma*. In contrast, in the *Asfār*, he writes, "*There is no doubt* that the entry [into Hell of] the creature whose end is that he should enter Hell" will be "agreeable" to "his nature and will be a perfection of his existence," and that which is agreeable "is not chastisement."[124] As we have seen, and as we shall see in the next chapter, making the case for the salvation of the damned is often a recipe for controversy.

Closing Thoughts

In relation to his argument for inclusivism, Ibn ʿArabī's case for quasi-universalism requires a deeper appreciation of his esoteric approach to scripture: he reinterprets certain Qur'anic verses (for example, 30:32 and 98:8) and terms (for example, *ʿadhāb*) in ways that a myriad of theologians have found especially unsettling and perplexing.[125] It is thus not surprising that aspects of his soteriology have often been misunderstood.[126] Yet Ibn ʿArabī maintains that any interpretation of scripture that differs from the "literal meaning" is a "most wondrous" error: how could one give preference to the authority of one's own "reflection and consideration" over that of the divine?[127] Many of Ibn ʿArabī's opponents, of course, would ask the same question of him. And his response would be that his reading of scripture is guided by insights gleaned through mystical "unveiling" (*kashf*) and is, therefore, inaccessible to many. It is true that compared with most philosophers (*falāsifa*) and speculative theologians (*mutakallimūn*) Ibn ʿArabī appears to be less concerned with utilizing outside systems of thought.

Nevertheless, given his obvious uniqueness, the claim made by Chittick that Ibn ʿArabī "places himself squarely in the mainstream of Islam by basing all his teachings upon the Koran and the Hadith" must be qualified.[128]

Be that as it may, it is difficult to overestimate Ibn ʿArabī's contribution to Islamic soteriology. Inspired by the notion that God is "all," he casts a new light on Islamic scripture—one that draws attention to passages and linguistic nuances that buttress the case for universal mercy. As with Ghazālī, Ibn ʿArabī's writings represent a challenge to coreligionists who fail to recognize the extent of God's compassion. Yet Ibn ʿArabī moves beyond Ghazālī, espousing a notably more inclusive inclusivism. In the absence of any direct evidence, it is reasonable to assume that he, like Ghazālī, conceived of Paradise as being the more popular final destination. But even if this were not the case, Ibn ʿArabī speaks of mercy and forgiveness being granted to the "people of the Fire who are its [true] inhabitants"—a group Ghazālī designates as "those who will perish." Given the "accidental" nature of sin, Ibn ʿArabī's quasi-universalism addresses the theodicean problem we encountered in the previous chapter, of whether a merciful God would punish His servants eternally for having committed temporal sins. But Ibn ʿArabī's conception of overwhelming mercy also manages to account for divine wrath, which is made manifest through the very existence of Hell (however paradisiacal it may seem) and "the veil" blocking its inhabitants from the *real* reward.

Ibn ʿArabī was not the first proponent of quasi-universalism. The heresiographer Abū al-Fatḥ al-Shahrastānī (d. 548/1153) in his *al-Milal wa-l-niḥal* (Sects and creeds) traces this doctrine back to at least the third/ninth century: Jāḥiẓ, the same Muʿtazilite who reportedly espoused liberal inclusivism, is also said to have maintained that the inhabitants of the Fire will eventually be transformed, adopting a fire-like constitution and experiencing pleasure within an abode that is agreeable to their nature.[129] Whether Jāḥiẓ actually advocated this is an issue of debate,[130] but this reference in a text that predates Ibn ʿArabī is one indication that this doctrine was, in some form or another, in circulation early on. Even so, it would be reasonable to assume that Ibn ʿArabī's particular elucidations and elaborations are all his own. In a telling passage, he confesses that he knows of no other person who has ever portrayed God's contentment with His creation in such a positive light: "I have called attention to it here," he explains, "only because mercy has overcome me at this moment."[131] (Interestingly, Ṣadrā, writing four centuries later, would claim that he himself had met no one who realized just how merciful God will be in the life to come.)[132]

To those traditionally trained scholars who deem quasi-universalism unjustifiable and overly optimistic, Ibn ʿArabī offers the following:

> [There is a] difference between him who desires the spreading of God's mercy among His servants—whether they be obedient or disobedient—and him who desires to take God's mercy away from some of His servants. This second person is the one who prohibits the mercy of God that embraces all things, but he does not prohibit it to himself. Were it not for the fact that God's mercy takes precedence over His wrath, the possessor of this attribute would never attain to God's mercy.[133]

Although Ibn ʿArabī's mercy-for-all approach has attracted many supporters, damnationist critics have long regarded it as a heretical innovation. Other critics include prominent advocates of an alternative vision of universal mercy. In the next chapter, we shall encounter a traditionalist rejection of quasi-universalism—in favor of universalism itself.

3

The Redemption of Humanity: The Case of Ibn Taymiyya

MANY HAVE BORNE the title "the master of Islam" (*shaykh al-Islām*). Foremost, however, is the dynamic Taqī al-Dīn Aḥmad Ibn Taymiyya (d. 728/1328). Having established himself as "one of the greatest religious leaders" of Islamic history, he rarely fails—centuries after his demise—to evoke passionate sentiments.[1] In stark contrast to Ibn ʿArabī, Ibn Taymiyya is regularly lauded by scores of Salafis and chastised by scores of Sufis. His notoriety has only ballooned in recent years, owing largely to the controversial view that "perhaps no medieval scholar-activist has had more influence on radical Islamic ideology."[2] As the debate over his legacy unfolds, what can be said with certainty is that he lived during a uniquely turbulent era. He was born in Ḥarrān, Syria, in 661/1263, roughly six years before the onslaught of invading Mongols. The young Ibn Taymiyya never forgot how he and his family were forced to flee for their lives, seeking refuge in Damascus. He was raised into a family of scholars, however, and his early life was stable enough for him to immerse himself in the Islamic sciences.[3]

He mastered an array of subjects but is remembered today mainly as a reviver of Ḥanbalite traditionalism and its "most celebrated representative."[4] Although a fierce detractor of speculative theology (*kalām*), he saw no real conflict between reason and revelation.[5] He himself "displays in his polemical broadsides a superb mastery of the methods of dialectical reasoning."[6] As an effective polemicist and occasional warrior, he was championed by even some theological opponents because of a perceived need for "a more aggressive ideological attitude" in confronting Mongols (who, as newly converted Muslims, laid siege to Damascus in 699/1300 and remained an imminent threat for some time) and their allied Crusaders.[7] This was also a period that witnessed the growing influence of Sufis who, inspired by Ibn ʿArabī, affirmed the "Oneness of Being" doctrine (*ittiḥādiyya*). Ibn Taymiyya's writings abound with condemnations of these and other factions.[8]

It was precisely this "aggressive attitude" and refusal to compromise that led to his persecution and imprisonment, not only in his Syrian homeland but in Egypt as well. Mamluk courts found him guilty of a wide range of offenses, from issuing innovative legal rulings to anthropomorphizing God (notwithstanding his insistence that the Almighty should never be likened to His creatures).[9] Thus it came to pass that Ibn Taymiyya took his final breath while incarcerated in the citadel of Damascus—the same city that had once been his safe haven.[10] And yet his defiant motto endures: "What can my enemies do to me? My Garden is in my heart; wherever I go, it goes with me. My prison is solitude! My death is martyrdom! Exile is a journey!"[11]

Ibn Taymiyya's numerous works, including his well-known and extensive *Fatāwā* (Fatwas), address various soteriological matters. When expounding on the salvation of Others on the Last Day, he promotes an inclusivism limited to the "unreached." Yet his belief in God's boundless mercy (*raḥma*), grounded in his particular reading of scripture, leads him to infer that, one day, everyone—even his most ardent enemies—will behold God in Paradise.

A Warning to All Recipients

While in his mid-fifties, Ibn Taymiyya received a gift from a group of Christians in Cyprus: a revised, expanded version of a treatise composed much earlier by a certain Paul of Antioch. This Paul, a Melkite bishop, had lived sometime between the mid–fifth/eleventh century and early seventh/thirteenth century in the Crusader see of Sidon (Saida). In the face of Muslim claims of Islamic supersessionism, Paul's tractate argues that Muḥammad himself never intended for his message either to be directed toward non-Arabs or to debunk Christianity.[12] Ibn Taymiyya's response was perhaps not surprising: a voluminous work entitled *al-Jawāb al-ṣaḥīḥ li-man baddala dīn al-Masīḥ* (The sound response to those who altered the religion of the Messiah). Addressed not only to Christians but to Muslims as well, this is "a work whose length and scope have never been equaled in [premodern] Muslim critiques of the Christian religion and whose depth of insight into the issues that separate Christianity and Islam sets it among the masterpieces of Muslim polemic against Christianity."[13]

The *Jawāb* affords Ibn Taymiyya an opportunity to rebuke Judaism as well. With Jews occupying one extreme and Christians the other, he positions "true" Muslims—"the best community singled out for people" (Q. 3:110)[14]—as "a middle nation" (Q. 2:143) in matters of ritual and theology. Jews, we are told, follow unusually stringent dietary and purity laws;

Christians are extremely lax and, in the case of monks, pride themselves on their uncleanliness.[15] Jews ascribe to the Creator attributes specific to creatures when they characterize Him as miserly, "poor" (Q. 3:181), and "tight-fisted" (Q. 5:64) and when they claim that "He created the world, then became tired."[16] Christians ascribe to creatures attributes specific to the Creator when they take bishops, monks, angels, and prophets "as lords."[17] On the topic of Jesus, Jews reject him and slander his mother (Q. 4:156), while Christians claim that he is God Himself—a more egregious form of unbelief.[18] The Qur'an, Ibn Taymiyya asserts, not only corrects and abrogates the older, "corrupted" religions but also explicitly affirms the universal nature of Muḥammad's message when it states, for example, "We have sent you [Prophet] only to bring good news and warning to all the people [*kāfatan li-l-nās*]" (34:28).[19] It is true that the Qur'an praises and promises reward to certain People of the Book (as in 2:62, for example). But, Ibn Taymiyya explains, these are not references to Jews and Christians who reject the final prophet and stray far from the "straight path."[20] As such, the claim that Islamic scripture itself upholds Christianity in a post-Muḥammadan world, or that Muḥammad was sent only to the Arabs, is "among the greatest lies."[21] History itself confirms this: the Prophet invited and welcomed both Arab People of the Book and non-Arabs to his remarkably successful, fast-growing, far-reaching religion.[22] It is true that many have not received his message. This, Ibn Taymiyya notes, is why the Qur'anic warning applies only to "everyone it reaches" (6:19), rather than to absolutely everyone.[23] The fact remains, however, that all who are "reached" must heed the warning.

Islamic supersessionism is fundamental to Ibn Taymiyya's soteriology. In his *Fatāwā*, we find the following two pronouncements:

> God the Exalted sent the messengers and revealed the books, so that all worship would be "devoted to God alone" [Q. 8:39]....God sent Muḥammad*. He does not accept [a religion] from anyone whom the call [to Islam] [*al-daʿwa*] has reached, except the religion with which He sent [Muḥammad], for his invitation is, in general, for all created beings.... So all people should follow Muḥammad*.[24]

> It is obligatory upon [every] human to know that God the Exalted sent Muḥammad* to all...humans and *jinn*. And [that] He made obligatory upon them belief in [Muḥammad] and what he brought, and obedience to him....And that everyone for whom proof [*al-ḥujja*] of Muḥammad's* messengership has been established,

> from among humans and *jinn*, [but] does not believe in him, deserves the punishment of God the Exalted, just as those… from among the unbelievers to whom the Messenger was sent deserve it.[25]

Accordingly, those who receive "the call" of the final message and reject it disqualify themselves from receiving forgiveness,[26] intercession on Judgment Day,[27] and admittance into Paradise.[28] But not all unbelievers are equal: the Prophet's oppressive uncle Abū Lahab, for example, will receive a greater punishment than the Prophet's protective uncle Abū Ṭālib.[29] Even so, the chastisement of both uncles is predicated on the belief that the authenticity of Muḥammad's prophethood is recognizable to anyone of sound mind (*ʿāqil*) who uses reason (*al-ʿaql*) and reflects on the content of the message and the miracles of the Messenger, which are known via diffuse and congruent reports (*tawātur*).[30] This, Ibn Taymiyya explains, is why the people of Hell will lament, "If only we had listened, or reasoned, we would not be with the inhabitants of the blazing fire" (Q. 67:10).[31] Thus, anyone who comes to know of the Prophet's message in its "true" form and either "opposes" it or fails to investigate and follow it, giving precedence to personal "desire" over "the truth" due to a preoccupation with worldly matters, is deserving of punishment.[32]

But are there not such people as "sincere" non-Muslims who, upon encountering the final message, fail to recognize that which is supposed to confirm its authenticity? Ibn Taymiyya considers this question in the *Jawāb* and provides a sharp response: anyone of sound mind among the reached who does not accept the truthfulness of the Prophet manifests unbelief and is worthy of Hell, period.[33] Again, Ibn Taymiyya presents Muḥammad's message as inherently compelling; among the reached, sanity plus sincerity can only equal submission. (This is notwithstanding the fact that Ibn Taymiyya felt compelled to produce the *Jawāb* in the first place.) An explicit acknowledgment of those "earnest" non-Muslims who actively investigate the final message (Ghazālī's "fourth category" of non-Muslims) is absent here. Similarly absent is a general sense of optimism regarding salvation on the Last Day.[34] Nevertheless, Ibn Taymiyya is willing to concede one thing: since revelation only informs us of the fate of certain individuals (such as Abū Lahab), these are matters that are ultimately and entirely up to God.[35]

This recognition of human limitation, however, does not inhibit Ibn Taymiyya from making the case for the salvation of righteous, unreached non-Muslims.[36] How, then, will they be distinguished? There are, after all, different types of unreached non-Muslims, from those who have never encountered any revelation to those People of the Book who know only their respective scriptures. As for the former, the truly unreached, Ibn Taymiyya, like Ibn ʿArabī, asserts that they will receive a messenger on the Last Day. Referencing the hadith corpus, Ibn Taymiyya simply informs us that this messenger-of-resurrection will test his community in the "courtyards of the resurrection" (*ʿaraṣāt al-qiyāma*).[37] (Although Ibn Taymiyya speaks briefly of the limbo of "the heights" [*al-aʿrāf*] between Heaven and Hell [Q. 7:46–49], he seems to reserve it for believers who do not fear and turn to God and whose good and evil deeds are equal.)[38] In one way or another, every single individual of sound mind will be tested at some point in his or her existence and will thus be liable for chastisement if he or she fails.[39]

Some theologians would dismiss the notion of a messenger-of-resurrection as superfluous. Centuries before Ibn Taymiyya's time, numerous Muʿtazilites and other rationalists—and even a Ḥanbalite named Abū al-Khaṭṭāb (d. 410/1116)—argued that anyone of sound mind has the ability to arrive at a belief in one God, and to differentiate to some extent between acts that are "good" (*ḥasan*) and those that are "detestable" (*qabīḥ*), in the absence of revelation. Thus, the argument continues, even for the unreached, unbelief and detestable acts, including "acts" of *shirk* (associating partners with God), are potentially punishable.

Ibn Taymiyya acknowledges that the truly unreached can distinguish and be deemed guilty of committing acts that are detestable. This is why the Qur'an describes Pharaoh as having "exceeded all bounds" (79:17) before receiving Moses' message; the people of Thamūd are commanded to repent for actions committed before the prophet Ṣāliḥ conveys to them the divine threat (11:61). But what the Muʿtazilites and their kind fail to account for, Ibn Taymiyya explains, is another scriptural statement: "We do not punish until We have sent a messenger" (17:15)—a proclamation interpreted broadly here to encompass virtually all forms of divine chastisement. It is, therefore, only "transgressors" who encounter the message who must mend their ways to avoid chastisement.[40] Thus, even though Ibn Taymiyya regards the existence of the one God as "self-evident" to humanity's pure natural disposition (*fiṭra*),[41] and even though he characterizes atheism as the greatest of sins,[42] he insists that "no one will be punished until [the message of] a messenger comes to him," even if he encounters a religious leader (*imām*).[43]

Does this, then, mean that the advent of messengers is detrimental, inasmuch as it provides a justification for chastisement? Ibn Taymiyya considers this question and responds with a simile: messengers are like rain. Rain may lead to destruction, but it also provides benefits. Messengers indicate specifically what is good and what is detestable, pointing the way to a richer life and allowing one to be in line with God's will.[44] Those who suffer as a result show their true colors. The reason God commands and proscribes to begin with is simply to test people, to see if they will submit or rebel.[45]

Ibn Taymiyya's stance regarding unreached Jews and Christians fits well within his soteriology: since they already have a share of the message, their responsibility is limited to that share. They may make erroneous deductions based on that share (and what is missing from it)—as when Christians arrive at problematic beliefs regarding Jesus. But as long as they earnestly strive for the truth, they will be no more blameworthy before God than a sincere Muslim scholar (specifically, a *mujtahid*) who, similarly, strives for the truth yet arrives at mistaken interpretations of Islamic scripture.[46] Accordingly, the Jews and Christians commended in the Qur'an in passages such as 2:62 are not limited to those living before the first/seventh century.[47]

Working with these soteriological principles, one might wonder if a case could be made for the salvation of reached People of the Book who, in Ibn Taymiyya's words, "admit that the religion of Muslims is authentic" and even "superior to their religion" yet claim that Muḥammad's message was never intended to be universal and that the various religions merely represent different schools of thought (*madhāhib*).[48] Given that such Jews and Christians recognize the authenticity and divine origins of the final message yet remain adherents of their respective faiths on the basis of what Ibn Taymiyya regards as flawed logic, could at least some of these individuals be saved from chastisement on the grounds that they simply do not recognize their error? The answer one deduces from Ibn Taymiyya's writings is a resounding no. It is one thing to make an honest mistake but quite another to reject what Ibn Taymiyya regards as the obvious, fundamental truths of Islamic scripture. It is precisely for this reason that he condemns certain Muslim sects on account of their doctrines: they expose their "insincerity" by failing to recognize that which is evident to those possessing "sound hearts."[49] Thus, it is worth reiterating that, according to Ibn Taymiyya, the denial of the Qur'an's unambiguous universality is "among the greatest lies."[50] Those of sound heart and with access to the holy book would never claim such a thing.

Nevertheless, given Ibn Taymiyya's reputation for being antipathetic toward Others—thanks in part to his recurring warning against imitating

Jews, Christians, and other outsiders[51]—his openness to the salvation of unreached non-Muslims has been described as "surprising."[52] Yet his limited inclusivism is merely an interim position. What is truly astonishing is what follows.

The Grand Finale

Shortly before he passed away, Ibn Taymiyya was presented with another thought-provoking gift. This time, however, the gift-giver was none other than his prized disciple Ibn Qayyim al-Jawziyya (d. 751/1350), and the gift was a volume of commentary on the Qur'an by the third/ninth-century hadith specialist ʿAbd ibn Ḥamīd al-Kissī (d. 249/863).[53] Ibn Qayyim had instructed the messenger delivering the book to point Ibn Taymiyya to a marked section. There the "master of Islam" encountered, possibly for the first time in his life, the following statement attributed to the prominent Companion and second caliph ʿUmar ibn al-Khaṭṭāb (d. 23/644): "If the people of the Fire [*ahl al-nār*] remain in the Fire [for a period of time comparable to] the amount of sand of ʿĀlij"—the name of a desert located on the path to Mecca[54]—"then theirs would be a day in which they would leave it."[55]

In a work entitled *Shifāʾ al-ʿalīl* (Healing the sick), Ibn Qayyim informs us that, much earlier, he had asked his teacher whether Hell's chastisement would be everlasting. A seemingly undecided Ibn Taymiyya had only this to say: "This is a very great matter."[56] Ibn Qayyim suggests that his gift served as the impetus for Ibn Taymiyya's composition of what became, as I discuss below, his final work, a "well-known" treatise that makes the case for temporal punishment and the eventual salvation of all people.[57] Although its existence is well documented, its title is disputed, and today it is considerably more obscure than, for example, the *Jawāb*. It was first published in its entirety in 1995 in Saudi Arabia under the somewhat misleading title *al-Radd ʿalā man qāla bi-fanāʾ al-janna wa-l-nār* (The rejoinder to those who maintain the annihilation of the Garden and the Fire). I shall simply refer to it as *Fanāʾ al-nār* (The annihilation of the Fire).[58]

Ibn Taymiyya opens the *Fanāʾ* with an exposition of three views regarding the fate of Heaven and Hell: (1) both persist eternally; (2) both eventually perish; and (3) Hell eventually perishes, while Heaven persists eternally—Ibn Taymiyya's own position. He strongly rebukes those who maintain the eventual annihilation of both abodes (that is, the second view) precisely because of their denial of Heaven's eternality—a position he regards as innovative, as it was never known to be held by anyone among the *salaf* (the first three generations of Muslims). The "innovators" include the likes of Jahm ibn Ṣafwān and his followers, the Jahmites, who argued that the Garden and the Fire must be temporal since both are accidents with beginnings, and whatever begins to exist cannot be eternal; only God endures.[59] Ibn Taymiyya rejects this line of reasoning: why must that which has a beginning have an end? Could not God's will suffice in sustaining everlasting life? Are not His capabilities boundless?[60] Since the blessings of Paradise are derived from God's essence, and since "what God has endures" (Q. 16:96), His reward is necessarily everlasting. Indeed, the righteous "will have a reward that never fails" (Q. 41:8).[61] Additionally, Heaven's temporality has been disavowed by the "leaders" of the faith, and affirming it serves as grounds for declaring someone an unbeliever (*takfīr*). And this charge of unbelief, Ibn Taymiyya asserts, is justified on the basis of the following four unambiguous Qur'anic pronouncements: (1) "[The Garden's] food is perpetual [*dā'im*]" (13:35); (2) "Our provision for you [in the Gardens of lasting bliss] will never end [*mā lahu min nafād*]" (38:54); (3) "[Heaven's provisions will] neither be limited nor forbidden [*lā maqṭūʿa wa-lā mamnūʿa*]" (56:33); and (4) "[The Garden will be] an unceasing gift [*ʿaṭā'an ghayr majdhūdh*]" (11:108).[62]

Much less problematic although still disconcerting to Ibn Taymiyya is the more widely recognized position that both Heaven and Hell persist without end (that is, the first view). He identifies four arguments employed to establish the endless perpetuity of Hell: (1) It is in accordance with the consensus of the *salaf*—opposing viewpoints are simply innovative; (2) the Qur'an explicitly and definitively affirms it; (3) the hadith corpus indicates that unbelievers will never be spared perpetual torment (unlike those with an iota of faith, who will eventually be saved); and (4) it is necessary and in accordance with reason.[63]

Ibn Taymiyya rejects all four of these claims. The question of Hell's duration, he maintains, has actually been a subject of debate among both the *salaf* and the later generations (*khalaf*).[64] The idea that there was ever a consensus is common yet unfounded. And while not one of the Prophet's Companions is known to have explicitly affirmed the eternality of Hell and its chastisement,[65] we have already encountered an unambiguous report—ascribed to no less than ʿUmar—of the eventual salvation of the "people of the Fire." This report was related by the über scholar of the *salaf*, al-Ḥasan al-Baṣrī (d. 110/728), and subsequently transmitted through two chains of reliable narrators (*isnādān*, sing. *isnād*).[66] But might not ʿUmar's report refer only to sinning believers and not *all* of Hell's inhabitants?

Ibn Taymiyya offers a reasonable response: the phrase "people of the Fire" (*ahl al-nār*) would not be an appropriate designation for Muslims who are eventually removed from Hell, leaving others behind; it could only refer to unbelievers who remain in Hell as long as it endures, that is, the *real* people of the Fire.[67] (The phrase "people of the Fire" should not be confused with "party of the Fire" [*baʿth al-nār*], which designates those whom God dispatches [*yabʿath*] to Hell or, as Ghazālī argues, those who simply deserve to be chastised.) As we shall soon see, there are additional accounts of a noneternal punishment ascribed to other prominent Companions.

"But this contradicts scripture," Ibn Taymiyya's imaginary interlocutor exclaims. The Qur'an plainly states that unbelievers will "remain" in their "state of rejection: their punishment will not be lightened, nor will they be reprieved" (2:162). Even so, Ibn Taymiyya insists that not one statement in either the Qur'an or the hadith corpus explicitly affirms the eternality of this unrelenting punishment. In other words, one could be chastised without reprieve for a finite period of time. The unrighteous will be tormented in Hell "for a long time" (*abadan*) (Q. 72:23), but not forever.[68] What is more, the Qur'an itself hints at the impermanence of Hell in at least three places: 6:128, 11:106–108, and 78:23. Ibn Taymiyya examines each of these passages carefully, beginning with 6:128, which reads:

> On the day He gathers everyone together [saying], "Company of *jinn*! You have seduced a great many humans," their allies [*awliyāʾ*] among humankind will say, "Lord, we have profited from one another, but now we have reached the appointed time You decreed for us." He will say, "Your home is the Fire, and there you shall remain [*khālidīn fīhā*]"—*unless* God wills otherwise [*illā mā shāʾa Allāh*]: your Lord is Wise, Aware.

After all is said and done, God alone determines who is saved and who is damned. A statement to this effect is attributed to the Companion Ibn ʿAbbās (d. 68/687). With this in mind, Ibn Taymiyya proceeds to argue that both the divine threat in Q. 6:128 ("Your home is the Fire, and there you shall remain") and the exception ("unless God wills otherwise")—the latter of which leaves open the possibility of eventual salvation—are addressed not to Muslims (*ahl al-qibla*) but to unbelievers. Who else could the "allies" (*awliyāʾ*) of the satanic *jinn* be? This, Ibn Taymiyya explains, is the only interpretation in line with the Qur'anic statements "We have made the devils allies [*awliyāʾ*] to those who do not believe" (7:27) and "Fight the allies [*awliyāʾ*] of Satan"—"allies" described as "those who reject faith" (4:76).[69]

That the torment of unbelievers will one day cease is, to Ibn Taymiyya's mind, confirmed by Q. 78:23, which states that the "transgressors" will "remain" in Hell "for ages" (*aḥqāban*), not forever. Reports ascribed to the *salaf* indicate that each "age" is of *limited* duration, although how long exactly was an issue of debate: was it forty, seventy, eighty, or seventy thousand years—wherein a day may be "like a thousand years by your reckoning" (Q. 22:47)—or an amount known only to God?[70] Although the Qur'an provides no specific limit (say, three ages, or 240 years), Ibn Taymiyya insists that the ages are, by definition, finite.[71] Furthermore, the verses immediately surrounding Q. 78:23 reveal that the transgressors in question can only be unbelievers and that the term *ages* is employed to describe the stay in Hell and not simply a particular form of punishment:[72]

> Gehenna [*jahannam*] lies in wait, a home for the transgressors [*al-ṭāghīn*], where they will remain for ages, where they will not taste any coolness or drink save one that is scalding and one that is dark—a fitting requital, for they did not fear a reckoning, and they rejected Our messages as lies. (78:21–28)

Corroborating Ibn Taymiyya's reading of Q. 78:23 is a statement ascribed to the Companion Ibn Masʿūd (d. 32/652) that foretells "a time" in which "no one" will remain in Hell and that this "time" will arrive after the passing of "ages" (*aḥqāban*). We are informed that a similar proclamation is attributed to the Companion Abū Hurayra (d. 58/678).[73]

To bolster his argument, Ibn Taymiyya cites Q. 11:106–108:

> The wretched ones will remain in the Fire, sighing and groaning, there to remain [*khālidīn fīhā*] for as long as the heavens and earth endure, unless your Lord wills otherwise [*illā mā shāʾa rabbuka*]: your Lord carries out whatever He wills. As for those who have been blessed, they will be in Paradise, there to remain as long as the heavens and earth endure, unless your Lord wills otherwise—an unceasing gift.

Although both the threat of eternal damnation and the promise of eternal bliss are qualified ("unless your Lord wills otherwise"), they conclude differently: while the gift of Paradise is "an unceasing gift"—a confirmation of Heaven's permanence—we read that "your Lord carries out whatever

He wills" with regard to the damned—a declaration that seems to leave the door open for eventual salvation from Hell (and not simply, as Ibn ʿArabī argues, salvation *within* Hell). In fact, some Companions reportedly held that this passage qualifies every Qur'anic threat (*waʿīd*).[74]

Ibn Taymiyya stresses that Heaven is fundamentally dissimilar to Hell. According to the Qur'an and prophetic reports, Hell is nothing more than the abode of those guilty of sins. In contrast, the inhabitants of the Garden include former sinners who had previously spent time in the Fire, deceased children whose parents were righteous,[75] and beings created specifically for Heaven (to accompany the blessed). More important, Paradise is derived from God's mercy and forgiveness, thus reflecting His essence. Hell, meanwhile, is the abode of chastisement, which is distinct from God's essence. Wrath is not, as Ibn ʿArabī claims, an everlasting divine attribute. The Qur'an itself suggests this in the way that it carefully words the following statements, differentiating between God's merciful nature and His punishing acts: "[Prophet], tell My servants that I am the Forgiving, the Merciful, but My torment is the truly painful one" (15:49–50); "Know too that God is severe in punishment yet most forgiving and merciful" (5:98); and "Your Lord is swift in punishment, but He is most forgiving and merciful" (7:167).[76] As such, God's severe, swift chastisement is simply a creation that will be terminated once the wisdom behind its existence has been obtained. Has not God "taken it upon Himself to be merciful" (Q. 6:12)? Is it not true that His "mercy encompasses all things" (Q. 7:156) and, as prophetic reports indicate, "outstrips" and "overcomes" His wrath?[77] Thus, and here the argument becomes theodicean, if chastisement really were eternal, there would be no mercy in that. It is established in the hadith corpus that punishment in this life is actually a manifestation of compassion since it purifies the soul of its sins. In light of Ibn Taymiyya's theodicy of optimism—he often sought to discern the wisdom in the evils and calamities of this life[78]—he asserts that it is reasonable to maintain that Hell's inhabitants will continue to be chastised until, finally, they become completely purified and rectified. Once this occurs, the raison d'être of chastisement will cease to exist. From Ibn Taymiyya's vantage point, the realization that there is wisdom and mercy in the very existence of Hell is nothing short of momentous. It was on account of the belief that some individuals would never see the light of Heaven that certain theologians, including Jahm, emphasized God's omnipotence and omniscience and de-emphasized His wisdom and compassion, effectively denying His status as "the most merciful of the merciful" (*arḥam al-rāḥimīn*) (Q. 7:151).[79]

Ibn Taymiyya's case for a noneternal Hell generally supports a universalist paradigm: the "people of the Fire" will not simply perish along with Hell, they will spend the rest of eternity in Paradise. But in his attempt to debunk the notion that Hell's eternality was the consensus view of the *salaf*, he occasionally cites reports that seem to support an annihilationist paradigm. He quotes, for example, the Companion Ibn ʿAbbās, who reportedly proclaimed that God will command Hell to consume its inhabitants.[80] Other reports that appear in the *Fanā*ʾ could support either annihilationism or universalism. The following statement is ascribed to the Companion ʿAbd Allāh ibn ʿAmr (d. 63/682): "There will come a time when the gates of Gehenna will be shut, and no one will remain in it."[81] According to an early authority named al-Shaʿbī (d. 103/721), "Gehenna is the fastest of the two abodes in being inhabited, and the fastest in becoming desolate."[82] (This latter report could just as well be cited by the Jahmites since it arguably implies that both abodes will become desolate.) Nevertheless, given the preponderance of evidence offered for the salvation of all, Ibn Taymiyya's preference for universalism is clear. Working out the implications of ʿUmar's report, Ibn Taymiyya submits that the people of the Fire will proceed to another phase of existence when Hell ceases to exist. Why should the end of Hell necessitate the end of its inhabitants? Consider the example of the people of this world: one day, they will all die, perish (Q. 55:26), and become "annihilated" (*yuhlakūn*) and the earth will be transformed "into another earth" (Q. 14:48), serving as the site of Gehenna. The "annihilation" of the people of this world, however, is by no means absolute. They will simply enter a new state of being. Since "what God has endures" (Q. 16:96), and since this includes each and every soul, all of humanity will live on in one form or another.[83]

Ibn Taymiyya's closing remarks leave no doubt as to his preference for universalism. He begins his conclusion by paraphrasing a famous hadith:

> Death will come in the form of a spotted ram, and will be slaughtered between Heaven and Hell. It will be said, "people of the Garden, [there is] abiding [*khulūd*]; there is no death [in the Garden]. People of the Fire, [there is] abiding; there is no death [in the Fire]."[84]

Accordingly, the ultimate termination of Hell could not entail the absolute annihilation of its denizens, as death itself will have been slaughtered. Ibn Taymiyya avers that those who were once damned will proceed into the only remaining abode, the Garden, "the abode of felicity," where they will enjoy "everlasting pleasure."[85] To all former evildoers, Hell and, it would seem, "the heights" will be nothing more than a memory, if that. Recognizing that many will find this conclusion troubling, Ibn Taymiyya prefaces it with a warning: no one, not even the Prophet, will enter Paradise on account of his or her faith or deeds; it is a gift from God's magnanimity. And since "your Lord carries out whatever He wills" (Q. 11:107), there is nothing to stop Him from one day granting bliss to even the most unworthy of His creatures—creatures whom He chose to bring into existence.[86]

The Denial

Ibn Taymiyya was not the first to make the case for the salvation of all. If we accept his reasonable reading of the report ascribed to the Companion ʿUmar and cited by ʿAbd ibn Ḥamīd, and if we assume that the latter's volume of Qur'anic commentary had not been tampered with during the intervening centuries between its composition and Ibn Taymiyya's encounter with it, then we can trace Islamic universalism to the third/ninth century at the latest and the beginnings of Islam at the earliest. (Although, as I noted in the introduction, debates over the duration of both Heaven and Hell intensified during the second/eighth century, it is not clear to what extent, if any, universalists played a role in these discussions. This, after all, was the era of Jahm.) Still, before Ibn Taymiyya's time, we find widely recognized exegetes, including Muḥammad ibn Jarīr al-Ṭabarī (d. 310/923), Abū al-Qāsim al-Zamakhsharī (d. 538/1144), Ibn ʿAṭiyya al-Andalusī (d. 541/1146), Fakhr al-Dīn al-Rāzī (d. 606/1209), and Muḥammad ibn Aḥmad al-Qurṭubī (d. 671/1273), citing and refuting arguments in circulation for a finite Hell, most of which Ibn Taymiyya employs.[87] Interestingly, Rāzī makes a vague reference to a "group" (*qawm*) that rejects Hell's eternality; they cite Q. 11:107 and 78:23 as evidence and insist that everlasting chastisement would be both unjust and futile. Might this be a reference to universalists, rather than annihilationists?[88] Whatever the case may be, Ibn Taymiyya was undoubtedly the earliest prominent figure of the post-*salaf* era to claim that Paradise is for all of humanity; he challenged what was widely regarded then as the consensus opinion and moved beyond Ibn ʿArabī's quasi-universalism, with which Ibn Taymiyya was familiar (and which may explain some of the similarities in their arguments for universal salvation, notwithstanding their sharp differences regarding Sufi philosophy).[89] To say that the *Fanāʾ* is a source of controversy would be an understatement.

Perhaps the best indication of this is the fact that many of Ibn Taymiyya's modern supporters, including certain scholars of the Wahhabi (or Najdī) tradition, deny that this was his real position.[90] The contemporary scholar ʿAlī al-Ḥarbī, for instance, asserts that Ibn Taymiyya never authored the *Fanāʾ*, at least in the form we have it today, and that this can be known on the basis of its peculiar content.[91] This is despite the fact that, as we shall soon see, Ibn Taymiyya's contemporaries, namely, his universalist student Ibn Qayyim and his damnationist adversary Taqī al-Dīn al-Subkī, cite much of the *Fanāʾ*, often verbatim. Additionally, we do not have a single report of any of Ibn Taymiyya's contemporaries claiming that his universalist proclamations were misattributions. Since Ḥarbī published his denial of Ibn Taymiyya's universalism in 1990 (five years before the publication of the complete edition of the *Fanāʾ*), two studies have drawn attention to the fatal shortcomings of Ḥarbī's arguments.[92]

Another apologetic tactic is to suggest that Ibn Taymiyya composed the *Fanāʾ* before mastering the religious sciences, that is, during a radically different period in which, he himself admits, he had held a favorable view of Ibn ʿArabī.[93] This theory was advanced by the renowned hadith specialist Muḥammad Nāṣir al-Dīn al-Albānī (d. 1999), who cites passages from Ibn Taymiyya's other writings that seem to affirm eternal chastisement.[94] To be sure, Ibn Taymiyya occasionally appears to be a firm damnationist. In his *Fatāwā*, for example, he speaks, without qualification, of the Prophet's parents remaining in Hell and enduring "unrestricted burning" (*al-ṣalī al-muṭlaq*).[95] Elsewhere he asserts that the *salaf*, the leaders of the Muslim community, and the generality of Sunnis are in agreement that "Heaven, Hell, the Throne [of God], and other [things]" will "not perish completely" (*bi-l-kulliyya*); it is only a group of innovative rationalists, such as Jahm and certain (not most) Muʿtazilites, who say that "all of creation" will cease to be. He goes on to proclaim that, according to the consensus of the *salaf* and the leaders of the Muslim community, Heaven and its inhabitants, as well as "other than that," are everlasting.[96] Ibn Taymiyya's wording here may be intentional: he avoids using the term *consensus* when speaking of the perpetuity of Hell, and it is in response to the claim of a finite afterlife that he states that Heaven and Hell will not "completely" perish.[97] It is certainly plausible that, by assuming qualifications that never made it onto paper, he disguised his universalism in writings that he knew would be more accessible to the broader public.

Yet even if every one of his ostensibly anti-universalist statements represents an earnest alignment with the majority, this was not Ibn Taymiyya at his most mature. In the aforementioned report in the *Shifāʾ*, we are informed that Ibn Qayyim sent a book of Qur'anic commentary (containing

ʿUmar's report) to Ibn Taymiyya and that the latter subsequently composed his "well-known" treatise, that is, the *Fanāʾ*. The report in the *Shifāʾ* indicates that Ibn Taymiyya received the book of commentary during the latter's "final session" (*fī majlisihi al-akhīr*). (It is not clear whether this was a teaching "session" or a tribunal.)[98] According to another of Ibn Taymiyya's disciples, Ibn Rushayyiq (d. 749/1348), the *Fanāʾ* was produced during his master's "final imprisonment" (*fī maḥbasihi al-akhīr*) in the citadel of Damascus.[99] This places the *Fanāʾ* sometime during the last two years of Ibn Taymiyya's life but before his paper and pen were confiscated just a few months prior to his death.[100] According to the biographer Ṣalāḥ al-Dīn al-Ṣafadī (d. 764/1363), the *Fanāʾ* was "the last work he composed in the citadel."[101] The available evidence leads only to the conclusion that it was most likely Ibn Taymiyya's final work.

Assuming Ibn Taymiyya composed the *Fanāʾ* without subsequently repudiating it, some apologists caution against characterizing him as a universalist, insisting that he merely *leaned* toward universalism. This is the position Muḥammad al-Samharī takes in his introduction to the 1995 Saudi publication of the *Fanāʾ*.[102] According to Samharī, the "master of Islam" never explicitly states his own opinion, and so one cannot say that he abandoned the Sunni doctrine of an eternal Hell.[103] It is true that Ibn Taymiyya never prefaces his case for universalism with "I say" or "My doctrine is." But if this becomes the unnecessarily stringent criterion by which we ascribe positions to scholars, then we shall have to rethink much of Islamic intellectual history. The fact remains that in the *Fanāʾ* Ibn Taymiyya refutes the doctrine of an eternal Hell (which he does not regard as *the* Sunni position) while developing arguments in favor of universalism, giving it the final word. Yet even if we decide that he simply preferred universalism, the implications remain profound. Samharī, therefore, finds it necessary to warn his audience: since Hell's eventual annihilation is "improbable," it is the duty of the "common" Muslim to side with the doctrine indicated by the Qur'an and Sunna and adopted by many of the *salaf*, namely, Hell's eternality; only a good-intentioned and qualified scholar (specifically, a *mujtahid*) may be excused for leaning toward any other position, even if it is wrong.[104]

The predicament of Ibn Taymiyya's universalism is accentuated by the fact that it has inspired rejoinders by scholars as diverse as the Syrian Taqī al-Dīn Abū Bakr al-Ḥiṣnī (d. 829/1426),[105] the Yemeni Muḥammad ibn Ismāʿīl al-Ṣanʿānī (d. 1182/1768),[106] and more recently, the Jordanian ʿUmar al-Ashqar.[107] Perhaps most significant of all, however, and most relevant for our purposes is Subkī's *al-I'tibār bi-baqā' al-janna wa-l-nār* (Consideration of the permanence of the Garden and the Fire). The *I'tibār*, which was produced approximately two decades after Ibn Taymiyya's demise, represents the most well-known refutation by a contemporary. It served as the vehicle by which many later scholars were introduced to Ibn Taymiyya's universalism and was a model for later refutations.

The Rejoinder

Taqī al-Dīn 'Alī ibn 'Abd al-Kāfī al-Subkī had at least a few things in common with Ibn Taymiyya. Both bore the name Taqī al-Dīn and the title "the master of Islam," and both spent the majority of their lives in Syria and Egypt. Yet Subkī is remembered today as one of Ibn Taymiyya's fiercest detractors. Born in 683/1284 in the Egyptian province of Subk and trained in Cairo, Subkī eventually taught at the Manṣūriyya madrasa, located at the grandiose Ibn Ṭūlūn mosque. He then moved to Damascus and became the city's chief judge before once again returning to Egypt, where he passed away in 756/1355. He was an Ash'arite theologian, Shāfi'ite jurist, and prolific author, and is said to have penned approximately 150 works on a variety of topics, from theology to law to poetry.[108] In the *I'tibār*, which was composed in 748/1347,[109] he sets himself the task of undermining the Taymiyyan concept of a finite Hell–infinite Heaven, which, by this time, was being promoted by "some of the people of [his] era."[110] As Subkī would have it, Ibn Taymiyya regularly conflated what he transmitted as revelation with his own personal views, and, thus, he "is not one to be relied upon."[111] His universalism in particular is an "innovation [*bid'a*] from among the most ominous and ugliest of innovations"[112] and warrants a charge of unbelief (*kufr*) (although Subkī here avoids openly calling Ibn Taymiyya an unbeliever).[113]

Subkī commences the *I'tibār* by affirming that there is in fact a consensus regarding not only the eternality of Heaven but also the eternality of Hell and that this was documented long ago by the fifth/eleventh-century Andalusian scholar Ibn Ḥazm (d. 456/1064).[114] It is also a doctrine supported by clear scriptural evidence. Subkī goes on to quote thirty-four Qur'anic passages he regards as explicit indications of Hell's permanence, including three verses that speak of unbelievers "remaining" (*khālidīn*) in Hell "forever" (*abadan*) (4:169, 33:65, 72:23)—a markedly different interpretation from that offered by Ibn Taymiyya. Subkī asserts that such an abundance of unambiguous statements, which are corroborated by many other verses, means that only a literal, straightforward interpretation could do justice to the passages in question.[115] After all, they parallel Qur'anic statements of Heaven's permanence, thirty-eight of which he quotes to illustrate this point.[116]

As for the three key Qur'anic passages that supposedly qualify and clarify all other divine threats, that is, 6:128, 11:106–108, and 78:23, Subkī provides a counterexegesis. Much, he observes, has been written about the exceptions in 6:128 ("unless God wills otherwise") and 11:107 ("unless your Lord wills otherwise") concerning the stay in Hell. Abū ʿAmr al-Dānī (d. 444/1052), another Andalusian scholar of the same era as Ibn Ḥazm, compiled a comprehensive list of twenty-seven doctrines in circulation regarding these exceptions. Not one of these doctrines involves the eventual salvation of unbelievers.[117] What is included in this list and is, therefore, justifiable is the view that the exceptions refer to the period of time preceding entry into the Fire. This would mean that the exceptions should be interpreted as "except whatever [period of time] God/your Lord wills." Otherwise, the exceptions may be an indication of the temporality of the punishment of the Fire but not of punishment itself. As I indicated earlier, the hadith corpus (and arguably the Qur'an) attests to the reality of the *zamharīr*, the extremely cold alternative to the extremely hot Fire. (The Fire here is construed as an aspect of Hell, rather than its synonym.) Thus, the declaration immediately following the exception in Q. 11:107, "your Lord carries out whatever He wills," connotes not the termination of punishment but the variation and intensification of chastisement.[118] It is true that the "transgressors" will remain in Gehenna "for ages" (Q. 78:23), but this need not mean that the ages are finite. Even if each age is equivalent to a limited number of years, this need not mean that there is a limited number of ages.[119]

Subkī similarly contests the claim that, of the two abodes, only Heaven can persist since only it reflects the essence of the divine, the Forgiving, the Merciful (Q. 15:49). Here the universalists fail to account for the fact that God is also the Subduer (al-Qahhār) (Q. 12:39), the Compeller (al-Jabbār) (Q. 59:23), the Avenger (al-Muntaqim) (derived from Q. 44:16, which uses an indefinite form of this term in describing God on a "day" that lies ahead), the Humiliator (al-Mudhill) (derived from Q. 3:26, which states that God humiliates), and Severe in Punishment (Shadīd al-ʿiqāb) (Q. 5:98) (Subkī presents the latter as a divine name, although it is typically not considered as such and does not appear in the standard list of God's ninety-nine "most beautiful names"). Yet even if we ignore these particular attributes, there is another problem with Ibn Taymiyya's claim: if God's names must translate into eternal realities (eternal here interpreted to mean not bound by time), since God is the Creator (al-Khāliq) (Q. 59:24), the universe would have to be infinitely old—a position notoriously associated with many of the philosophers (*falāsifa*).

Countering Ibn Taymiyya's theodicean contention, Subkī insists that everlasting damnation is in no way incongruous with God's attribute of mercy. Paradise—mercy par excellence—awaits the virtuous; unbelievers deserve their fate, and the Almighty is free to do with them as He pleases. While it is true that, according to Q. 7:156, His "mercy encompasses all things," this same verse goes on to state, "I shall ordain My mercy for those who are conscious of God," not those who turn away. The wisdom, then, behind the creation of the "people of the Fire" is that it manifests divine omnipotence while honoring the believers and their beliefs. God could have created everyone as upright, but He desired to distinguish certain entities from their corrupting opposites, such as belief and unbelief, knowledge and ignorance. Thus, He produced not only angels and pious people, including prophets and "the best of creation," Muḥammad, but also the Prophet's hostile kinsman Abū Jahl, Pharaoh, and satanic beings, including Satan (Iblīs) himself, "the chief of misguidance."[120]

It is, therefore, unthinkable that Satan, Pharaoh, and all other unbelievers could and would eventually rectify themselves and take up residence in Paradise, where they would spend the rest of eternity—a point Subkī makes after quoting the universalist conclusion to the *Fanā'*. Thus, Subkī opines that Ibn Taymiyya's doctrine not only violates the consensus of the community but is also bizarre—a doctrine one would have only expected from a non-Muslim![121] (And yet, as Subkī notes a few pages earlier, even non-Muslim religious sects accept everlasting damnation.)[122] The Qur'an could not be clearer: the unbelievers, who "have no hope of receiving [God's] grace" (29:23), will remain in a Fire that will be made to "blaze more fiercely" each time it "goes down" (17:97). This will not be a time of reformation: "God has sealed their hearts" (Q. 2:7); "no soul will profit from faith if it had none before" (Q. 6:158).[123] This is a strong counterargument, provided one takes these scriptural declarations to reflect eternal realities. (It is worth noting that the statement quoted from Q. 6:158 is immediately prefaced by the phrase "*on the day* some of your Lord's signs come.")

How, then, does one account for the universalist proclamations attributed to the Prophet's Companions, particularly ʿUmar's report of the salvation of the "people of the Fire"? Subkī casts doubt on the latter's authenticity: the alleged narrator, al-Ḥasan al-Baṣrī, who was born in 21/641 (a mere two years before ʿUmar's assassination), could not have learned anything directly from ʿUmar.[124] Even if this report were genuine, however, one should only assume the best of the Companions: ʿUmar's report does not specify where the people of the Fire will go after leaving their abode. Their destination could very well be the torturous, freezing *zamharīr*. Still, if their end is Paradise, this report could simply be in reference to sinning believers.[125] (Subkī never seriously addresses Ibn Taymiyya's argument that the "people of the Fire" could only be unbelievers.) Why would this and similar accounts be in circulation among the *salaf* in the first place? According to Subkī, since the Qur'an never explicitly states that sinning believers will be saved—this is only made clear in the Sunna—the early Muslims, dreading the thought of everlasting damnation, made it a point to affirm the ultimate salvation of all believers, in the face of Muʿtazilite objections.[126] (The view that all unrepentant sinners, believers or otherwise, will be forever chastised was common among the Muʿtazilites.)[127] In reality, not one pious individual among the *salaf* ever held that Hell itself is finite.[128] Thus, whereas Ibn Taymiyya regards the statements ascribed to ʿUmar and other early Muslims as proof that there have always been differences of opinion on this matter, Subkī invokes the consensus documented by Ibn Ḥazm, a scholar living in Muslim Spain four centuries after the Prophet (and, as we saw in the introduction, one whose consensus claims are not always reliable), in order to justify his own view of the *salaf*.[129]

In the final analysis, Subkī's critique demonstrates just how underdeveloped some of the arguments in the *Fanāʾ* are, even if his own contentions are no less problematic. But universalists would find a stronger case for Ibn Taymiyya's position in the works of his disciple Ibn Qayyim—even though the latter's own conclusions are, as we shall soon see, ostensibly more cautious. Given that Ibn Qayyim's writings on this matter have been much more accessible than the *Fanāʾ*, universalists inspired by Ibn Taymiyya are likely to have encountered only those passages of the *Fanāʾ* quoted by Ibn Qayyim.

The Rearticulation

If Ibn Taymiyya is the most influential Ḥanbalite of all time, a strong candidate for second place is his student Shams al-Dīn Abū Bakr Ibn Qayyim al-Jawziyya. A true son of Damascus, Ibn Qayyim was born there in 691/1292 and passed away there in 751/1350. As his name indicates, his father was the superintendent (*qayyim*) of the city's Jawziyya madrasa, which also served as a Ḥanbalite court of law. Ibn Qayyim's upbringing and training may account for at least some of his scholarly accomplishments. His works, which today are in wide circulation, cover subjects as varied as rhetoric, mysticism, legal philosophy, politics, and theology. Ibn Qayyim was hardly an imitator of Ibn Taymiyya, although he did have much in common with his teacher. He, too, clashed with the Mamluk government and was imprisoned in the citadel of Damascus. He, too, opposed Ibn ʿArabī–inspired Sufis (*ittiḥādiyya*). He, too, adopted limited inclusivism as an interim soteriological position.[130] He, too, adhered to a theodicy of optimism.[131] And, building on the *Fanāʾ*, he, too, developed arguments for universal salvation. The latter are laid out not only in the *Shifāʾ* but, most famously, in a work entitled *Ḥādī al-arwāḥ ilā bilād al-afrāḥ* (Spurring souls on to dominions of joys).[132] A more forceful version of these arguments appears in one of his final works, *Ṣawāʿiq al-mursala* (The dispatched thunderbolts); however, all we have of the relevant discussion in the *Ṣawāʿiq* survives in an ostensibly reliable abridgment by a certain Muḥammad ibn al-Mawṣilī (d. 774/1372), a contemporary of Ibn Qayyim.[133]

Although he quotes extensively from the *Fanāʾ* (especially in the *Ḥādī*), it is clear that Ibn Qayyim had reflected on its inadequacies. The *Ḥādī*, for instance, examines and refutes doctrines not treated in the *Fanāʾ*, including Ibn ʿArabī's quasi-universalism and a position ascribed to the Prophet's Jewish contemporaries, namely, that the inhabitants of Hell will be chastised for a limited—and relatively brief—period of time before entering Paradise and being replaced by another group.[134] According to Ibn Qayyim, this doctrine—held by the "enemies of God"—violates the consensus of the Companions, the succeeding generation, and the leaders of Islam, and is rejected in the Qur'an:[135]

> [The Jews] say, "The Fire will only touch us for a few days." Say to them, "Have you received a promise from God—for God never breaks His promise—or are you saying things about Him of which you have no real knowledge?" Truly those who do evil and are surrounded by their sins will be the inhabitants of the Fire, there to remain [*khālidūn*]. (2:80–81)

> Have you considered those who were given a share of the scripture? They were asked to accept judgment from God's scripture, and yet some of them turn their backs and walk away, all because they declare, "The Fire will only touch us for a limited number of days."[136] The lies they have invented have led them astray in their own religion. (3:23–24)

The Qur'an, Ibn Qayyim adds, affirms that "[the followers of evildoers] shall not leave the Fire" (2:167); "whenever, in their anguish, [the unbelievers] try to escape, they will be pushed back in and told, 'Taste the suffering of the Fire' " (22:22); "[those who reject the truth] will neither be finished off by death, nor be relieved from Hell's torment" (35:36); and

> the gates of Heaven will not be open to those who rejected Our revelations and arrogantly spurned them; they will not enter the Garden until [*ḥattā*] the camel [*al-jamal*] passes through the eye of the needle. This is how We punish the guilty. (7:40)[137]

This, Ibn Qayyim declares, is the "most eloquent" indication of "the impossibility" of unbelievers "entering the Garden."[138] But in light of Ibn Qayyim's universalist stance, it is clear that he regards these passages as being qualified: they are true as long as Hell exists. Nevertheless, his attempt to debunk a doctrine that was never seriously championed by Muslims seems to demonstrate defensive posturing on his part in response to damnationist critics who may have invoked passages such as Q. 2:80–81 and 3:23–24 in an attempt to link the universalists to the Prophet's Jewish nemeses. Polemics may also explain why Ibn Qayyim would bother denying the view that all of Hell's inhabitants will leave the Fire while it persists, with no one remaining in it—a case of everlasting futility.[139]

Although the *Ḥādī* is believed to have been composed in 745/1344,[140] which is approximately three years before Subkī penned the *I'tibār*, the latter makes no reference to Ibn Qayyim's specific contributions to Ibn Taymiyya's case for universalism (which I discuss below). Meanwhile, Ibn Qayyim's rearticulation suggests that he was familiar with at least some of the points raised by Subkī. For example, when enumerating arguments for damnationism, Ibn Qayyim rehashes Ibn Taymiyya's list of four and adds the following two: (1) it is the unambiguous belief not simply of the *salaf* but of Sunnis in general; and (2) it is unreasonable to speak of the salvation of insolent unbelievers who, if reprieved from their chastisement, would simply return to their evil ways.[141] If the *I'tibār* was indeed produced after the *Ḥādī*, we have good reason to think that Ibn Taymiyya's universalism inspired a host of Subkī-like critics before Subkī himself.

This would help to explain Ibn Qayyim's lengthy final section of this discussion in the *Ḥādī*, as he presents twenty-five arguments for a temporal Hell and an eternal Heaven for all. This *Fanā'*-inspired exposition constitutes the most extensive known case for universalism in premodern

Islamic thought.[142] The twenty-five arguments, which greatly overlap, may be summarized into two basic claims.

First, scripture indicates that the Garden is fundamentally dissimilar to the Fire. While God admits into Paradise individuals who may not have proved themselves worthy of it, only sinners land in Hell.[143] And whereas the denizens of Heaven will have "an unceasing gift" (Q. 11:108), one can only conclude that, for a time, the "people of the Fire" will remain in Hell, unable to escape it (Q. 32:20), neither dying nor living in it (Q. 20:74). What is more, the Qur'an points to Hell's finitude, not only in 6:128, 11:107, and 78:23 but also in passages that mention "the punishment of a dreadful *day*" (*yawm ʿaẓīm*) (6:15) and "a painful *day*" (*yawm alīm*) (11:26).[144] In contrast, the Qur'an never describes the felicity of Paradise as the felicity of a "day." (It is not entirely clear how Ibn Qayyim would choose to interpret a passage like Q. 50:34: "So enter [Heaven] in peace. This is the *day* of abiding" [*yawm al-khulūd*].) Thus, sinners will be punished only in accordance with the finite extent of their sins. But this does not necessarily mean that the chastisement will be swift: a "day" could last (or feel like) thousands and thousands of years.[145]

An important supplement to this argument appears in the *Shifāʾ*. As I noted earlier, a common damnationist claim is that because the Qur'an employs the terms *khālidīn* (from the root *kh-l-d*) and *abadan* (from the root *ʾ-b-d*) when describing the punishment of the Fire, there should be no doubt concerning the eternality of punishment. In other words, a statement such as *khālidīn fīhā abadan* (72:23) can only mean "they will remain in [Hell] forever." Not so, says Ibn Qayyim: it is known that words derived from the root *kh-l-d* may connote an extended yet ultimately limited period of time (for example, *qayd mukhallad*, "a lasting shackle"). The same is true of the root *ʾ-b-d*. The Qur'an itself states that the evildoers among the Jews "will never long for [death]" (*lan yatamannawhu abadan*) (2:95). Here the term *abadan* establishes the perpetuity of their aversion to dying. This, however, could only reflect a temporal reality, as it is known that, in the next life, the people of Hell will cry, if only God would "put an end to us!" (Q. 43:77).[146] *Abadan*, therefore, connotes perpetuity, but only within a particular context, for instance, this life or life in Hell. But this presents a problem: while the term *abadan* appears thrice in the Qur'an in reference to the duration of chastisement (4:169, 33:65, 72:23), it is employed nine times in reference to heavenly reward (4:57, 122; 5:119; 9:22, 100; 18:3; 64:9; 65:11; 98:8). If *abadan* need not signify an eternal reality, what assurance does the believer have of everlasting bliss? Ibn Qayyim defends the selective interpretation of *abadan* as "forever" in the case of Paradise by pointing to Qur'anic passages that describe heavenly reward as "never-ending" (*ghayr mamnūn*) (84:25) and—as Ibn Taymiyya had noted—"an unceasing gift" (11:108) whose provisions "will never end" (38:54).[147] These attestations are to be sharply contrasted with the clear indications of temporal chastisement that appear not only in the Qur'an (as in 78:23) but also in reports ascribed to the Companions. The latter include the aforementioned statement attributed to ʿUmar. As Ibn Qayyim may have encountered Subkī's *Iʿtibār* by the time he composed the *Shifāʾ*—it is known to be among his later works and, unlike the *Ḥādī*, is quite dissimilar structurally to Ibn Taymiyya's *Fanāʾ*[148]—he makes it a point to defend the report's authenticity: the narrator of the report, al-Ḥasan al-Baṣrī, learned of ʿUmar's statement not from ʿUmar directly (which would have been virtually impossible given their respective ages) but indirectly from unnamed individuals among the Successors to the Companions (*al-tābiʿūn*). (A similar clarification appears on the margins of one of the two extant manuscripts of the *Fanāʾ*.)[149] If the report were truly controversial—due to either its content or the manner of its transmission—we would expect earlier generations to have rejected and refuted it.[150] (Conspicuously, ʿUmar's statement—but not the aforementioned reports ascribed to Ibn Masʿūd, Abū Hurayra, ʿAbd Allāh ibn ʿAmr, and al-Shaʿbī—is absent from the abridged remains of the *Ṣawāʿiq*.)

Second, the divine attributes of mercy, wisdom, and omnipotence necessitate the annihilation of the Fire and the salvation of all. According to the hadith corpus, God's mercy outstrips and overcomes His wrath and, in the life to come, will be multiplied ninety-nine times.[151] This is because mercy, not wrath, is of God's essence. Thus, mercy, not wrath, is everlasting. Accordingly, the Compassionate, on account of His immense good will, will rescue the wicked.[152] To quote Ibn Qayyim, "Forgiveness is more beloved to [God]—praise be to Him—than vengeance, mercy is more beloved to Him than punishment, acceptance is more beloved to Him than wrath, and grace is more beloved to Him than justice."[153]

Incidentally, in response to Subkī, Ibn Qayyim in the *Shifāʾ* maintains that the proclamation in Q. 7:156, "[God's] mercy encompasses all things," should indeed be read as a general statement; the latter part of the verse, "I shall ordain"—literally, "I shall write out" (*aktub*)—"My mercy for those who are conscious of God," refers to a specific, special form of mercy reserved for the virtuous, those who will be saved from all forms of chastisement.[154] If mercy truly embraces "all things," nothing in creation is barred from mercy.

Back in the *Ḥādī*, Ibn Qayyim invites his audience to reflect on the mercy before their eyes. In fact, he writes, it is already evident in this life that God's mercy outstrips His wrath:[155] "He created [unbelievers] by His mercy, nourished them by His mercy, provided for them and healed them by His mercy, and sent them messengers by His mercy."[156] And yet even His agonizing punishments—past, present, and future—are the products of mercy. According to one hadith, if the disobedient repent, God will be "their beloved" (*ḥabībuhum*); if they persist, He will be "their physician" (*ṭabībuhum*), healing them through afflictions—a familiar metaphor.[157] As Ibn Qayyim explains, the treatment for an obdurate disease can be exceedingly onerous, and even the most compassionate of physicians must sometimes resort to cauterizing with fire to eliminate harm. Painful chastisement, therefore, allows for rectification. This is known to be true of the divinely ordained punishments of this life (that is, the *ḥudūd* punishments), which resolve one's affairs with God. Thus, in chastisement we find not only justice but also mercy and perfection.[158] The Fire, then, is "the grand remedy."[159]

But the treatment is not generic; rather, it is specific to each individual. Unlike sinners who have at least an iota of good in them, some will never be saved from Hell as long as it exists. They require a thorough cleansing: "those who were blind in this life will be blind in the hereafter, and even further off the path" (Q. 17:72); "even if they were brought back, they would only return to the very thing that was forbidden to them" (Q. 6:28); "if God had known there was any good in [those who are willfully deaf and dumb], He would have made them hear, but even if He had, they would still have turned away and taken no notice" (Q. 8:23).[160] Yet even these miscreants can be rectified: if one were to tarry in Hell "for ages" (Q. 78:23), and if, according to one prophetic report, each age is as long as fifty thousand years (an amount not mentioned by Ibn Taymiyya), it would be unfathomable for anyone to maintain even an iota of *shirk* (associationism), arrogance, or wickedness after such a lengthy chastisement.[161]

All things considered, Hell serves the dual purpose of creating fear among believers and purifying evildoers. Wickedness not purged through sincere repentance, good deeds, and afflictions in this life will melt away in the Fire. Once all of its inhabitants have been restored to their pure natural disposition (*fiṭra*), God will have no interest in punishing His servants without cause: "Why should God make you suffer torment if you are thankful and believe in Him? God always rewards gratitude and He knows everything" (Q. 4:147). Again, all punishments are means, not ends.[162]

And all scriptural threats cease to be in effect once the basis for those threats no longer exists, as in the case of an unbeliever who submits to God before passing away.[163]

Even if we assume that scriptural warnings of damnation that use terms like *khālidīn* and *abadan* connote endlessness, Ibn Qayyim offers the following: while it is known that God's promises are absolute, when it comes to His threats, "your Lord carries out whatever He wills" (Q. 11:107). This is widely recognized: the prevailing opinion among Muslim scholars is that God, out of His generosity and nobility, will save sinning believers despite the following threats (translated here to reflect the majority view): "whoever disobeys God and His messenger will have the Fire of Gehenna; they will remain in it forever [*khālidīn fīhā abadan*]" (Q. 72:23); "if anyone kills a believer deliberately, the punishment for him [or her] is Hell, and there he [or she] will remain forever [*khālidan*]" (Q. 4:93). According to prophetic reports, whoever commits suicide will be barred from Paradise, and whoever kills himself or herself using a piece of iron will continually kill himself or herself with that piece of iron, remaining in Hell "forever" (*abadan*).[164] Although these passages and reports are often employed to rebut universalism, most theologians recognize that even these threats are not absolute, particularly in the case of believers, however sinful they may be. Is it not, then, at least conceivable that the Compassionate, the Noble, qualifies all of His threats?[165]

Developing Ibn Taymiyya's distinction between God's names and His actions, Ibn Qayyim observes that, although "God is severe in punishment" (Q. 5:98), scripture never once refers to Him as the Punisher (al-Muʿāqib) or the Torturer (al-Muʿadhdhib).[166] God avenges transgressions (Q. 44:16), but once His creatures desist from transgressing, He desists from punishing them. Harm (*sharr*), therefore, results from divine wisdom and ceases once it becomes futile; we have no scriptural reason to suppose that harm is itself of the divine essence.[167] Ibn Qayyim advises his audience to reflect deeply on the Qur'an's careful portrayal of God: "Contemplate this…and a gate from among the gates [that lead to] knowing and loving Him will open for you."[168]

Still unclear, however, is how Ibn Qayyim would respond to Subkī's contention that if God's attributes translate into eternal realities (eternal here meaning timeless), then one would be compelled to accept the controversial doctrine that the universe is eternally old. (Again, one of the divine names is the Creator.) Perhaps Ibn Qayyim would argue that prior to creation, the divine attributes were made manifest primarily through the divine will: because God always willed to create, He was always the Creator. And an eternally old will to create at a specific point in time precludes the possibility of an eternally old universe.[169]

Ibn Qayyim acknowledges that his specific arguments for universal salvation are anomalous; his audience may not encounter them elsewhere. Perhaps this is why he concludes his discussion in the *Ḥādī* conservatively, announcing that his own position on the matter is the Qur'anic statement "your Lord carries out whatever He wills" (11:107). He also cites a report attributed to the Prophet's cousin, the fourth caliph ʿAlī ibn Abī Ṭālib (d. 40/661), which states that after the "people of the Garden" enter Paradise and the "people of the Fire" enter Hell, "God will do what He pleases."[170] Ibn Qayyim proceeds to make a common declaration of humility, granting that whatever in his book is sound is from God and whatever is unsound is either from him or from Satan and that, ultimately, "God knows best."[171] Despite these final qualifications, a similar version of which appears in the *Shifāʾ*,[172] it is evident that Ibn Qayyim, at the very least, prefers universalism. He advocates what I would call "cautious universalism."

In the *Ṣawāʿiq*, which was composed after both the *Ḥādī* and the *Shifāʾ*,[173] he goes a step further, suggesting that the temporality of Hell is a doctrine of the enlightened:

> Those who say that the chastisement of unbelievers is a benefit to them and a mercy to them circle around this sense and do not penetrate its depth. But what benefit to them is there in chastisement that does not end, that is [eternally] perpetual by virtue of the perpetuity of the Lord—Most High is He? Ponder this point very thoroughly, and give it its due reflection. Join that with the senses of His names and His attributes, with what His word and the word of His Messenger indicate, and with what the Companions and those after them said. Do not rush to speak without knowledge or to condemn. If the dawn of what is correct shines on you, [that is good]. If not, then ascribe the judgment to what God ascribes it in His statement, "Your Lord carries out whatever He wills" [Q. 11:107], and hold firm to the statement of ʿAlī ibn Abī Ṭālib, may God be pleased with him.[174]

It would have been odd if such sentiments did not generate the kind of agitation instigated by Ibn Taymiyya. Yet for apologists like ʿAlī al-Ḥarbī, rejecting the authenticity of Ibn Qayyim's case for universalism would have been a more daunting task: it appears in three popular and readily available works. Ḥarbī, therefore, takes another route: he asserts that these writings contain no evidence that Ibn Qayyim ever affirmed universal deliverance (even if he was leaning in that direction) and that, looking to his other works, we can know for certain that he passed away a damnationist.[175] The first part of Ḥarbī's claim—that Ibn Qayyim never advocates universalism in the *Ḥādī*, the *Shifāʾ*, and the *Ṣawāʿiq*—distracts from the thrust of all three discussions and, more important, fails to account for the passage in the *Ṣawāʿiq* quoted above. But is there something to the second part of the claim? Did Ibn Qayyim actually come to prefer the more common view that chastisement is everlasting?

In a recent study, Jon Hoover identifies some of the weaknesses of Ḥarbī's approach but finds at least three of the seemingly anti-universalist passages marshaled by Ḥarbī to be supportive of the latter's assertion. First, in what may have been Ibn Qayyim's final work, *Zād al-maʿād* (Provisions for the hereafter), he proclaims that

> when an associationist [*mushrik*] is foul in constitution and foul in essence, the Fire does not cleanse his foulness. On the contrary, if he were to come out of it, he would return as foul as he was [before], like a dog when it enters the sea and then comes out of it.

This, he continues, is why the Almighty "forbade the Garden" to associationists.[176] God created the "fair" and the "foul," and both will be distinguished in the life to come.[177] Second, in another late manuscript, *Ṭarīq al-hijratayn* (The path of the two emigrations), Ibn Qayyim describes Heaven and Hell as the "two perpetual abodes" (*dārā al-qarār*)[178] and, despite an extensive discussion of the hereafter and the divine wisdom it reflects, leaves the reader with the impression that damnation is endless.[179] Finally, in *al-Wābil al-ṣayyib* (The abundant downpour), which is difficult to date, Ibn Qayyim states that both the "abode of pure fairness" and the "abode of pure foulness" will remain and will "not pass away" (*lā tafnayān*), unlike the transient "abode for those accompanied by something foul and something fair." The latter is the "abode of the disobedient." And "none of the disobedient among those who confess [God's] unity will remain in Hell," as belief in God's unity is the "key" to Paradise.[180]

As we saw in the previous chapter in the case of Mullā Ṣadrā, arguing for temporal chastisement can be perilous. Hoover speculates that Ibn Qayyim may have stopped promoting universal deliverance after Subkī produced the *Iʿtibār* in order to ward off a charge of unbelief.[181] It was a mere two years earlier that Subkī, as chief judge of Damascus, had denounced Ibn Qayyim's anomalous legal stance on the permissibility of certain horse races involving stakes; when summoned by Subkī, Ibn Qayyim gave in to the majority. Four years later (that is, two years after the *I'tibār* was composed and shortly before Ibn Qayyim passed away), the two were at odds again—this time regarding, of all topics, divorce laws—before being publicly reconciled a second time.[182]

It is highly unlikely that the aforementioned references to Hell's perpetuity in Ibn Qayyim's later works represent a true conversion to the prevailing view. Neither these nor any of his other known writings offer a retraction or refutation of any of his crucial and well-developed arguments for universalism, let alone an admission of error. Given that he gradually acquired more confidence in the universalist paradigm, as evidenced in the *Ṣawā'iq* (again, one of his final works), it is difficult to imagine that he suddenly changed his mind and had little to say about it (again, after having devoted much space to the universalist agenda in three separate works). As such, I submit that Ibn Qayyim made his ostensibly damnationist statements with qualifications in mind: associationists will not be purified by the Fire—until they have been tormented for ages; the "fair" will be separated from the "foul" in the hereafter—although the "foul" will eventually become "fair"; unlike the short-term "abode of the disobedient," Hell will "not pass away"—until much later. Indeed, in the *midst* of presenting his case for universal salvation in the *Shifā'*, Ibn Qayyim states that "it is necessarily known through the religion of Islam that the Garden and the Fire do not perish [*lā tafnayān*], rather, they both remain [*bāqiyatān*]." Unlike monotheists, he continues, unbelievers will be unable to leave Hell; but this is because it requires "long ages" for them to be reformed: "the wisdom that necessitates their entry [into Hell] is that which necessitates their abiding [in it]."[183] Regardless of whether Ibn Qayyim was attempting to appease Subkī by disguising his doctrinal orientation in some of his final works, there is nothing there that is incongruous with his previous arguments for temporal damnation.

Ultimately, it was through Ibn Qayyim's writings that many subsequent scholars were introduced to and swayed by Ibn Taymiyya's universalism.[184] Just over a generation later, Ibn Abī al-'Izz al-Ḥanafī (d. 792/1390) produced his classic commentary on the (damnationist) creed of Abū Ja'far al-Ṭaḥāwī. In it, he cites portions of the *Ḥādī* and presents Ibn Qayyim's cautious universalist stance therein as one of only two viable doctrines regarding the fate of Hell and its inhabitants (the other being damnationism).[185] Centuries later, we find an astonishing variety of individuals and groups boldly aligning themselves with Ibn Taymiyya and Ibn Qayyim. These include some of their traditional supporters among Wahhabis[186]—notwithstanding the denials and objections I noted earlier; the Salafi thinker Muḥammad Rashīd Riḍā, whose views we examine in the next chapter; the famed Egyptian scholar and former rector of al-Azhar University, Mahmoud Shaltout (d. 1963), who writes about how he was moved by Ibn Qayyim's contentions;[187] and Yusuf al-Qaradawi, arguably the most influential contemporary scholar in the Arab world, who, in a 2002 issue of a major Egyptian newspaper, explicitly promotes Ibn Qayyim's cautious universalist stance as presented in the *Shifāʾ*.[188] As we shall now see, those impacted by Ibn Taymiyya's Paradise-for-all doctrine also comprise individuals not known for being particularly fond of either him or his school of thought.

Excursus

The Ibn Taymiyya Controversy Resurfaces in a Twentieth-Century Dispute: The Case of Maulana Muhammad Ali and James Robson

In 1889, British India witnessed the birth of a movement called the Ahmadiyya. Its eponym, Mirzā Ghulām Aḥmad (d. 1908), claimed to be the "Promised Messiah" who would restore the purity of Islam. After his death, his followers split into two major factions: the Ahmadiyya Muslim Community, which declares Aḥmad to be a prophet of sorts—notwithstanding the Qur'anic proclamation that Muḥammad was the "seal of the prophets" (33:40)—and the Lahore Ahmadiyya Movement, which stops short of this, thereby rendering it the less controversial of the two among most Muslims. At some point in the early twentieth century, the Ahmadiyya came to be regarded as the "chief form" of Islam portrayed to the West.[189] This was, in large part, due to the writings of Maulana Muhammad Ali (d. 1951) of the Lahore Ahmadiyya Movement. Ali's 1917 English translation of the Qur'an, which was reprinted in the 1920s and 1930s, and a 1936 work entitled *The Religion of Islam* were (and, thanks to revised editions, still are) particularly popular. Although hardly an enthusiast of the traditionalist theology of Ibn Taymiyya and Ibn Qayyim, in *Religion* Ali invokes the authority of both in his justification of universal salvation, to which we now turn.

Ali writes that, owing to God's mercy, chastisement can be likened to "a hospital wherein different operations are performed only to save life."[190]

While Hell "only represents the evil consequences of evil deeds," its purpose is to make evildoers fit for "spiritual advancement."[191] It is, therefore, purgatorial. The Qur'an hints at this when it describes the Fire as the sinners' "friend" (*mawlā*) (57:15) and "mother" (*umm*) (101:9): as a good friend, Hell elevates the spiritual state of its inhabitants and, like a mother, nurtures their growth. And when referring to the "trials" experienced by both believers in this life (29:2) and evildoers in the Fire (37:63), the Qur'an employs the term *fitna*—a term originally used to refer to the purification of gold through fire.[192]

The ultimate salvation of "non-Muslim sinners" is a minority view, Ali explains, because "great misunderstanding prevails" among Muslims.[193] Ali concedes that the terms the Qur'an uses when referring to the stay in Hell, for example, *khulūd* (from the root *kh-l-d*) and *abadan*, can connote "eternity." But, much like Ibn Qayyim, he avers that, according to "all authorities on Arabic lexicology," both terms can also signify "a long time."[194] The word *khulūd*, he observes, is used "freely" in the Qur'an when referring to the chastisement in Hell of both Muslim and non-Muslim sinners (as in 4:14).[195] The term *abadan* is the accusative form of the word *abad*; the mere fact that *abad* has dual and plural forms in Arabic that "are in use" shows that it need not mean "forever" (as it makes little sense to speak of a duality or plurality of "eternities"). Thus, when something exists for *abad*, it "is taken to mean *what remains for a long time*."[196]

In Ali's translation of the Qur'an, he generally renders *abadan* as "forever" in reference to Paradise but as "for long ages" and "for a long time" in reference to the Fire.[197] This, he explains in *Religion*, is because the Qur'an speaks of punishment—but not reward—as lasting ages (78:23).[198] He also cites two other familiar passages, Q. 6:128 and 11:106–107, as proof that chastisement is limited by divine volition. This is to be contrasted with Paradise, God's "unceasing gift" (Q. 11:108).[199] While certain Qur'anic verses indicate that the damned will be unable to escape their punishment, Ali insists that "not a word is there in any of these verses to show that God will not [eventually] take them out of it, or that the tortures of Hell are endless."[200]

To seal his argument, Ali turns to reports of the Prophet and his Companions. According to one hadith, God will save "a handful" of Hell's inhabitants, and these will be "people who have never done any good."[201] As Ali would have it, this means that Hell will be empty, as "the handful of God cannot leave anything behind."[202] Ali also cites the familiar sayings ascribed to the Companions ʿUmar ibn al-Khaṭṭāb and

Ibn Mas'ūd and notes that similar statements have been made by "many other Companions."[203] Lest one assume that Ali's reading of the sources is uniquely his own, he ascribes universalism to "later" leaders ("Imāms"), "such as Ibn 'Arabī, Ibn Taimiya, Ibn Qayyim and many others."[204] Although Ibn 'Arabī is known to have influenced the Ahmadiyya,[205] Ali's reference to him here—as is clear now—is problematic. What is equally evident is that Ali's conception of Paradise for all demonstrates at least the indirect influence of Ibn Taymiyya and Ibn Qayyim. This is known not simply through Ali's reliance on Q. 6:128, 11:106–108, and 78:23, but—perhaps most significantly—through his use of the reports ascribed to 'Umar and other Companions. Unlike Ibn Qayyim, however, Ali is much more forthright: any sign of doubt, or even the traditional formula "God knows best" (*Allāhu a'lam*), is conspicuously absent from his exposition. Instead, he presents the eventual salvation of all matter-of-factly and concludes his argument with a hadith that, he insists, "establishes beyond all doubt that all men will ultimately be set on the way to the higher life":

> Then will Allāh say, "Bring out (of the fire) every one in whose heart there is faith or goodness to the extent of a mustard seed, so they will be taken out having become quite black; then they will be thrown into the river of life and they will grow as grows a seed by the side of a river."[206]

Ali's presumption is that no one can be an absolute unbeliever. This may be supported by Qur'anic passages such as 2:88, which says about the unbelievers among the Jews, "they have little faith" (*qalīlan mā yu'minūn*). But here we have a complication: there are some hadiths that explicitly describe certain individuals as not having even a "mustard seed" of faith.[207] Perhaps Ali would concede that such individuals exist in this life but add that those who endure the purification of Hell will necessarily acquire the iota of faith necessary for their eventual salvation.

Be that as it may, Ali's influence meant that his case for universal deliverance would shape the views of a great many people, particularly in the English-speaking world. This seems to include the Honorable Elijah Muhammad (d. 1975) of the Nation of Islam, the well-known African American movement founded in Detroit in 1930. In Elijah Muhammad's manifesto, *The Supreme Wisdom: Solution to the So-Called Negroes's Problem,* he teaches his followers that, unlike Heaven, Hell "is not eternal."[208] Although Elijah Muhammad here generally avoids citing the names of scholars, he concludes by recommending two translations of the Qur'an: "you can find a good one of it by Maulana Muhammad Ali and one by Allama Yusuf Ali."[209] Given that Yusuf Ali's (d. 1953) translation generally leaves one with the impression that Hell is eternal,[210] it was likely Muhammad Ali—who presents a brief version of his case for universalism in the introduction to his translation—who helped shape Elijah Muhammad's doctrine of Hell. This is supported by the fact that other aspects of Muhammad Ali's approach to eschatology (and Islam in general) were adopted by Elijah Muhammad.[211] (The latter's "white devil" polemics and his anticipation of the destruction of the white race are unique, although it is unclear if this destruction was meant to be literal or figurative. In a 1972 interview, Elijah Muhammad noted that even whites could be saved.)[212] If there is, indeed, a soteriological connection between Muhammad Ali and Elijah Muhammad, this would mean that Ibn Taymiyya's arguments for universal salvation may have played a role—however minor or indirect—in the theological development of an indigenous, nontraditionalist American movement centuries later.[213] And yet, whatever the context, these very arguments always seem to serve as catalysts for Subkīan rejoinders. I now examine a non-Muslim scholarly response to Muhammad Ali—a response that constitutes what is, to the best of my knowledge, Western academia's first serious engagement with Islamic universalism.

In an article entitled "Is the Moslem Hell Eternal?" which was published in *The Moslem World* in 1938, James Robson (d. 1981), a onetime professor of Arabic at the University of Manchester, sets out to assess Ali's universalist claims. Robson critiques Ali on the basis of the latter's translation of the Qur'an, whose introduction, as noted earlier, includes a short defense of Hell's temporality. Robson does not treat Ali's more extensive discussion in *Religion*, of whose existence—but not necessarily content—Robson was aware when he wrote his article.[214]

Robson concedes that the term *abadan* can mean either "forever" or "for a long time." Even so, he asserts that Ali is

> mistaken [in] assuming that one is free to use either [definition] arbitrarily, for it is extremely unlikely that the same word would be used in similar contexts and be left to the ingenuity of readers to recognize that in one place it has one meaning and in another a different meaning. The words [*khālidīn*] *fīhā abadan* must surely mean the same thing, whether they apply to the blessed or the damned.[215]

Ali here would say that *abadan* in both cases does connote something similar: perpetuity *within a given context.* In any case, that the finitude of Hell is indicated by the term *ages* in Q. 78:23 is, Robson admits, a "seemingly more effective line of argument."[216] Yet he dismisses it on the grounds that both early and later commentators, such as Ṭabarī, Zamakhsharī, and ʿAbd Allāh ibn ʿUmar al-Bayḍāwī (d. 685/1286), took *ages* to mean an endless, limitless series of epochs.[217] As for Alī's reading of Q. 11:106–108 (that the duration of punishment is limited by divine volition, whereas Paradise is neverending), Robson describes it as "interesting" and grants that "there are grounds for it in the actual words of the passage."[218] But, again, he rejects Alī's interpretation since it is contrary to the traditional understanding.[219]

Robson proceeds to cite prophetic reports that are presumed to be congruous with damnationism. These include the aforementioned hadith of death appearing in the form of a ram and being slaughtered. According to Robson, this report supports the notion of an eternal Hell since—in the variant that he cites—it concludes with the statement (as Robson translates it), "Then joy will be added to the joy of the people of Paradise and sorrow to the sorrow of the people of Hell."[220] Another variant adds, "Then will be said to the two parties, (You will spend) eternity in what you find (yourselves); there is no death in it for ever (*abadan*)."[221] Robson also invokes reports of certain people being removed from the Fire (such as those whose hearts contain the equivalent of "a mustard-seed of faith") as evidence for restricted salvation.[222] Although Robson never discusses ʿUmar's report (which appears at the end of Alī's brief argument for universalism in the introduction to his translation),[223] he notes that Ṭabarī did not accept the report ascribed to the Companion Ibn Masʿūd (which speaks of a time—after ages have passed—in which no one will remain in Hell).[224]

All this shows that Alī's universalist declarations violate "the clear teaching of the community of which Muhammad is reported to have said, 'My people will never agree upon an error.'"[225] Robson justifies his consensus claim by citing certain Ḥanafite creedal affirmations of an eternal Hell.[226] By both preferring the damnationist interpretations of scripture and appealing to doctrines popularized and assumed by most Muslim scholars of the post-*salaf* era, Robson follows the path trod by Subkī, even though the former gives no indication that he was aware of either the latter's *Iʿtibār* or the eminent medieval scholar refuted therein. (Ibn Taymiyya's name appears in *Religion* but not in the introduction to Alī's translation.) Robson concludes his piece by casting universalism as an odd doctrine, one that could be propagated only by an unconventional sect such as the Ahmadiyya. Again, he writes, everlasting damnation is "the generally accepted belief of the Moslem community."[227]

Closing Thoughts

I began this chapter by discussing Ibn Taymiyya's limited inclusivism. Although both Ibn Taymiyya and Ibn ʿArabī cite Q. 17:15 (specifically, "We do not punish until We have sent a messenger") as a proof text for an inclusivist soteriology, the differences in their interpretations and, by extension, their inclusivisms are profound: while both maintain that the unreached may be saved, Ibn ʿArabī includes those who cannot perceive the "proofs" of the Messenger. The disparity between these two stances reflects alternative emphases. In other words, the crucial hermeneutic question is, Which aspect of Q. 17:15 should one accentuate: the delivery of the message (Ibn Taymiyya's emphasis) or its reception (Ibn ʿArabī's emphasis)? Perhaps it is an unwillingness to privilege one or the other that explains why Ghazālī and many other inclusivists opted for a middle-of-the-road form of inclusivism—an inclusivim that encompasses truth-seeking non-Muslims while affirming the inherent persuasiveness of the message.

Of the three scholars examined thus far, that is, Ghazālī, Ibn ʿArabī, and Ibn Taymiyya, the latter is generally regarded as the least tolerant. Some might be shocked that he was an inclusivist at all. And yet he was the universalist of the three. In the *Ḥādī*, his student Ibn Qayyim dismisses Ibn ʿArabī's vision of the Fire as an abode of felicity, but his and his master's position is seemingly more radical: the people of Thamūd, Abū Lahab, Pharaoh, and Satan himself will one day inhabit Paradise.[228] Yet in the writings of these two traditionalists, they turn the tables on the damnationists: true absurdity lies in restricting God's mercy and wisdom and denying His volition to save whomever He pleases. Such bold proclamations continue to reverberate and innervate. The fact that Muhammad Ali and James Robson could engage in the same dance that the very different Ibn Taymiyya and Subkī engaged in centuries earlier suggests that the universalist–damnationist impasse is here to stay.

Ibn Taymiyya and Ibn Qayyim's case for universal deliverance is a formidable challenge to those on the side of the majority. And there are yet other arguments that might be adduced to support their doctrine. For instance, Q. 57:13 states that a "wall with a gate will be erected" between the people of Heaven and the people of Hell. Perhaps the existence of this "gate" suggests that the barrier between both afterlife abodes is not in fact permanently impenetrable. In Q. 7:40, we see the declaration that "those who rejected" the message arrogantly "will not enter the Garden until [*ḥattā*] the camel [*al-jamal*] passes through the eye of the needle." As I noted earlier, Ibn Qayyim presents this verse as evidence that, initially at least, some will have no chance of entering Paradise. But the qualification in Q. 7:40 ("until the camel passes through the eye of the needle") might in fact be seen as a sign of hope. An analogous and well-known statement appears in the Gospels: "It is easier for a camel to go through the eye of a needle than for a rich man to enter the kingdom of God" (Revised Standard Version, Mark 10:25).[229] Countless Christian exegetes and theologians take this to mean that the wealthy will encounter additional hurdles on the path to glory, not that they will be barred. This is because, as we read two verses later, "all things are possible with God" (Mark 10:27). Similarly, a Muslim universalist might argue that Q. 7:40 in fact leaves the door of ultimate salvation open to unbelievers. After all, "God has power over all things" (Q. 35:1)—including camels and needles. To be sure, Judgment Day will be "a day of anguish" (*yawm ʿasīr*) for the wicked; "they will have no ease" (*ghayr yasīr*) (Q. 74:9–10). But Judgment Day is but a "day," and, as the Qur'an assures us, "With every hardship [*al-ʿusr*] comes ease [*yusr*]; truly, with every hardship comes ease" (94:5–6).

But the matter is not this simple. The universalist who holds that scripture is internally consistent must also hold that numerous Qur'anic passages are implicitly qualified: "there is no doubt that [the unbelievers] will be the losers in the hereafter" (16:109)—until they are purified; "their deeds go to waste in this world and the next" (9:69)—but they will be purified; "they will have no share in the hereafter" (2:200)—until they are purified; "such people will have nothing in the hereafter but the Fire" (11:16)—until they are purified; and so on. There are, of course, other ways of reconciling these passages with universalist doctrine. Consider the last two examples cited here: the first states that some "will have no share in the hereafter." This statement appears in the following context:

> There are some who pray, "Our Lord, give us in this world," and they will have no share [*khalāq*] in the hereafter; others pray, "Our Lord, give us good in this world and in the hereafter, and protect us from the torment of the Fire." They will have the portion [*naṣīb*] they have worked for: God is swift in reckoning. (Q. 2:200–202)

The term *share* (*khalāq*) here is vague and might simply denote the blessings awarded to the righteous: immediate salvation and the first and best paradisiacal gifts.

The second example states that some "will have nothing in the hereafter but the Fire." Hell is no doubt torturous, but as we saw earlier, the

Qur'an itself describes the Fire as a "friend" and a "mother." Assuming that these descriptions are not intended to be ironic, the passage in question could be understood to mean that some "will have nothing in the hereafter" but a purgatorial "friend" who guides them along a path leading to Paradise and a purgatorial "mother" who disciplines them and raises them to be among the righteous. In other words, the phrase "the Fire" itself could imply eventual rectification and bliss.

Whatever one makes of the various arguments marshaled for universal salvation, its advocates face a colossal challenge: accounting for the fact that their reading of Islamic scripture has not been obvious to most Muslim theologians. Indeed, Ibn Taymiyya has to rely on controversial interpretations and reports to defend a position whose theological significance could hardly be understated. But here the universalist might simply echo a statement attributed to the Companion Ibn Masʿūd, which appears in passing in the *Fanāʾ*: "If the people of the Fire came to know that they will stay in the Fire the duration of this world they would certainly rejoice."[230] Accordingly, it is on account of God's wisdom that He only provides hints of the final outcome. And although these hints may not be obvious, they were enough for the likes of the "master of Islam."

But if we assume that Companions as prominent as ʿUmar believed in universal salvation, why is it that by the fifth/eleventh century, his view came to be regarded as a violation of consensus? It is here that the universalist may have to resort to a questionable conspiracy theory. I offer the following as a possible example: the Khārijites and, later, the rationalist Muʿtazilites, whose influence was far-reaching during the formative period of Islamic thought, popularized a particular conception of justice, whereby even sinning believers would be barred from Paradise. Those groups that came to dominate Islamic theological discourse during and following the demise of the Muʿtazilites found themselves in the difficult position of having to defend the eventual salvation of believers without appearing to undermine God's attribute of justice. This, along with the promotion of conversion to Islam, resulted in the suppression of an already obscure scriptural message of universal deliverance.[231] It would take the disruption of the Mongol incursion to shake the firmaments of Islamic thought and allow for an Ibn Taymiyya to appear on the scene and unearth this message. And it would take European ascendancy and Muslim decline to allow for a Rashīd Riḍā to repopularize it.

4

The Modern Scene: Rashīd Riḍā and Beyond

MUCH HAS CHANGED since Ibn Taymiyya passed away in the citadel of Damascus, now a tourist attraction. Non-Muslim Europe discovered the New World, rediscovered ancient Greece and Rome, and became *the West*. European colonization of Muslim lands inspired secular, nationalist movements and fostered both deep appreciation for and unrelenting resentment against the colonizers. Traditional Islamic institutions declined, yet classical Islamic texts became more accessible than ever before, and the key contributors to Islamic discourse—and its revival—came to include the laity: physicians, engineers, school teachers, university professors, and others. The growing Muslim presence in the West and other predominantly non-Muslim regions—a result of immigration and conversion—meant that mosques were erected for the first time in cities such as Paris and Tokyo, York and New York. It also meant new kinds of relationships between Muslims and Others. And thanks to the global nature of the Internet, the world shrunk to the size of a computer monitor (and even smaller), fostering the creation of countless virtual communities. The outcome of all this has been great, unprecedented diversity in Muslim writings on the salvific status of Others.

Muḥammad Rashīd Riḍā (d. 1935), hailed as the "undoubted intellectual leader" of the far-reaching modern Salafi movement,[1] was a crucial link in the transition to contemporary Islamic thought. Born in 1865 near Tripoli (in present-day Lebanon), Riḍā had the benefit of attending a traditional Qur'anic school, a government school, and a school established by Shaykh Ḥusayn al-Jisr (d. 1909), a traditionally trained thinker known for his relatively open attitude to the modern sciences. Having grappled with and been inspired by the writings of the legendary scholars of old (particularly Ghazālī and, later, Ibn Taymiyya), Riḍā was convinced that the Muslim world needed to be saved from both its intellectual stagnation and the moral malaise induced by popular Sufism.[2] He found the enlightenment he was looking for in the writings of the Iranian (or, less likely, Afghani) modernist Jamāl al-Dīn al-Afghānī (d. 1897)[3] and his Egyptian disciple Muḥammad ʿAbduh (d. 1905). Today, both Afghānī and ʿAbduh are remembered as leading reformers who opposed antiquated religious decrees and emphasized the role of reason and science. The following is Riḍā's account of his first meaningful exposure to Afghānī and ʿAbduh's celebrated Paris-based periodical *al-ʿUrwa al-wuthqā* (The strongest link):

> I found several copies of the journal among my father's papers, and every issue was like an electric current striking me, giving my soul a shock, or setting it ablaze, and carrying me from one state to another.... My own experience and that of others, and history, have taught me that no other Arabic discourse in this age or the centuries that preceded it has done what it did in the way of touching the seat of emotion in the heart and persuasion in the mind.[4]

This pull toward Islamic modernism eventually led Riḍā to Cairo in 1897 to study under ʿAbduh, who soon became the Grand Mufti of Egypt. Together, they propagated their ideas and ideals through their own even more famous periodical *al-Manār* (The lighthouse), which was established in 1898 and remained a joint project until ʿAbduh's death in 1905. Riḍā steered *al-Manār* for the next three decades until his own demise. Afghānī and ʿAbduh laid the foundations for the Salafi movement, and Riḍā became its "spokesman."[5] It is largely due to Riḍā that Salafism spread relatively quickly throughout North Africa, the Middle East, and the rest of the Muslim world. But under Riḍā, the movement also became relatively more "conservative," especially as he came to appreciate the writings of Ibn Taymiyya and the Wahhabi movement that claimed the "master of Islam" for itself. Riḍā is thus widely considered an intermediary between the reformism of Afghānī and ʿAbduh and the activism of the Egyptian Muslim Brotherhood (al-Ikhwān al-Muslimīn), the now global Islamist organization established in 1928 by Ḥasan al-Bannā (d. 1949).[6]

Most relevant for our purposes is Riḍā's Qur'anic commentary in *al-Manār*, which provides a summary of ʿAbduh's lectures on the Qur'an, Riḍā's own interpretations, and vindications and emendations of various premodern doctrines. Taken as a whole, this exegetical corpus, first collected and republished separately in 1927 under the title *Tafsīr al-Manār*

(The Qur'anic commentary of *al-Manār*), runs from Q. 1:1 to 12:107.[7] Because of his death, ʿAbduh's indirect involvement in this project through his lectures on the Qur'an did not go beyond Q. 4:125, although the commentary on this passage was first published in *al-Manār* several years after his passing.[8] Even while he was alive, his failing health prevented him from reviewing and even reading the commentary on passages beyond Q. 2:121.[9] This, along with the fact that Riḍā himself changed over time, means that the *Tafsīr* is occasionally yet significantly inconsistent. (We shall see a stark example of this below.) Today, owing to its propagation of both "liberal" and "conservative" ideas (the former typically linked to ʿAbduh), *al-Manār* is utilized by a wide variety of Muslim scholars.[10] Concerning the fate of Others, whereas some of ʿAbduh's precise views are ultimately difficult to discern, Riḍā develops a soteriology that is not particularly "conservative": one that liberalizes Ghazālī's criterion for non-Muslim salvation while also borrowing from Ibn Qayyim's case for noneternal damnation.

Beyond Religious Affiliations

Relying solely on English works, it would be difficult to discern the "real" Riḍā. Abdulaziz Sachedina and Farid Esack utilize Riḍā's writings to support their respective cases for pluralism. According to Sachedina, Riḍā "grudgingly concedes the validity of salvation for the 'People of the Book.'"[11] From Esack's perspective, Riḍā affirms "the validity of other religious paths" in a post-Muḥammadan world,[12] despite anti-Jewish and anti-Christian polemics that sometimes appear to "counterbalance his ideas on the validity of religious pluralism."[13] In a rejoinder to Esack, the inclusivist T. J. Winter characterizes Esack's defense of pluralism as a "revival of Rashīd Riḍā's project of redefining the Koranic concept of 'believer' (*mu'min*), generally understood by the exegetic tradition as a subset of 'Muslim,' to include all believers in God."[14] (I shall return to this pluralist–inclusivist debate.) Meanwhile, Jane McAuliffe asserts that Riḍā "harshly condemns the majority" of Christians (and others), "leaving them the sole prospect of torment in the Fire."[15]

So who, exactly, was Riḍā: reluctant redeemer, pluralist pioneer, callous condemner, or none of the above? Our starting point in answering this question is Riḍā's commentary on Q. 2:62, a familiar pronouncement:

> The believers, the Jews, the Christians, and the Sabians—all those who believe in God and the Last Day and do good—will have their rewards with their Lord. No fear for them, nor will they grieve.

Here Riḍā approvingly cites ʿAbduh's teaching that this verse should be read in conjunction with what immediately precedes it:

> Remember when you [the Children of Israel] said, "Moses, we cannot bear to eat only one kind of food, so pray to your Lord to bring out for us some of the earth's produce, its herbs and cucumbers, its garlic, lentils, and onions." He said, "Would you exchange better for worse? Go to Egypt and there you will find what you have asked for." They were struck with humiliation and wretchedness, and they incurred the wrath of God because they persistently rejected His messages and killed prophets contrary to all that is right. All this was because they disobeyed and were transgressors. (Q. 2:61)

According to ʿAbduh, the promise of reward in Q. 2:62 precludes those among the Children of Israel censured in Q. 2:61, as what matters soteriologically is not to which religion (*dīn*) or religious community (*milla*) one belongs but "true faith" (*ṣidq al-īmān*) in and servitude to the Almighty.[16]

With this in mind, Riḍā cites Q. 4:123:

> It will not be according to your hopes or those of the People of the Book: anyone who does wrong will be requited for it and will find no one to protect or help him [or her] against God.

This verse was reportedly revealed following a debate between certain Medinan Jews and Companions of the Prophet over who could (now) rightfully claim to be preferred by God. As these particular early Muslims would have it, as long as their Jewish counterparts remained members of their respective religious community, they could not hope to be saved. According to Riḍā, the fact that this dispute was the backdrop to the revelation of Q. 4:123 demonstrates the superiority of sound belief and righteous deeds over religious identity[17]—a point Riḍā repeats years later when his commentary had reached Q. 4:123 and later again (this time without referencing the reported quarrel) at Q. 5:69 ("For the believers, the Jews, the Sabians, and the Christians—all those who believe in God and the Last Day and do good—there is no fear: they will not grieve").[18]

This position is further elucidated in Riḍā's treatment of Q. 3:19, which reads:

> True religion [*al-dīn*], in God's eyes, is *islām*. Those who were given the Book disagreed out of rivalry, only after they had been given

> knowledge—if anyone denies God's revelations, God is swift to take account.

As Riḍā explains, "true religion" is *islām*, or submission to God, and not specifically the religion formally called Islam. After all, Abraham himself was a *muslim*, a submitter to God (Q. 3:67). A "true" *muslim*, therefore, is one whose faith and deeds are pure, whatever the context. It is with this understanding of *islām* that one should also read Q. 3:85: "If anyone seeks a religion [*dīn*] other than *islām*, it will not be accepted from him [or her]: he [or she] will be one of the losers in the hereafter."[19]

The Qur'anic verse 5:48 is significant in this light, as it indicates that the commandments directed to Muḥammad's community by no means constitute the only divinely ordained law:

> We have revealed to you [Muḥammad] the scripture in truth, confirming the scriptures that came before it and as a guardian [*muhaymin*] over them: so judge between them according to what God has sent down. Do not follow their whims, which deviate from the truth that has come to you. We have assigned a law [*shirʿa*] and a path [*minhāj*] to each of you. If God had so willed, He would have made you one community, but He wanted to test you through that which He has given you, so race to do good: you will all return to God and He will make clear to you the matters about which you differed.

In his explication of this passage, Riḍā maintains that the various revealed laws constitute different aspects of a single religion (*dīn*).[20] It is, therefore, easy to see why Riḍā is sometimes classified as a pluralist. But a closer look reveals a different picture.

In this very section of his commentary, Riḍā, ever the polemicist, contrasts Muḥammad's perfect, moderate path with the corrupted, extreme paths of Judaism, with its fixation on law, and Christianity, with its obsession with the spiritual realm. Noting that the following verse (Q. 5:49)[21] commands the Prophet to judge the People of the Book according to what he received from God, Riḍā asserts that the pre-Muḥammadan laws have been abrogated and distorted and cannot be followed in a world in which the Prophet's universal message is available.[22] In his discussion of Q. 5:69, Riḍā adds that in light of the surrounding verses—verses that are ostensibly critical of Jews and Christians—one can only conclude that "the People of the Book did not uphold the religion [*dīn*] of God."[23] An example of Christian "deviation," for instance, is the doctrine of the trinity, which Riḍā elsewhere presents as an irrational, pagan-inspired violation of true monotheism (*tawḥīd*): "It is, as the commoners say, 'nonsense' [*kalām fārigh*]."[24]

Returning to Riḍā's commentary on Q. 3:19, it is true that he makes a distinction between *islām* and Islam. But he also draws attention to the fact that immediately after the declaration "True religion, in God's eyes, is *islām*," God rebukes the People of the Book on account of their divisions and deviations. This, according to Riḍā, indicates that by Muḥammad's time, their religions no longer represented *islām*. Riḍā illustrates this point by citing the history of the Christian church, its internal schisms, and the various councils it convened, beginning with the Council of Nicaea in 325 CE and the subsequent excommunication of Arius (d. 336 CE) and the Arians.[25] Accordingly, the Prophet ushered in a new era in which his path became the primary path of *islām*. It is, as Riḍā declares in his 1933 book *al-Waḥy al-muḥammadī* (The Muḥammadan revelation), "the religion of all peoples."[26] If certain Muslims fail to adhere to it, they fail to qualify as *muslims*. Conversely, if Others adhere to it, they qualify as *muslims*, even if they are not affiliated with Muslims. An example of the latter would be the Christian Negus (al-Najāshī) of Ethiopia, who famously allowed followers of the Prophet to remain within his kingdom following their flight from Meccan persecution. According to Muslim sources, the Negus discreetly abandoned Christianity in favor of the Muḥammadan path, and the Prophet prayed for him when he passed away. In *al-Manār*, Riḍā identifies the Negus and other People of the Book who accepted the Muḥammadan message and law as the subject of the following Qur'anic passage:[27]

> Some of the People of the Book believe in God, in what has been sent down to you and in what was sent down to them, humbling themselves before God; they would never sell God's revelation for a small price. These people will have their rewards with their Lord; God is swift in reckoning. (Q. 3:199)

In contrast, "wicked" People of the Book are those who reject the Prophet and his teachings, for "there is no difference between disbelieving in all of the messengers and disbelieving in some."[28] Thus,

> no one can be credited with belief (*īmān*) who knows [the Qur'an] and yet disagrees with it by preferring his own scriptures.... Everyone reached by the call (*da'wa*) of Muḥammad and to whom its truth is evident, as it is to [certain self-absorbed, stubborn People of the Book], but who rejects and resists, as they reject and resist, gains no positive credit for his belief in former prophets and their books. His belief in God is not an authentic belief, one linked to fear of God and submission (*khushū'*).[29]

Notice that Riḍā here qualifies his condemnation of non-Muslims, limiting it to those who have received "the call of Muḥammad and to whom its truth is evident."

Excusing Others

This brings us back full circle to Riḍā's commentary on Q. 2:62, where we find a relevant discussion regarding the people of the gap (*ahl al-fatra*), those who are truly "unreached." Riḍā surveys competing claims concerning their fate: 'Abduh is quoted as stating that the majority view—but ascribed only to the Ash'arites—is that the people of the gap will be saved and that this is predicated on familiar scriptural statements, such as "We do not punish until We have sent a messenger" (Q. 17:15).[30] In contrast, the Mu'tazilites and many Ḥanafites insisted that the intellect (*'aql*) suffices as the means by which one is made responsible. In other words, even unreached evildoers will be taken to account for their sins and unbelief in God and the Last Day. Viewed from this standpoint, messengers are not the cause of damnation; instead, they confirm the truth and provide humanity with greater insights into those things that would otherwise be unknowable, such as the precise manner of worship that is pleasing to God, as well as details regarding the life to come. As for Q. 17:15, one could argue that it refers only to the punishments of this life. As Riḍā notes, however, this argument is undermined by the fact that, linguistically, the phrase "We do not" (*mā kunnā*) in "We do not punish until We have sent a messenger" is used to indicate a general negation.[31] An alternative argument, which Riḍā cites and dismisses elsewhere, is that the term *messenger* in passages like Q. 17:15 connotes "reason." As Riḍā notes, the Qur'an is clear on this matter: the "messengers" are individuals commissioned by God; we know their names and their narratives.[32]

Back in his discussion of Q. 2:62, Riḍā proceeds to cite Ghazālī's three categories of non-Muslims: (1) those who never heard of the Prophet;

(2) damned unbelievers who learned of the Prophet's true nature but were arrogant, resistant, or negligent in looking into his message; and (3) those who were "improperly" exposed to the message because what they encountered was an erroneous representation of it or because its "precondition" (*sharṭ*) was not satisfied, meaning that it was not presented to them in a manner that would spur the "sincere" among them to investigate it.[33] The careful observer will notice that Riḍā's description of this third category is subtly different from Ghazālī's, in that the latter presents exposure to the message in its "true" form to be itself the source of motivation for sincere investigation—a point to which I shall soon return.

Here Riḍā promotes, supplements, and emends Ghazālī's categorization. For instance, he provides a new example of Ghazālī's first category (those who never heard of the Prophet): the inhabitants of America "of that era" (*li-dhālika al-ʿahd*)—presumably Ghazālī's era—assuming they did not receive another sound message.[34] Additionally, Riḍā posits that the first and third categories (the latter being those who were improperly exposed to the message) should be regarded as one and the same: both are unreached. He also asserts that, per Q. 17:15, such non-Muslims will be excused for not following the Prophet (or any other prophet to whom they were never "properly" exposed). But, Riḍā adds, this does not mean that they have absolute immunity: to be unreached is not to be saved and granted Paradise without further consideration, for this would be unreasonable; it would mean that the messengers are a source of harm for many people. As we saw in chapter 1, Ghazālī never clarifies how or whether the unreached will be distinguished from one another. Yet, as Riḍā observes, the unreached are not a monolithic group: some are righteous (despite not having access to the message), others are wicked. What is reasonable and consistent with scripture is to hold that God the Just will judge the unreached according to what they know of the truth and falsehood, and good and evil.[35] As vague as this criterion might seem, Riḍā assures us elsewhere that people (including the unreached) generally have a sense of what is good and what is evil. What is occasionally unclear is the details, however consequential they may be (at least in this life).[36]

Despite all this, in his various writings, Riḍā never excludes the possibility of a test on Judgment Day for those who never encounter any form of the message. This is evident in Riḍā's discussions of the Prophet's parents, whom Riḍā classifies as true people of the gap. According to various hadiths, either one or both of them are "in the Fire." Riḍā clarifies that these reports indicate only their condition when they passed away; no one is actually consigned to an abode until after the Judgment.

This, he writes, means that there is yet hope for their salvation should they encounter the reported test of the messenger-of-resurrection and pass it.[37] Interestingly, Riḍā only ever mentions the possibility of such a test in the context of redeeming the Prophet's parents. What he never suggests is that the people of the gap will collectively occupy the limbo of "the heights" (Q. 7:46–49), which he regards as simply the abode of those whose good and evil deeds are of equal weight.[38]

What, then, of unreached Jews and Christians? Returning to the commentary on Q. 2:62, Riḍā writes that although their religious traditions are compromised, there is enough of the original message within their scriptures to render them distinct from the people of the gap. Jews, for instance, "have the Torah with God's judgment" (Q. 5:43); the same is true of Christians, who have also preserved at least some of the core teachings of Jesus[39]—this is notwithstanding Riḍā's belief that the Bible contains pagan elements.[40] As for the Sabians (referenced in Q. 2:62 and elsewhere), they are either a group similar to pre-Islamic Arab monotheists (*ḥunafā'*, sing. *ḥanīf*) or an offshoot of Christianity—one that engaged in star-worship. If the former, then they are more likely to be considered people of the gap. If the latter, then "like the Jews and Christians," they are expected to follow their respective path, having understood its obligations, "until another form of guidance reaches them."[41]

But what of those who learn of the final message and investigate it yet never convert? Can they, too, be regarded as *muslims*? In this commentary, which was first published in April 1903 in *al-Manār*,[42] Riḍā only cites Ghazālī's three categories of non-Muslims. He does not explicitly mention what I labeled earlier as the "fourth category": the sincere who actively investigate the message upon encountering it in its true form yet die without ever converting. Nevertheless, Riḍā seems to have them in mind when describing Ghazālī's second category, the damned, as arrogant, resistant, and negligent.[43]

Shortly after publishing his commentary on Q. 2:62, Riḍā took the additional step of explicitly accounting for the sincere truth-seekers among the "reached." In June 1903, *al-Manār* published a letter from a certain ʿAbd al-Ḥamīd of the northern Egyptian city of Zagazig. The latter inquires as to whether a Muslim could justifiably believe that God's mercy (*raḥma*) does not extend to non-Muslims. In his response, Riḍā explains that while divine mercy "encompasses all things," it is ordained "for those who are conscious of God and pay the prescribed alms, who believe in [His] revelations, who follow the Messenger" (Q. 7:156–157). It is, therefore, not ordained for non-Muslims who are properly exposed to God's final message and then reject it. But, Riḍā clarifies, God excuses both the unreached and the reached who investigate the message "with sincerity" but who never succeed in discerning its truth.[44] Riḍā reiterates this doctrine a year later in *al-Manār* in a reply to a letter from a certain Muḥammad, a prison clerk residing in Sudan, who asks, "Is it true that the unbeliever and the Christian will remain in Hell?"[45] Interestingly, Riḍā in this case places the boundary between the reached and the unreached at the point at which a non-Muslim encounters the message "in a sound way, one that moves [the sincere] to investigate [it]" (*ʿalā wajh ṣaḥīḥ yuḥarrik ilā al-naẓar*).[46]

As I indicated earlier, Riḍā, in his commentary on Q. 2:62, subtly rewords Ghazālī's description of non-Muslims who have been improperly exposed to Islam, that is, Ghazālī's third category of non-Muslims. According to Ghazālī, God will excuse such people unless they come to learn of the Prophet's real message and then reject it. This is because merely encountering the divine truth should provide sincere non-Muslims with "enough incentive to compel them to investigate."[47] Riḍā, meanwhile, presents the third category of non-Muslims as those who *either* have not encountered the message in its true form *or* have not encountered it in a manner that would provide "enough incentive" for investigation.

Riḍā affirms this distinction in later writings, including a fatwa published in the September 1910 edition of *al-Manār*. This fatwa was issued in response to a query by an anonymous Tunisian scholar concerning whether contemporary People of the Book could be considered true believers. In his reply, Riḍā approvingly and, for the first and only time, explicitly cites Ghazālī's discussion of the sincere truth-seekers who encounter the message and subsequently investigate it before passing away. Yet Riḍā goes further: immediately after citing Ghazālī, he comments that those things that prompt investigation of the Islamic message vary from era to era. If merely learning of the Prophet's message, his attributes, and his miracles were sufficient for prompting investigation during Ghazālī's era, such is not necessarily the case in the age of modernity. And as long as there is no incentive for non-Muslims to investigate the message, the "precondition" for being counted among the reached is not satisfied.[48]

What, then, would prompt investigation in a modern context? According to Riḍā, whatever the context, it depends entirely on the state of mind of the person in question and what is clear or unclear to him or her. He opines, for instance, that it would be unthinkable that sincere People of the Book who already believe in God and the Last Day and who do righteous deeds would simply reject Islam once its superior and progressive nature were "made clear" to them; instead, they would find themselves compelled to accept it.[49] Accordingly, the only non-Muslims whom God will hold accountable for not heeding his final message are (1) those who, besides encountering it in its true form, are provided with "enough incentive" to look into it and yet fail to do so and (2) those who investigate it (or encounter it somehow), and its truth is made apparent to them, yet rather than accept it, resist it out of stubbornness and arrogance.[50] Notice that both of these categories involve (obviously reached) non-Muslims who recognize the truth of Islam or an aspect of this truth, the latter of which should at least prompt investigation.

Riḍā finds support for his liberal form of inclusivism in Q. 4:115:[51]

> If anyone opposes the Messenger, after guidance has been *made clear* to him [or her], and follows a path other than that of the believers, We shall leave him [or her] on his [or her] chosen path—We shall burn him [or her] in Hell, an evil destination.

Muslim exegetes typically report that this verse was revealed in reference to an apostate named Ṭuʿma ibn Ubayriq. While in Medina, Ṭuʿma falsely accused a Jew of theft, when in fact he himself was the thief. When his guilt became evident, he abandoned the Muslim community and fled to Mecca, which was at the time under pagan control.[52] As Riḍā observes in his commentary on Q. 4:115, which appeared in *al-Manār* in March 1912,[53] the divine threat in this verse is worded in a general way.[54] It is, therefore, directed not just at apostates like Ṭuʿma but at anyone who refuses to accept or investigate Islamic revelation after its reality as a source of guidance (and not simply its content) is made evident to that individual. And for Riḍā, this threat is general enough that its qualification ("after guidance has been made clear") applies to other Qur'anic threats directed at Others.

Here Riḍā further elucidates his lenient form of inclusivism, which, we discover, was previously espoused by ʿAbduh.[55] Particularly insightful is Riḍā's discussion of human diversity. To illustrate the different ways in which people relate to Islamic revelation, Riḍā designates ten groups of people. The first two of these groups are (1) those who have unwavering conviction in the final message and (2) those who may not have attained absolute certainty but to whom the truth of the message is "made clear," meaning that they see it as a source of divine guidance or, at the very least, a better guide than all others. Individuals of either group who "oppose" the

Prophet and choose not to follow his path are those most worthy of damnation. These are people who take "desire as a god" and "whom God allows to stray in the face of knowledge" (Q. 45:23). But few people—examples being Ṭuʿma and some of the Jewish scholars in contact with the Prophet—have actually rejected the message after its truth was made clear to them.[56] This is because most people, on account of their pure natural disposition (*fiṭra*), prefer "guidance over error, truth over falsehood, and good over evil" when these are evident.[57] As for why anyone would oppose the Messenger "after guidance has been made clear," ʿAbduh had provided two possible explanations: (1) stubbornness associated with tribalism (*ʿaṣabiyya*) or (2) the pursuit of desire at the expense of guidance.[58] Riḍā provides an expanded list of explanations: "envy, transgression, love of leadership, arrogance, desire that overcomes the intellect, and tribalism."[59]

The next eight groups of people are as follows: (3) those who adhere to Islam through imitation of their parents and leaders, even though the truth of its message is not "made clear" to them; (4) those who adhere to error through imitation and thus turn away from the message and avoid investigating it when it is presented to them in its true form—these include most of the People of the Book and Zoroastrians living during the era of the Prophet (who conveyed his message to their leaders and held the latter responsible for their respective "blind" followers); (5) those who adhere to error through imitation but whose inclination to imitate is not as strong as that of the previous group, and so they are more likely to investigate the message—these include the generality of Arab pagans living during the era of the Prophet; (6) the argumentative scholars of world religions who, deluded by their incomplete knowledge, "shun" the message when they are invited to it because they follow their masters and fail to investigate it with sincerity; (7) those who were exposed to Islam but not properly, meaning that they did not encounter the version of the message that is true and that stimulates investigation—these include the majority of non-Muslims of Riḍā's era ("this era");[60] (8) those who, after having been exposed to Islamic revelation (either properly or improperly), investigate it with sincerity yet cease investigating when the truth is not made apparent to them; (9) the sincere truth-seekers who actively investigate the message and, even when they fail to recognize its complete truth, continue their investigation—these are the same as Ghazālī's fourth category of non-Muslims; and (10) those who never received any form of the message, such as the people of the gap (*ahl al-fatra*).[61]

Riḍā maintains that Q. 4:115 does not condemn individuals belonging to these last eight groups, even though not all are monotheistic.[62] Of course, if the truth were ever made clear to them and they were then to defy it, they would be counted as rebels of either of the first two groups. But this is not to say that individuals of the last eight groups could not be condemned at all. As we saw earlier, Riḍā holds that those who will be excused for not believing in the final message will still be judged by what they could recognize as being true and moral (owing to their share of the message, if they have any, and their own deductions). As such, Riḍā clarifies that the evil described in Q. 4:115 ("opposing" the Prophet and not following his path) represents just one form of unbelief and error.[63] So rather than guess the respective fates of the individuals of the last eight groups, Riḍā proffers that the most appropriate statement concerning them actually appears in Q. 4:115 itself: "We shall leave him [or her] on his [or her] chosen path."[64]

Notice that Riḍā counts most of his contemporary non-Muslims among the unreached, specifically those who were improperly exposed to the final message (the seventh group). And he makes this assessment in an age of widespread literacy and increased contact between different cultures. Returning to his September 1910 fatwa, Riḍā bemoans the fact that his fellow Muslims have generally failed to understand their own religion and have thus failed miserably in presenting it properly to non-Muslims.[65] In a piece published in *al-Manār* in April 1933, Riḍā asserts that even the intellects of Europe were never exposed to the final message in a manner that would move them to contemplate its divine origins.[66]

In his commentary on Q. 4:115, Riḍā observes that most modern non-Muslims have heard nothing about Islam "except that it is a religion among the many human-invented religions" and that both the religion itself and its adherents propagate "falsehoods."[67] This distorted image of Islam, Riḍā adds, is comparable to that created by the leaders of Christianity and others just before the Crusades. Accordingly, most modern non-Muslims think of Islam as being "obviously false." They do not bother to investigate it "just as Muslims [generally] do not investigate, for example, Mormonism."[68]

The obvious implication of this is that God will excuse most early-twentieth-century non-Muslims for not accepting or even investigating the Islamic message. God will also excuse other kinds of modern non-Muslims, such as the truth-seekers for whom the truth of the final message is not evident. God will even excuse the majority of non-Muslims of the Prophet's era, whom Riḍā mentions as examples of his fourth group, the blind imitators of error. Because they were generally not inclined to consider anything outside of their own tradition, they were oblivious to the truth of the final message, finding no incentive to investigate it. Of course, had they ever recognized this incentive and then failed to contemplate Islam, then they would cease to belong to Riḍā's fourth group; at that point, preferring to close their minds and resume their blind imitation of error would be a cause for their damnation.[69]

Given Riḍā's belief that God will excuse so many people of both his and the Prophet's era, we have reason to think that Riḍā, much like Ghazālī, was an optimist regarding people's potential for salvation on the Last Day, despite Riḍā's expectation that God will still judge the unreached. As we have seen, Riḍā asserts that most people, on account of their natural disposition, prefer guidance, truth, and goodness over their opposites. This explains why those who reject Islam after its truth is made clear to them are small in number. Thus, when the Qur'an states that "most people do not have faith" (11:17), Riḍā clarifies that "faith" here means "complete faith" (*al-īmān al-kāmil*) and that "people" here may simply refer to the people residing in Mecca when this (Meccan) passage was revealed.[70] Now consider the following: when Riḍā cites Ghazālī's criterion for non-Muslim salvation, he cites the same section of the treatise *Fayṣal al-tafriqa bayna al-Islām wa-l-zandaqa* (The decisive criterion for distinguishing Islam from masked infidelity) that presents Ghazālī's case for optimism. Had Riḍā taken issue with Ghazālī's optimistic outlook, it would have been odd if he had not at least made a brief note to this effect. Furthermore, throughout his writings, Riḍā never gives any clear indication that he was anything but an optimist. This, however, does not mean that his optimism is always obvious. For instance, when the Qur'an states that "most" of the People of the Book "are wrongdoers" (*fāsiqūn*) (3:110), Riḍā takes this to be a general statement applicable to contemporary People of the Book. (As we should expect, Riḍā refutes the claim made by some of his coreligionists that *all* contemporary Jews and Christians are "wrongdoers.") He also argues that "corruption" (*fisq*) tends to become more prevalent over time within all religions.[71] But "sinfulness" need not warrant damnation "for ages" (Q. 78:23). It should be recalled that Ghazālī's optimism is not predicated on a belief that the great bulk of humanity is so righteous that it will attain immediate salvation. Instead, Ghazālī assumes that throughout the lengthy period known as Judgment Day, countless sinners may be briefly chastised "for a second or an hour or some period of time, by virtue of which they earn the title, 'party of the [Fire].'"[72] This is besides the fact that many individuals will "simply" be taken to account or saved from Hell through intercession. It is only those who are extremely evil, constituting a small proportion of the "party of the Fire," who will remain in Hell beyond the Last Day. This seems to be precisely what Riḍā has in mind when, as we shall soon see, he asserts that the kinds of evildoers who would only continue to sin if granted everlasting life in this world are a "minority" of the people consigned to Hell.[73]

Yet while there is much overlap between the soteriological frameworks of Ghazālī and Riḍā, it is their dissimilarities that are most striking. Although he cites Ghazālī, Riḍā's standard for determining who qualifies as a sincere non-Muslim is decidedly more lenient. It even converges with the doctrines ascribed to Jāḥiẓ and Ibn ʿArabī, namely, that non-Muslims who fail to recognize the authenticity of the message will be excused—a doctrine that Ghazālī explicitly refutes, although one would never know this relying solely on Riḍā's writings. As we saw in chapter 1, Ghazālī argues that blind imitators are culpable if they encounter an accurate representation of the message and then fail to accept or investigate it—even if the truth of the message were never made clear to them. Because God provided them with intellects capable of recognizing the proofs of the Prophet, their failure to see the truth is symptomatic of the "disease in their hearts" (Q. 2:10).

From Riḍā's standpoint, however, the inability to appreciate prophetic proofs may have nothing to do with impure hearts and much to do with less-than-ideal intellects—although not necessarily "stupidity." Consider, for instance, Riḍā's ten groups: each group represents a different level of intellectual development. For instance, blind imitators (such as Riḍā's fourth group) are inferior to truth-seekers (the eighth and ninth groups). The truth-seekers who cease investigating after failing to discern the truth of the message (the eighth group) are not as far along as those truth-seekers who can see that there is good reason not to give up (the ninth group). And the latter, Riḍā indicates in a 1905 piece, lag behind those who succeed in recognizing the truth of the message (as would be the case for individuals of Riḍā's first two groups).[74] As Riḍā would have it, those with a "disease in their hearts" are those who reject the final message after seeing the truth, and not necessarily those whose "mental vision" is impaired in the first place.

To this Riḍā adds another layer of nuance: the inability to see clearly may in fact have less to do with the quality of one's intellect than with one's social, cultural, and political environment. As I intimated in chapter 1, it would be challenging in a modern context to affirm both the particulars of Ghazālī's inclusivist criterion for salvation and his optimism without either modifying the former or rethinking the latter. Again, Ghazālī maintains that the unreached cease to be so once they come to know of the Prophet, his character, and his miracles. Because so many non-Muslims of Ghazālī's era never came to know of these things, it was relatively easy for Ghazālī to justify his claim that the overwhelming majority of humanity will be saved without violating or modifying his criterion. But early-twentieth-century non-Muslims, especially the many intellectuals among them, would have been much more likely to hear of Muḥammad and the noble qualities and miracles ascribed to him.[75] Even if most modern non-Muslims had heard only negative things about Islam, there were yet many others whose knowledge of the basic principles and features of the religion was generally accurate. If these numerous non-Muslims had generally not seen the light, and if this were likely to be true of many more non-Muslims of future generations in an age of technological advancement, damning all these people would surely undermine Ghazālī's optimism.

Riḍā deeply appreciated the fact that social, cultural, and political paradigms often serve as the lenses through which individuals and communities view the world.[76] And certain paradigms make it unlikely that encountering Islamic revelation would induce the kind of response that Ghazālī took for granted. This is precisely why those things that would prompt the contemplation of Islam must vary from era to era. In the age of modernity, proper exposure to the message could not simply entail exposure to the Prophet's attributes and his miracles. The prevailing paradigms must be sufficiently counterbalanced. But how or at what point this occurs is not entirely clear. What is clear is that Riḍā regarded his work and that of ʿAbduh as attempts to rehabilitate the tarnished image of Islam, to provide "enough incentive" to at least some non-Muslims to take it seriously.[77] And despite the gloomy state of affairs in the early twentieth century, Riḍā was hopeful that the world would eventually progress to the point that it would be more likely for people—including Europeans—to investigate and ultimately accept the final, universal message.[78]

Although Riḍā's thought evolved over the years (we shall soon see a striking example of this), and although his polemics intensified in response to increased Christian missionary activity,[79] we have no evidence that he ever abandoned his liberal, Ghazālī-inspired (arguably Ghazālīan) form of inclusivism for, say, Ibn Taymiyya's limited inclusivism. As I noted earlier, Riḍā republished his exegetical discussions in *al-Manār* as *Tafsīr al-Manār* in 1927, years after they first appeared in the periodical. Although he occasionally provides corrigenda and addenda (for instance, at the end of the first volume of the *Tafsīr*),[80] none have any bearing on his soteriological inclusivism. Furthermore, none of the later volumes of his *Tafsīr* or any of his other later writings present an alternative vision regarding the fate of Others on Judgment Day.[81]

Cautious Universalism

If we are to speak of a change in Riḍā's soteriology, it appears in his discourse on the damned. In early volumes of *al-Manār*, Riḍā never gives serious consideration to the possibility that even the wicked may be saved. To the contrary, he generally appears content with the prevailing view of eternal chastisement. Consider, for instance, his treatment of Q. 2:162, which reads, "[The unbelievers] will remain in this state of rejection: their punishment will not be lightened, nor will they be reprieved." As Riḍā sees it (he notes that he does not recall anything by ʿAbduh on this verse), the Qur'an here indicates that Hell's inhabitants will remain in the Fire and will be "banished from the mercy of God the Exalted, permanently [*dāʾiman*]."[82] There is no hope for them: when they passed away, their deeds were cut off, and they were prevented from reflecting. God will neither pay attention to nor purify them.[83]

These damnationist pronouncements first appeared in the June 1904 issue of *al-Manār* and were reprinted toward the end of Riḍā's life in the second volume of his *Tafsīr*.[84] When they were reprinted, however, they no longer represented his position. He corrects himself in the eighth volume of his *Tafsīr*, specifically his treatment of Q. 6:128, which was first published as a two-part series in the December 1920 and January 1921 issues of *al-Manār*.[85]

It should be recalled that the latter half of Q. 6:128 reads as follows: "[God] will say, 'Your home is the Fire, and there you shall remain [*khālidīn fīhā*]'—unless God wills otherwise [*illā mā shāʾa Allāh*]: your Lord is Wise, Aware." In his commentary on this verse, Riḍā delves into the topic of Hell's duration. He warns early on that, ultimately, one must leave this matter to God and "avoid passing a verdict [*al-ḥukm*] concerning His will," for it pertains to the "unseen"; no one can truly know which of His creatures He chooses to place in Paradise and which He chooses to place in Hell.[86] Among the reports Riḍā cites early in his discussion is a hadith that quotes the Prophet as saying, "If God wills to remove from the Fire and admit into Paradise a people from among those who were made wretched, He will do so."[87] Before long, we encounter the familiar statements ascribed to ʿUmar ibn al-Khaṭṭāb, Ibn Masʿūd, Abū Hurayra, ʿAbd Allāh ibn ʿAmr, and al-Shaʿbī, all of which point to the eventual desolation of Hell. We also find mention of Ibn Abī al-ʿIzz al-Ḥanafī's commentary on the Ṭaḥāwī creed, specifically his claim that God's choice to save whomever He wills and terminate Hell is one of two justifiable Sunni doctrines, the other being everlasting wretchedness.[88] Riḍā then proceeds to rehash the entirety of Ibn Qayyim's lengthy discussion of universal salvation in *Ḥādī al-arwāḥ ilā bilād al-afrāḥ* (Spurring souls on to dominions of joys).[89] It is primarily for this reason that Riḍā was compelled to publish his commentary on Q. 6:128 in *al-Manār* as a two-part series.

In support of Ibn Qayyim's arguments for the salvation of all, Riḍā adds a now familiar linguistic observation: Qur'anic terms used in reference to the stay in Hell, such as *khulūd* and *abadan*, need not indicate that which is without end; they often simply connote an extended period of time.[90] Although Ibn Qayyim himself makes a similar observation in *Shifāʾ al-ʿalīl* (Healing the sick),[91] Riḍā here and in later works only ever references Ibn Qayyim's universalist exposition in the *Ḥādī*. As we saw in the previous chapter, the *Ḥādī* devotes twenty-five arguments to the Paradise-for-all paradigm; however, its concluding note is that God does as He pleases. Riḍā makes no mention of Ibn Qayyim's later and more confident case for universalism in *Ṣawāʿiq al-mursala* (The dispatched thunderbolts), which presents leaving the matter to God as an appropriate approach for those who have not yet been illuminated by the "dawn of what is correct."[92] Although Riḍā was aware of the existence of the *Ṣawāʿiq*, we have no evidence that he ever actually read it.[93] As for Ibn Qayyim's universalist exposition in the *Ḥādī*, we do not know when exactly Riḍā discovered it, although the first time he ever mentions the *Ḥādī* at all is in the November 1909 issue of *al-Manār*, as an announcement of its publication by the Egyptian press Maṭbaʿat al-Nīl.[94] This was well over a decade before Riḍā first published his commentary on Q. 6:128.

Whenever it was that Riḍā first encountered the case for universalism in the *Ḥādī*, it undoubtedly moved him. After citing it, Riḍā showers Ibn Qayyim with praise and avers that the latter's arguments for universal salvation not only provide important insights but also reveal the great error committed by adherents of all the major religious traditions when they claim that only they will be saved and that "the majority of humankind will be punished severely, perpetually, with no end—ever."[95] Thus, Riḍā continues,

Ibn Qayyim challenges us to reconsider God's overwhelming mercy—mercy that "encompasses all things" (Q. 7:156) and far exceeds that of a loving mother for her only child. As such, Riḍā adds, this discussion may in fact be of benefit to those astray (while the prevailing damnationist doctrine is of no detriment to believers).[96]

As one might expect, some of Riḍā's readership took him to task for such daring remarks. At the end of the March 1921 issue of *al-Manār*, two months after these remarks first appeared, Riḍā takes note of the brewing controversy and addresses his detractors. He reiterates that there is no consensus on the duration of the Fire; the universalist statements published in *al-Manār* are by no means novel. In response to the claim that *shirk* (associating partners with God) necessitates everlasting damnation because it is an unforgivable sin (Q. 4:116), Riḍā insists that this transgression only necessitates chastisement, not everlasting chastisement. He concedes that Ibn Qayyim's discussion may confound some troublemaking atheists and apostates; however, it also assists those sincere believers who doubt that God would forever chastise beings that He created. Interestingly, Riḍā divulges that while in the past he may have found it relatively easy to convince different kinds of people of the existence of God and the logical underpinnings of various doctrines, his most difficult challenge was to convince some sincere skeptics of the rationale behind everlasting chastisement—a hint as to what may have led Riḍā to rethink damnationism. It is appropriate, he adds, to demonstrate to such skeptics that their views are acceptable within the Islamic tradition—the same tradition whose net was wide enough to include the supporters of Jahm.[97]

Nevertheless, Riḍā was a tactful editor of a major periodical. He knew that he could not alienate a segment of his readership and risk being branded a heretic by his peers because of what appeared to be an enthusiastic endorsement of a controversial belief. Accordingly, although he had just recently published and endorsed Ibn Qayyim's lengthy case for universal deliverance in two consecutive issues of *al-Manār* (and would later republish them in his *Tafsīr*), Riḍā comments that the temporality of Hell and the cessation of chastisement are not the kinds of doctrines he would "propagate and stand up for" (*adʿū ilayhā wa-anāḍil ʿanhā*).[98] He even promises to publish rejoinders by readers—a promise fulfilled in the very next issue of *al-Manār*.[99] But in the process of appeasing his critics, he makes a peculiar statement: it would be a mistake to assume that either he or Ibn Qayyim favors [*yurajjiḥ*] the doctrine of the annihilation of Hell and chooses it [*yakhtāruh*]."[100] In truth, he insists, both he and Ibn Qayyim leave the matter to God.

It is, however, one thing to leave the matter to God after highlighting the strengths and weaknesses of competing doctrines; it is quite another to do so after devoting tens of pages to refuting eternal chastisement—and not following it with counterarguments (at least not until pressured to do so). It is difficult to imagine a scholar as brilliant as Riḍā not deducing from the *Ḥādī* that Ibn Qayyim at least favors universalism. As such, I read Riḍā's statement above as a denial that either he or Ibn Qayyim "favors" *and subsequently* "chooses" the temporal Hell doctrine, the operative word being *chooses*. If neither Riḍā nor Ibn Qayyim even favors the view that Hell is temporal, it would be superfluous to mention their not taking the additional step of choosing it as their doctrine. Accordingly, their leaving the matter to God is an act of caution, not a sign of agnostic indifference. Thus, elsewhere in this missive, when describing Ibn Qayyim's stance toward the competing doctrines of an eternal Hell and a temporal Hell, Riḍā states that Ibn Qayyim "was not absolutely certain of this one or that one" (*lam yajzim bi-hādhā wa-lā dhāka*). Why use such strong language ("absolutely certain") if Ibn Qayyim did not even prefer either doctrine? (Of course, had Riḍā encountered Ibn Qayyim's statements in the *Ṣawāʿiq*, he would have had to reconsider this claim altogether.) It should be recalled that early in his commentary on Q. 6:128, Riḍā warns against "passing a verdict [*al-ḥukm*] concerning [God's] will."[101] He is, therefore, consistent when he states that the temporality of chastisement is not a doctrine that he himself would "propagate and stand up for." Again, notice the strong language.

That Riḍā would extol Ibn Qayyim, reproduce his relatively lengthy discussion in the *Ḥādī*, and initially omit damnationist rejoinders leads me to believe that at this stage of his life Riḍā favored universalism but, recognizing the controversy surrounding it, preferred to remain on solid ground by leaving the matter to God. Preferring the Paradise-for-all paradigm yet abstaining from "choosing" it as a doctrine worth "standing up for" because of some uncertainty concerning the divine will is an orientation that I classify as "cautious universalism." Such a cautious approach was not at all unusual for Riḍā. In a piece published in 1905, for instance, he briefly describes Heaven and Hell and follows it with a warning: both abodes "are of the unseen realm; it is not permissible for us to investigate their reality"; when it comes to the afterlife, the "obligation of deferring" to God is "established."[102] Assuming that Riḍā in his later years continued to view the afterlife with such circumspection, the mere fact that he would devote considerable space in *al-Manār* to the topic of universal salvation and the annihilation of the Fire is telling.

But how, then, do we account for Riḍā's bold declarations regarding the salvation of Others on Judgment Day? Although Riḍā occasionally qualifies these assertions with the traditional formula "God knows best,"[103] he does not insist that these matters should be deferred to God. But are these not affairs of the "unseen realm"? In fact, not entirely: unlike the topic of Hell's annihilation, Riḍā's inclusivist doctrine pertains to the state in which one passes away; it concerns the question of how one should live in this world and, in particular, when it is obligatory to follow the way of Muḥammad. Thus, Riḍā regarded his criterion for non-Muslim salvation as being significantly "safer" than a doctrine allowing for the eventual salvation of people like Pharaoh and Abū Lahab.

Be that as it may, not long before he died, Riḍā revisited the question of universal salvation in his commentary on Q. 11:106–108. Here he refers back to his discussion of Q. 6:128 and continues where he left off. He reminds his audience that God, out of His generosity, rewards those who do good deeds by multiples of ten to seven hundred (numbers that appear in the hadith corpus and that are congruous with Qur'anic statements of increased reward),[104] whereas unbelievers receive only what they deserve. Riḍā presents as problematic the claim that eternal chastisement is just recompense for those consigned to Hell because they would only continue to sin if granted everlasting lives in this world. As Riḍā would have it, people generally rectify themselves when various impediments to faith are removed. Did not the people of Mecca accept the Prophet after having fiercely opposed him? Those who would perpetually transgress in this life are the stubborn and arrogant leaders of sin, and these are a minority of the people who will be punished in Hell. Riḍā concedes, however, that it would be "plausible" to hold that some people deserve everlasting chastisement on account of their deeply ingrained "unbelief, iniquity, and depravity."[105] With this, Riḍā ends his discussion abruptly, promising to return to the topic of Hell's duration at the end of his treatment of sura 11 ("Hūd").

And return he would. Riḍā's concluding commentary on this sura consists of a relatively brief yet remarkable discussion of damnation that betrays his preference for universal salvation. Riḍā reiterates that the term *abadan* need not mean "forever"; yet he finds hidden wisdom in the fact that in four instances in the Qur'an, where paradisiacal reward and hellish torment appear together (specifically, 4:56–57, 121–122; 64:9–10; and 98:6–8), *abadan* is only employed to describe the duration of heavenly bliss. (We find no mention of Paradise immediately preceding or succeeding the three verses where *abadan* appears in reference to chastisement, that is, 4:169, 33:65, and 72:23.) This, Riḍā asserts, is not random or without purpose.[106] It is true that most Muslim exegetes affirm the eternality of Hell. But, Riḍā writes, some hold a different opinion due to "explicit" (*ṣarīḥa*) passages of the Qur'an and hadith corpus that convey the true nature of God's expansive mercy and justice. According to these exegetes, it would be contrary to reason and scripturally baseless to hold that God the Just would punish sinners with a chastisement that is of greater magnitude than their sins warrant.

Riḍā adds that although he had originally promised his readers that he would discuss all of the known doctrines regarding the duration and purpose of chastisement, he found himself satisfied with Ibn Qayyim's discussion in the *Ḥādī*. In sum, "the mercy of God the Exalted is most expansive and most complete and His will is most universal and most inclusive. So nothing can restrict them, and nothing but His knowledge can fully grasp them."[107] As a halfhearted attempt to mitigate the appearance of deferential consideration, Riḍā immediately follows this remark with a brief note: two "late exegetes," the Yemeni traditionalist Muḥammad al-Shawkānī (d. 1834) and the Indian Salafi thinker Ḥasan Ṣiddīq Khān (d. 1890), also discuss this topic in their Qur'anic commentaries. Riḍā does not mention their arguments, their merits, or even the fact that both advocate damnationism. Instead, he simply concludes, "Whoever wishes may consult both."[108] One, therefore, must comb through their respective writings to discover that, according to Shawkānī, the unbelievers will remain in Hell for "ages" followed by "ages," ad infinitum;[109] and according to Khān, Ibn Qayyim's twenty-five arguments for universalism are problematic, erroneous, and contrary to the consensus view.[110]

Beyond Riḍā: A Survey of Some Modern Trends

In Riḍā's soteriology we observe a common tendency to invoke different, sometimes competing, theological doctrines of past centuries as a way of garnering support among both scholars and the laity for one's own unique vision while also allaying suspicion that one's own stances are merely signs of the times. Riḍā's success may be measured by the fact that other notable scholars were able to follow suit and corroborate his brand of interim inclusivism–ultimate universalism. Consider, for instance, the case of the influential Egyptian jurist and theologian Yusuf al-Qaradawi. As a member of the Muslim Brotherhood, he was once a student of Ḥasan al-Bannā, who was himself greatly influenced by Riḍā. As I noted in the previous chapter, Qaradawi defends Ibn Qayyim's case for cautious universalism in a 2002 article. In a 2003 fatwa, Qaradawi also promotes a familiar form of inclusivism: citing Q. 17:15 and 4:115, he argues that while the general principle is that faith in Islam is required for salvation, God, out of His justice, exempts those who are unaware of the final (or any other) message, those who never encounter it in a manner that is "attractive" (*mushawwiqan*) enough to prompt investigation, and those who never convert because of impediments beyond their control. Damnation, then, awaits those for whom the truth of the message was "made clear" but who rejected it out of arrogance, envy, love of this world, a preference for blind imitation, and so on. Thus, when the Qur'an condemns those guilty of *shirk* (associating partners with God), it is specifically condemning individuals who are arrogant and stubborn, and not simply anyone who adheres to a problematic creed. To buttress his conclusion, Qaradawi cites a similar position held by the ʿAbduh-influenced former rector of al-Azhar, Mahmoud Shaltout, who, as we saw earlier, was also influenced by Ibn Qayyim's universalist arguments.[111] But just as Riḍā was selective in his use of Ghazālī and Ibn Qayyim, those influenced by Riḍā were also discriminating in their choices. This is true of Sayyid Qutb, a leading ideologue of the Muslim Brotherhood, who appears not to have been swayed by either Riḍā's inclusivism or his universalism.

Sayyid Qutb and Modern Exclusivism

On August 29, 1966, Sayyid Qutb was executed in his Egyptian homeland. What he left behind was a controversial Islamist legacy and an extremely influential modern commentary on the Qur'an: *Fī ẓilāl al-Qurʾān* (*In the Shade of the Qur'an*). Notwithstanding his secular education, Qutb demonstrates in the *Ẓilāl* a deep familiarity with the rich legacy of Islamic thought. Relative to classical exegetical works, however, the *Ẓilāl* (volumes of which were published from 1952 to 1965) is both au courant and accessible to nonscholars. And, significantly, one finds in it no obvious endorsement of either soteriological inclusivism (let alone pluralism) or universalism.

In his explication of Q. 2:62, Qutb affirms that what matters before God is proper belief, not communal affiliation. But, he quickly clarifies, in a post-Muḥammadan world, there is only one community for all to join.[112] Accordingly, he notes in his commentary on Q. 3:19, "there is no *islām* without submission to God, obedience to His Prophet, observance of His order [*manhaj*], and judging by His book in life's affairs."[113] In his treatment of Q. 17:15 and 4:115, Qutb draws attention to God's mercy: He only chastises those who have received a warner and who recognize the warning for what it is.[114] This warning is God's proof against humanity; those who have not received the warning have a proof against God. But as Qutb informs us (in his discussion of Q. 4:165), the proof against God no longer exists on account of His final message—a message that is universal, for all people and all times. What keeps this proof intact is Muslim efforts to spread their religion, even if through armed struggle (*jihād*). And yet, Qutb adds, it is proselytizing that allows Muslims to save Others.[115]

In the absence of any clarification or explanation of how one qualifies as a recipient of the message (would simply hearing something, *anything*, about it suffice as an incentive to convert because of its inherent persuasiveness?), Qutb leaves the reader with the impression that there may no longer be individuals who qualify as unreached. Additionally, Qutb, like Riḍā, reserves "the heights" (Q. 7:46–49) simply for those whose good and evil deeds are equal.[116] It seems, then, that the overwhelming majority of—and possibly all—non-Muslim adults of sound mind will face God's wrath. Elsewhere (in his analysis of sura 98 ["al-Bayyina"]), Qutb states that because of the finality and universality of Muḥammad's message, it is the only path to salvation. Anyone who appears to be good but does not accept God's universal revelation undoubtedly exhibits false goodness.[117] In his 1964 Islamist manifesto *Maʿālim fī al-ṭarīq* (*Milestones*), Qutb presents reified Islam as the only way to God and asserts that only one group of people—righteous Muslims—is upright; all others are ignorant and astray.[118]

When commenting on the Qur'anic verses typically employed by universalists, Qutb gives no clear indication that the unbelievers residing in the Fire could ever be saved. The fact that the divine threat in Q. 6:128 ("Your home is the Fire, and there you shall remain") is followed by an exception ("unless God wills otherwise") is merely a reminder of God's unlimited volition.[119] The same is true of Q. 11:106–107.[120] The fact that the "transgressors" will "remain" in Hell "for ages" (Q. 78:23) means that their torment will be renewed "ages after ages."[121] In his discussion of Q. 4:169, which states that—according to the prevailing interpretation—the unbelievers will remain in Hell "forever" (*abadan*), Qutb states that it is not God's business to forgive and guide the wicked: they "deserve" their fate; they have no hope of escaping it.[122] In his treatment of a similar passage (Q. 33:65), Qutb broaches the possibility of a noneternal chastisement: the damned will remain in the Fire for "a long time, the duration of which only God knows. It has no end save in God's knowledge, inasmuch as God desires." He continues, however, by asserting that "there is no hope for salvation" from the Fire.[123] Even if chastisement in Hell were to come to an end, this would seem to entail the annihilation of the unbelievers and not their relocation to Paradise. Qutb was well aware of the writings of Riḍā and Ibn Qayyim, but he cites both elsewhere, not here.[124]

The reader is thus left with the impression that, in the modern world, only Muslims will ever be saved; it is only through Islam that one can attain the key to soteriological (and, for that matter, political) success. With the *Ẓilāl* serving as a source of inspiration for multitudes of Muslims, the implication of this is far-reaching. Here I should add that some of Qutb's strongest exclusivist and particularist statements (in the *Maʿālim* and his commentary on suras 78 and 98) appear toward the end of his life, during what had become a long prison term imposed on him by, in his eyes, an ignorant, barbaric, and not truly Muslim Egyptian government.

Qutb was by no means the first major modern figure to popularize the exclusivist paradigm. A similar sentiment appears, for instance, in some of the writings of Abul Ala Maududi (d. 1979), the Pakistani scholar and journalist and Ḥasan al-Bannā–inspired revivalist who founded the Islamist organization Jamaat-e-Islami and whose thought influenced Qutb.[125] And, needless to say, there are numerous contemporary personalities who propagate a message of exclusivism.

One unique example is the popular Indian Sunni preacher Zakir Naik. Naik's influence is magnified by modern technology: one can view numerous online clips of Naik giving public lectures and taking questions from the audience. In one such clip, he is asked to comment on the fate of non-Muslims. Naik cites the following passage as evidence that God will guide to Islam anyone who is sincere: "We shall show them Our signs on the far horizons [*al-āfāq*] and in themselves, until it becomes clear to them that this is the Truth" (Q. 41:53).[126] Leaving aside the fact that "them" here is an apparent reference to the Meccan pagans referenced throughout sura 41 ("Fuṣṣilat")—the majority of whom eventually professed their faith in the final message—Naik's point is, in effect, that anyone who dies a non-Muslim must have rejected God's clear signs and is therefore a damnable unbeliever.

In another clip, a young woman in the audience asks Naik about the salvific status of Nobel Peace laureate and Catholic nun Mother Teresa (d. 1997). In his response, Naik references Q. 5:72, which reads:

> Those who say, "God is the Messiah, son of Mary," have defied God. The Messiah himself said, "Children of Israel, worship God, my

Lord and your Lord." If anyone associates others with God, God will forbid him [or her] from the Garden, and Hell will be his [or her] home. No one will help such evildoers.

According to Naik, Mother Teresa, whatever her deeds, failed the test of faith by associating partners with God.[127] Without qualifying this statement, Naik leaves the audience with the impression that, whatever the circumstances, any Christian who affirms Jesus' divinity is damned.

For many Muslims in close contact with Christians and other non-Muslims, this is a hard pill to swallow: ruthless Muslim tyrants may one day behold God in Paradise, while seemingly saintly non-Muslims will remain forever in the Blazing Fire? Is this fair? Is it reasonable to believe that God would create multiple religions yet designate only one as salvific—and then allow that one religion to flourish only in specific regions of the world? Such questions and the anxieties they induce have often served as an impetus for rethinking Islamic soteriology. What follows is a brief look at some pluralist proposals by Muslim thinkers who may not be as well known in the Muslim world as, say, Qutb or Maududi but whose ideas are worthy of consideration.

A Plurality of Pluralisms

Having experienced the struggles of apartheid and post-apartheid South Africa, and having observed Christian activists working with others in the region to effect positive change, Sunni academic and activist Farid Esack could not accept the exclusivist sentiments and tendencies of his coreligionists. In *Qur'ān, Liberation, and Pluralism*, Esack develops "a theology of pluralism for liberation" that emphasizes virtuous deeds rather than theological doctrines, thereby making "space"—in both this life and the next—"for the righteous and just Other."[128] Esack utilizes a methodology that critically incorporates the exegetical writings of medieval and modern scholars on Qur'anic passages such as 2:62 and 5:48. In so doing, he attempts to uncover a Qur'anic message of ecumenism—"explicit" in 2:62[129]—that has been suppressed historically because of hermeneutic tendencies that privilege reified Islam. As I indicated earlier, when making his case for pluralism, Esack often invokes Riḍā's Qur'anic commentary and presents him as a pluralist of sorts; yet, as we have seen, it would be more precise to think of Riḍā as a liberal inclusivist. Nevertheless, Esack himself recognizes that his sources may not necessarily accommodate his particular vision and he goes to great lengths to overcome potential scriptural impediments to his project.

One such impediment is Qur'anic criticisms of the People of the Book. These criticisms, Esack argues, must not be generalized, for they are typically directed at specific groups of Jews and Christians. For instance, the following rebuke and others like it are intended only for certain exclusivist factions in contact with the Prophet: "They also say, 'No one will enter Paradise unless he is a Jew or a Christian.' This is their own wishful thinking" (Q. 2:111).[130] When the Qur'an accuses the People of the Book of having "distorted" their respective revelations, the accusation is usually directed at "some" of them (as in 2:75, 3:78, and 4:46). We must not assume, therefore, that all People of the Book are "distorters" or even that their scriptures are now completely invalid. If the latter were true, the Qur'an would not instruct certain People of the Book to "judge" according to the Torah and the Gospel (as in 5:43–47).[131] As for the pronouncement that those who ascribe divinity to Jesus are guilty of *kufr* (unbelief, dissent, concealment of the truth, rejection, ingratitude) (Q. 5:17, 72), Esack reads this not as a "purely doctrinal" matter.[132] This is because the Qur'anic notion of *kufr* is multidimensional and intrinsically linked to a rejection of morality and justice. Thus, Christians guilty of *kufr* are those who maintained an antagonistic attitude toward *islām* and *muslims* and who presumably "recognized the unity of God and Muhammad as His Prophet, but... willfully refuse[d] to acknowledge it," thereby deliberately concealing the truth.[133] It is their arrogant hostility toward Muḥammad and his path, and not simply their decision to remain Christian, that the Qur'an denounces.

As Esack explains, "Muhammad's basic responsibility in inviting was to call to God. For some components of the Other, the response to this call was best fulfilled by a commitment to Islam. Thus they were also invited to become Muslims. For others, the call was limited to *islam*."[134] An example of the latter group is the Christian delegation of Najrān (a city located in southern Arabia) that the Prophet welcomed in Medina shortly before he passed away. When they chose not to become Muslim, they were simply invited to "arrive at a statement that is common to us all: we worship God alone, we ascribe no partner to Him, and none of us takes others beside God as lords" (Q. 3:64). While many exegetes read this as a call to Islamic monotheism or, at best, a recognition of at least some commonality between Muslims and Christians, Esack sees in this verse an explicit affirmation of the ecumenical nature of *islām*.[135] Esack develops this point in his treatment of Q. 5:48. Consider the wording of the latter half of the verse:

> We have assigned a law and a path to each of you. If God had so willed, He would have made you one community, but He wanted to test you through that which He has given you, so race to do good: you will all return to God and He will make clear to you the matters about which you differed.

Exegetes often claim that this statement is addressed only to Muslims and pre-Muḥammadan People of the Book who passed away before their laws were abrogated by Islam. Esack challenges the exegetes on this point: why would Islamic scripture speak to the deceased in this manner ("to each of you," "race to do good," etc.)?[136] As such, although there is only one true *dīn*, or "religion," it is a *dīn* consisting of multiple, nonabrogated approaches; it is not bound by the conventional conceptions of religion.[137] Indeed, the Qur'an itself informs us that God has "appointed [different] acts of devotion for every community to observe" (22:67).[138]

All this is not to suggest that the competing truth claims of the divinely sanctioned religious traditions are equally valid. Even so, one need not believe that, for example, Jesus is divine in order to affirm that Christians can achieve closeness to God through Christianity. What matters most soteriologically is the attainment of righteousness, not one's precise conception of reality. On the path to Heaven, therefore, virtuous Christian deeds trump various Christian creeds.

Again, when the Qur'an deplores *kufr*, it is not simply debunking inaccurate dogma. *Kufr* is "something conscious, deliberate and active rather than a casual ignoring or disregard of the existence of God."[139] Thus, the Qur'anic term for a Hell-bound unbeliever, *kāfir*, is not simply a doctrinal designator, and it does not apply to those who adopt a passive approach to divine truth and divine gifts. There is, therefore, no good reason to think that agnostics and even atheists are necessarily "unbelievers." The same is true of adherents of non-Abrahamic faiths, including traditions that have long been dismissed as religions of *shirk* (associationism), such as Hinduism.[140]

According to Esack, the Qur'anic denunciation of *shirk* must be read historically and in context, as it was "intrinsically connected to the socioeconomic practices of the Arabs,"[141] which led to the oppression of the disenfranchised.[142] In short, it was a "disturbance 'in the balance.'"[143]

When the Qur'an condemns advocates of certain "erroneous" truth claims, it often does so when there is a perceived "relationship" between such claims and "the socio-economic exploitation of others."[144] This is evident in the case of certain Medinan Jews: despite their relative proximity to Muslims theologically, some of the Qur'an's harshest criticisms—doctrinal or otherwise—are reserved for these individuals. By the same token, however, the Qur'an includes other Jews among those who may be saved (as in 2:62 and 5:69). The same is true of certain Sabians, even though many exegetes report that they "worshipped stars, even angels."[145]

Much like Esack, Abdulaziz Sachedina, a U.S.-based academic of Indian heritage, underlines the Qur'anic emphasis on good works and argues that Islamic scripture accepts the salvific efficacy of "other Abrahamic traditions."[146] Particularly poignant for Sachedina is Q. 2:213, which reads:

> Humanity was a single community, then God sent prophets to bring good news and warning, and with them He sent the scripture with the Truth, to judge between people in their disagreements. It was only those to whom it was given who disagreed about it after clear signs had come to them, because of rivalry between them. So by His leave God guided the believers to the truth they had differed about: God guides whomever He will to a straight path.

This verse, according to Sachedina, "command[s] Muslims to build bridges of understanding and co-operation between the once united human community."[147] Invoking Q. 2:62 and the exegetical writings of Riḍā and the Iranian Shī'ite scholar Muḥammad Ḥusayn Ṭabāṭabā'ī (d. 1981), both of whom rejected the claim that this verse (2:62) had been abrogated, Sachedina, himself a Shī'ite, insists that salvation is made available to righteous monotheists who do not affirm Muḥammad's prophethood.[148] (It should be recalled that Q. 2:62 promises salvation to "all those who believe in God and the Last Day and do good.") Yet Sachedina's focus on Jews and Christians, along with his observation that the Qur'an never mentions "the fate of non-monotheistic traditions, such as particular south Asian and east Asian religions," leaves the reader with the impression that he is an "Abrahamic pluralist."[149] Thus, relative to Esack at least, Sachedina lays more emphasis on the role of doctrines in securing salvation.

A more restrictive form of pluralism appears in the writings of another U.S.-based Shī'ite academic (in this case, of Lebanese heritage), Mahmoud Ayoub. Utilizing the exegetical writings of modern Sunni and Shī'ite scholars, including the Iranian Ayatollah Mahmoud Taleghani (d. 1979), Ayoub draws attention to Q. 2:62 and the similarly worded 5:69. He notes that 2:62 was revealed shortly after the Prophet's emigration to the city of Medina (originally known as Yathrib), while 5:69 was revealed nearly a decade later and at a time in which the Prophet had become the most dominant figure in Arabia. This, according to Ayoub, indicates that the principle of pluralism is general in nature and cannot be contextualized away.[150] To support his particular reading of scripture, which, he concedes, is "selective,"[151] he draws attention to the Qur'anic reference to "those who say, 'We are Christians,' " who are

> closest in affection toward the believers...for there are among them people devoted to learning and ascetics. These people are not given to arrogance, and when they listen to what has been sent down to the Messenger, you will see their eyes overflowing with tears because they recognize the Truth [in it]. They say, "Our Lord, we believe, so count us among the witnesses. Why should we not believe in God and in the Truth that has come down to us, when we long for our Lord to include us in the company of the righteous?" For saying this, God has rewarded them with Gardens graced with flowing streams, and there they will stay: that is the reward of those who do good. (5:82–85)

According to Ayoub, this passage—appearing just ten verses after the aforementioned condemnation of those who ascribe divinity to Jesus—"confirm[s] the People of the Book in their own religious identities and expect[s] from them no more than the recognition of Muḥammad as a messenger of God and of the Qur'ān as a genuine divine revelation confirming their own scriptures."[152] On account of this significant qualification, Ayoub is promoting what I would call "limited pluralism."

Here Ayoub bears some resemblance to the U.S.-based Pakistani Sunni academic Fazlur Rahman (d. 1988). According to Rahman, the Qur'an not only rejects exclusivist sentiments (such as those of the Jews and Christians rebuked in Q. 2:111–124) but "repeatedly recognizes the existence of good people in other communities." This is exemplified in Q. 2:62 and 5:69, even though "the vast majority of Muslim commentators exercised themselves fruitlessly to avoid having to admit the obvious meaning: that those—from any section of humankind—who believe in God and the last day and do good deeds, are saved."[153] Yet, Rahman declares, "if Muḥammad and his followers believe in all prophets, all people must also and equally believe in him. Disbelief in him would be equivalent to disbelief in all, for this would arbitrarily upset the line of prophetic succession."[154]

Toward the other end of the pluralist spectrum we find Muslim scholars of the Sophia Perennis school of thought. Inspired by the French philosopher René Guénon (d. 1951), these thinkers, often called "perennialists" or "traditionalists," hold that the various world religions are ultimately different manifestations of the same truth, which has as its source God, or the Real. Accordingly, Muslims, Christians, Jews, Hindus, Buddhists, and others describe the same Reality from different perspectives—much like the blind men in the well-known Indian parable who touch and describe different parts of the same elephant. Perennialists often employ the metaphysical writings of Sufis such as Ibn ʿArabī to support their worldview and their pluralist (rather than liberal inclusivist) soteriological outlook. A well-known perennialist among Islamicists is Seyyed Hossein Nasr, a U.S.-based academic of Iranian Shīʿite heritage.[155] Utilizing his and other perennialist writings,[156] as well as some of the same Sufi sources referenced in these works, Reza Shah-Kazemi, a Shīʿite scholar from the United Kingdom, makes a scriptural case for a form of pluralism he calls "universalism." He opts for this term in order to distance himself from the famous pluralist John Hick (of Christian heritage) and his teaching that all religions are "human 'cognitive responses' to the ineffable Real."[157] In contrast, Shah-Kazemi's universalism—buttressed by passages such as Q. 2:62 and 5:48—recognizes the major religions (including Hinduism and Buddhism) as "valid paths to salvation, but parts company with the pluralist in asserting that this salvific efficacy stems from the fact that these religions are divinely revealed, not humanly constructed."[158] According to Shah-Kazemi, because these diverse religions are distinct manifestations of the same infinite Reality and because this Reality determined that these religions should assume particular, irreducible forms, "one disagrees with the kind of pluralism which is constrained to deny the uniqueness of each religion in order to subsume them all under some putatively 'global theology.' For it is by the same token constrained to contradict the self-definition of all religions."[159] Shah-Kazemi's proposal, which I would label as a form of "perennial pluralism" (rather than universalism), upholds some aspects of exclusivism, including the normative aspects of each religious tradition and even the personal "belief that one's own religion"—be it Christianity, Islam, Hinduism, or others—"is the best religion" while maintaining that other religions are equally salvific and true at some level.[160]

Although many Muslims find unqualified claims of non-Muslim damnation to be unsettling, many are also uncomfortable with a paradigm that seems too unconventional (notwithstanding pluralist claims to the contrary). This uneasiness has inspired rejoinders by inclusivists. Qaradawī's aforementioned 2003 fatwa, for instance, makes the case for inclusivism only in passing; Qaradawi devotes more space in this brief fatwa to rebutting the unqualified claim that Jews and Christians need not become Muslim to be saved.[161] What follows is a look at the responses of two inclusivists to some of the pluralist arguments examined thus far.

Inclusivist Rebuttals

Is it possible to harmonize the ostensibly contradictory propositions that undergird the world's major religious traditions? What is one to make of the Christian claim that Jesus is divine and the Muslim insistence that he is only human? According to the British academic T. J. Winter (Abdal Hakim Murad), attempting to reconcile these disparate creeds is a problem, one that could lead to what Gavin D'Costa terms "transcendental agnosticism."[162] What is more, there is no historical evidence that the earliest Muslims were pluralists, and the pluralist project only appears tenable when it entails a rejection of the hadith tradition and "the theory of scholarly consensus (*ijmāʿ*) as a transhistorical expression of God's will."[163] Thinkers such as Esack and Ayoub, Winter notes, "characteristically deploy complex hermeneutic strategies of contextualisation and deconstruction in order to unearth the seeds of a theological pluralism from the Koran's discourse."[164] But as Winter sees it, the Qur'an itself presents Islam as a supersessionist, universal faith with an "abrogationist salvation history."[165] This, he maintains, is precisely why Q. 5:48—in the occasionally overlooked first half of the verse—describes the Qur'an as a "guardian" (*muhaymin*) over the preceding scriptures. All this, however, is not to say that anyone who is Jewish or Christian is damned eternally—the presumed fate of Arab pagans.[166] Looking to the theological writings of Ashʿarites and Māturīdites, Winter affirms the possibility that divine mercy will be available to multitudes of non-Muslims. He cites, for example, a short selection from Ghazālī's *Fayṣal* to show that individuals who have been "inadequately" exposed to Islamic revelation are blameless.[167]

It is Winter's belief in "non-categoric supercession" that leads him to proclaim that salvation in a post-Muḥammadan world may be granted to certain members of monotheistic communities that predate Islam.

In particular, he singles out individuals who, because of their circumstances, could not be expected to recognize the truth of Islam but nonetheless submit to God through "natural reason" and adherence to

> remnant teachings handed down from the founders of their own religions, whose detailed instructions are abrogated or have been mislaid, but whose general teachings of the unity and justice of God may be remembered sufficiently to trigger or to reinforce the inference of God's existence and qualities from the natural order.[168]

This in fact is a common Māturīdite view. Winter warns that this form of inclusivism, which one might call "monotheistic inclusivism," is to be distinguished from the "intricate theories of prevenient grace or postmortem conversion" advocated by many contemporary Christian inclusivists who speak of the salvation of "anonymous Christians," a term coined by the German Roman Catholic theologian Karl Rahner (d. 1984).[169] According to Winter, while those non-Muslims who will be saved are in the same category as Muslims, "given Islam's assurance of multiple and equivalently saving interventions in history, there is no need to engage in the patronising exercise of regarding [such] non-Muslims as 'anonymous Muslims,' if we take the term 'Muslim' in the denominational sense." This dichotomy between Islam and Christianity, he avers, is in part the result of the Islamic "insistence on a cyclic process of prepositional revelation whose details are modulated in each prophetic episode, instead of a single personal revelation which tends to divide history and also geography into categorically different parts."[170]

Muhammad (Gary) Legenhausen, an Iran-based American scholar, drawing much from Shī'ite sources, makes a somewhat similar defense of Islamic inclusivism, which he terms "non-reductive pluralism" to distinguish it from Rahner's inclusivism and Hick's "reductive pluralism" ("reductive" because it reduces religions to their commonalities at the expense of beliefs and doctrines that are widely considered fundamental to each tradition).[171] In response to pluralists who see Islam as being equal to other religions, Legenhausen cites the following Qur'anic passages as evidence of Islam's supersessionist character:[172]

> It is He who has sent His Messenger with guidance and the religion of truth, to show that it is above all [other] religions, however much the associationists [*al-mushrikūn*] may hate this. (9:33)

> We have sent you [Prophet] only to bring good news and warning to all people, but most of them do not understand. (34:28)

> As for those who ignore God and His messengers and want to make a distinction between them, saying, "We believe in some but not in others," seeking a middle way, they are really unbelievers: We have prepared a humiliating punishment for those who disbelieve. (4:150–151)[173]

Nevertheless, building on the writings of the Iranian Ayatollah Morteza Motahhari,[174] Legenhausen argues that salvation is not simply predicated on proper belief, as numerous sincere non-Muslims may be saved as long as their lack of faith in Islam is not the result of negligence. This, he claims, would explain a Qur'anic passage like 2:62. Thus, although Islam remains the most effective path for attaining felicity, enough of the truth inherent in the original message has been preserved in the belief systems of the People of the Book that they, too, may be saved if they are unable to recognize the truth of Islam—notwithstanding the irreconcilability of doctrines such as the trinity and Islamic monotheism.[175] Thus, like many pluralists, Legenhausen holds that the concepts of *kufr* and *shirk* are more than simply matters of dogma: they reflect one's purity of heart—a conclusion that requires an appreciation of the context of revelation. The reason Arab paganism may lead to damnation is that it is so far removed from the truth that it fosters wretchedness, thereby reflecting negligence on the part of its adherents. As for Hindus and Buddhists, Legenhausen speculates that, since they may in fact be People of the Book not mentioned in Islamic scripture, the righteous among them may be saved.[176] One, therefore, might think of Legenhausen as a seemingly optimistic "People-of-the-Book inclusivist." Even so, Legenhausen is careful to stress that there is no limit to divine grace: God may choose to forgive all.[177]

Now a pluralist might ask, If, according to inclusivists, numerous non-Muslims could attain righteousness outside of Islam, what is the logic behind Islamic supersessionism? Why would God require conversion or investigation following proper exposure to the final message if inexposure is not in and of itself damnable? An inclusivist might respond that while many Muslims themselves may not fully appreciate Islam, it is through this path that God guides select sincere truth-seekers to a deeper understanding of reality and a more fulfilling spiritual experience. As we have seen, the common inclusivist claim is that the sincere necessarily feel compelled to adhere to the Islamic message once they see it for what it really is. It is also, therefore, one of the many means by which God, out of His wisdom, tests His servants.

Considering that this kind of reasoning will likely not satisfy most pluralists and given that our world is becoming increasingly interconnected and seemingly smaller, we should expect to encounter more debates between pluralists and inclusivists in the years ahead.[178] But as we have seen, exclusivist sentiments have also become ostensibly more prevalent in modern Islamic discourse. In response, pragmatic pluralists might choose to draw attention to certain inclusivist alternatives. Whereas they might find it difficult to persuade their many exclusivist detractors—scholars or otherwise—that the Qur'an promotes pluralism, a mere reference to, say, Ghazālī might go a long way. Even Ibn Taymiyya's limited inclusivism, with his reminder that only God knows which non-Muslims are damned, is quite unlike modern exclusivism. Indeed, most versions of inclusivism, including those advocated by the four theologians featured in this book, effectively reduce or diminish the soteriological barrier between Muslims and Others: who can say with certainty that any specific non-Muslim in today's world is culpable before God? How can anyone declare this Christian or even that atheist a Hell-bound unbeliever? (This is besides the fact that many Muslims may not themselves qualify as Heaven-bound *muslims*.)

Closing Thoughts: Back to the Question

In this book I have examined the works of key intellectual figures in an effort to reveal their insights on a pressing matter. I never traveled with Ghazālī; I was veiled from Ibn ʿArabī's "illuminations"; I was barred from Ibn Taymiyya's prison cell; and I arrived in Cairo decades too late to converse with Riḍā. But what these four giants left behind in their writings is itself a treasure of ruminative thoughts and penetrating observations.

Ghazālī taught that most of humanity will be saved. God's mercy will cover the unreached and those sincere non-Muslims who actively investigate the message after having been properly exposed to it. Only a small minority, iniquitous unbelievers, should expect everlasting torment. According to Ibn ʿArabī, because Allah is a God of overwhelming mercy, He excuses those non-Muslims who do not recognize the message for what it is, not to mention those who have never encountered it. Yet even the wicked, those who can see the path of perfection but refuse to take it, will be delivered from the pain and anguish of the Fire—without having to move an inch. The inhabitants of Hell may be forever veiled from God, but they will find both pleasure and contentment where most would least expect it. Ibn Taymiyya's Hell is quite different. Its gates are much looser: anyone who has already encountered the message and fails to accept it is destined for the Fire. This is because the message should be inherently convincing to the sincere. But the gates of Ibn Taymiyya's Hell are so loose that all those inside it will eventually make their way out. Mercy will triumph over wrath, and all of humanity will one day walk in the Garden. Standing on the shoulders of his predecessors, Riḍā developed his own doctrine. Allowing for the modern condition, he held that all people will be judged according to what they know to be true and good. But even those who choose evil will all likely be restored to goodness and saved from the depths of Hell.

Their insights were many, their positions dissimilar. But despite their unwavering belief in Islamic supersessionism, all four felt compelled and justified to take what I would term a "hermeneutic leap of mercy," going beyond what is obviously stated in scripture without necessarily contradicting it. And considering the views held by many of their peers, their leaps were prodigious. In the end, all four affirmed the existence of the righteous Other; they recognized that God, as the Grand Designer, willed that felicity could be attained through paths other than their own; and they conceived of an afterlife that will, ultimately, be bustling with joy.

We may not have complete access to their reasoning and claims. (Consider, for instance, Ibn ʿArabī's 5,105 "degrees of the Garden.") And we may find some or most of their arguments wanting. But what is significant here is to recognize what these masters—people who devoted their entire lives to their faith—considered viable, and indeed true, interpretations. These interpretations, considered individually or, especially, collectively, challenge and problematize many common assumptions about the nature of Islam.

Our imaginary interlocutor asks yet again, "What does Islam say about the fate of non-Muslims?" As we have seen, Muslim theologians provide a complex array of responses. These responses offer points of departure for further contemplation and, more important, constructive dialogue. What none of them offer, however, is an indisputable resolution. Yet if one accepts the premise that the ethos of the Qur'an and Sunna compels a hermeneutic leap of mercy, then the end result is a positive ambiguity—the kind of ambiguity that leaves believers with a deep sense of humility and hope for humanity.

Glossary of Select Terms

Abbasid. A major Sunni dynasty that ruled circa 750–1258 and initially encompassed much of the early Muslim world. The Abbasid capital during most of its reign was Baghdad.

Allah. The proper name for God in Arabic.

Ashʿarite. A member of a rationalist school of theology whose eponym is Abū al-Ḥasan al-Ashʿarī (d. 324/935). Today, Ashʿarism and Māturīdism constitute the two popular schools of Sunni rationalism that have thrived since the Abbasid era.

fatwa. A formal scholarly opinion or ruling.

hadith. A report of the Prophet's actions and/or sayings. The most respected hadith collections among Sunnis are *Ṣaḥīḥ al-Bukhārī* and *Ṣaḥīḥ Muslim*, both of which were compiled during the third/ninth century.

Ḥanafite. A member of the oldest and largest of the four major Sunni schools of legal thought, whose eponym is Abū Ḥanīfa (d. 150/767). The Ḥanafite creeds mentioned in this book are widely accepted in the Māturīdite school of theology.

Ḥanbalite. A member of the youngest and smallest of the four major Sunni schools of legal thought, whose eponym is Aḥmad ibn Ḥanbal (d. 241/855). Ḥanbalism also refers to traditionalist theology; its proponents often claim to follow a methodology that is more scripture-based than that of the rationalists (such as the Muʿtazilites, Ashʿarites, and Māturīdites).

ḥudūd. Literally, "limits," as in "God's limits." This refers to the penal code of Islamic law.

īmān. A term that can mean belief, faith, assent, sincerity, or fidelity.

***islām* (*or al-islām*).** Submission or surrender (to God). Whether this Qur'anic term specifically designates the religion of Islam is an issue of debate among Muslims.

Islamist. One who subscribes to the belief that Islam is a comprehensive way of life, inclusive of a political and economic dimension.

Jahmite. A member of an obscure early sect whose eponym is Jahm ibn Ṣafwān (d. 128/745). This sect is remembered for its emphasis on predestination and denial of free will.

jinn. Invisible beings made of "smokeless fire" (Q. 55:15) or "the fire of scorching wind" (Q. 15:27). These include both virtuous and satanic entities, as well as Satan (Iblīs) himself.

kāfir. One who is guilty of *kufr*. In scholarly discourse, the term *kāfir* is often used to refer to anyone who is non-Muslim.

Khārijite. A member of an early and relatively small sect of Islam that was reportedly established by individuals who rejected and then assassinated the fourth caliph, ʿAlī ibn Abī Ṭālib (d. 40/661). The Khārijites are remembered for their emphasis on deeds and their claim that a Muslim who commits major sins ceases to be a believer (*muʾmin*).

kufr. A term that can mean unbelief, rejection, dissent, concealment of the truth, or ingratitude.

madrasa. A school or university.

Māturīdite. A member of a rationalist school of theology whose eponym is Abū Manṣūr al-Māturīdī (d. 333/944). Today, Māturīdism and Ashʿarism constitute the two popular schools of Sunni rationalism that have thrived since the Abbasid era.

mufti. One who is vested with authority to issue fatwas.

mujtahid. One who is vested with authority to engage in *ijtihād*, or independent interpretation.

muʾmin. A believer; a person of faith; one who has *īmān*.

Murjiʾite. A member of an early sect that developed in response to the Khārijites; it is remembered for its emphasis on faith (rather than deeds) and its claim that sin does not disqualify one from being considered a believer.

muslim. One who submits or surrenders (to God). An adherent of Islam is called a Muslim.

Muʿtazilite. A member of a rationalist school of theology that came to prominence during the reign of the Abbasids. Widely considered the first systematic school of Islamic theology, the Muʿtazilites gradually lost influence to the new rationalist schools of Ashʿarism and Māturīdism.

Ottoman. A major Turkish Sunni dynasty that ruled circa 1299–1923 and whose dominions once included much of the Near East and eastern Europe.

Qadarite. A member of an early sect that affirmed humanity's ability to choose and act freely (and not by divine force).

Qur'an (or Koran). Literally, "the recitation"; the Islamic holy book, believed to be the "word of God" transmitted to the Prophet Muḥammad.

Qurayshite. A member of the tribe of Quraysh, the principal tribe of Mecca during the lifetime of the Prophet.

Safavid. A major Shiʿite dynasty centered in Iran that ruled circa 1501–1722.

salaf. The first three generations (however defined) of Muslims; often shorthand for *al-salaf al-ṣāliḥ*, the pious ancestors.

Salafi. A member of a movement that calls for a return to the way of the pious ancestors (*al-salaf al-ṣāliḥ*), who are presumed to have interpreted the Qur'an and Sunna directly, without relying on the authority of specific scholars and their precedents.

Shāfiʿite. A member of one of the four major Sunni schools of legal thought, whose eponym is Muḥammad ibn Idrīs al-Shāfiʿī (d. 204/820).

Shiʿite (or Shīʿī). A member of the second largest branch of Islam, which comprises 10 to 20 percent of the Muslim population worldwide.

shirk. Associating partners with God (associationism).

Sufi. An individual affiliated with Sufism.

Sufism (*taṣawwuf*). An orientation of self-purification that is often called "Islamic mysticism" and the "mystical dimension of Islam."

Sunna. The Prophet's normative example.

Sunni. A member of the largest branch of Islam, which comprises 80 to 90 percent of the Muslim population worldwide.

sura. A chapter (or book) of the Qur'an. The Qur'an consists of 114 suras.

Wahhabi. A member of an Arabian reform movement established by its eponym Muḥammad ibn ʿAbd al-Wahhāb (d. 1207/1792).

Notes

INTRODUCTION

1. Harris, *End of Faith*, 117.
2. Aslan, *No god but God*, 100. As Aslan clarifies, Qur'anic criticisms of Christian doctrines concern "Imperial Byzantine (Trinitarian) Orthodoxy"—a relatively unpopular form of Christianity in central Arabia during the era of revelation—not "Christianity *per se*" (ibid., 101). All the same, Aslan insists that scriptural condemnations must be contextualized. The Qur'an is critical of polytheism, for instance, because it (the Qur'an) was revealed during the Prophet's often bloody conflict with Arab pagans. In the final analysis, God desires theological diversity, and, notwithstanding this diversity, Jews, Christians, Muslims, and presumably others constitute a single community (*umma*) of believers. See ibid., 99–104, 262–263.
3. The Qur'an in fact describes Muḥammad as being *only* a "bearer of good news" and "a warner" (7:188), thus making him a "witness" (*shāhid*) (33:45), rather than a "keeper" (*ḥafīẓ*) (4:80), "guardian" (*wakīl*) (6:107), or "tyrant" (*jabbār*) over the unbelievers (50:45), over whom he has no control (88:22).
4. See, for instance, Q. 6:128, 7:188, 10:49, 11:107–108.
5. Izutsu, *Ethico-religious Concepts in the Qur'ān*, 107. *Kufr* "naturally comes to mean 'to cover, i.e. to ignore knowingly the benefits which one has received,' and thence, 'to be unthankful'" (ibid., 119–120). *Īmān* is the antithesis of this. See Izutsu, *Concept of Belief in Islamic Theology*.
6. Although this is the only instance in which the Qur'an uses the Arabic noun for salvation, *najāh*, it employs related words elsewhere, for example, the verbs *nunajjī* (19:72) and *yunjī* (70:14); it also uses other terms that imply salvation, such as *fawz* (triumph) (85:11).

7. Consider, for instance, the popular Qur'anic invocation, "Our Lord, grant us good in this world and in the hereafter, and protect us from the torment of the Fire" (2:201).
8. Fazlur Rahman (d. 1988) in *Major Themes of the Qur'an*, 63, writes, "For Islam, there is no particular 'salvation': there is only 'success [*falāḥ*]' or 'failure [*khusrān*].'" More problematic is Max Weber's (d. 1920) assessment: "Islam was never really a religion of salvation; the ethical concept of salvation was actually alien to Islam.... An essentially political character marked all the chief ordinances of Islam.... There was nothing in ancient Islam like an individual quest for salvation" (*Sociology of Religion*, 263–264). For a related critique of Weber, see Salvatore, "Beyond Orientalism?"
9. This notion of a "bridge to salvation" is arguably implied by the Qur'anic pronouncement that "every one of you will approach [Hell].... We shall save the devout and leave the evildoers there on their knees" (19:71–72); the hadith corpus (including the *Ṣaḥīḥ al-Bukhārī* collection, in "Kitāb ṣifat al-ṣalāh") explicitly refers to it as "the path" (*al-ṣirāṭ*). The earliest known source to mention a "bridge to salvation" is the teachings of the ancient Persian sage Zoroaster. According to the Gathas (Yasna 46:10–16, 51:13–21), each individual will have his or her fate decided at the Chinvat bridge. The elect will cross it successfully, while the rest will fall into a netherworld.
10. According to the Qur'an, Hell has "seven gates" (15:44); in the hadith corpus, it also has seven levels. Certain theologians and exegetes regard the Qur'anic terms for Hell as names for each of its seven levels: the Bottomless Pit (*al-hāwiya*) (101:9); the Blazing Fire (*al-jaḥīm*) (44:47); the Scorching Fire (*al-saqar*) (74:26); the Raging Flame (*al-laẓā*) (70:15); the Crusher (*al-ḥuṭama*) (104:4–6); the Inferno (*al-sa'īr*) (22:4); and, usually highest of all (meaning the least severe), Gehenna (*jahannam*) (3:12). Proponents of this schema have not reached a consensus regarding the precise order of the seven levels. See Lange, *Justice, Punishment, and the Medieval Muslim Imagination*, 122–124; O'Shaughnessy, "Seven Names for Hell in the Koran"; Hamza, *To Hell and Back* (especially chap. 3). (See also note 50 below.) Some scholars maintain that Paradise has seven levels on the basis of Q. 23:17, which states, "We created seven levels above you." Others assert that there are eight levels corresponding to eight different Qur'anic references to Heaven: the Home of Peace (*dār al-salām*) (6:127); the Lasting Home (*dār al-qarār*) (40:39); the Abiding Garden (*jannat al-khuld*) (25:15); Gardens of Refuge (*jannāt al-ma'wā*) (32:19); Gardens of Delight (*jannāt al-na'īm*) (5:65); Gardens of Perpetual Bliss (or Eden; *jannāt 'adn*) (9:72); *'Illiyyūn*, where a lofty "record" of those who are virtuous is "witnessed by those brought near," that is, the elect (83:18–21); and Gardens of Paradise (*jannāt al-firdaws*) (18:107), which many proponents of the eight-tiered Heaven consider to be the highest level. According to the hadith corpus, Heaven also has eight gates. See Smith and Haddad, *Islamic*

Understanding of Death and Resurrection, 86–88. For an extensive discussion of both afterlife abodes in Islamic thought, see Rustomji's recent book *The Garden and the Fire*.

11. Murata and Chittick, *Vision of Islam*, 211.
12. These companions are called houris (*ḥūr al-ʿayn* or *ḥūr ʿīn*). While the notion of the houris does not appear in canonical biblical texts, we find it in Zoroastrianism. W. St. Clair-Tisdall (d. 1928) noted this over a century ago. See his *Sources of Islam*, 82–83. For a critical review of the contemporary theory offered by the pseudonymous Christoph Luxenberg that the term *ḥūr ʿīn* is actually a Syriac expression meaning "white grapes," see Stewart, "Notes on Medieval and Modern Emendations of the Qurʾān," 242–245. The topic of the houris has long attracted the attention of Christian Europe. See, for instance, Smith, "Old French Travel Accounts of Muslim Beliefs Concerning the Afterlife," 227–230. As John Esposito observes, the Qur'anic depiction of Heaven "stands in sharp contrast to the Christian tendency to compartmentalize life into the sacred and the profane, body and soul, sensual and spiritual" (*Islam*, 33).
13. Sells, *Approaching the Qurʾán*, 24.
14. Ibid., 57. Sells makes these comments in reference to the first suras revealed chronologically (that is, early Meccan suras), but they apply to much of the Qur'an.
15. See, for example, Shahrastānī, *Milal*, 85–86; Cornell, "Fruit of the Tree of Knowledge," 71; Fakhry, "Philosophy and Theology," 277–279, 281.
16. The Qur'anic verse 7:172 reads, "When your Lord took out the offspring from the loins of the Children of Adam and made them bear witness concerning themselves, He said, 'Am I not your Lord?,' and they replied, 'Yes, we bear witness.' So you cannot say on the Day of Resurrection, 'We were not aware of this.'" Some Muslim thinkers, such as Muhammad Asad (d. 1992), take this passage to be a metaphor for a "continuous recurrence" rather than an account of a single event in the past. See Asad, *Message of the Qurʾān*, 261n139.
17. Nasr, *Heart of Islam*, 7.
18. Other examples of Qur'anic passages that seem to affirm the universality of the Prophet include 7:158, 12:104, 21:107, 34:28, 38:87, 68:52, and 81:27. Elsewhere in this book we shall encounter some responses to the claim that the Prophet was sent only to the Arabs.
19. See, for instance, Riḍā's discussion of this in his *Tafsīr*, 6:73.
20. Complicating matters is the fact that the distinction between Qur'anic references to and threats of punishment in this life and those of eschatological punishments can sometimes be blurred. Tor Andrae (d. 1947) acknowledges this in *Mohammed*, 54. The same is true of David Marshall in *God, Muhammad and the Unbelievers*, 64. Marshall, however, takes issue with Andrae's claim that it was only in Muḥammad's "last days in Mecca" that the Qur'an began to make threats of punishment in this world, rather than purely eschatological threats.

According to Marshall, "As early as the middle Meccan period there is evidence, direct and indirect, of expectation of a temporal punishment" (ibid., 64–65).

21. It is worth noting that while the overwhelming majority of Muslims have deduced from Islamic scripture that Satan and Pharaoh are damned evildoers, there have been some interesting exceptions. The famous Sufi al-Ḥallāj (d. 309/922) is remembered for, among other things, describing Satan as a true monotheist: he prostrated only before God, refusing to do the same before Adam (as we read, for instance, in Q. 2:34). See Peter Awn's discussion of this in *Satan's Tragedy and Redemption*, 122ff. As for Pharaoh, some regard his last-minute repentance (Q. 10:90) as having been sufficient for his salvation. See Ormsby, "Faith of Pharaoh." See also chapter 2, note 42.
22. Looking to certain earlier authorities, Asad translates the expression "people of the heights" as "persons who [in life] were endowed with the faculty of discernment [between right and wrong]" (*Message of the Qur'ān*, 239). See Muḥammad ibn Jarīr al-Ṭabarī's (d. 310/923) commentary *Jāmiʿ al-bayān*, 5:3518, where Ṭabarī cites the view that these are individuals who "know [*yaʿrafūn*] [the true nature of] people." The prevailing view, however, and the one that Ṭabarī accepts, is that these are people who are in a temporary state of limbo, in a place called the heights (see ibid., 5:3517–3524).
23. Alan Race's landmark book *Christians and Religious Pluralism* (1983) is often credited for having popularized this tripartite typology in the context of Christian thought. But whereas various versions of this classification system concern truth claims, mine is strictly soteriological; whereas most define, for example, "pluralists" as those who hold multiple religions to be equally salvific and equally true ontologically, I define "pluralists" simply as those who hold multiple religions to be equally salvific.
24. As the Qur'an indicates, the Prophet was "not told anything that the previous messengers were not told: your Lord is a Lord of forgiveness, but also of painful punishment" (41:43). Elsewhere we read that Muḥammad and his followers were given "the same commandment" that God "gave Noah" and "enjoined on Abraham, Moses, and Jesus: 'Uphold the religion [*al-dīn*] and do not divide into factions within it' " (Q. 42:13).
25. See Huda, "Knowledge of Allah and the Islamic View of Other Religions," 297, where Huda explains that, according to the dominant view in Islamic thought, the "distortion" of previous scriptures "is not limited to interpretations but substituting (*tabdîl*) revealed words with more acceptable colloquial words, or the exchanging of revealed words with words that did not appear originally in scripture, or the *kitmân*, the suppressions of the truth with falsehood."
26. As I indicate in chapter 4, there is a difference of opinion as to who the Sabians (al-Ṣābi'ūn) are, with one camp regarding them as star worshipers, another considering them akin to pre-Islamic Arab monotheists, and there are yet others. On the various groups that Muslim exegetes have identified as Sabians, see McAuliffe, "Exegetical Identification of the Ṣābi'ūn."

27. Ayoub, *Qur'an and Its Interpreters*, 110. See, for instance, the Qur'anic commentary of Ṭabarī. In his explication of Q. 2:62, Ṭabarī cites a report ascribed to the Prophet's Companion Ibn ʿAbbās (d. 68/687) in which the latter claims that this Qur'anic verse was abrogated. Ṭabarī also references a report indicating that God revealed this verse after the Prophet had mistakenly indicated to his Persian adherent Salmān al-Fārisī that God would damn the Christian monks whom Salmān had befriended before coming to Arabia and becoming Muslim. Through this revelation, therefore, God announced that He would redeem these particular Christians. But as this report clarifies, these Christians had anticipated the coming of the Prophet and were committed to following him were they to encounter him (Ṭabarī, *Jāmiʿ*, 1:447–450). For a critical assessment of the pluralist approach to Q. 2:62, see Madhany, "Pooh-Poohing Pluralism."
28. In the Prophet's Arabian context, terms such as *Jew* and *Christian* often denoted tribal membership. See Bamyeh, *Social Origins of Islam*, 79–80.
29. See Nawawī, *Rawḍat*, 10:70. Here Nawawī presents Christians as an example of unbelievers. As I note later in the introduction, however, Nawawī's exclusionary statements are in fact qualified.
30. See Abdel Haleem, *Qur'an*, 118, where Abdel Haleem renders the phrase "who do not follow the religion of truth" (*lā yadīnūn dīn al-ḥaqq*) as "who do not obey the rule of justice." This is an uncommon translation, but one that is nevertheless plausible and significant for its implications.
31. The Qur'anic verse 9:29 has historically been employed to justify aggressive jihad against Christian, Jewish, and other communities that were either not already under Muslim rule or not protected by a peace treaty or armistice. Even so, thinkers such as Muhammad Asad, citing the modernist Muḥammad ʿAbduh (d. 1905), argue that this passage should be "read in the context of the clear-cut Qur'anic rule that war is permitted only in self defence" (*Message of the Qur'ān*, 294–295nn40–41). (Here Asad has in mind Q. 2:190 and 8:61.) In his article "Jihad and the Modern World," Sherman Jackson presents aggressive jihad as a tactic that was only effective and meaningful when the presumed state of relations between tribes and states was one of perpetual warfare, when the absence of a peace treaty or armistice meant that communities (often theocratic in nature) were only as safe as they were aggressive. Jackson asserts that this is hardly the current state of affairs thanks to the U.N. Charter. Much less contentious is the issue of indiscriminate killing, which was traditionally deemed strictly forbidden and severely punishable. See Jackson, "Domestic Terrorism in the Islamic Legal Tradition."
32. See Firestone, *Children of Abraham*, 34–36.
33. See also Q. 2:99 and 4:150–151. The Qur'anic verse 5:72 appears to indicate that those who ascribe divinity to Jesus are also guilty of *shirk*: "Those who say, 'God is the Messiah, son of Mary,' have defied God [*kafara*]. The Messiah himself said, 'Children of Israel, worship God, my Lord and your Lord.' If anyone associates others [*yushrik*] with God, God will forbid him [or her] from the Garden, and Hell will be his [or her] home. No one will help such evildoers." The sura goes on to

condemn those "who say that God is the third of three" (Q. 5:73), as well as those who claim that Jesus and Mary are "two gods alongside God" (Q. 5:116). Such statements, particularly the last two, may represent the sentiments of minority Christian sects, as the overwhelming majority of Christians historically would have found them to be similarly condemnable; however, they may also represent a particular Qur'anic critique of Christians who, like those who took "their monks as lords" (9:31), failed to preserve the kind of devotion owed to God alone. Cf. Watt, "Christianity Criticized in the Qur'an," where W. Montgomery Watt (d. 2006), a Christian scholar of Islam, argues that what often appears to be a Qur'anic rejection of common Christian doctrines concerning Jesus is not necessarily so. For instance, according to Watt, when the Qur'an denies that Jesus is God's son (as in 4:171), it is denying that Jesus "was a deity separate from God." Islamic scripture also refutes "the assertion of complete identity between Jesus and God, an assertion sometimes made by Christians but generally regarded as the heresy of confusing the hypostases" (Watt, "Christianity Criticized in the Qur'an," 199). According to the Muslim pluralist Seyyed Hossein Nasr, "Doctrines such as the question of the nature of Christ or the Trinity can be understood metaphysically in such a way as to harmonise" the Islamic and Christian perspectives (*Islamic Life and Thought*, 209–210). The wedge, then, between the two traditions is the following Qur'anic declaration: the Jews "did not kill [Jesus], nor did they crucify him, although it was made to appear like that to them" (4:157). Most Muslims take this statement to be a denial of the crucifixion. This statement, Nasr suggests, is precisely what separates Christianity and Islam. It is an "irreducible 'fact'" that is placed in Islamic scripture "providentially to prevent a mingling of the two religions" (Nasr, *Islamic Life and Thought*, 209). On the portrayals of Jesus in the Qur'an and in Islamic thought, see Cragg, *Jesus and the Muslim* (especially pages 17–74); Khalidi, *Muslim Jesus*.

34. Consider, for instance, the following Qur'anic passage: "In matters of religion [*al-dīn*], [God] has laid down for you [people] the same commandment that He gave Noah, which We have revealed to you [Muḥammad] and which We enjoined on Abraham, Moses, and Jesus: 'Uphold the religion [*al-dīn*] and do not divide into factions within it'" (42:13).

35. Asad, *Message of the Qur'ān*, 1011n17. Cf. Abdel Haleem's similar note in *Qur'an*, xxiv. This understanding of *islām* is supported by various modern scholarly and theological studies, including Cantwell-Smith, *Meaning and End of Religion*; Smith, *Historical and Semantic Study of the Term "Islām" as Seen in a Sequence of Qur'ān Commentaries*; Shahrur, *al-Kitāb*, 716–719; Esack, *Qur'ān, Liberation and Pluralism*, 126–134; Donner, "From Believers to Muslims"; Donner, *Muhammad and the Believers*, 68–74. As Esack notes in *Qur'ān, Liberation and Pluralism*, 131, Qur'anic passages such as the following clearly employ the term *islām* to refer not to the religion called Islam but to the personal surrender to God: "[The desert Arabs] think they have done you [Prophet] a favor by submitting [*aslamū*].

Say, 'Do not consider *your* submission [*islām*] a favor to me; it is God who has done you a favor, by guiding you to faith, if you are truly sincere'" (49:17).

36. Aydin, "Religious Pluralism," 342.
37. Soroush, *Reason, Freedom, and Democracy in Islam*, 72. For a fuller exposition of Soroush's pluralism, see his *Ṣirāṭhā*, 137–196. As for Rūmī, the Persian mystic illustrates the "differences of perspective" of the world's religions in the following lines from his epic poem, the *Masnavī*: "The lamps are different, but the Light is the same: it comes from Beyond. If thou keep looking at the lamp, thou art lost: for thence arises the appearance of number and plurality.... O thou who art the kernel of Existence, the disagreement between [Muslim], Zoroastrian and Jew depends on the standpoint. Some Hindus bought an elephant, which they exhibited in a dark shed. As seeing it with the eye was impossible, every one felt it with the palm of his hand. The hand of one fell on its trunk: he said, 'This animal is like a water-pipe.' Another touched its ear: to him the creature seemed like a fan. Another handled its leg and described the elephant as having the shape of a pillar. Another stroked its back. 'Truly,' said he, 'this elephant resembles a throne.' Had each of them held a lighted candle, there would have been no contradiction in their words" (*Rūmī*, 166).
38. Madhany, "Pooh-Poohing Pluralism," 408 (emphasis added). This hadith (in the *Ṣaḥīḥ Muslim* collection, in "Kitāb al-īmān") arguably parallels Q. 98:1–6, which speaks of unbelievers among pagans and People of the Book being damned after having received "clear evidence, a messenger from God, reading out pages [blessed with] purity, containing true scriptures."
39. Chapter 2 offers an example of a nonlimited inclusivist interpretation of Q. 17:15. With regard to the "*who hears about me*" hadith, one might ask, Under what circumstances did the Prophet make this statement? What does it mean to "hear" about him? To hear *anything* about him? Would not one at least have to hear about "that with which" he was sent before one could be expected to believe in it? And what would this particular belief entail? Belief in the universal message of monotheism, which certain Jews and Christians are said to have abandoned (as noted, for example, in Q. 5:72–73, 116; 9:29–31), or the specifics of the final message? Even if we assume the latter, are there implicit exceptions to this hadith (as there are in many other prophetic reports)?
40. According to Winter, "Last Trump Card," 151, the hadith corpus seems to indicate that while each prophet will intercede for his people, "the Greatest Intercession, which is to be exercised by the Prophet Muḥammad alone... will extend beyond the boundaries of Muslim affiliation to allow a pleading for adherents of previous versions of faith."
41. Stöckle, *Doctrine of Islam and Christian Belief*, 48.
42. Abul Quasem, *Salvation of the Soul and Islamic Devotions*, 31–35.
43. Versions of this hadith appear, among other places, in the *Ṣaḥīḥ al-Bukhārī* collection (in "Kitāb al-anbiyā'," "Kitāb al-tafsīr," and "Kitāb al-riqāq").

44. Abul Quasem, *Salvation of the Soul and Islamic Devotions,* 25–26.
45. Crone, *God's Rule,* 22, 56ff. According to Crone, if conditions prevented the establishment of a true imam, then, at the very least, one would have to affirm the obligation of following such a leader.
46. Ibid., 22–23. Crone supports this assertion by citing a report found in the *Ṭabaqāt* of Ibn Saʿd (d. 230/845) that quotes Muḥammad as saying, "He who dies without an imam dies a pagan death" (ibid., 22).
47. See Donner's recent book *Muhammad and the Believers,* especially pages 68–74. See also Donner, "From Believers to Muslims."
48. According to the Qur'an, if the unbelievers "were brought back [to this life], they would only return to the very thing that was forbidden to them" (6:28). In chapter 3, I cite an interpretation of this verse that allows for the eventual rectification of Hell's inhabitants.
49. See Abrahamov, "Creation and Duration of Paradise and Hell in Islamic Theology," 87. As I note in chapter 3, some of these early discussions of Hell's duration revolve around the issue of accidents (in the philosophical sense) and are not necessarily related to notions of mercy and justice. As for when Heaven and Hell were/will be created, this, too, has been a point of controversy among Muslim scholars, with the majority maintaining that both already exist (ibid., 87–93).
50. See Watt, *Islamic Creeds,* 52–54 (Ṭaḥāwī), 82 (Nasafī), 88 (Ījī); Fyzee, *Shiite Creed,* 80–82 (Ṣadūq). This position is also found in the anonymous *Waṣiyya* ascribed to Abū Ḥanīfa (d. 150/767) (Watt, *Islamic Creeds,* 60), at least one version of the Ḥanbalite creed (ibid., 36), and the Ashʿarite scholar ʿAbd al-Qāhir al-Baghdādī's (d. 429/1037) *Uṣūl al-dīn,* 238, 242–244. As a means of distinguishing between sinning believers and unbelievers, various Muslim scholars, as early as the second/eighth century, conceptualized the seven levels of Hell as follows (with minor variations): (1) Gehenna (*jahannam*), reserved for sinning believers; (2) the Inferno (*al-saʿīr*), for Christians; (3) the Crusher (*al-ḥuṭama*), for Jews; (4) the Raging Flame (*al-laẓā*), for Zoroastrians; (5) the Scorching Fire (*al-saqar*), for Sabians; (6) the Blazing Fire (*al-jaḥīm*), for those who associate partners with God; and (7) the Bottomless Pit (*al-hāwiya*), the lowest level, for hypocrites. According to this hierarchy, only sinning believers (in Gehenna) could ever leave Hell. See Lange, *Justice, Punishment, and the Medieval Muslim Imagination,* 123–125. Cf. O'Shaughnessy, "Seven Names for Hell in the Koran"; Smith and Haddad, *Islamic Understanding of Death and Resurrection,* 85; Thomassen, "Islamic Hell," 407–408, 412. Needless to say, the notion of an eternal Hell is also commonplace in modern Muslim works, scholarly or otherwise. Three examples are Abul Quasem's *Salvation of the Soul and Islamic Devotions,* 26; the Iranian scholar Sayyid Mujtaba Musavi Larī's *Resurrection Judgement and the Hereafter,* 216–217, 226–227; and the popular pseudonymous Turkish writer Harun Yahya's *Basic Tenets of Islam,* 63. I provide additional examples in chapter 3.

51. Watt, *Islamic Creeds*, 44. The same may be said of Ibn Abī Zayd al-Qayrawānī (d. 386/996), who speaks only of believers leaving Hell (ibid., 70–71).
52. Pre-twentieth-century examples include Ibn Ḥazm (d. 456/1064), *Marātib al-ijmāʿ fī al-ʿibādāt wa-l-muʿāmalāt wa-l-iʿtiqādāt*, 167–173; Ibn ʿAṭiyya al-Andalusī (d. 541/1146), *al-Muḥarrar al-wajīz fī tafsīr al-kitāb al-ʿazīz*, 2:346; Fakhr al-Dīn al-Rāzī (d. 606/1209), *Muḥaṣṣal afkār al-mutaqaddimīn wa-l-mutaʾakhkhirīn min al-ʿulamāʾ wa-l-ḥukamāʾ wa-l-mutakallimīn*, 237; Sayf al-Dīn al-Āmidī (d. 631/1233), *Akbār al-afkār fī uṣūl al-dīn*, 4:360; Muḥammad ibn Aḥmad al-Qurṭubī (d. 671/1273), *al-Tadhkira fī aḥwāl al-mawtā wa-umūr al-ākhira*, 2:211; ʿAḍud al-Dīn al-Ījī (d. 756/1355), *Kitāb al-mawāqif*, 3:397 (cited in Hoover, "Islamic Universalism," 197n3); Taqī al-Dīn al-Subkī (d. 756/1355), *Shifāʾ al-saqām fī ziyārat khayr al-anām*, 163; Saʿd al-Dīn al-Taftāzānī's (d. 791/1389) commentary on the creed of Nasafī, *Sharḥ al-ʿaqāʾid al-nasafiyya*, 106, 114–115; Marʿī ibn Yūsuf al-Karmī (d. 1033/1624), *Tawqīf al-farīqayn ʿalā khulūd ahl al-dārayn*, 76; Ḥasan Ṣiddīq Khān (d. 1890), *Yaqẓat ūlī al-iʿtibār mimmā warada fī dhikr al-nār wa-aṣḥāb al-nār*, 15–17, 125. The notion of a damnationist consensus persists today. In a recent publication of a contemporary American Muslim journal, Hamza Yusuf provides an eloquent refutation of exclusivism and, in passing, characterizes the view of a noneternal punishment as "heterodoxic" ("Who Are the Disbelievers?" 47). I provide additional examples of the damnationist consensus claim in chapter 3.
53. This version of the hadith appears in the *Sunan Ibn Māja* collection (in "Kitāb al-fitan").
54. Esposito, *Islam*, 33–34. See Esposito, *What Everyone Needs to Know about Islam*, 29, where Esposito writes, "Hell is a place of endless pain, suffering, torment, and despair. . . . The destiny of the damned, their eternal punishment, is a just punishment."
55. Rahman, *Major Themes of the Qur'an*, 120.
56. Sells, *Approaching the Qur'án*, 199.
57. Ibid., 106.
58. As the Muʿtazilite exegete Abū al-Qāsim al-Zamakhsharī (d. 538/1144) (*Kashshāf*, 2:405) explains, this expression either functions as a common Arabic formula for indicating eternality, or refers to the everlasting heavens and earth of the hereafter, which are mentioned in Q. 14:48 and 39:74. This is corroborated by, among many others, Ibn Qayyim al-Jawziyya (see *Ḥādī*, 569–572) and Muḥammad Rashīd Riḍā (see *Tafsīr*, 12:160).
59. Robson, "Is the Moslem Hell Eternal?"
60. Some additional examples include O'Shaughnessy, *Muhammad's Thoughts on Death*, 68; Watt, *What Is Islam?* 48; Stöckle, *Doctrine of Islam and Christian Belief*, 49; Winter, "Last Trump Card," 137; Calder, "Limits of Islamic Orthodoxy," 224; Rustomji, *The Garden and the Fire*, 2, 40, 80, 82.

61. Smith and Haddad, *Islamic Understanding of Death and Resurrection*, 94–95. It is not entirely clear if this is a reference to reports about the Prophet, his Companions, or early Muslim theologians.
62. Abrahamov, "Creation and Duration of Paradise and Hell in Islamic Theology," 94–95. Other works that at least *mention* the doctrine of a temporal Hell and an eternal Heaven (without claiming that it represents the majority view) include (but are not limited to) El-Saleh's 1971 monograph *La Vie future selon le Coran* and four recent works: Lange, *Justice, Punishment, and the Medieval Muslim Imagination*, 117; Hoover, "Islamic Universalism"; Hoover, "Against Islamic Universalism"; and Thomassen, "Islamic Hell."
63. Knietschke, "Koran Doctrine of Redemption," 62–63.
64. Rahbar, *God of Justice*, 223–225.
65. Ibid., 226.
66. Bouman, *Gott und Mensch im Koran*, 173, 178–179.
67. Murata and Chittick, *Vision of Islam*, 77.
68. Rahman, *Major Themes of the Qur'an*, 1–2.
69. Marshall, *God, Muhammad and the Unbelievers*, 80–82; Baljon, *Modern Muslim Koran Interpretation*, 58. Nevertheless, Marshall recognizes that the Qur'an "repeatedly refers to God's mercy and its many manifestations" (*God, Muhammad and the Unbelievers*, 78).
70. Marshall, *God, Muhammad and the Unbelievers*, 83.
71. As such, and so as not to lose focus, I do not examine, at least not thoroughly, discussions of the nature of intercession (*shafāʿa*); free will and predestination; theodicy; gender-specific issues (for example, the ratio of males to females in either Heaven or Hell); specific features of Heaven, Hell, and the Day of Judgment; and the fate of sinning Muslims, deceased children, animals, etc.
72. As Q. 5:19 indicates, the Prophet came "after a break in the sequence of messengers."
73. For this, see Smith and Haddad, *Islamic Understanding of Death and Resurrection*, 31–61, 99–126. Cf. Ragnar Eklund's dated yet thorough *Life between Death and Resurrection According to Islam* (1941). For a treatment of Muslim eschatological motifs, see Cook, *Studies in Muslim Apocalyptic*.
74. Winter, "Last Trump Card," 134.
75. See ibid., 134n2.
76. See Sophia Vasalou's discussion of this in *Moral Agents and Their Deserts*, 119, 121–132.
77. See ibid. See also Shahrastānī, *Milal*, 45. Significant for the Muʿtazilites in this regard was the following Qur'anic pronouncement: "Whoever disobeys God and His Messenger will have Hell's fire, dwelling therein continuously [*khālidīn fīhā abadan*]" (72:23). It must be noted, however, that the Muʿtazilites famously maintained that sinning believers would occupy a "station between two stations": although barred from Paradise, they would not be punished

as severely as the other inhabitants of Hell. This is to be contrasted with the view ascribed to the Khārijites that sinning believers are on the same level as unbelievers.

78. Smith and Haddad, *Islamic Understanding of Death and Resurrection*, 94–95.
79. Ibid., 95, 220n98. Elsewhere, when discussing modern Islamic thought, Smith and Haddad state that the "majority of Qur'ān exegetes generally hold" the view that "as long as the Fire lasts, so will at least some of those consigned to it remain there; but because of the mercy of God, we can be sure that the Fire itself will not last eternally" (ibid., 143). In the note that follows this characterization of the majority opinion, we read that according to the Egyptian author ʿAbbās al-ʿAqqād (d. 1964), "this view is supported by the many reliable *ḥadīths* illustrating God's mercy in delivering from the Fire those in whose hearts is even an atom of faith" (ibid., 230n48; ʿAqqād, *Falsafa*, 216–217). Otherwise, we only find references to the "noneternalist" sentiments of a select group of scholars, such as Maulana Muhammad Ali and Mahmoud Shaltout (see Smith and Haddad, *Islamic Understanding of Death and Resurrection*, 143–144), whose universalist views I discuss later in this book.
80. Ṭaḥāwī never qualifies his statement regarding the perpetual nature of the Fire and explicitly states that only those who have (true) monotheistic faith can be saved, even if they pass away as unrepentant sinners (Watt, *Islamic Creeds*, 52–54). Nasafī's pronouncements are comparable to this: Hell is everlasting, its inhabitants "will not pass away," and sinning believers will not remain forever in Hell (ibid., 82). As for Ashʿarī, he never once suggests that punishment will cease for unbelievers (cf. ibid., 44). Needless to say, commentaries on these creeds may lend themselves to alternative conclusions. See, for example, chapter 3, where I briefly refer to Ibn Abī al-ʿIzz al-Ḥanafī's (d. 792/1390) discussion of Ṭaḥāwī's doctrine of Hell.
81. Jackson, *On the Boundaries of Theological Tolerance in Islam*, 30–32. Various scholars have denied the very notion of orthodoxy in Islam. These include Islamicists such as Watt, Ignaz Goldziher (d. 1921), and George Makdisi (d. 2002). As Jackson rightly notes, however, "all that is needed to establish and sustain any orthodoxy is authority, full stop, which may be formal *or informal*" (ibid., 30). See ibid., 78n77.
82. This is precisely what happened when the universalist (apocatastatic) vision ascribed to the Christian theologian Origen (d. 254 CE) by many of his later supporters was declared heretical by the Fifth Ecumenical Council of Constantinople in 553 CE. See Elizabeth Clark's discussion of this in *The Origenist Controversy*. There are, of course, instances in the history of Islam in which some have attempted to establish a formal Sunni orthodoxy. The most memorable example is the Abbasid *miḥna* (inquisition) (218–234/833–848), which ultimately failed.
83. Shahrastānī, *Milal*, 87–88. See also Baghdādī's related discussion of Jahm in the *Uṣūl*, 333. I briefly treat Ibn Taymiyya's rejection of Jahm's position in chapter 3.

84. This, of course, is not to say that scholars of religion should not interpret Islamic scripture as they see fit. But in this case, it should be made clear that theirs is a particular, not a universal, reading.
85. See Rūmī, *Discourses of Rumi*, 134–136, where Rūmī affirms the superiority of Muḥammad's way and censures al-Jarrāḥ for accepting the belief that Jesus is God, a belief that he adopted from his father. Rūmī writes, "God gave you an intelligence of your own other than your father's intelligence, a sight of your own other than your father's sight, a discrimination of your own. Why do you nullify your sight and your intelligence, following an intelligence which will destroy you and not guide you?" (ibid., 135). See Legenhausen's discussion of this other side of Rūmī in "Islam and Religious Pluralism." See also here Legenhausen's note on how even the philosophers (*falāsifa*) privileged Islam.
86. See Nawawī, *Minhāj*, 2:342.
87. On the former, see, for instance, Ṭabarī, *Jāmiʿ*, 1:442–450 (on Q. 2:62); Rāzī, *Tafsīr*, 3:96–98 (on Q. 2:62), in conjunction with 11:73–74 (on Q. 4:150–151); Ibn Kathīr (d. 774/1373), *Tafsīr*, 1:179–182 (on Q. 2:62), in conjunction with 2:424–425 (on Q. 4:150–151); Jalāl al-Dīn al-Maḥallī (d. 864/1459) and Jalāl al-Dīn al-Suyūṭī (d. 911/1505), *Tafsīr*, 19 (on Q. 2:62), in conjunction with 106 (on Q. 4:115) and 200 (on Q. 9:29). These commentaries all affirm Islamic supersessionism.

    On the latter, see, for instance, Ṭabarī, *Jāmiʿ*, 1:446–449 (on Q. 2:62), in conjunction with 4:2642–2643 (on Q. 4:165) and 4:3146–3148 (on Q. 6:19); Rāzī, *Tafsīr*, 12:147–148 (on Q. 6:19), in conjunction with 11:87–88 (on Q. 4:165) and 20: 138–139 (on Q. 17:15); Maḥallī and Suyūṭī, *Tafsīr*, 139 (on Q. 6:19), in conjunction with 293 (on Q. 17:15); Ibn Kathīr, *Tafsīr*, 3:11–12 (on Q. 6:19), in conjunction with 4:286–288 (on Q. 17:15). These discussions indicate that only the reached will be held accountable for not adhering to God's final message.
88. This quote by A. Kevin Reinhart appears in a draft of his paper tentatively entitled "Failures of Practice or Failures of Faith: Are Non-Muslims Subject to the Sharia?" Here Reinhart examines the soteriological discourse of Ibn Ḥazm (cited below in notes 89 and 90). This paper appears in my forthcoming edited volume *Islam, Salvation, and the Fate of Others* (tentative title). It goes without saying that "*Reconquista* angst" would have been but one of several factors that could have shaped Ibn Ḥazm's soteriological outlook.
89. Ibn Ḥazm, *Iḥkām*, 1:63.
90. Ibid., 5:117–8.
91. I should note that Ṭabarī (in the *Jāmiʿ*, 4:3147 [on Q. 6:19]) cites a report dated to the second/eighth century in which the question is raised, "Is there anyone remaining who has not received the invitation [to Islam] [*al-daʿwa*]?" It is unclear whether this is referring to "anyone" in a particular region or "anyone" in the entire world. The response is a statement attributed to the early exegete Mujāhid (d. 104/722): "Wherever the Qur'an comes, it is a caller [to the faith]

and a warner." Ṭabarī himself never comments on this report and simply cites it among others that affirm the reached status of those who come to learn of the Islamic message. He concludes that the Qur'anic warning applies to whoever receives it; he never suggests that it applies to everyone, meaning he never suggests that everyone has been reached.

92. Harris, *End of Faith*, 117.
93. The relationship between this-worldly realities and next-worldly soteriologies is a subject taken up in my forthcoming edited volume *Islam, Salvation, and the Fate of Others* (tentative title).

CHAPTER 1

1. Fakhry, *History of Islamic Philosophy*, 37.
2. Watt, *Muslim Intellectual*, 180.
3. Although most scholars date Ghazālī's birth at 450/1058, here I follow Frank Griffel's recent estimate in *Al-Ghazālī's Philosophical Theology*, 23–25, 42.
4. See Ghazālī, *Munqidh*, 64–71; ʿArwānī's (ed.) comments in Ghazālī, *Arbaʿīn*, viii–x. See also Griffel, *Al-Ghazālī's Philosophical Theology*, 20, 43, 49–50, where Griffel corrects the common misconception that Ghazālī spent all of the next ten years of his life in "Sufi wandering," neither teaching nor writing; evidently, he did both in phases during this period.
5. Jackson, *On the Boundaries of Theological Tolerance in Islam*, 36. Jackson adds monism to this list, but this is a point of controversy. Cf. Treiger, "Monism and Monotheism in al-Ghazālī's *Mishkāt al-anwār*."
6. Ghazālī, *Munqidh*, 29–32.
7. Griffel, *Al-Ghazālī's Philosophical Theology*, 25, 50.
8. Ghazālī, *Munqidh*, 29–32.
9. Ibid., 31.
10. According to Eric Ormsby, Ghazālī began writing the *Iḥyāʾ* in 488/1095 and completed it within two years (*Ghazali*, 25). Most scholars maintain that the *Iḥyāʾ* was in its final form by 495/1102. As for the *Kīmiyā*, Ghazālī may have composed it sometime between 490 and 495/1097 and 1102 (ʿUthmān, *Sīrat*, 203–204). Contrary to popular belief, the *Kīmiyā* is not merely a Persian summary of the *Iḥyāʾ*.
11. Ghazālī, *Iḥyāʾ*, 1:80.
12. Ghazālī, *Kīmiyā*, 61–62. The metaphor of the mirror appears elsewhere in Ghazālī's writings, as in the *Iḥyāʾ*, 3:13ff.
13. Ghazālī, *Iḥyāʾ*, 1:80–81.
14. According to Ghazālī, belief in Muḥammad need not entail complete comprehension of every aspect of revelation. In the *Iḥyāʾ*, 3:9, for example, he states, "While we believe in prophethood and the Prophet, and accept his existence, the reality [*ḥaqīqa*] of prophethood is nevertheless only known to the Prophet."

15. Ghazālī, *Iqtiṣād*, 207–209.
16. Ibid., 209. Here I use the terms *atheists* and *deists* in their most inclusive sense. The "atheists," *al-dahriyya* in the original, were materialists who, in this case, denied divine creation. The "deists," *al-barāhima* in the original, reportedly believed in one God but denied that He sends prophets. This qualifies as deism if we consider the meaning that was given it by the sixteenth-century Swiss Protestant theologian Pierre Viret, who used it in a Christian context as a "term of opprobrium" against people who, "in contrast to the atheists, believed in God but accepted nothing of Christ and his teachings" (Jackson, *On the Boundaries of Theological Tolerance in Islam*, 134n11). In the present context, a deist is one who rejects divine revelation (rather than Christ per se).
17. ʿUthmān, *Sīrat*, 203. Griffel speculates that the *Iqtiṣād* may have been completed before Ghazālī's arrival in Baghdad in 484/1091 (*Al-Ghazālī's Philosophical Theology*, 35).
18. Ghazālī, *Iḥyāʾ*, 1:84–85.
19. According to Griffel (*Al-Ghazālī's Philosophical Theology*, 245–246), we cannot be certain when exactly the *Mishkāt* was written. What we do know is that it was sometime after 490/1097 and that it was probably later than the *Iḥyāʾ* and a work I discuss later entitled *al-Maqṣad al-asnā fī sharḥ asmāʾ Allāh al-ḥusnā* (ibid., 264). Cf. ʿUthmān, *Sīrat*, 205, where ʿUthmān dates the *Mishkāt* to shortly before 500/1107.
20. "God is the Light of the heavens and earth. His light is like this: there is a niche, and in it a lamp, the lamp inside a glass, a glass like a glittering star, fueled from a blessed olive tree from neither east nor west, whose oil almost gives light even when no fire touches it—light upon light—God guides whoever He wills to His Light; God draws such comparisons for people; God has full knowledge of everything" (Q. 24:35).
21. "God has seventy veils of light and darkness; were He to lift them, the august glories of His face would burn up everyone whose eyesight perceived Him" (Ghazālī, *Mishkāt* [trans. Buchman], 44). Variants of this hadith mention 700 and 70,000 veils. No version of this report appears in the canonical hadith collections.
22. Alexander Treiger rightly rejects W. Montgomery Watt's claim (in "Forgery in al-Ghazālī's *Mishkāt*?") that this section of the *Mishkāt* was not really authored by Ghazālī because of its Neoplatonist character. As Treiger notes (in "Monism and Monotheism in al-Ghazālī's *Mishkāt al-anwār*," 23n49), "There are (partial) parallels to this section in other works of al-Ghazālī," including the *Kīmiyā* and other sources listed in Landolt, "Ghazālī and 'Religionswissenschaft,'" 27n34. Other scholars unconvinced by Watt's claim include A. ʿAfīfī, H. A. Davidson, Hava Lazarus-Yafeh, and David Buchman. See Buchman's (trans.) remarks in Ghazālī, *Mishkāt* (trans.), xxvii. See also Griffel, *Al-Ghazālī's Philosophical Theology*, 9–10.

23. See Gairdner's (trans.) remarks in Ghazālī, *Mishkāt* (trans.), 14.
24. Ghazālī, *Mishkāt*, 85.
25. Ibid.
26. Ibid.
27. Ibid., 86.
28. Ibid., 87–90.
29. Ibid., 90–93. See Landolt, "Ghazālī and 'Religionswissenschaft,'" 39, where Landolt relates Ghazālī's hierarchy to Abraham's progressive discovery of the one true God, as depicted in Q. 6:75–79: "In this way We showed Abraham [God's] mighty dominion over the heavens and the earth, so that he might be a firm believer. When the night grew dark over him he saw a star and said, 'This is my Lord,' but when it set, he said, 'I do not like things that set.' And when he saw the moon rising he said, 'This is my Lord,' but when it too set, he said, 'If my Lord does not guide me, I shall be one of those who go astray.' Then he saw the sun rising and cried, 'This is my Lord! This is greater.' But when the sun set, he said, 'My people, I disown all that you worship beside God. I have turned my face as a true believer toward Him who created the heavens and the earth. I am not one of those who associate [partners] with God.'"
30. Ghazālī, *Kīmiyā*, 112–113.
31. Ibid., 89.
32. Griffel, *Al-Ghazālī's Philosophical Theology*, 252.
33. See Ghazālī, *Iḥyā'*, 1:107–108.
34. See Ghazālī, *Iqtiṣād*, 207–208.
35. Griffel, *Al-Ghazālī's Philosophical Theology*, 101. Cf. ʿUthmān, *Sīrat*, 204, where ʿUthmān dates the *Fayṣal* to 497/1104.
36. See Baghdādī, *Uṣūl*, 234, 267, 335. See also Griffel, *Apostasie*, 187–199, where Griffel discusses Baghdādī's teachings on belief and orthodoxy.
37. See Ghazālī, *Fayṣal*, 61–74. Cf. Jackson's translation of Ghazālī, *Fayṣal*, in *On the Boundaries of Theological Tolerance in Islam*, 112–120. Here Ghazālī adds that the status of those who reject doctrines agreed upon by consensus (*ijmāʿ*) is "unclear." Cf. Ghazālī, *Mustaṣfā*, 399, where Ghazālī writes that although the Muʿtazilites, Khārijites, Shīʿites, and innovators may espouse sinful doctrines, they remain within the fold of Islam. As Griffel observes, this distinction between apostasy and "simple heterodoxy" is "one of al-Ghazālī's most important contributions" (*Al-Ghazālī's Philosophical Theology*, 105).
38. According to Ghazālī, the physical nature of reward and punishment effectively incites most people to do good and deters them from evil (Griffel, *Al-Ghazālī's Philosophical Theology*, 102).
39. A similar sentiment appears in Ghazālī's *Tahāfut al-falāsifa* (*The Incoherence of the Philosophers*). See, for instance, Ghazālī's concluding remarks on pages 376–377. From the perspective of the philosophers, the Prophet did not speak untruths

due to any ill will on his part; rather, they argued, he spoke to his followers at a level at which they could both understand and appreciate his message.

40. Ghazālī, *Fayṣal*, 25–26. My translation here loosely follows that of Jackson in *On the Boundaries of Theological Tolerance in Islam*, 92–93. I should note that the edition of the *Fayṣal* I cite here is a 1993 publication edited by M. Bījū, which is widely regarded as one of the most reliable of all published editions of the *Fayṣal*. Even so, Bījū's edition here contains what I consider to be an error: in place of the phrase "all of these parties are associationists [*mushrikūn*] inasmuch as all of them deem the Messenger* to be one who speaks untruths," Bījū's edition reads, "all of these parties are participants [*mushtarikūn*] in deeming the Messenger* to be one who speaks untruths" (Ghazālī, *Fayṣal*, 26). The former version, which uses the term *associationists* (*mushrikūn*) and which I have adopted in my translation, appears in Jackson's translation, earlier editions of the *Fayṣal* (including the first printing in 1901 and the popular 1961 edition of S. Dunyā), and the well-known manuscript of the *Fayṣal* located in Istanbul (MS Istanbul, Shehit Ali Pasha 1712, fol. 59b). I am grateful to Frank Griffel for his assistance in examining this last source. See note 43 below.

41. See, for example, Ghazālī, *Iḥyā'*, 1:35.

42. Ghazālī, *Faḍā'il*, 49, translated and discussed by Ebrahim Moosa in *Ghazālī and the Poetics of Imagination*, 149. This statement appears in a collection of Ghazālī's (originally Persian) letters, which were likely compiled shortly after his death (reportedly by an unnamed relative). Interestingly, as Moosa notes in *Ghazālī and the Poetics of Imagination*, 17, some early twentieth-century Western scholars regarded Ghazālī as being Christian-like. Consider, for instance, the Orientalist and American missionary Samuel Zwemer's (d. 1952) observations in *Moslem Seeker after God*, 12–13: "There is a real sense in which al-Ghazālī may be used as a schoolmaster to lead Moslems to Christ. His books were full of references to the teaching of Christ. He was a true seeker after God. . . . No one can read the story of al-Ghazālī's life, so near and yet so far from the Kingdom of God, eager to enter and yet always groping for the doorway, without fervently wishing that al-Ghazālī could have met a true ambassador of Christ. Then surely this great champion of the Moslem faith would have become an apostle of Christianity in his own day and generation. By striving to understand al-Ghazālī we may at least better fit ourselves to help those who, like him, are earnest seekers after God amid the twilight shadows of Islam."

43. As Jackson speculates, when Ghazālī states that the rejection of the Prophet (or prophets) constitutes associationism (*shirk*), he means that "these groups directly or indirectly attribute the capacity to identify supernatural ways and means of extracting service from nature to an entity other than God" (*On the Boundaries of Theological Tolerance in Islam*, 134n14).

44. See Jackson's translation of Ghazālī, *Fayṣal*, in *On the Boundaries of Theological Tolerance in Islam*, 126–128; Ghazālī, *Fayṣal*, 84–87.

45. See Winter, "Last Trump Card," 149.

46. Baghdādī, *Uṣūl*, 263, translated by Winter in "Last Trump Card," 148.
47. Most manuscripts and editions of the *Fayṣal* render this name as al-Muqaffaʿ, a reference to ʿAbd Allāh ibn al-Muqaffaʿ (d. ca. 139/756), a Persian literary genius who criticized the Prophet and Islamic scripture and claimed to have produced a scripture comparable to the Qur'an. But as Griffel notes, this is a scribal error that occurred "very early in the manuscript tradition" (*Al-Ghazālī's Philosophical Theology*, 315). Earlier manuscripts refer to another, less well-known Persian, al-Muqannaʿ ("the veiled one," d. 164/780), a propagandist who claimed to be an incarnation of God.
48. See Jackson's translation of Ghazālī, *Fayṣal*, in *On the Boundaries of Theological Tolerance in Islam*, 126; Ghazālī, *Fayṣal*, 84. Here I replaced al-Muqaffaʿ with al-Muqannaʿ (see previous note).
49. See Jackson's translation of Ghazālī, *Fayṣal*, in *On the Boundaries of Theological Tolerance in Islam*, 126; Ghazālī, *Fayṣal*, 84.
50. See Jackson's translation of Ghazālī, *Fayṣal*, in *On the Boundaries of Theological Tolerance in Islam*, 128; Ghazālī, *Fayṣal*, 86. Ghazālī's list of "miracles that defied the laws of nature" is virtually identical to Baghdādī's list of "evidentiary signs" of Muḥammad's prophethood, which appears in Baghdādī, *Uṣūl*, 161–162.
51. Ghazālī, *Fayṣal*, 86–87. Cf. Jackson's translation of Ghazālī, *Fayṣal*, in *On the Boundaries of Theological Tolerance in Islam*, 128.
52. Ghazālī, *Iḥyāʾ*, 1:104. This argument appears elsewhere in Ghazālī's writings, such as the *Mustaṣfā*, 1:121–123.
53. Ghazālī, *Iqtiṣād*, 12.
54. Ibid., 175.
55. Ghazālī, *Kīmiyā*, 792.
56. This is a point Ghazālī makes in the *Munqidh*, to which he adds: "Seek certain knowledge about prophecy from this method and not from the turning of a stick into a serpent or from the splitting of the moon. For if you consider that event by itself, and do not include the many circumstances that accompany this event you may think that it is sorcery [*siḥr*] and imagination [*taḥyīl*]" (*Deliverance from Error*, 86).
57. Ghazālī, *Iḥyāʾ*, 1:103.
58. Ghazālī, *Iqtiṣād*, 172ff. For example, in ibid., 172–174, Ghazālī examines a claim made by Jews belonging to the messianic ʿĪsāwiyya sect that Muḥammad was a prophet sent only to the Arabs. Since this constitutes a recognition of Muḥammad's status as a true prophet and since prophets never lie, Ghazālī argues that such Jews would have to accept Muḥammad as a universal prophet, as he declared himself to be a messenger to both humans and *jinn* (*al-thaqalayn*) and sent his own messengers to Khosraw (Kisrā) of Persia, Caesar (Qayṣar) of Byzantium, and other non-Arab kingdoms. Ghazālī then addresses two other claims put forth by certain Jews: (1) abrogation of God's law is impossible since that would imply the alteration of God's perfect law, and (2) Moses declared himself to be the seal

(*khātam*) of the prophets. (This assumes a specific understanding of prophethood, as there were numerous biblical prophets after Moses; however, it was only Moses who presented the Israelites with God's foundational commandments.) Ghazālī's response is that times have changed; what was best for humanity during Moses' era is no longer best. Abrogation, therefore, was necessary. Furthermore, whatever led people to believe in the prophethood of Moses should lead people to believe in the prophethood of Jesus and Muḥammad. This means that whoever first transmitted the statement of Moses being the seal of the prophets must have uttered an untruth; as Ghazālī notes, even the Jews of the Prophet's age never made this assertion while he was in their midst. (Similar contentions appear in Ibn Taymiyya's *al-Jawāb al-ṣaḥīḥ li-man baddala dīn al-Masīḥ*, which I briefly discuss in chapter 3.) To those who maintain that the Qur'an is not miraculous, Ghazālī points to its "purity and eloquence, with [its] wondrous arrangement and style, which is foreign to the manners of speech of the Arabs." It is "the combination of this arrangement and this purity" that "is beyond human capability" (Ghazālī, *Iqtiṣād*, 175). Ghazālī proceeds to address those who deny the Prophet's other miracles, such as the splitting of the moon and the springing forth of water from his fingers, on the grounds that these episodes were not transmitted through diffuse and congruent reports. According to Ghazālī, we can have confidence in these miracle narratives: there exist *numerous* "solitary" (*aḥād*) reports of such events. And, he continues, if Christians argue otherwise, then on what basis could they claim to have knowledge of Jesus' miracles, the reports of which are no more reliable? (ibid., 174–177).

59. Ghazālī, *Iḥyā'*, 1:88–90.
60. See Jackson's translation of Ghazālī, *Fayṣal*, in *On the Boundaries of Theological Tolerance in Islam*, 128; Ghazālī, *Fayṣal*, 87.
61. See Jackson's translation of Ghazālī, *Fayṣal*, in *On the Boundaries of Theological Tolerance in Islam*, 128; Ghazālī, *Fayṣal*, 87. Ghazālī presumably would have regarded the "*who hears about me*" hadith (discussed in the introduction) as being implicitly qualified.
62. Although 'Uthmān dates the *Mustaṣfā* to 503/1109 (see *Sīrat*, 205), it is ultimately difficult to determine when exactly it was written.
63. Ghazālī, *Mustaṣfā*, 2:401.
64. With regard to the unbelievers, we read in the Qur'an, "It is not their eyes that are blind, but their hearts within their breasts" (22:46).
65. Ghazālī, *Mustaṣfā*, 2:401–402.
66. Ghazālī, *Iḥyā'*, 1:97. Cf. related remarks in Ghazālī, *Kīmiyā*, 68–88.
67. Ghazālī, *Fayṣal*, 77. Cf. Jackson's translation of Ghazālī, *Fayṣal*, in *On the Boundaries of Theological Tolerance in Islam*, 122.
68. Ghazālī states that knowledge of God may be attained through meditation on the nature of our bodies and soul, with emphasis on the latter. A simple consideration of each individual's lowly origins and evolution would suffice. No one,

Ghazālī maintains, is capable of creating even a single strand of hair, and even if the wisest of the wise collaborated, they would be unable to effect a single improvement to the human body. To the mind of Ghazālī, atheists, including those who are scientists, are so deep in error that they are akin to those who come across a well-written letter and deem it to have either always existed or produced itself (*Kīmiyā*, 68–88). Similar teleological contentions appear elsewhere, for instance, in Ghazālī, *Iḥyā'*, 1:96–97, 4:294–295. Ghazālī's cosmological argument for God's existence, which he presents, among other places, in the *Iqtiṣād*, 29ff., and the *Iḥyā'*, 1:97, is related to what modern philosophers term the *kalām* cosmological argument. See, for instance, Craig, *Kalām Cosmological Argument*, especially pages 42ff. In much of the *Tahāfut*, Ghazālī justifies the premise that the universe had a beginning in time.

69. Ghazālī, *Kīmiyā*, 58. Should one argue that there could be more than one god, Ghazālī in the *Iqtiṣād*, 69–74, attempts to demonstrate through logic that God is necessarily indivisible, perfect, and unique.
70. Ghazālī, *Iḥyā'*, 1:104.
71. Consider, for instance, Ghazālī's advice in the *Kīmiyā*, 126–127, to the Muslim seeking to respond to those who deny the afterlife: he should rhetorically ask the deniers if they sincerely trust that they (the deniers) are right and that 124,000 prophets—a number derived from the hadith corpus—and numerous saints were wrong. If they persist in disbelieving—and according to Ghazālī, the probability that they will recant is low—they are to be ignored, and the Muslim has done all he is expected to do in conveying the message. If, however, they reach a state in which they are simply unsure of the reality of the Last Day, Ghazālī puts forth an argument that appeals to both revelation and practical considerations (an argument to which the seventeenth-century French philosopher Blaise Pascal's "wager" bears some resemblance): given what is at stake and given the severity of Hell, it is in the best interest of all to believe. After all, if one were about to enjoy a hearty meal and were then informed that it is contaminated with poisonous snake venom, it is to be expected that one would abstain from eating. And in the pursuit of great reward, it is common for people to take risks; there are numerous individuals who embark on hazardous voyages at sea for the sake of profit that is not promised. That this line of argumentation assumes some form of exposure to revelatory promises and threats points to the fact that, in the absence of such exposure, the reality of the life to come is not necessarily self-evident. Thus, Ghazālī in the *Iḥyā'*, 1:19, bothers to state that new Muslims should be informed of the life to come if they were previously unaware of it.
72. This is in keeping with the position of Juwaynī and other Ash'arites and that ascribed to Ash'arī himself. See Juwaynī, *Kitāb*, 258ff.; Jackson, "Alchemy of Domination?" 190, 199; Reinhart, *Before Revelation*, 25–26; Ormsby, *Theodicy in Islamic Thought*, 232–234.

73. Ghazālī, *Mustaṣfā*, 1:112–119. See Jackson's discussion of this in "Alchemy of Domination?" 187–191. As Jackson observes, Ghazālī's "seminal contribution" was his redirection of Ash'arite "ethical discourse away from ontology toward psychology" such that later Ash'arites would conceive of the appetitive self (*al-ṭab'*), rather than the intellect, as being "the instrument of moral judgment" (ibid., 190–191).
74. See Ghazālī, *Iḥyā'*, 1:103.
75. See Ghazālī, *Mustaṣfā*, 1:120; Ghazālī, *Iqtiṣād*, 157–158. Although Ghazālī had much to say about the importance of thanking God, he maintained that not even this act can be described as an "absolute good" (Reinhart, *Before Revelation*, 119).
76. As I noted in the introduction, many Muslim scholars restrict the meaning of this passage (and Q. 5:69) in such a way that it excludes Jews, Christians, and other non-Muslims living in a post-Muḥammadan world. In Ghazālī's case, we may presume that the only non-Muslims excluded would be those of the second category, that is, those who were properly exposed to the message yet rejected it or failed to investigate it.
77. Ghazālī, *Fayṣal*, 81. Cf. a similar translation of this hadith in Jackson, *On the Boundaries of Theological Tolerance in Islam*, 125. This hadith appears, among other places, in the *Ṣaḥīḥ al-Bukhārī* collection (in "Kitāb al-anbiyā'," "Kitāb al-tafsīr," and "Kitāb al-riqāq").
78. Ghazālī, *Fayṣal*, 82. Cf. Jackson, *On the Boundaries of Theological Tolerance in Islam*, 125, where Jackson translates this last expression as "unbelievers who will abide forever in Hellfire."
79. See Jackson's translation of Ghazālī, *Fayṣal*, in *On the Boundaries of Theological Tolerance in Islam*, 125; Ghazālī, *Fayṣal*, 82. Although Ghazālī does not mention it here, well-known variants of this report indicate that 999 out of the aforementioned one thousand will come from Ya'jūj and Ma'jūj—evildoers who appear in the Qur'an (18:83–98, 21:96–97) and whom exegetes often identify as the biblical Gog and Magog. In Islamic thought, these are widely regarded as apocalyptic figures, as they will one day—as a sign of Judgment Day—be "let loose" and will "swarm swiftly from every highland" (Q. 21:96) after having been once contained (Q. 18:93–98).
80. See Jackson's translation of Ghazālī, *Fayṣal*, in *On the Boundaries of Theological Tolerance in Islam*, 125; Ghazālī, *Fayṣal*, 81; Wensinck, *Mu'jam*, 5:135–136.
81. Ghazālī, *Fayṣal*, 85. My translation here loosely follows that of Jackson in *On the Boundaries of Theological Tolerance in Islam*, 127. This hadith appears, among other places, in the *Ṣaḥīḥ al-Bukhārī* collection (in "Kitāb al-riqāq"). Also humiliating for those who are not "saved" will be the physical manifestation of their imperfections. According to Ghazālī, in the hereafter, people will be transfigured into bodies that reflect their particular flaws. See Griffel's discussion of this in "Divine Actions, Creation, and the Human Fate after Death in 9th/15th-Century Imāmī Shi'ite Theology," 75.

82. Ghazālī, *Fayṣal*, 85. Cf. Jackson's translation of Ghazālī, *Fayṣal*, in *On the Boundaries of Theological Tolerance in Islam*, 127. Throughout Ghazālī's writings, the philosophers (*falāsifa*) and Ismāʿīlites are "effectively the only two Muslim groups that he brands as unbelievers" (Griffel, *Al-Ghazālī's Philosophical Theology*, 102). We may presume that Ghazālī lumps the two together when speaking of a single sect of "heretics."
83. See Jackson's translation of Ghazālī, *Fayṣal*, in *On the Boundaries of Theological Tolerance in Islam*, 127; Ghazālī, *Fayṣal*, 86.
84. Ghazālī, *Fayṣal*, 86. Cf. Jackson's translation of Ghazālī, *Fayṣal*, in *On the Boundaries of Theological Tolerance in Islam*, 127–128.
85. See Jackson's translation of Ghazālī, *Fayṣal*, in *On the Boundaries of Theological Tolerance in Islam*, 125–126; Ghazālī, *Fayṣal*, 82–83. As Jackson notes, there exist slightly different versions of this hadith, several of which do not mention "bedouin who neither prayed nor fasted" (*On the Boundaries of Theological Tolerance in Islam*, 140n63).
86. See Jackson's translation of Ghazālī, *Fayṣal*, in *On the Boundaries of Theological Tolerance in Islam*, 126; Ghazālī, *Fayṣal*, 84.
87. See Jackson's translation of Ghazālī, *Fayṣal*, in *On the Boundaries of Theological Tolerance in Islam*, 129; Ghazālī, *Fayṣal*, 87.
88. Ghazālī, *Fayṣal*, 87–88. My translation here loosely follows that of Jackson in *On the Boundaries of Theological Tolerance in Islam*, 129. The statement ascribed to God, "My mercy outstrips My wrath," appears in the *Ṣaḥīḥ al-Bukhārī* hadith collection (in "Kitāb al-tawḥīd"). On God's expansive mercy, see Ghazālī's related remarks at the conclusion of the *Iḥyāʾ*, 4:495–499.
89. See also Q. 2:100; 3:110; 5:59; 7:17, 102; 12:103, 106; 13:1; 26:8, 67, 103; 36:7; 37:71; 41:4. The Qur'anic verse 6:116 states, "[Prophet], if you obeyed most of those on earth, they would lead you away from the path of God." This, however, does not necessarily mean that most of humanity is insincere and headed toward damnation; it could simply be a statement on the nature of personal judgment in the absence of revelation.
90. Ghazālī, *Iqtiṣād*, 157–159; Ghazālī, *Iḥyāʾ*, 1:96.
91. Field (trans.), in Ghazālī, *Kīmiyā* (trans.), xiii–xiv.
92. Ghazālī, *Iḥyāʾ*, 1:108. Ghazālī makes this statement in response to the assertion that believers will never enter Hell. The Qur'anic passage cited here continues, "We shall save the devout and leave the evildoers there on their knees" (19:72).
93. See Jackson's translation of Ghazālī, *Fayṣal*, in *On the Boundaries of Theological Tolerance in Islam*, 125; Ghazālī, *Fayṣal*, 82.
94. The claim that Ghazālī was inconsistent because he was writing for different audiences—a claim that is often abused for polemical purposes—appears not long after his death in the works of medieval Muslim thinkers, including the Andalusians Ibn Rushd (d. 595/1198) and Ibn Ṭufayl (d. 581/1185)

(see Gianotti, *Al-Ghazālī's Unspeakable Doctrine of the Soul*, 19–21). According to Moosa, Ghazālī was working "within a maelstrom" and was thus "forced to negotiate multiple antithetical positions. And if he appears tentative and undecided from time to time, it suggests that he did not entirely subscribe to a totalitarian epistemology, but one that was partly open to reconstruction" (*Ghazālī and the Poetics of Imagination*, 140). This, of course, does not mean that most claims of inconsistency in Ghazālī's corpus are warranted. As Griffel warns, these allegations are, often, "a hermeneutic device to mask the failure of interpreters to understand the texts" (*Al-Ghazālī's Philosophical Theology*, 286).

95. Hourani, *History of the Arab Peoples*, 188.
96. Ghazālī, *Iḥyā'*, 1:87.
97. Ibid., 3:16.
98. Ibid., 1:10ff.
99. Ibid., 1:16–17.
100. Ghazālī, *Kīmiyā*, 106.
101. When speaking of Islamic scholarship, Ghazālī explicitly espouses the notion that some forms of knowledge are potentially dangerous: "Knowledge... either destroys [its possessor] eternally or grants him eternal life. For this reason, the Prophet* said, 'The person who will be most severely punished on the Day of Resurrection will be a learned person'" who does not truly benefit from his or her knowledge (*Iḥyā'*, 1:47).
102. Ibid., 4:29–30.
103. Those in favor of the limbo interpretation of this passage tend to ascribe it to the Prophet's Companion Ḥudhayfa ibn al-Yamān (d. 36/656).
104. Ghazālī, *Iḥyā'*, 4:29–30.
105. For a survey of the various well-known hadiths and theological views on the fate of deceased children, see Ibn Kathīr, *Tafsīr*, 4:288–295 (on Q. 17:15); Smith and Haddad, *Islamic Understanding of Death and Resurrection*, 168–182.
106. Ghazālī, *Iḥyā'*, 4:30.
107. See, for instance, Ṭabarī, *Jāmi'*, 5:3519–3520 (pre-Ghazālī); and Ibn Kathīr, *Tafsīr*, 3:171–175 (post-Ghazālī). The going view is that the people of the heights are those whose good and evil deeds were of the same measure (for instance, sinning believers who were martyred for God's sake while having been disobedient to their parents) and that God, out of His mercy, will eventually place them in Paradise. Incidentally, one could read the conclusion of Q. 7:49 as an indication that God will instruct the people of the heights (and not those headed directly to Paradise), "Enter the Garden! No fear for you, nor shall you grieve."
108. Ghazālī, *Iqtiṣād*, 207–209.

109. Griffel, *Al-Ghazālī's Philosophical Theology*, 236. Cf. Bouyges, *Essai*, 46–47; Hourani, "Revised Chronology of Ghazālī's Writings," 298–299. According to ʿUthmān, *Sīrat*, 204, the *Maqṣad* was written from 490/1097 to 495/1102.
110. The overwhelming majority of Muslim scholars consider the opening verse of the Qur'an to be what is called the *basmala* formula: "In the Name of God, the Compassionate, the Caring." (A minority insist that the Qur'an opens with the next verse, or Q. 1:2.) With one exception (sura 9), this formula precedes all subsequent suras. Here and elsewhere I use Michael Sells's translation of *al-Raḥmān* (the Compassionate) and *al-Raḥīm* (the Caring). See Sells, *Approaching the Qur'án*, 20–21, where Sells explains why he chose this particular translation.
111. See Juwaynī, *Kitāb*, 145.
112. Cupping is an antiquated therapeutic practice of drawing blood from the body.
113. Ghazālī, *Maqṣad*, 68. See Ghazālī, *Iḥyā'*, 4:498–499, where Ghazālī concludes the *Iḥyā'* by citing a report in which the Prophet tells his Companions that God is more merciful to His servants than a woman who, having been parted from her young son during battle, was seen lovingly embracing him, moving the onlookers to tears.
114. Ormsby, *Theodicy in Islamic Thought*, 257. See Griffel's recent treatment of Ibn Sīnā's influence on Ghazālī's worldview in *Al-Ghazālī's Philosophical Theology*.
115. Ghazālī, *Maqṣad*, 68–69. This inevitably leads to a classic philosophical question: could not all good have been obtainable without evil? Ghazālī's warning is that one should not doubt God's compassion, nor should one think that anything that is conceivable is in fact a better alternative. This discussion overlaps with Ghazālī's theodicean assessment of this life, that is, that this is the "best of all possible worlds"—the subject of Ormsby's *Theodicy in Islamic Thought*. See also Griffel's discussion of this in *Al-Ghazālī's Philosophical Theology*, 223–231.
116. Ghazālī, *Iḥyā'*, 4:22–31.
117. Ibid., 4:24.
118. Ibid., Cf. related remarks in Ghazālī, *Kīmiyā*, 791–792.
119. Ghazālī, *Mustaṣfā*, 1:171–174.
120. See Jackson's translation of Ghazālī, *Fayṣal*, in *On the Boundaries of Theological Tolerance in Islam*, 127; Ghazālī, *Fayṣal*, 85.
121. Ghazālī, *Iḥyā'*, 1:86, 4:28. Cf. similar remarks in Baghdādī, *Uṣūl*, 242–244.
122. Ghazālī, *Iḥyā'*, 4:26.
123. Ibid., 1:86, 4:28.
124. This statement ("what God wills, is") appears in Ghazālī's *Iqtiṣād* and is translated and discussed by Ormsby in *Theodicy in Islamic Thought*, 195.
125. See ibid., 40.
126. Ibid., 256. According to Juwaynī, the punishment of the damned is in fact what is best for them; if they were ever saved, they would only engage in even worse

sins, the result being that they would be banished to an even lower level of Hell (ibid., 22).

127. Ghazālī, *Maqṣad*, 69. My translation here loosely follows that of Burrell and Daher in Ghazālī, *Maqṣad* (trans.), 57.
128. Even so, the ninth/fifteenth-century Yemeni traditionalist Ibn al-Wazīr (d. 840/1436) appears to depict Ghazālī as a proponent of universal salvation in his *Īthār al-ḥaqq ʿalā al-khalq*, 216.
129. This connection to Ashʿarism is especially evident in Walī Allāh's *al-Khayr al-kathīr* (The abundant good). See Hafiz A. G. Khan's discussion of this in "Shah Wali Allah," 734.
130. Hermansen, "Shāh Walī Allāh of Delhi's *Ḥujjat Allāh Al-Bāligha*," 143.
131. Aside from Ghazālī, Walī Allāh was greatly influenced by Ibn ʿArabī.
132. See Hermansen's (trans.) remarks in Walī Allāh, *Ḥujjat*, xxvi–xxvii. Walī Allāh describes this vision in two books: (1) *Fuyūḍ al-Ḥaramayn*, 65–66; and (2) *al-Tafhīmāt al-ilāhiyya*, 2:300.
133. See Walī Allāh, *Ḥujjat*, 165–167.
134. Ibid., 238.
135. Ibid., 340–360.
136. Ibid., 187, 253–254.
137. Ibid., 339.
138. Ibid., 198.
139. See Hermansen's (trans.) remarks in Walī Allāh, *Ḥujjat*, xxxvi.
140. Walī Allāh, *Ḥujjat*, 250. See ibid., 250–256, and Hermansen's (trans.) related note in ibid., 154n6.
141. Walī Allāh, *Ḥujjat*, 336–337. "Those who excel" and the "people of the right" are expressions from the Qur'an (56:7–11, 27).
142. Walī Allāh, *Ḥujjat*, 339. *Jāhiliyya*, translated as the "Ignorant Age," is a term that denotes the "barbaric" period in Arabian history that immediately preceded the era of the Prophet.
143. Ibid., 334–339. Cf. related remarks in Walī Allāh, *Budūr*, 193–196, 203–204.
144. Walī Allāh, *Budūr*, 196.
145. Walī Allāh, *Ḥujjat*, 338.
146. Ibid.
147. Walī Allāh, *Budūr*, 203.
148. Ibid., 196.
149. See Hermansen's (trans.) remarks in Walī Allāh, *Ḥujjat*, xxviii–xxix; Jalal, *Partisans of Allah*, 50–57.
150. Cf. Winter's remarks on Ghazālī's and Walī Allāh's respective soteriologies in "Last Trump Card," 150–151.
151. Ghazālī, *Iḥyāʾ*, 4:498. This hadith appears in the *Ṣaḥīḥ Muslim* collection (in "Kitāb al-tawba").
152. See Yusuf, "Who Are the Disbelievers?"

CHAPTER 2

1. Andrae, *In the Gardens of Myrtles*, 3.
2. Nasr, *Garden of Truth*, 30.
3. See, for example, ibid., 210. From James Morris's vantage point, one "could say that the history of Islamic thought subsequent to Ibn ʿArabī (at least down to the eighteenth century and the radically new encounter with the modern West) might largely be construed as a series of footnotes to his work. To the degree that such a statement is justifiable, this wide-ranging influence must be explained not simply by reference to the intrinsic characteristics of Ibn ʿArabī's own life and works . . . but also by their coincidence with a broader historical movement of institutionalization of Sufism (with a concomitant penetration of 'Sufi' forms and allusions in virtually every domain of the arts and intellectual life) that seems to have touched the most scattered regions of the Islamic world at almost the same time, and with a broad range of inescapable intellectual and practical problems posed by that institutionalization" ("Ibn ʿArabī and His Interpreters," 106:733).
4. Ibn ʿArabī also reportedly had visions of other noble figures, including al-Khiḍr ("the green one"), a mysterious individual typically identified as the wise man who teaches Moses an important lesson on knowledge and patience in Q. 18:65–82.
5. For a more detailed account of Ibn ʿArabī's travels and mystical experiences, see Addas, *Quest for the Red Sulphur*. See also Michel Chodkiewicz's discussion of Ibn ʿArabī's status as "seal of the saints" in *Seal of the Saints*.
6. In the mid-1960s, Osman Yahia (in *Histoire*) estimated that Ibn ʿArabī had composed roughly seven hundred works (some significantly longer than others), approximately four hundred of which are extant. There is, however, an ongoing debate as to the exact number of his works. Complicating matters is the fact that there are many spurious writings in his name, a good example of which is a popular commentary on the Qur'an commonly called *Tafsīr Ibn (al-)ʿArabī* or *Tafsīr al-shaykh al-akbar*. This exegetical work appears to have been written by ʿAbd al-Razzāq al-Kāshānī (d. 736/1335), a student of Muʾayyid al-Dīn Jandī (d. 690/1291), who was a student of Ibn ʿArabī's renowned disciple Ṣadr al-Dīn al-Qūnawī (d. 673/1274). Despite much overlap, soteriological or otherwise, it would be a mistake to assume that Kāshānī's views mirror those of Ibn ʿArabī. On this point, see Morris, "Ibn ʿArabī and His Interpreters," 107:101ff.; Lory, *Commentaires*.
7. See Q. 7:180 and 17:110, both of which refer to God's "most beautiful names." The notion that God has ninety-nine names comes from the hadith corpus, for instance, the *Ṣaḥīḥ al-Bukhārī* collection (in "Kitāb al-shurūṭ," "Kitāb al-daʿawāt," and "Kitāb al-tawḥīd"). It is widely recognized that the "standard" list of ninety-nine names was produced long after the Prophet passed away.

8. Chittick, *Sufi Path of Knowledge*, 10.
9. Chittick, *Imaginal Worlds*, 169. On this point, see Rustom, "Is Ibn al-ʿArabī's Ontology Pantheistic?" According to Knysh, this so-called Oneness of Being doctrine "shocked" Ibn ʿArabī's "opponents who (mis)took it for a veiled acknowledgment of the substantial identity between God and the world that effectively disposed with divine transcendency and self-sufficiency. In such a theory, God was no longer the absolutely otherworldly and impregnable entity" to which Muslim theologians were accustomed (*Ibn ʿArabi in the Later Islamic Tradition*, 14).
10. Chittick, *Imaginal Worlds*, 46.
11. Ibid., 168–169. God is unbounded by the limitations that distinguish all that is other than Him (see ibid.).
12. See Chittick's translation of Ibn ʿArabī, *Futūḥāt* (4:3), in *Imaginal Worlds*, 45. One proof of this is the human "potential to know everything," which is inferred from the Qur'an itself: God "taught Adam all the names" (2:31) (Chittick, *Imaginal Worlds*, 168).
13. See Ibn ʿArabī, *Futūḥāt*, 4:3.
14. Ibid., 4:386. Unlike God Himself, our perceptions and understanding of Him are transient. On this point, see Chittick, *Ibn ʿArabi*, 111–112.
15. This statement comes from Ibn ʿArabī's *Fuṣūṣ* and is translated and discussed by Chittick in *Imaginal Worlds*, 150. Ibn ʿArabī makes a similar observation in the *Futūḥāt*, 3:132.
16. Ibn ʿArabī, *Futūḥāt*, 4:386.
17. Ibid.
18. Ibid., 4:391.
19. Ibid., 3:309.
20. Ibid., 3:510.
21. See Chittick's translation of Ibn ʿArabī, *Futūḥāt* (4:133), in *Imaginal Worlds*, 151. See also Chittick's related remarks in *Imaginal Worlds*, 152.
22. See Chittick's translation of Ibn ʿArabī, *Futūḥāt* (3:398), in *Imaginal Worlds*, 154. See also Chittick's related remarks in *Imaginal Worlds*, 149, 168–169.
23. See Ibn ʿArabī, *Futūḥāt*, 3:410.
24. See Chittick, *Imaginal Worlds*, 147–148. Cf. related remarks in ibid., 137.
25. See Chittick's translation of Ibn ʿArabī, *Futūḥāt* (2:148), in *Imaginal Worlds*, 146. On this point, see Knysh, "Realms of Responsibility in Ibn ʿArabi's *al-Futuhat al-makkiya*," 88–89.
26. See Chittick's translation of Ibn ʿArabī, *Futūḥāt* (2:248), in *Imaginal Worlds*, 147. Thus, it is only the divine prescriptions that make "the entity of evil manifest from Satan." See Chittick's translation of Ibn ʿArabī, *Futūḥāt* (4:223), in *Imaginal Worlds*, 147.
27. See Chittick's translation of Ibn ʿArabī, *Futūḥāt* (4:186), in *Imaginal Worlds*, 146. Ibn ʿArabī goes on to say, "Your taking from the Messenger is nondelimited, but your taking from God is delimited. The Messenger himself is delimited,

but taking from him is nondelimited. God is not delimited by any delimitation, but taking from Him is delimited. So consider how wonderful this affair is!" (ibid.).

28. See Chittick's translation of Ibn ʿArabī, *Futūḥāt* (3:410), in *Imaginal Worlds*, 145–146 (diacritics added).
29. Ibn ʿArabī, *Futūḥāt*, 3:153.
30. Schuon, *Transcendent Unity of Religions*, 35–36.
31. Ibn ʿArabī, *Tarjumān*, 67. I am here citing the dated yet classic translation by R. A. Nicholson.
32. Winter, "Last Trump Card," 134n2.
33. Ibn ʿArabī makes this statement and elaborates on it in the chapter (*faṣṣ*) on Jesus. See Ibn ʿArabī, *Fuṣūṣ*, chap. 15, particularly page 141. Winter briefly discusses this in a paper tentatively entitled "Realism and the Real: Islamic Theology and the Problem of Alternative Expressions of God." This appears in my forthcoming edited volume *Islam, Salvation, and the Fate of Others* (tentative title).
34. See, for example, Ibn ʿArabī, *Muḥāḍarat*, 2:284; Ibn ʿArabī, *Tadhkirat*, 274. In fact, it was common for premodern Muslim scholars to refer to Christians and Jews as associationists (see Friedmann, *Tolerance and Coercion in Islam*, 70–72). On Ibn ʿArabī's sometimes less than ecumenical attitude toward Christians in matters of this life, see Keller, "Perceptions of Other Religions in Sufism," 189–190.
35. See Ibn ʿArabī, *Futūḥāt*, 3:153.
36. Ibid. See Ibn ʿArabī's related remarks in ibid., 3:141, particularly his claim that if Moses were alive during the era of the Prophet, he would have been compelled to adhere to the latter's more progressive law. See also ibid., 3:311, where Ibn ʿArabī writes of the obligation to worship God in the manner prescribed by the revealed law (*sharīʿa*).
37. See Chittick's translation of Ibn ʿArabī, *Futūḥāt* (4:100), in *Imaginal Worlds*, 150.
38. See Chittick's translation of Ibn ʿArabī, *Futūḥāt* (3:469), in *Imaginal Worlds*, 156–157. See also *Imaginal Worlds*, 155–160, where Chittick discusses Ibn ʿArabī's conception (and handwritten diagram) of the relationship between revealed religions and the "diversity of human dispositions." Incidentally, Ibn ʿArabī's particular elucidation of the significance of the term *messenger* in Q. 17:15, as quoted above, is absent from the discussion of this verse in the Qur'anic commentary commonly and mistakenly ascribed to him (see Kāshānī [pseudo–Ibn ʿArabī], *Tafsīr*, 1:712).
39. According to Q. 67:9, Hell's inhabitants will confess that they had received a "warner" but "denied" him. If this implies that they had recognized this fact (that is, that they had received a warner but refused to listen to him or heed his warnings) during this lifetime, then this passage would serve as additional support for Ibn ʿArabī's reading of Q. 17:15.

40. See Ibn ʿArabī, *Futūḥāt*, 3:172, where Ibn ʿArabī writes that even Trinitarians may qualify as true monotheists who will hopefully be saved.
41. See Ibn ʿArabī, *Fuṣūṣ*, 95.
42. Ibn ʿArabī, *Futūḥāt*, 1:319. Cf. Chittick's discussion of this in *Imaginal Worlds*, 137–138.
43. I should note that in chapter 25 of Ibn ʿArabī's *Fuṣūṣ*, which features Moses, we find an alternative, positive portrayal of Pharaoh: a Pharaoh who, despite his apparent arrogance, actually discerns the reality of the one God and is thus saved. (The Qur'anic verse 10:90 indicates that, as most interpret it, Pharaoh's body—not his soul—was saved as a "sign" to others.) On this point, see Ormsby, "Faith of Pharaoh." ʿĀ'isha al-Manāʿī seems to overlook the depiction of Pharaoh in the *Fuṣūṣ* when dismissing the claim that Ibn ʿArabī regarded Pharaoh as a believer bound for Paradise. See her "ʿAqīdat," 96–97.
44. Ibn ʿArabī, *Futūḥāt*, 1:301–304.
45. See ibid., 2:690.
46. See Ibn ʿArabī, *Fuṣūṣ*, 137. The notion of the messenger-of-resurrection appears in well-known exegetical works, such as Ṭabarī, *Jāmiʿ*, 6:5135–5136, and well-known hadith compilations, such as the *Musnad Aḥmad* collection.
47. This is the impression one gets from Qur'anic passages such as 2:214, 216; 29:2–4; 33:9–11; 47:31.
48. See Ibn ʿArabī, *Futūḥāt*, 3:145, where Ibn ʿArabī states that the Jews and Christians living under Muslim rule attain happiness by paying the *jizya*, a tax levied on certain non-Muslim males. According to ʿAbd al-Ghanī al-Nābulusī (d. 1143/1731), an advocate of Ibn ʿArabī and a onetime mufti of Damascus, this statement need not mean that these particular People of the Book will attain contentment in the life to come; it may simply be a reference to happiness (or at least relative happiness) in this life. Nevertheless, Nābulusī adds, those Jews and Christians residing in Muslim lands who have faith in God in their hearts will indeed attain bliss in the hereafter. They are believers, even though they are legally non-Muslim and pay the *jizya* to Muslim authorities (see Winter, "Polemical Treatise by ʿAbd al-Ġanī al-Nābulusī against a Turkish Scholar on the Religious Status of the Ḏimmīs," 97–100).
49. See Ibn ʿArabī, *Futūḥāt*, 1:301–302.
50. See Chittick's translation of Ibn ʿArabī, *Futūḥāt* (2:281), in *Ibn ʿArabi*, 131–132.
51. Ibn ʿArabī, *Futūḥāt*, 1:534, 3:77. Cf. related remarks in Kāshānī (pseudo–Ibn ʿArabī), *Tafsīr*, 1:580–581.
52. Ibn ʿArabī, *Futūḥāt*, 3:77.
53. See Rustom, *Triumph of Mercy*, chap. 7, where Rustom comments on the use of the word *taste* in this passage (and in Q. 32:14).
54. See Chittick's translation of Ibn ʿArabī, *Futūḥāt* (3:466), in *Ibn ʿArabi*, 137. Cf. related remarks in Ibn ʿArabī, *Futūḥāt*, 1:534, 3:77. In this vein, Ibn ʿArabī in the *Futūḥāt* (3:390, translated in Chittick, *Ibn ʿArabi*, 143–144), provides the following observation regarding the Qur'anic statement "with God is the most beautiful

place of return" (3:14): "God does not explicitly link any ugliness whatsoever to the place of returning to Him.... For His mercy is all-embracing, and His blessing is abundant and all-comprehensive.... This explains why all the world will be mustered on the [Day of Resurrection] 'like scattered moths' [Q. 101:4]. Mercy will be scattered in all the homesteads, so the world will scatter in search of it, for the world has diverse states and various forms. Through the scattering they will seek from God the mercy that will remove from them the forms that lead to wretchedness."

55. Ibn ʿArabī, *Futūḥāt*, 3:9. Cf. related remarks in ibid., 3:551, 4:405.
56. Ibid., 3:418. Cf. related remarks in ibid., 1:297, 656.
57. Ibid., 4:405. Cf. related remarks in ibid., 3:382.
58. See Chittick's translation of Ibn ʿArabī, *Futūḥāt* (3:25), in *Ibn ʿArabi*, 128–129. (Chittick capitalizes "most merciful.") On Ibn ʿArabī's "good opinion" of God, see Ibn ʿArabī, *Futūḥāt*, 2:474; Chittick, "Ibn al-ʿArabī's Hermeneutics of Mercy," 155–160, 163–167.
59. See Chittick, "Ibn al-ʿArabī's Hermeneutics of Mercy," 157; Chittick, *Ibn ʿArabi*, 129–130.
60. See Chittick's translation of Ibn ʿArabī, *Futūḥāt* (3:478), in *Ibn ʿArabi*, 130.
61. See Ibn ʿArabī, *Futūḥāt*, 3:255; 4:4, 163, 405. Cf. related remarks in ibid., 3:550–551.
62. Ibid., 2:206.
63. See Ibn ʿArabī, *Fuṣūṣ*, 93–94. In treating the Qur'anic declaration "Those who malign God and His Messenger will be rejected by God in this world and the next—He has prepared a humiliating torment for them" (33:57), Ibn ʿArabī submits the following: owing to God's attribute of patience—the final name in the widely recognized list of God's ninety-nine "most beautiful names" is the Patient (al-Ṣabūr)—He waits until the hereafter to take the disobedient to task; however, as mercy takes precedence over wrath, there will be "no escape from mercy and the removal of wrath. Inescapably, mercy will include everything, through God's bounty, God willing." See Chittick's translation of Ibn ʿArabī, *Futūḥāt* (2:206), in *Ibn ʿArabi*, 139.
64. Ibn ʿArabī, *Futūḥāt*, 3:553.
65. Ibid., 3:9.
66. See ibid.
67. See ibid., 3:147.
68. Ibid., 3:346. Fifty thousand years is presented as the duration of Judgment Day in the *Ṣaḥīḥ Muslim* hadith collection (in "Kitāb al-zakāh"). According to the Qur'an, fifty thousand years is also the duration of a "day" (*yawm*) on which angels and the Spirit (often identified as the archangel Gabriel) journey to God (70:4).
69. Ibn ʿArabī, *Futūḥāt*, 2:447. Cf. related remarks in ibid., 4:296.
70. The wretched ask, "Why did such and such happen?" and claim, "If such and such had been, it would have been better and more appropriate." See Chittick's translation of Ibn ʿArabī, *Futūḥāt* (2:447), in *Ibn ʿArabi*, 141.

71. See Chittick's translation of Ibn ʿArabī, *Futūḥāt* (2:213), in *Ibn ʿArabi*, 135–136. Cf. related remarks in Ibn ʿArabī, *Futūḥāt*, 2:690.
72. Ibn ʿArabī, *Futūḥāt*, 3:418.
73. Ibid., 1:312.
74. Ibid., 3:402. Cf. related remarks in ibid., 3:461.
75. It is, then, only natural to expect God to be merciful to them all (ibid., 3:433). Is not "essential worship" worthy of greater consideration than "accidental wretchedness"? See Chittick's translation of Ibn ʿArabī, *Futūḥāt* (3:402), in *Ibn ʿArabi*, 134.
76. Knysh, "Realms of Responsibility in Ibn ʿArabi's *al-Futuhat al-makkiya*," 93.
77. See Chittick's translation of Ibn ʿArabī, *Futūḥāt* (3:300), in *Imaginal Worlds*, 137. On this understanding of human freedom, see Chittick's related discussion in *Imaginal Worlds*, 143–144. Cf. Knysh's discussion of this in "Realms of Responsibility in Ibn ʿArabi's *al-Futuhat al-makkiya*."
78. See Chittick's translation of Ibn ʿArabī, *Futūḥāt* (3:356), in *Imaginal Worlds*, 143.
79. See Chittick's translation of Ibn ʿArabī, *Futūḥāt* (3:353), in *Ibn ʿArabi*, 137. The verse immediately following Q. 39:53 suggests that the latter is in reference to those who seek forgiveness in this life: "Turn to your Lord. Submit to Him before the punishment overtakes you and you can no longer be helped." Nevertheless, one could read 39:53 as a general statement, which would mean that forgiveness can be granted to unrepentant "immoderates" *after* they have been punished.
80. See Chittick's translation of Ibn ʿArabī, *Futūḥāt* (3:405), in *Sufi Path of Knowledge*, 343.
81. See Chittick's translation of Ibn ʿArabī, *Futūḥāt* (3:24), in *Ibn ʿArabi*, 136. See also Ibn ʿArabī, *Futūḥāt*, 1:534. Cf. related remarks in ibid., 3:382.
82. "Exoteric scholars," we are told, mistakenly interpret the word *qadā* here to mean "commanded." See Chittick's translation of Ibn ʿArabī, *Futūḥāt* (3:117), in *Sufi Path of Knowledge*, 343.
83. Ibn ʿArabī, *Futūḥāt*, 3:471.
84. Ibid., 2:244. Cf. related remarks in ibid., 3:495.
85. Ibn ʿArabī famously characterized the Qur'an as an "ocean without shore." See Chodkiewicz, *Ocean without Shore*.
86. Ibn ʿArabī, *Futūḥāt*, 2:207.
87. Ibn ʿArabī, *Fuṣūṣ*, 94.
88. Ibn ʿArabī, *Futūḥāt*, 4:256. In the *Fuṣūṣ*, 211, Ibn ʿArabī characterizes chastisement as "the absence of mercy." Although this might appear to constitute a contradiction, it is important to bear in mind the different senses in which Ibn ʿArabī uses certain terms (recall that all people are both "idol worshipers" and "knowers" of God). Punishment could very well be regarded as both "the absence of mercy"—consider the agony—and the tool of mercy—consider the outcome.

89. See Chittick's translation of Ibn ʿArabī, *Futūḥāt* (3:9), in *Ibn ʿArabi*, 132. Cf. related remarks in Ibn ʿArabī, *Futūḥāt*, 3:551. From one perspective, the "cosmos is identical with mercy, nothing else." See Chittick's translation of Ibn ʿArabī, *Futūḥāt* (2:437), in *Ibn ʿArabi*, 130.
90. Ibn ʿArabī, *Futūḥāt*, 3:171. The Qur'anic verse 66:6 refers to "stern and strong" angels who stand over the Fire, "angels who never disobey God's command to them, but do as they are ordered."
91. Ibn ʿArabī, *Futūḥāt*, 3:463. See also Ibn ʿArabī, *Fuṣūṣ*, 169–170.
92. See Chittick's translation of Ibn ʿArabī, *Futūḥāt* (4:306), in *Self-Disclosure of God*, 181. Cf. related remarks in Ibn ʿArabī, *Futūḥāt*, 4:307.
93. Ibn ʿArabī, *Futūḥāt*, 4:14.
94. See ibid., 1:87, 188, 215, 316, 429, 509–510; 2:250, 680; 3:204, 439, 472; 4:10, 48. This conflation of the wall with the heights appears in earlier exegetical works. See, for instance, Ṭabarī, *Jāmiʿ*, 5:3517–3519. See also ibid., 5:3519–3524, where Ṭabarī cites (but does not accept) the view that the heights are occupied by righteous and knowledgeable people (that is, the elect) and a competing claim that it is angels who reside there; in neither of these cases are the people of the heights in a state of limbo. See Kāshānī (pseudo–Ibn ʿArabī), *Tafsīr*, 1:434–435, where Kāshānī asserts that the people of the heights are in fact the elect, righteous and knowledgeable people who are superior to those below them in Paradise.
95. Ibn ʿArabī, *Futūḥāt*, 4:14.
96. See Chittick's translation of Ibn ʿArabī, *Futūḥāt* (3:418), in *Imaginal Worlds*, 155.
97. Ibn ʿArabī, *Futūḥāt*, 3:25.
98. Ibid., 1:169.
99. See Chittick's translation of Ibn ʿArabī, *Futūḥāt* (3:119), in *Imaginal Worlds*, 115. As Chittick notes, divine wrath should not be confused with pure wrath, which does not exist (*Imaginal Worlds*, 112).
100. See Chittick's translation of Ibn ʿArabī, *Futūḥāt* (3:346), in *Imaginal Worlds*, 116. On account of such statements, many mistakenly assume that Ibn ʿArabī completely dismisses the reality of punishment, even during the Last Day (see Manāʿī, "ʿAqīdat," 96ff.).
101. See intoduction, note 10.
102. Ibn ʿArabī, *Futūḥāt*, 1:299. Cf. Chittick's discussion of this in *Imaginal Worlds*, 117.
103. Ibn ʿArabī, *Futūḥāt*, 2:335.
104. See Chittick's translation of Ibn ʿArabī, *Futūḥāt* (3:245), in *Ibn ʿArabi*, 140.
105. See Chittick's translation of Ibn ʿArabī, *Futūḥāt* (3:119), in *Imaginal Worlds*, 117.
106. On this point, see Lange, *Justice, Punishment, and the Medieval Muslim Imagination*, 127n160.
107. Ibn ʿArabī, *Futūḥāt*, 2:207. My translation here loosely follows that of Chittick in *Ibn ʿArabi*, 140. Cf. related remarks in Ibn ʿArabī, *Futūḥāt*, 1:534; 3:172, 440.
108. See Chittick's translation of Ibn ʿArabī, *Futūḥāt* (3:387), in *Ibn ʿArabi*, 140.

109. Ibn ʿArabī, *Fuṣūṣ*, 114.
110. See Lory, *Commentaires*, 129–132; Rustom, *Triumph of Mercy*, chap. 6; Winter, "Ibn Kemāl," 157n97.
111. Morris (trans.) in Mullā Ṣadrā, *Ḥikma*, 3.
112. See Rizvi, *Mullā Ṣadrā Shīrāzī*; Morris's (trans.) introduction to Mullā Ṣadrā, *Ḥikma*.
113. Rustom, "Nature and Significance of Mullā Ṣadrā's Qurʾānic Writings," 130.
114. Mullā Ṣadrā, *Tafsīr*, 1:40–41, cited and discussed in Rustom, *Triumph of Mercy*, chap. 5.
115. Mullā Ṣadrā, *Tafsīr*, 1:153–154, cited and discussed in Rustom, *Triumph of Mercy*, chap. 5. Seyyed Hossein Nasr discusses Ṣadrā's adoption of the "Oneness of Being" doctrine in "Mullā Ṣadrā and the Doctrine of the Unity of Being."
116. Mullā Ṣadrā, *Tafsīr*, 1:111, cited and discussed in Rustom, *Triumph of Mercy*, chap. 7. Given that humanity is predisposed to love existence and perfection, Ṣadrā teaches that it is natural for people (or at least those who do not have a sickness in their hearts) to desire a return to God, the source of all love (*Asfār*, 9:347, cited and discussed in Rustom, *Triumph of Mercy*, chap. 6). The text of the *Asfār* cited here was published under the variant title *al-Ḥikma al-mutaʿāliya fī al-Asfār al-ʿaqliyya al-arbaʿa*.
117. See Mullā Ṣadrā, *Asfār*, 9:350–351, cited and discussed in Rustom, *Triumph of Mercy*, chap. 6.
118. Mullā Ṣadrā, *Asfār*, 9:352–353; Mullā Ṣadrā, *Tafsīr*, 1:42, 70–71. These passages are cited and discussed in Rustom, *Triumph of Mercy*, chap. 6.
119. Mullā Ṣadrā, *Tafsīr*, 1:156, cited and discussed in Rustom, *Triumph of Mercy*, chap. 7. See also ibid., chap. 6.
120. Mullā Ṣadrā, *Tafsīr*, 1:70–71, cited and discussed in Rustom, *Triumph*, chap. 7. Neither the *Asfār* nor Ṣadrā's commentary on the Qur'an's first sura contains any reference to "imaginal chastisement."
121. Mullā Ṣadrā, *Ḥikma*, 240.
122. Rustom, *Triumph of Mercy*, chap. 7. Quasi-universalism was undoubtedly regarded as controversial. It was for precisely this reason that, not long after Ṣadrā passed away, he was condemned by Muḥammad Bāqir Majlīsī (d. 1111/1699), author of the celebrated Shīʿite hadith collection *Biḥār al-anwār* (Oceans of lights) (see Rizvi, *Mullā Ṣadrā Shīrāzī*, 33).
123. Morris (trans.) in Mullā Ṣadrā, *Ḥikma*, 237n283. Cf. ibid., 43.
124. See Rustom's translation of Mullā Ṣadrā, *Asfār* (9:352), in *Triumph of Mercy*, chap. 6 (emphasis added).
125. According to Chittick, Ibn ʿArabī "launches a massive assault on straightforward assertions.... [He] does not deny the relative validity and usefulness of dogma, and he often reaffirms the standard formulations.... But, the moment he begins to meditate on the meanings explicit and implicit in the sources of the tradition, he destabilizes unreflective minds" (*Ibn 'Arabi*, 111).

126. Among the common misattributions to Ibn ʿArabī are the following two claims: (1) Heaven and Hell are merely conceptions, and (2) no one will ever be physically punished in the Fire (Manāʿī, "ʿAqīdat," 96ff., 126ff.).
127. See Chittick's translation of Ibn ʿArabī, *Futūḥāt* (1:288), in *Imaginal Worlds*, 118–119.
128. Chittick, *Sufi Path of Knowledge*, xv.
129. See Shahrastānī, *Milal*, 75.
130. See Manṣūr, *World-View of al-Jāḥiz in Kitāb al-Ḥayawān*, 123ff.
131. See Chittick's translation of Ibn ʿArabī, *Futūḥāt* (2:244), in *Ibn ʿArabi*, 138.
132. Mullā Ṣadrā, *Tafsīr*, 1:42, cited and discussed in Rustom, *Triumph of Mercy*, chap. 7.
133. See Chittick's translation of Ibn ʿArabī, *Futūḥāt* (3:370), in *Imaginal Worlds*, 114–115.

CHAPTER 3

1. See Watt, *Islamic Philosophy and Theology*, 159. Donald Little speculates that what has been recorded about Ibn Taymiyya in Muslim sources, from chronicles to biographical dictionaries, "is quite possibly greater in bulk and detail than that for any other medieval Muslim with the obvious exception of Muhammad himself" ("Did Ibn Taymiyya Have a Screw Loose?" 94; cf. Little, "Historical and Historiographical Significance of the Detention of Ibn Taymiyya," 318).
2. Esposito, *Unholy War*, 45. As Jon Hoover notes, "Ibn Taymiyya is seen widely today as the key inspiration for contemporary Islamic militancy, primarily because militants quote him as a key authority. However, accepting this linkage uncritically... is anachronistic and distorts Ibn Taymiyya into a more militant figure than he was" (*Ibn Taymiyya's Theodicy of Perpetual Optimism*, 5n12). Hoover identifies the following sources as "antidotes to this problem": Heck, "*Jihad* Revisited"; Jansen, "Ibn Taymiyyah and the Thirteenth Century"; Sivan, "Ibn Taymiyya"; and Ibn Taymiyya, *Mardin*. See also Delong-Bas, *Wahhabi Islam*, 247ff.
3. See Hāshimī, *Ibn Taymiyya*, 12–13.
4. See Martin and Woodward, *Defenders of Reason in Islam*, 123–126; Laoust, "Ḥanābila."
5. See Abrahamov, "Ibn Taymiyya on the Agreement of Reason with Tradition," 271–272. It would be erroneous to assume, as many do, that the Ḥanbalites are "anti-reason." In fact, they have engaged in some of the same rationalist discourses as the Muʿtazilites have, and have occasionally espoused similar doctrines (see, for example, Reinhart, *Before Revelation*, 33–34). As Jackson explains, traditionalists "use *reason*—even aspects of Aristotelian reason—but they [unlike the rationalists] do not recognize the tradition of Aristotelian reason as an ultimate authority" (*On the Boundaries of Theological Tolerance in Islam*, 19–20).

6. Arberry, *Revelation and Reason in Islam*, 18. A vivid demonstration of Ibn Taymiyya's dialectical skills appears in the accounts of his trials in Damascus, during which he took on some of the leading rationalists of his day, such as Ṣafī al-Dīn al-Hindī (d. 715/1315). See Jackson, "Ibn Taymiyyah on Trial in Damascus."
7. See Gutas, *Greek Thought, Arabic Culture*, 170–171. According to Gutas, it was not just the Ḥanbalites who supported Ibn Taymiyya during the Mongol incursions but also "reformed" (here meaning post-Ghazālī) Ashʿarites.
8. See, for example, Ibn Taymiyya, *Fatāwā*, 2:172–173, 11:227.
9. See Laoust, "Ibn Taymiyya"; Ibn Taymiyya, *Fatāwā*, 5:262–263. Among the well-known statements attributed to Ibn Taymiyya—and one reason he continues to be accused of anthropomorphism—is the following proclamation, which he allegedly made before a mosque congregation in Damascus as he descended one step of the pulpit (*minbar*): "God comes down to the sky of this world just as I come down now" (Little, "Did Ibn Taymiyya Have a Screw Loose?" 96).
10. Hāshimī, *Ibn Taymiyya*, 116–117.
11. Ibn Rajab, *Dhayl*, 2:402, translated by Little in "Did Ibn Taymiyya Have a Screw Loose?" 106.
12. See Michel's (trans. and ed.) remarks in Ibn Taymiyya, *Jawāb* (trans.), vii. Here Michel places Paul's death date at 575/1180. For an extensive treatment of Paul's treatise, see Ebied and Thomas, *Muslim–Christian Polemic during the Crusades*.
13. Michel (trans. and ed.) in Ibn Taymiyya, *Jawāb* (trans.), vii.
14. As Tariq Ramadan observes, many exegetes "explain that the precondition for this election is the promotion of the good, being a model and bearing witness, and demonstrating ethical consistency towards all men" (*Quest for Meaning*, 70).
15. See Ibn Taymiyya, *Jawāb*, 1:11–12, 206.
16. Ibid., 1:208.
17. Ibid., 1:209.
18. Ibid., 1:26, 209–210.
19. Ibid., 1:106–107. Ibn Taymiyya makes a similar assertion in the *Iqtiḍāʾ*, 211.
20. Ibn Taymiyya, *Jawāb*, 1:233–243, 270, passim; Ibn Taymiyya, *Fatāwā*, 4:201–209; Ibn Taymiyya, *Iqtiḍāʾ*, 3ff., 453–456.
21. Ibn Taymiyya, *Jawāb*, 1:242.
22. Ibid., 1:74–108, 242, passim. See related remarks in Ibn Taymiyya, *Nubuwwāt*, 28–30.
23. Ibn Taymiyya, *Jawāb*, 1:272; Ibn Taymiyya, *Fatāwā*, 22:41. Ibn Taymiyya reminds his audience that, as stated in Q. 4:165, messengers were sent "so that people would have no excuse before God" (*Fatāwā*, 22:41). Being unreached, therefore, means being excused. In this vein, Ibn Taymiyya quotes the Prophet as saying, "No one loves excuses more than God; for this reason, He sent messengers as bearers of good news and as warners" (ibid., 3:288). Accordingly, people's obligations to God commence only when they encounter the message (ibid., 20:200, 22:41–42).

24. Ibn Taymiyya, *Fatāwā*, 11:522–523.
25. Ibid., 19:9. See related remarks in ibid., 10:430; Ibn Taymiyya, *Iqtiḍā'*, 452–453.
26. Ibn Taymiyya, *Fatāwā*, 4:325.
27. Ibid., 1:149.
28. Ibid., 4:305.
29. Ibid., 4:305–306.
30. Ibid., 4:203, 210–215. See related remarks in ibid., 11:377–380. According to Ibn Taymiyya, it is miracles that allow people to distinguish prophets from others; however, miracles should not be regarded as the sole proof of prophethood (see Ibn Taymiyya, *Sharḥ*, 88ff.; cf. Ibn Taymiyya, *Nubuwwāt*, 9, 13ff., 108ff., passim). One reason Jews and Christians in particular should recognize the authenticity of the Prophet is his corroboration of their narratives, despite having had no meaningful contact with any People of the Book, as well as his being foretold in their scriptures (see Ibn Taymiyya, *Jawāb*, 2:265–302, passim; Ibn Taymiyya, *Nubuwwāt*, 26ff.). Cf. Q. 7:157.
31. Ibn Taymiyya, *Fatāwā*, 9:286–287. He goes on to quote the Qur'anic question "Have these people not traveled through the land with hearts to understand[?]" (22:46). In a separate but related discussion, he cites the following two Qur'anic statements: (1) "We have created many *jinn* and people who are destined for Hell, with hearts they do not use for comprehension, eyes they do not use for sight, ears they do not use for hearing" (7:179); and (2) "There truly is a reminder in this for whoever has a heart, whoever listens attentively" (50:37) (*Fatāwā*, 9:310–311).
32. Ibn Taymiyya, *Jawāb*, 1:272.
33. Ibid., 1:272–273. This is one reason Ibn Taymiyya condemns the philosophers (*falāsifa*) and other self-professing Muslims who claim that the Prophet spoke untruths for the greater good. See, among other works, Ibn Taymiyya, *Sharḥ*, 89ff., passim; Ibn Taymiyya, *Ḥamawiyya*, 22.
34. This also pertains to the salvation of self-professing Muslims. Whereas Ghazālī (in the *Fayṣal*) cites less popular versions of the hadith on the sects in order to challenge the soteriological pessimism that many derive from the "standard" version (which states that only one of "seventy-odd sects" of the Prophet's community will be saved), Ibn Taymiyya limits himself to the latter and similarly worded versions. See, for example, Ibn Taymiyya, *Iqtiḍā'*, 37; Ibn Taymiyya, *Ḥamawiyya*, 14. See also Ibn Taymiyya, *Nubuwwāt*, 95–96, where Ibn Taymiyya states that the damned sects stem from four groups: Shī'ites, Khārijites, Murji'ites, and Qadarites; other groups, such as the Jahmites, do not adhere to Islamic scripture in the first place.
35. Ibn Taymiyya, *Jawāb*, 1:273.
36. See Ibn Taymiyya, *Fatāwā*, 17:308, where Ibn Taymiyya divides people into three categories: followers of prophets, deniers of prophets, and "people of ignorance" (*ahl al-jāhiliyya*)—an expression used in this context to extend beyond its customary application to pre-Islamic Arabs. Cf. related remarks in Ibn Taymiyya, *Nubuwwāt*, 6.

37. Ibn Taymiyya, *Jawāb*, 1:273–274; Ibn Taymiyya, *Fatāwā*, 11:686, 17:308–310. Complicating matters is Ibn Taymiyya's discussion of the Prophet's parents. While Ibn Taymiyya affirms the soundness of hadiths that speak of one or both parents being in Hell, he dismisses a report of their being raised from the dead for the sake of Muḥammad and submitting to God before dying a second time. According to Ibn Taymiyya, both passed away as unbelievers, and even if they were both raised from the dead, neither could benefit from faith at that point (*Fatāwā*, 4:324–327). Given that their deaths occurred well over three decades before their son's prophethood (it is reported that the father, ʿAbd Allāh, passed away before Muḥammad was born, while the mother, Āmina, passed away when he was only six years old), one is left wondering whether they are damned because they failed to accept a portion of the message (possibly through their encounters with Arab People of the Book) or—as true people of the gap—if they received nothing, yet the Prophet was made aware of their wickedness, which would presumably be confirmed in their encounter with the messenger-of-resurrection. As we shall see in the next chapter, Rashīd Riḍā similarly accepts reports of their chastisement but suggests that there may yet be hope for their salvation on Judgment Day.
38. Ibn Taymiyya, *Fatāwā*, 16:177.
39. See Ibn Taymiyya, *Jawāb*, 1:273–274, where Ibn Taymiyya states that deceased children and those who are mentally impaired will also be tested by the messenger-of-resurrection. See also Ibn Taymiyya's related remarks in ibid., 1:278. Meanwhile, in the *Fatāwā*, 10:431–432, Ibn Taymiyya suggests that these two groups will never be chastised and that the deceased children of Muslims will be reunited with their parents in Paradise. See note 75 below.
40. Ibn Taymiyya, *Jawāb*, 1:273–274, 276–278; Ibn Taymiyya, *Fatāwā*, 11:675–686. Cf. Ibn Taymiyya, *Fatāwā*, 22:101–102; Ibn Taymiyya, *Nubuwwāt*, 103–105. On the Muʿtazilite approaches to this issue, see Reinhart, *Before Revelation* (particularly pages 157–160).
41. See, for example, Ibn Taymiyya, *Fatāwā*, 14:108–114. Ibn Taymiyya concedes that reason, including the rational argumentation that the Qur'an employs, can also lead to true monotheism. See, for instance, his *Fatāwā*, 1:46–49. For a more detailed account of Ibn Taymiyya's approach to this subject, see Hoover, *Ibn Taymiyya's Theodicy of Perpetual Optimism*, particularly pages 32–44; cf. Wael Hallaq's helpful yet somewhat dated study, "Ibn Taymiyya on the Existence of God."
42. Ibid., 8:218–229, 14:323.
43. Ibid., 19:68.
44. Ibid., 8:93–94.
45. Ibid., 8:436.
46. Ibn Taymiyya, *Jawāb*, 1:272–275. Cf. related remarks in Ibn Taymiyya, *Iqtiḍā'*, 36ff.; Ibn Taymiyya, *Fatāwā*, 2:200, 22:101–102.

47. Ibn Taymiyya, *Jawāb*, 1:238–239, passim. Cf. related remarks in Ibn Taymiyya, *Fatāwā*, 4:208.
48. Ibn Taymiyya, *Fatāwā*, 4:203. Cf. related remarks in ibid., 4:203–209; Ibn Taymiyya, *Jawāb*, 1:389–390, passim.
49. Ibn Taymiyya, *Iqtiḍāʾ*, 39.
50. Ibn Taymiyya, *Jawāb*, 1:242, passim.
51. Ibn Taymiyya, *Iqtiḍāʾ*, 12–14, 27–28, 44ff., passim. Unlike Ghazālī, Ibn Taymiyya is often presented as having been unusually hostile in his polemics against Christians. See, for example, Saab, "Communication between Christianity and Islam," 54; Ruthven, "Introduction," xi–xii.
52. Michel (trans. and ed.) in Ibn Taymiyya, *Jawāb* (trans.), 134. Michel likens Ibn Taymiyya's inclusivism to that of Ghazālī (ibid., 420n4); as is clear now, this is problematic.
53. See Ibn Qayyim, *Shifāʾ*, 2:245, where Ibn Qayyim refers to ʿAbd ibn Ḥamīd al-Kissī as ʿAbd ibn Ḥamīd (or Ḥumayd) al-Kiththī. It appears that ʿAbd ibn Ḥamīd's commentary is no longer extant. See Hoover, "Islamic Universalism," 198n7. Cf. Sezgin, *Geschichte*, 113.
54. See Ḥamawī, *Muʿjam*, 4:69–70.
55. Ibn Qayyim, *Shifāʾ*, 2:231, 245; Ibn Taymiyya, *Radd*, 53. Cf. Hoover, "Islamic Universalism," 182–183; Albānī's (ed.) remarks in Ṣanʿānī, *Raf*, 8. Although Ibn Qayyim's report does not explicitly state that Ibn Taymiyya received the volume, it is clearly implied.
56. Ibn Qayyim, *Shifāʾ*, 2:245.
57. Ibid.
58. According to the editor of this Saudi publication, Muḥammad al-Samharī, its published title (*al-Radd ʿalā man qāla bi-fanāʾ al-janna wa-l-nār*) is derived from the opening line of the body of the treatise in one of the two extant manuscripts, in this case, the manuscript located in Cairo's Dār al-Kutub, not the one in Beirut's al-Maktab al-Islāmī, which is incomplete and significantly shorter (see Samharī's [ed.] remarks in Ibn Taymiyya, *Radd*, 9–11, 30–31). Although this title may conceal the controversial core of the treatise, it is congruent with at least a portion of the *Fanāʾ*, assuming one interprets it to mean that it is a rejoinder to those who affirm the annihilation of both the Garden and the Fire, considered collectively, that is, the afterlife itself. And this title is not without precedent: Ibn Taymiyya's student Ibn Rushayyiq al-Maghribī (d. 749/1348) refers to the *Fanāʾ* as *Qāʿida fī radd ʿalā man qāla bi-fanāʾ al-janna wa-l-nār* (A foundation for the rejoinder to those who maintain the annihilation of the Garden and the Fire [see "Asmāʾ," 225]). More ambiguous but less misleading is the title offered by the biographer Ṣalāḥ al-Dīn al-Ṣafadī (d. 764/1363): *Fī baqāʾ al-janna wa-l-nār wa-fanāʾihimā* (On the perpetuity and annihilation of the Garden and the Fire [*Aʿyān*, 1:242]).

Others merely speak of it as a work on *Fanā' al-nār* (The annihilation of the Fire) (see Samharī's [ed.] remarks in Ibn Taymiyya, *Radd*, 11; Hoover, "Islamic Universalism," 184). Because of its content, *Fanā' al-nār* is its most appropriate title.

59. Ibn Taymiyya, *Radd*, 42–52. See ibid., 44–45, where Ibn Taymiyya likens the Jahmite view to that of the Mu'tazilite theologian Abū al-Hudhayl (d. 226/840), who held that the inhabitants of Heaven and Hell will eventually cease to move. The latter doctrine, according to Josef van Ess, can be traced back at least to certain early Christians, including the Gnostics ("Begrenzte," 121).
60. According to Ibn Taymiyya, *Radd*, 50–51, passages such as the following indicate that God's words alone are boundless: "If all the trees on earth were pens and all the seas, with seven more seas besides, [were ink,] still God's words would not run out: God is almighty and all wise" (Q. 31:27).
61. Ibn Taymiyya, *Radd*, 81–84.
62. Ibid., 42–44.
63. Ibid., 71.
64. Ibid., 52–55.
65. Ibid., 71–72.
66. Ibid., 53–56.
67. Here Ibn Taymiyya cites a well-known hadith (that appears in the *Ṣaḥīḥ Muslim* collection, in "Kitāb al-īmān") in which the Prophet declares, "As for the people of the Fire who are its [true] inhabitants [*alladhīna hum ahluhā*], they will neither die in it nor will they live." The wording of this hadith suggests that not everyone chastised in the Fire is among its "[true] inhabitants" (Ibn Taymiyya, *Radd*, 56).
68. Ibn Taymiyya, *Radd*, 71ff. See ibid., 72–74, where Ibn Taymiyya cites the following Qur'anic passages as evidence of an extended (but ultimately temporal) stay in Hell for unbelievers: 2:161–162, 6:27–28, 23:107–108, 35:36–37, 40:49–50, 43:74–78, 69:25–27.
69. Ibn Taymiyya, *Radd*, 57–60. Other Qur'anic verses that Ibn Taymiyya cites to support this link to unbelievers include 6:121, 7:201–202, 16:99–100, 18:50, and 58:19. Yet another report ascribed to the Companion Ibn 'Abbās seems to limit the threat and exception in Q. 6:128 to those sinners who submit to God in this life. Ibn Taymiyya dismisses this account, in large part because it conflicts with the Qur'an itself (*Radd*, 60–61).
70. The Qur'an uses the singular form of *ages* (*aḥqāb*) in 18:60: "Moses said to his servant, 'I will not rest until I reach the place where the two seas meet, even if it takes me years [or an age (*ḥuquban*)]!' "
71. Al-Ḥasan al-Baṣrī reportedly stated that while one age may be equivalent to seventy thousand years, each day of which is like a thousand years, no one can say with certainty what the ages signify other than an "abiding" stay (*khulūd*). This is true, Ibn Taymiyya adds, as long as Hell exists (*Radd*, 62–63).

72. Ibid., 60–66. See ibid., 64, where Ibn Taymiyya dismisses as baseless the following two claims: (1) the ages are the duration of only one kind of torment, namely, excruciating drinks that are "scalding" and "dark" (Q. 78:25); and (2) the statement "where they will remain for ages" (Q. 78:23) was abrogated by Q. 78:30: "So taste. We will only increase your punishment." See Ṭabarī, *Jāmiʿ*, 10:8422, where Ṭabarī rejects the latter claim on the grounds that scriptural abrogation pertains to commandments and prohibitions, not depictions of the life to come.
73. Ibn Taymiyya, *Radd*, 60–62.
74. Ibid., 66–68. There is some uncertainty as to which of the Companions were of this opinion. One report, for example, cites "Jābir [ibn ʿAbd Allāh (d. 78/697)], Abū Saʿīd [al-Khudrī (d. 74/693)], or some [other] Companions of the Prophet" (ibid., 68).
75. As Ibn Taymiyya notes in the *Fatāwā*, 10:431, the notion that deceased children will reunite with their righteous fathers in Paradise may be deduced from Q. 52:21: "We unite the believers with their offspring who followed them in faith—We do not deny them any of the rewards for their deeds: each person is in pledge for his [or her] own deeds." Of course if all of humanity will one day arrive in Heaven, then every child will—at some point—be reunited with his or her parents.
76. To illustrate the point at hand, I am here translating *raḥīm* as "merciful," rather than "caring."
77. Ibn Taymiyya, *Radd*, 81–82. These reports appear, among other places, in the *Ṣaḥīḥ al-Bukhārī* hadith collection (in "Kitāb al-tawḥīd").
78. See Hoover, *Ibn Taymiyya's Theodicy of Perpetual Optimism.*
79. Ibn Taymiyya, *Radd*, 82–83. Here Ibn Taymiyya adds that Ashʿarī "and others" developed a similar conception of God. Taqī al-Dīn al-Subkī rejects this depiction of Ashʿarī (*Rasāʾil*, 207).
80. Ibn Taymiyya, *Radd*, 68.
81. Ibid., 69.
82. Ibid.
83. Ibid., 55–57.
84. Ibid., 87. This hadith appears in the *Ṣaḥīḥ al-Bukhārī* collection (in "Kitāb al-tafsīr") and, with some variation, in the *Ṣaḥīḥ Muslim* collection (in "Kitāb al-janna").
85. Ibn Taymiyya, *Radd*, 87.
86. Ibid., 85–87. Here Ibn Taymiyya cites a hadith in which the Prophet says that even he will not enter Paradise on account of his deeds. (One version of this report appears in the collection of *Ṣaḥīḥ al-Bukhārī*, in "Kitāb al-riqāq.") Ibn Taymiyya also cites Qur'anic verses that affirm the role of divine grace in guiding and saving believers, namely, 3:164, 7:43, 37:57, 49:17, and 52:27.
87. See Ṭabarī, *Jāmiʿ*, 6:4424–4426; Zamakhsharī, *Kashshāf*, 2:405–406; Ibn ʿAṭiyya, *Muḥarrar*, 2:346, 5:426; Rāzī, *Tafsīr*, 18:51; Qurṭubī, *Tadhkira*, 2:211–212; Qurṭubī, *Jāmiʿ*, 11:214. Discussions of the duration of Hell most often appear

in commentaries on the three aforementioned passages: Q. 6:128, 11:106–108, and 78:23.

88. Rāzī, *Tafsīr*, 18:51.
89. See Manāʿī, "ʿAqīdat," 101ff. Cf. Ibn Taymiyya, *Fatāwā*, 2:464–465.
90. See Samharī's (ed.) remarks in Ibn Taymiyya, *Radd*, 18–19.
91. See Ḥarbī, *Kashf*, 31, 58–71, 82–83. The apologist ʿAbd Allāh Ibn Jibrīn (d. 2009) similarly denies Ibn Taymiyya's universalism in his introduction to Karmī, *Tawqīf*, 5–6, 17–49 (especially 30–35). There are also various denials published online. See, for example, "Fanāʾ al-nār ʿind Ibn Taymiyya wa-Ibn al-Qayyim"; Abu Rumaysah, "Reply to Accusations against Shaykh ul-Islâm ibn Taymiyyah."
92. See Samharī's (ed.) remarks in Ibn Taymiyya, *Radd*, 6, 12–16, 23ff.; Hoover, "Against Islamic Universalism." Cf. Manāʿī, "ʿAqīdat," 101. One major deficiency of Ḥarbī's analysis is that it fails to account for the entire content of the *Fanāʾ*. This may be explained by the fact that prior to 1995, only a small portion of the *Fanāʾ*—the version found in Beirut's al-Maktab al-Islāmī—had been published (in 1984, in Albānī's [ed.] introduction to Ṣanʿānī, *Rafʿ*, 9–14, with photographs of the manuscript on 53–55). This portion is found on pages 52–57 and 80–83 of Samharī's edition of the complete manuscript, which is located in Cairo's Dār al-Kutub (the entirety of the *Fanāʾ* runs from pages 41 to 87 of Samharī's edition, with photographs of the first and last pages of the Cairo manuscript on 34–35). Naturally, scholars unfamiliar with the complete version of the *Fanāʾ* have claimed that the various statements ascribed to Ibn Taymiyya (by Ibn Qayyim, for example) are nowhere to be found in his original works (Manāʿī, "ʿAqīdat," 100). Even Ibn Jibrīn, in his introduction to the 1998 edition of Karmī's *Tawqīf*, presents the *Fanāʾ* as something of a mystery. A footnote, presumably by the editor of the *Tawqīf*, Khalīl al-Sabīʿī, explains Ibn Jibrīn's oversight: Samharī's edition of the *Fanāʾ* had been printed only recently (Karmī, *Tawqīf*, 31n1).
93. See Ibn Taymiyya, *Fatāwā*, 2:464–465.
94. See Albānī's (ed.) remarks in Ṣanʿānī, *Rafʿ*, 23–28, 32, 38. See also Ḥarbī, *Kashf*, 44–48, where Ḥarbī discusses this theory; however, as I noted earlier, he maintains that Ibn Taymiyya never held the universalist views ascribed to him. Ḥarbī's portrayal of Ibn Taymiyya as a damnationist appears in ibid., 60–69, while Ibn Jibrīn's appears in Karmī, *Tawqīf*, 30–35. It is worth noting that Albānī (ed.), however fond he may have been of the "master of Islam," criticizes (not condemns) the latter for having ever argued for temporal damnation and warns against following him in this matter (in Ṣanʿānī, *Rafʿ*, 23–26, 28–32, 46, 48).
95. Ibn Taymiyya, *Fatāwā*, 4:326. Beyond the *Fatāwā*, Ibn Taymiyya writes that Heaven and Hell will remain "absolutely" (*baqāʾan muṭlaqan*) (*Bayān*, 1:157; cf. Ḥarbī, *Kashf*, 66).
96. Ibn Taymiyya, *Fatāwā*, 18:307. Ḥasan Ṣiddīq Khān (d. 1890) cites a portion of this particular discussion by Ibn Taymiyya shortly after dismissing the latter's and Ibn Qayyim's arguments for universalism. Here Khān does not bother

to explain what appears to be a contradiction in Ibn Taymiyya's writings. See Khān, *Yaqẓat*, 16–28.

97. It is noteworthy that Ibn Taymiyya makes this statement in the context of denying the authenticity of a hadith that states that, among other things, "Hell and its inhabitants" will "neither perish nor taste annihilation" (*Fatāwā*, 18:307).
98. Ibn Qayyim, *Shifā'*, 2:245.
99. Ibn Rushayyiq, "Asmā'," 225.
100. Hoover, "Islamic Universalism," 184–185.
101. Ṣafadī, *A'yān*, 1:242. (Ṣafadī refers to the *Fanā'* as *Fī baqā' al-janna wa-l-nār wa-fanā'ihimā*.) Here Ṣafadī notes in passing that Subkī had "refuted" the *Fanā'*.
102. Samharī was not the first to take this position. He was preceded by Muḥammad al-Safārīnī (d. 1188/1774), Ḥasan Ṣiddīq Khān, and Nu'mān al-Alūsī (d. 1899). See Samharī's (ed.) remarks in Ibn Taymiyya, *Radd*, 19, 25–27.
103. See ibid., 25–27.
104. See ibid., 28. Cf. similar remarks in Ashqar, *Janna*, 43–44.
105. See Ḥiṣnī, *Daf'*, 62, 331–333, 338–340. See also 'A. Muṣṭafā's (ed.) contributing notes in ibid., especially pages 331n1, 333n7, 338n1. Cf. Ḥarbī's related remarks in the *Kashf*, 15–17.
106. See Ṣan'ānī, *Raf'*. (In ibid., 63n7, Albānī [ed.] observes that Ṣan'ānī unjustifiably attributes certain passages in Ibn Qayyim's *Ḥādī al-arwāḥ ilā bilād al-afrāḥ* [discussed later in this chapter] to Ibn Taymiyya.) A rejoinder with a similar title (*Kashf al-astār fī ibṭāl kalām man qāla bi-fanā' al-nār*) is ascribed to another well-known Yemeni traditionalist, Muḥammad al-Shawkānī (d. 1834) (see Ḥarbī, *Kashf*, 21–22). As Ibn Jibrīn would have it, this unpublished manuscript, located in Sanaa, rejects the universalist interpretations of Q. 6:128, 11:106–107, and 78:23 but should not be regarded as a refutation of either Ibn Taymiyya or Ibn Qayyim. Ibn Jibrīn states this in his introduction to the 1998 edition of Mar'ī ibn Yūsuf al-Karmī's (d. 1033/1624) damnationist manifesto *Tawqīf al-farīqayn 'alā khulūd ahl al-dārayn*, 23–24. Karmī, writing nearly a century and a half before Ṣan'ānī's time, was a Cairo-based Ḥanbalite who, in the *Tawqīf*, 61–80, upholds eternal damnation, providing "corrective" interpretations of Q. 11:106–107 and 78:23 but never referencing Q. 6:128 or the seemingly universalist statements ascribed to the Companions. Here Karmī never explicitly cites (let alone criticizes) either Ibn Taymiyya or Ibn Qayyim.
107. See Ashqar, *Janna*, 39–46. See also Shinqīṭī, *Daf'*, 122–128, where Muḥammad al-Shinqīṭī discusses Q. 6:128 and, in the process, rebuts Ibn Taymiyya and Ibn Qayyim without mentioning either by name. Even more recently, American Muslim thinker Hamza Yusuf characterizes both Ibn 'Arabī's quasi-universalism and Ibn Taymiyya's universalism as "heterodoxic" ("Who Are the Disbelievers?" 47). Historical condemnations of Ibn Taymiyya's doctrines (including his noneternal Hell) are documented in Ḥabashī, *Maqālāt* (see, for example, pages 13, 170–173).

108. See Schacht, "Al-Subkī."
109. Whoever transcribed the manuscript notes this at the conclusion of the *I'tibār*. See Subkī, *Rasā'il*, 208. The volume cited here, *al-Rasā'il al-subkiyya*, includes additional polemical attacks by Subkī against Ibn Taymiyya regarding other, often legal, matters.
110. Ibid., 200.
111. Ibid., 195. One should not assume, however, that Subkī had nothing good to say of Ibn Taymiyya. In a conversation with one of Ibn Taymiyya's students, Shams al-Dīn al-Dhahabī (d. 748/1347), Subkī was at least quoted as saying, "I am convinced of the great scope, the ocean-like fullness and vastness of [Ibn Taymiyya's] knowledge of the transmitted and intellectual sciences, his extreme intelligence, his exertions and his attainments, all of which surpass description. I have always held this opinion. Personally, my admiration is even greater for the asceticism, piety, and religiosity with which God has endowed him, for his selfless championship of the truth, his adherence to the path of our forebears, his pursuit of perfection, the wonder of his example, unrivalled in our times and in times past" (Ibn Ḥajar, *Durar*, 1:169, translated by Little in "Did Ibn Taymiyya Have a Screw Loose?" 100).
112. Subkī, *Rasā'il*, 201.
113. Ibid., 198. Subkī avoids mentioning Ibn Taymiyya by name in the *I'tibār*, referring to him simply as "the author" (*al-muṣannif*) or "this man."
114. See Ibn Ḥazm, *Marātib*, 167–173. Cf. Ibn Taymiyya's critique of some of Ibn Ḥazm's other consensus claims in the *Naqd*.
115. Subkī, *Rasā'il*, 196–198. As further support, Subkī cites three hadiths that can be summarized as follows: (1) whoever kills himself or herself using a piece of iron will continually kill himself or herself with that piece of iron while in Hell, remaining in it "forever" (*abadan*); (2) Hell's "[true] inhabitants" will neither live in it nor die in it (cf. Q. 20:74); and (3) death will come in the form of a spotted ram and be slaughtered, and the peoples of Heaven and Hell will be told that they will abide, which Subkī regards as proof that the unbelievers will be unable to escape Hell (*Rasā'il*, 198, 207). I shall discuss the first hadith later, the second is only vaguely pertinent, and I have already discussed the third.
116. Subkī, *Rasā'il*, 198–200.
117. See ibid., 203. Dānī himself advocates damnationism (see *Risāla*, 65–66).
118. Subkī, *Rasā'il*, 203–204.
119. Ibid., 201–202. Subkī considers alternative approaches to Q. 78:23 but avoids claiming that it simply refers to sinning believers who will spend a certain number of ages in Gehenna before proceeding to Paradise (*Rasā'il*, 202–203). Like Ibn Taymiyya, Subkī acknowledges that Q. 78:27–28 ("for they did not fear a reckoning, and they rejected Our messages as lies") clarifies that the punishment applies to unbelievers. Interestingly, however, when later analyzing the report of the Companion Ibn Mas'ūd, which states that after the passing of

ages there will be "a time" in which "no one" will remain in Gehenna, Subkī maintains that, if this report is indeed sound, it must refer to sinning Muslims and the ages must be limited in this context (*Rasā'il*, 205).

120. Subkī, *Rasā'il*, 206–208.
121. Ibid., 207. Ṣan'ānī, *Raf'*, 125–127, presents a similar contention.
122. Subkī, *Rasā'il*, 200.
123. Ibid., 207. According to Ṣan'ānī, it is impossible for satanic beings to reform themselves since they are by their very nature evil and resistant to God's oneness (*Raf'*, 122–127).
124. Subkī, *Rasā'il*, 204. For evidence of forgery in entire works ascribed to al-Ḥasan al-Baṣrī, see Mourad, *Early Islam between Myth and History*.
125. Ibid., 204–205. See Shinqīṭī, *Daf'*, 124, where Shinqīṭī cites the opinion that the reports of an empty Fire ascribed to the Companions are only in reference to the level of Hell containing believers.
126. Subkī, *Rasā'il*, 205.
127. On this point, see Vasalou, *Moral Agents and Their Deserts*, 119, 121–132.
128. Subkī, *Rasā'il*, 201. Here Subkī makes the unwarranted allegation that Ibn Taymiyya regarded the temporality of Hell as *the* doctrine of the *salaf* (*qawl al-salaf*).
129. See Ibn Qayyim, *Shifā'*, 2:235, where Ibn Qayyim draws attention to this methodological disparity between Ibn Taymiyya and Subkī. See also Hoover's related remarks in "Islamic Universalism," 187–188. Ashqar employs Ibn Ḥazm's documented consensus in much the same way that Subkī does (see *Janna*, 39).
130. In a work entitled *Hidāyat al-ḥayārā fī ajwibat al-Yahūd wa-l-Naṣārā* (Guidance to the perplexed in responding to the Jews and Christians), a continuation of his master's polemics against the People of the Book, we observe a decisive Ibn Qayyim: "To deny the prophethood of Muḥammad is to deny the Lordship of God the Exalted" (583). Ibn Qayyim then goes on to cite what he deems to be erroneous beliefs held by philosophers (*falāsifa*), Zoroastrians, Christians, and Jews. Yet, in his exegetical writings, Ibn Qayyim makes the familiar argument that God will only punish those who have been warned by a messenger; the wicked will only be taken to task for their responses to the warnings of messengers, as opposed to their faulty deductions or detestable deeds in the absence of revelation (Ibn Qayyim, *Ḍaw'*, 3:521). Ibn Qayyim was also a pessimist with regard to salvation on the Last Day. In various writings, he characterizes most of humanity as condemned "idol worshipers." This characterization, he insists, is in line with the aforementioned hadith on the 999, as well as the following Qur'anic statements: "most of [the people to whom the Qur'an was revealed] persist in disbelieving" (17:89); "most people will not believe" (12:103); "We found that most of [the people to whom messengers were sent] did not honor their commitments; We found that most of them were defiant" (7:102). See Ibn Qayyim, *Ighāthat*, 221; Ibn Qayyim, *Ḥādī*, 600; Ibn Qayyim, *Shifā'*, 2:246–249; Ibn Qayyim, *Ṣawā'iq*, 2:676–677.

131. See Hoover, *Ibn Taymiyya's Theodicy of Perpetual Optimism*, 5, where Hoover observes that Ibn Qayyim actually goes further than Ibn Taymiyya in affirming a theodicy of optimism (particularly in the *Shifāʾ*).
132. See Ibn Qayyim, *Shifāʾ*, 2:223–246; Ibn Qayyim, *Ḥādī*, 569–626.
133. See Ibn Qayyim, *Ṣawāʿiq*, 2:637–685. In ibid., 1:74–77, ʿAlawī (ed.) discusses the preservation of the *Ṣawāʿiq* in Mawṣilī's abridgment.
134. Ibn Qayyim characterizes Ibn ʿArabī's position as follows: the inhabitants of the Fire will be chastised until they transform and become fire-like, thereby enjoying their stay in an environment that conforms to their nature (*Ḥādī*, 579–580). After quoting Ibn ʿArabī's statement, "[The Fire] is called a chastisement [*ʿadhāb*] due to the sweetness [*ʿudhūba*] of its food" (*Fuṣūṣ*, 94), Ibn Qayyim proceeds to claim (erroneously) that Ibn ʿArabī held that the Fire would *never* be a source of true punishment—a position that Ibn Qayyim contrasts with another extreme: the Muʿtazilite view that none of Hell's inhabitants will ever be saved. Cf. related remarks in Ibn Qayyim, *Shifāʾ*, 2:246; Manāʿī, "ʿAqīdat," 92–93.
135. Ibn Qayyim, *Ḥādī*, 580–581. In the *Shifāʾ*, 2:246, Ibn Qayyim also dismisses the claim that the chastisement of unbelievers will last as long as the number of years they spent in this life.
136. Here the expression "a limited number of days" is in Arabic *ayyāman maʿdūdāt*. (This is a variant of the "few days" [*ayyāman maʿdūda*] mentioned in Q. 2:80.) Leaving aside grammatical endings, this particular phrase appears in two other passages of the Qur'an: verses that mention the limited number of days of required fasting (2:184) and pilgrimage rites (2:203).
137. See Abdel Haleem, *Qur'an*, 97, where Abdel Haleem renders the middle part of the verse (about the camel passing through the eye of the needle) as "even if a thick rope were to pass through the eye of a needle they would not enter the Garden." See also Asad, *Message of the Qurʾān*, 238n32, where Asad, looking to earlier sources, justifies his rendering of *al-jamal* as "a twisted rope" rather than "a camel," the latter of which is the more popular reading. See Ṭabarī's discussion of these competing interpretations in *Jāmiʿ*, 5:3508–3510.
138. Ibn Qayyim, *Ḥādī*, 581.
139. Ibid.
140. Hoover, "Islamic Universalism," 193–194.
141. Ibn Qayyim, *Ḥādī*, 591–593. Cf. related remarks in Ibn Qayyim, *Shifāʾ*, 2:235–239.
142. Cf. a similar observation by Samharī (ed.) in Ibn Taymiyya, *Radd*, 17. Alternative versions of the universalist arguments in the *Ḥādī* appear in Ibn Qayyim, *Shifāʾ*, 2:239–244, and Ibn Qayyim, *Ṣawāʿiq*, 2:637–685.
143. Ibn Qayyim, *Ḥādī*, 598, 615–618. Cf. related remarks in Ibn Qayyim, *Shifāʾ*, 2:240; Ibn Qayyim, *Ṣawāʿiq*, 2:644–646, 667–668, 678–679. This claim may seem at odds with a hadith in the *Ṣaḥīḥ al-Bukhārī* collection that states that

God will create beings specifically for Hell. According to Ibn Qayyim, Bukhārī himself recognized that this hadith was reported erroneously, as evidenced by the fact that he (Bukhārī) places it in a chapter whose corrective heading reads, "As for the Garden, God will create other beings for it" (Ibn Qayyim, *Ḥādī*, 598).

144. Ibn Qayyim, *Ḥādī*, 597, passim. Cf. related remarks in Ibn Qayyim, *Shifā'*, 2:225–226, 232–233; Ibn Qayyim, *Ṣawā'iq*, 2:647, passim.
145. Ibn Qayyim, *Ḥādī*, 613–614. Cf. related remarks in Ibn Qayyim, *Ṣawā'iq*, 2:672–673. See Ibn Qayyim, *Ḥādī*, 613, where Ibn Qayyim cites a hadith that places the length of the Day of Judgment at fifty thousand years. (This hadith appears in the *Ṣaḥīḥ Muslim* collection, in "Kitāb al-zakāh.") This, however, need not be what Ibn Qayyim regards as the precise duration of chastisement, as we shall see in his discussion of the "ages" (Q. 78:23). Cf. Q. 22:47, 32:5, and 70:4, which refer to one-thousand-year-long and fifty-thousand-year-long "days."
146. See Ibn Qayyim, *Ṣawā'iq*, 2:675, where Ibn Qayyim provides examples of common Arabic statements that use the term *abadan* when referring solely to matters of this life, such as "I will never marry" (*lā atazawwaj abadan*).
147. Ibn Qayyim, *Shifā'*, 2:228, 239. Cf. related remarks in Ibn Qayyim, *Ṣawā'iq*, 2:648, 674–675. In the *Ṣawā'iq*, 2:674–675, Ibn Qayyim draws attention to passages such as Q. 98:6–8, where both punishment and reward are mentioned but the word *abadan* is used only in reference to Paradise.
148. On this point, see Hoover, "Islamic Universalism," 191; Bell, *Love Theory in Later Ḥanbalite Islam*, 96, 102.
149. See Samharī's (ed.) remarks in Ibn Taymiyya, *Radd*, 53n4.
150. Ibn Qayyim, *Shifā'*, 2:231.
151. Ibn Qayyim, *Ḥādī*, 624. Cf. related remarks in Ibn Qayyim, *Shifā'*, 2:224, 241–243; Ibn Qayyim, *Ṣawā'iq*, 2:643, 666, 671, 676–677. The hadith on the ninety-nine parts of divine mercy reserved for the afterlife appears in the *Ṣaḥīḥ al-Bukhārī* collection (in "Kitāb al-adab"). The hadiths about God's mercy outstripping or overcoming His wrath are also in *Bukhārī* (in "Kitāb al-tawḥīd").
152. Ibn Qayyim, *Ḥādī*, 598–599. Cf. related remarks in Ibn Qayyim, *Shifā'*, 2:240–241; Ibn Qayyim, *Ṣawā'iq*, 2:642–643, 676–678.
153. Ibn Qayyim, *Ḥādī*, 606–607. Cf. related remarks in Ibn Qayyim, *Shifā'*, 2:243; Ibn Qayyim, *Ṣawā'iq*, 2:643.
154. Ibn Qayyim, *Shifā'*, 2:242. Cf. a related remark in Ibn Qayyim, *Ṣawā'iq*, 2:242.
155. Ibn Qayyim, *Ḥādī*, 610–613. See ibid., 623, where Ibn Qayyim reminds his audience that "if God took people to task for the evil they do, He would not leave one living creature on earth" (Q. 16:61).
156. Ibn Qayyim, *Ḥādī*, 613. Here Ibn Qayyim adds that God already grants mercy to the children of unbelievers, for He has prohibited killing them, and whoever sees them is compassionate toward them.

157. Ibid., 611. Cf. related remarks in ibid., 603–607, 610.
158. Ibid., 599–603. Cf. related remarks in Ibn Qayyim, *Shifāʾ*, 2:209ff., especially 224–225; Ibn Qayyim, *Ṣawāʿiq*, 2:646, 656–658, 665–668. Ibn Qayyim has more to say concerning spiritual treatments in his treatise *al-Dāʾ wa-l-dawāʾ* (The disease and the cure).
159. Ibn Qayyim, *Ḥādī*, 611. Prior to arriving at this conclusion, Ibn Qayyim references a hadith foretelling the fate of four men on Judgment Day: one is deaf, another feebleminded, another senile, and a fourth debilitated. Each will claim that his respective impediment prevented him from submitting to his Lord. God, presumably through the messenger-of-resurrection, will command them to enter the Fire. Those who obey will find peace and coolness. This, Ibn Qayyim opines, demonstrates that God's grace is bestowed upon those who readily submit to their punishment, who seek to surrender to God's will and please Him, allowing Him to love them in return (ibid., 607–608). (This hadith appears in the *Musnad Aḥmad* collection.) Thus, Ibn Qayyim notes in the *Ṣawāʿiq*, the Fire will become cool for those who truly reform themselves (2:658, 661). It is presumably at that point that they will proceed into the Garden. As for those who doubt that good could ever be the product of harmful punishment, Ibn Qayyim reminds them that even the angels did not immediately recognize God's wisdom in creating humanity: "When your Lord told the angels, 'I am putting a vicegerent on earth,' they said, 'How can You put someone there who will cause damage and bloodshed, when we celebrate Your praise and proclaim Your holiness?' but He said, 'I know things you do not' " (Q. 2:30) (Ibn Qayyim, *Ṣawāʿiq*, 2:637–638; cf. related remarks in Ibn Qayyim, *Shifāʾ*, 209–210).
160. Ibn Qayyim, *Ḥādī*, 600–603. Cf. related remarks in ibid., 617–618; Ibn Qayyim, *Ṣawāʿiq*, 2:647, 679.
161. Ibn Qayyim, *Ḥādī*, 616–617. Cf. related remarks in Ibn Qayyim, *Shifāʾ*, 2:234, 236, 244; Ibn Qayyim, *Ṣawāʿiq*, 2:679–680.
162. Ibn Qayyim, *Ḥādī*, 599–600, 603. Cf. related remarks in Ibn Qayyim, *Shifāʾ*, 2:241, 244; Ibn Qayyim, *Ṣawāʿiq*, 2:637–641, 658, 664–668, 679–680.
163. Ibn Qayyim, *Ḥādī*, 620–621.
164. The hadith on suicide by an iron weapon appears in the *Ṣaḥīḥ al-Bukhārī* collection (in "Kitāb al-ṭibb").
165. Ibn Qayyim, *Ḥādī*, 620–623. Cf. related remarks in Ibn Qayyim, *Shifāʾ*, 2:229–230. According to Albānī, Ibn Qayyim is mistaken, as the Qur'an itself indicates that God adheres to His threats: "I sent you a warning, and My word cannot be changed: I am not unjust to any creature" (Q. 50:28–29) (see Albānī's [ed.] remarks in Ṣanʿānī, *Raf*, 43–44). In fact, Albānī's point here is taken from Ibn Taymiyya himself in the *Fatāwā*, 14:497–498. Nevertheless, Albānī makes no attempt here to resolve the apparent incongruity of absolute divine threats and salvation for sinning believers, both of which he accepts. Additionally, his critique seems

to miss a crucial point: Ibn Qayyim never denies the fact that God's "word" of warning "cannot be changed"; his contention is that because threats are generally predicated on some form of sinfulness, once the damned rectify themselves, God will do as He pleases. Cf. Q. 46:16.

166. Typically included among the ninety-nine "most beautiful names" of God is the Harmer (al-Ḍārr), but this is derived, not taken directly, from the Qur'an: "If God touches you with harm [*ḍurr*], no one can remove it except him" (6:17). The same is true of the names Bringer of Death (al-Mumīt) (derived from passages such as 3:156), the Restrainer (al-Qābiḍ) (derived from 2:245), the Humiliator (al-Mudhill) (derived from 3:26), and the Abaser (al-Khāfiḍ) (arguably derived from 95:5). Other names such as the Subduer (al-Qahhār) (12:39) and the Compeller (al-Jabbār) (59:23), both of which appear in the Qur'an (with the definite article *al-*), could be interpreted in ways that avoid or minimize connotations of chastisement. For instance, see Asad, *Message of the Qur'ān*, 384, where Asad translates *al-Qahhār* in Q. 12:39 to mean the One "who holds absolute sway over all that exists," rather than simply "the Subduer." See also A. Yusuf Ali, *Holy Qur'ān*, 1528, where Ali translates *al-Jabbār* in Q. 59:23 to mean "the Irresistible," rather than "the Compeller."

167. Ibn Qayyim, *Ḥādī*, 609–610. Cf. related remarks in Ibn Qayyim, *Shifā'*, 2:223–224, 241; Ibn Qayyim, *Ṣawā'iq*, 2:638–644, 668–671. As Ibn Qayyim observes, the Qur'an states, "Anything good [*ḥasana*] that happens to you [Prophet] is from God; anything bad [*sayyi'a*] is from yourself" (4:79). Therefore, only the former ("anything good that happens to you") can be eternal (Ibn Qayyim, *Ṣawā'iq*, 2:668–670).

168. Ibn Qayyim, *Ḥādī*, 609. Cf. Ibn Qayyim's exposition of the divine attributes in *Asmā' Allāh al-ḥusnā*.

169. The claim that God's eternally old will to create necessitates an eternally old universe was famously refuted by Ghazālī in his rejoinder to the philosophers (*falāsifa*), *Tahāfut al-falāsifa* (*The Incoherence of the Philosophers*), and was similarly rejected by the vast majority of Muslim theologians.

170. Ibn Qayyim, *Ḥādī*, 626.

171. Ibid.

172. Ibn Qayyim, *Shifā'*, 2:245–246. Here Ibn Qayyim adds that the sacred texts never indicate that Hell and its torments are endless.

173. See Hoover, "Islamic Universalism," 193–194; Bell, *Love Theory in Later Ḥanbalite Islam*, 96, 242n34.

174. Ibn Qayyim, *Ṣawā'iq*, 2:663. My translation here loosely follows that of Hoover in "Islamic Universalism," 196.

175. Ḥarbī, *Kashf*, 9, 30, 34–57, 59, 78–84. Ibn Jibrīn presents a relatively similar apologia for Ibn Qayyim in Karmī, *Tawqīf*, 5–6, 17–49 (especially 24–27, 36–49). Albānī is much less charitable. See his sharp critique of Ibn Qayyim in Ṣan'ānī, *Raf'*, 17, 22, 35–44, 48–49.

176. Ibn Qayyim, *Zād*, 1:68. My translation here loosely follows that of Hoover in "Against Islamic Universalism."
177. See Ibn Qayyim, *Zād*, 1:42–68; Hoover, "Against Islamic Universalism."
178. Ibn Qayyim, *Ṭarīq*, 135.
179. See ibid., 135–140; Ḥarbī, *Kashf*, 50–51.
180. Ibn Qayyim, *al-Wābil*, 19–20, translated by Hoover in "Against Islamic Universalism." Albānī misattributes to Ibn Qayyim an additional ostensibly damnationist statement that was actually made by Jalāl al-Dīn al-Suyūṭī (Ṣanʿānī, *Raf*, 18). Ḥarbī notes this in the *Kashf*, 44, as does Ibn Jibrīn in Karmī, *Tawqīf*, 46 (Ibn Jibrīn mistakenly cites page 81 of Ṣanʿānī, *Raf*).
181. Hoover, "Against Islamic Universalism."
182. Ibid.; Laoust, "Ibn Ḳayyim al-Djawziyya."
183. Ibn Qayyim, *Shifāʾ*, 2:236. Cf. related remarks in Ibn Qayyim, *Ṣawāʿiq*, 2:673.
184. In the words of Binyamin Abrahamov, although the arguments employed by Ibn Qayyim are "not irrefutable," they are nonetheless "very convincing" ("Creation and Duration of Paradise and Hell in Islamic Theology," 101). This particular remark follows a brief discussion of Ibn Qayyim's *Ḥādī* and *Ṣawāʿiq*.
185. See Ibn Abī al-ʿIzz, *Sharḥ*, 535–542. Cf. Ibn Qayyim, *Ḥādī*, 579–582. According to Ḥarbī, *Kashf*, 6, 17–18, 25–28, the ninth/fifteenth-century Yemeni traditionalist Ibn al-Wazīr, citing Ibn Taymiyya and his supporters, initially rejected everlasting damnation before finally rethinking the matter. Cf. Ibn al-Wazīr, *Īthār*, 216–219, where Ibn al-Wazīr presents arguments for a finite Hell and briefly refers to the universalist writings of Ibn Qayyim ("Shams al-Dīn").
186. See, for example, Ḥumayd, *Inkār*. Incidentally, Ḥarbī, who was once a graduate student at the prestigious Umm al-Qurā University in Mecca, notes that a student at his alma mater named Fayṣal ʿAbd Allāh had recently defended a master's thesis entitled "al-Janna wa-l-nār wa-l-arāʾ fīhimā" (Heaven and hell and the viewpoints regarding them). The thesis argues for universalism by appealing to God's mercy, nobility, willingness to forgive, and wisdom, but it makes no explicit reference to either Ibn Taymiyya or Ibn Qayyim (Ḥarbī, *Kashf*, 22; cf. Samharī's [ed.] remarks in Ibn Taymiyya, *Radd*, 22–23).
187. See Shaltout, *ʿAqīda*, 43–44.
188. See Qaradawi, "Allāh." Here Qaradawi indicates that he has yet to encounter Ibn Taymiyya's *Fanāʾ*.
189. See Robson, "Is the Moslem Hell Eternal?" 392–393.
190. Ali, *Religion of Islam*, 308. In demonstrating God's merciful nature, Ali cites Q. 6:12, 54, 148; 7:156; 11:119 (which, according to Ali, shows that it is "for mercy" that God created humanity); 39:53; and 40:7. According to Ali, since the "ultimate object of the life of man is that he shall live in the service of God" (as indicated by Q. 51:56), purification "by fire" makes one "fit" again "for divine service" (*Religion of Islam*, 308–309).

191. Ali, *Religion of Islam*, 307. This notion of spiritual progress in a temporal Hell appears in his other writings. See, for example, Ali, *Translation of the Holy Quran*, lxvi.
192. Ali, *Religion of Islam*, 309; Ali, *Translation of the Holy Quran*, lxvii.
193. Ali, *Religion of Islam*, 309.
194. Ibid.
195. The Qur'anic verse 4:14 reads, "But those who disobey God and His messenger and overstep His limits will be consigned by God to the Fire, and there they will stay [*khālidan*]—a humiliating torment awaits them." The "limits" here include the inheritance guidelines mentioned earlier in the sura.
196. Ali, *Religion of Islam*, 310; emphasis in the original. See a similar discussion of *abad* in Ali, *Translation of the Holy Quran*, lxvii–lxviii.
197. One exception appears in Ali's translation of Q. 4:168–169: "Those who disbelieve and act unjustly—God will not forgive them nor guide them to a path, Except the path of hell, to abide in it for ever [*abadan*] and this is easy to God" (*Translation of the Holy Quran*, 105). Ali may have chosen this translation because he regarded the passage as a hypothetical statement: while it would be "easy" for God to "guide" some to everlasting damnation, this need not reflect what will actually occur. Interestingly, *abadan* here is translated as "for a long time" (not "for ever") in a revised edition of his translation. See M. Muhammad Ali, *The Holy Quran* (2002).
198. Ali, *Religion of Islam*, 310. Here Ali asserts that each age is equivalent to a year, many years, or eighty years. Since there is no mention of the possibility that these are years wherein a day "is like a thousand years by your reckoning" (Q. 22:47), the reader is left with the impression that Ali's "ages" are relatively(!) brief. Cf. Ali, *Translation of the Holy Quran*, lxviii, 589, where Ali translates *aḥqāban* as "long years," rather than "ages."
199. Ali, *Religion of Islam*, 312–313; Ali, *Translation of the Holy Quran*, lxviii. In *Translation of the Holy Quran*, lxviii, 233, Ali translates the end of Q. 11:108 ("an unceasing gift") as "a gift never to be cut off."
200. Ali, *Religion of Islam*, 311. Here Ali cites Q. 2:167, 5:36–37, 22:22, and 32:20.
201. Ali, *Religion of Islam*, 313; Ali, *Translation of the Holy Quran*, lxviii–lxix. This hadith appears in the *Ṣaḥīḥ al-Bukhārī* collection (in "Kitāb al-tawḥīd") and the *Ṣaḥīḥ Muslim* collection (in "Kitāb al-īmān").
202. Ali, *Religion of Islam*, 313. Both Ibn Taymiyya and Ibn Qayyim cite this hadith in the context of discussing deliverance from chastisement while Hell still exists; neither presents the "handful of God" as direct evidence for universal salvation (see Ibn Taymiyya, *Radd*, 76–77; Ibn Qayyim, *Ḥādī*, 617–618).
203. Ali, *Religion of Islam*, 313–314. Here Ali notes that these "other Companions" include "Ibn 'Umar, Jābir, Abū Sa'īd, Abū Huraira, etc." Assuming that "Ibn 'Umar" is actually Ibn 'Amr, then these are the very Companions cited by Ibn Taymiyya in the *Fanā'*. Of these Companions, Ali only mentions 'Umar ibn

al-Khaṭṭāb by name in the preface to his translation of the Qur'an when discussing evidence for the temporality of Hell (*Translation of the Holy Quran*, lxix).

204. Ali, *Religion of Islam*, 313–314.
205. See Friedmann, *Prophecy Continuous*, particularly pages 71–6; Friedmann, "Aḥmadīyah," 81.
206. Ali, *Religion of Islam*, 314. Ibn Qayyim cites this prophetic report in the *Ḥādī*, 617, but not as direct evidence for universalism. Versions of this hadith appear in the *Ṣaḥīḥ al-Bukhārī* collection (in "Kitāb al-īmān," "Kitāb al-riqāq," and "Kitāb al-tawḥīd"). Ali refers to this report in passing in *Translation of the Holy Quran*, lxix. In his own translation of the Qur'an, Muhammad Asad cites this report as evidence for universalism, which he, too, espouses. See Asad, *Message of the Qur'ān*, 813n10, where Asad quotes this hadith, and 1055n12 (a footnote to Q. 78:23), where he refers to it while making the case for noneternal damnation. In a footnote to Q. 6:128, he notes, "Some of the great Muslim theologians conclude from" Q. 6:128 and 11:107 and "several well-authenticated" prophetic reports "that—contrary to the bliss of paradise, which will be of unlimited duration—the suffering of the sinners in the life to come will be limited by God's mercy" (*Message of the Qur'ān*, 220n114). It would seem that Asad here has in mind Ibn Taymiyya, whom he elsewhere refers to as one "of the great Muslim thinkers" (ibid., 231n3).
207. See, for example, the *Ṣaḥīḥ al-Bukhārī* collection (in "Kitāb al-riqāq" and "Kitāb al-fitan").
208. Muhammad, *Supreme Wisdom*, 44. This statement also appears in Muhammad, *Supreme Wisdom: Vol. 2*, 53.
209. Muhammad, *Supreme Wisdom*, 51. This statement also appears in Muhammad, *Supreme Wisdom: Vol. 2*, 67.
210. A. Yusuf Ali often uses the expression "for ever" when translating passages pertaining to the duration of damnation. For instance, he translates a portion of Q. 6:128 as "The Fire be your dwelling-place: You will dwell therein for ever" (*Qur'ān*, 327; here the Qur'an has the word *khālidīn*). In a footnote following the exception within this verse (which he translates as "Except as God willeth"), he broaches the topic of limited chastisement: "Eternity and infinity are abstract terms. They have no precise meaning in our human experience. The qualification, 'except as God willeth,' makes it more intelligible, as we can form some idea—however inadequate—of a Will and Plan, and we know God by His attribute of Mercy as well as of Justice" (ibid., n951). In a footnote to Q. 11:107, however, Yusuf Ali notes that the "majority of Muslim theologians" reject the idea of a noneternal punishment and concludes, "This is not the place to enter into this tremendous controversy" (*Holy Qur'ān*, 543n1608).
211. It is perhaps no coincidence that of all the names Elijah Muhammad could have bestowed on legendary boxer Cassius Clay, he chose Muhammad Ali. If

The Supreme Wisdom is any indication, Muhammad Ali of Lahore seems to have left a profound impression on Elijah Muhammad. When quoting from the Qur'an, Elijah Muhammad usually follows Muhammad Ali's translation with minor modifications, replacing, for example, *Messenger* with *Apostle* (in Q. 61:9) (Muhammad, *Supreme Wisdom*, 43; Ali, *Translation of the Holy Quran*, 554) or *thee* with *you* (in Q. 7:18) (Muhammad, *Supreme Wisdom*, 25; Ali, *Translation of the Holy Quran*, 154). Additionally, some of Elijah Muhammad's pronouncements bear an uncanny resemblance to those made by Muhammad Ali. Consider, for instance, Elijah Muhammad's portrayal of Paradise (in *Supreme Wisdom: Vol. 2*, 40–41 and, in an alternative arrangement, in *Supreme Wisdom*, 25–26): "Everyone of us—the so-called Negroes—who accepts the religion of Islam and follows what Allah has revealed to me will begin enjoying the [Hereafter] life here, now! Yes, the glorious joy and happiness is yours for the asking, my people. Accept Islam and see your God in truth, and the righteous will meet and embrace you with peace (As-Salaam-Alaikum).... This is the time when you enter such life, for your God is here in Person.... The Righteous will make an unlimited progress in the Hereafter; peace, joy and happiness will have no end. Wars will be forgotten; there will be no place for disagreement.... 'O soul that is at rest, return to your Lord, well-pleased with Him, well-pleasing; So enter among My servants and enter into My Paradise' [Q. 89:27–30]." In the introduction to his translation—just before his discussion of universal salvation—Muhammad Ali writes, "Paradise and Hell begin in this very life... the fruits which the righteous shall find in paradise shall be the same as were given to them in this life.... These are the fruits of good deeds and the sustenance which the righteous find in the remembrance of God.... The soul that has found rest in God is admitted into paradise in this life: 'O soul that art at rest! return to thy Lord, well-pleased with Him, well-pleasing Him; so enter among My servants and enter into My garden' [Q. 89:27–30].... The highest bliss of paradise is plainly stated to be the pleasure of God, the greatest spiritual blessing which the righteous strive for in this life, and by attaining which they enter into paradise in this very life.... There is no grief, fatigue or toil therein, and the heart is purified of all rancour and jealousy, peace and security reigning on all sides.... 'They shall not hear therein vain or sinful discourse, except the word peace, peace' [Q. 56:25–26].... Not only does paradise admit the righteous to high places, but it is in fact the starting-point for a new advancement, there being higher and higher places still" (*Translation of the Holy Quran*, lxiv–lxvi). Cf. Curtis, *Black Muslim Religion in the Nation of Islam*, 46–47, 49, 205n43, where Edward Curtis discusses Elijah Muhammad's use and limited critique of Muhammad Ali's translation and commentary. Elijah Muhammad may have found Ali's depiction of the afterlife appealing, in part, because of its apparent consonance with the spiritual (rather than physical) conception of the afterlife advanced by proponents of the American New Thought Movement. For a treatment of this movement and the context in which it arose, see Albanese, *Republic of Mind and Spirit*; for a look at this movement's influence on the Nation of Islam, at least with regard to dietary ideals, see Griffith, *Born Again Bodies*, 155–159.

212. See Curtis, *Black Muslim Religion in the Nation of Islam*, 12, 196n51.

213. Another intriguing possible link is to Sir Muhammad Iqbal (d. 1938), the celebrated South Asian poet-philosopher. In his monumental work *The Reconstruction of Religious Thought*, a collection of several lectures by Iqbal that was first published in 1930 (and published with an additional chapter in 1934), Iqbal makes some statements that parallel those of Muhammad Ali: "Heaven and Hell are states, not localities.... There is no such thing as eternal damnation in Islam. The word 'eternity' used in certain verses, relating to Hell, is explained by the Quran itself to mean only a period of time (78:23). Time cannot be wholly irrelevant to the development of personality. Character tends to become permanent; its reshaping must require time. Hell, therefore, as conceived by the Quran, is not a pit of everlasting torture inflicted by a revengeful God; it is a corrective experience which may make a hardened ego once more sensitive to the living breeze of Divine Grace. Nor is Heaven a holiday. Life is one and continuous. Man marches always onward to receive ever fresh illuminations from an Infinite Reality" (123). Iqbal was certainly familiar with the Ahmadiyya. See, for example, his critique of the movement in *Islam and Ahmadism*. Despite his criticisms of the Ahmadiyya, Iqbal is known to have been an eclectic thinker. It is for future studies to determine whether there is indeed a link here of some sort between Iqbal and Ali or Iqbal and a medieval universalist such as Ibn Qayyim.

214. See Robson, "Is the Moslem Hell Eternal?" 393, where Robson, in his conclusion, makes a passing reference to *The Religion of Islam*, describing it as Ali's "more recent book," and warns readers not to consider the doctrines expounded therein to be representative of mainstream Muslim thought.

215. Robson, "Is the Moslem Hell Eternal?" 387. See also ibid., 388. Robson also takes issue with Ali's selective translation of the word *khuld*, which, like *khulūd*, has the root *kh-l-d* (ibid., 386). Ali translates *shajarat al-khuld*, which appears in Q. 20:120 in reference to Adam and the forbidden tree, as "the tree of immortality" and *jannat al-khuld*, which appears in Q. 25:15 in reference to Paradise, as "the abiding garden." In reference to Hell, however, he translates *dār al-khuld* (Q. 41:28) as "the house of long abiding."

216. Robson, "Is the Moslem Hell Eternal?" 387.

217. Ibid.

218. Ibid., 389.

219. Ibid., 388–390.

220. Ibid., 391.

221. Ibid. This account appears in the *Musnad Aḥmad* hadith collection.
222. Robson, "Is the Moslem Hell Eternal?" 391–392.
223. See Ali, *Translation of the Holy Quran*, lxix.
224. Robson, "Is the Moslem Hell Eternal?" 389.
225. Ibid., 392.
226. Ibid., 390.
227. Ibid., 392–393.
228. Although Ibn Qayyim states in the *Shifāʾ* that satans (*shayāṭīn*) are beings who only commit evil (207), one should not take from this that they could never be rectified. In fact, Ibn Qayyim's argument for universalism in the *Ṣawāʿiq* appears in the context of addressing the question of why God would create satans and unbelievers in the first place (see 2:630–631).
229. As with Muslim interpretations of Q. 7:40, some scholars of the Bible argue that "camel" here should be "rope."
230. Ibn Taymiyya, *Radd*, 62.
231. Of course, if we privilege the Khārijite and Muʿtazilite perspectives, we would have to consider an alternative conspiracy theory: the earliest Muslims conceived of Hell as being completely inescapable, and later theologians, particularly during the second/eighth century, reimagined Gehenna as a gateway to Heaven for sinners who were believers. See Feras Hamza's fascinating discussion of this in his book *To Hell and Back* (especially chap. 3). This theory is only tenable if we assume that a great many reports ascribed to the Prophet and his Companions were fabricated relatively early in Islamic history and then later deemed reliable by most exegetes and authentic by most hadith collectors.

CHAPTER 4

1. Haim, *Arab Nationalism*, 20.
2. See Hourani, *Arabic Thought in the Liberal Age*, 224–226; Shahin, "Rashīd Riḍā, Muḥammad," 508–509.
3. Although he claimed to be an Afghan and spent much of his youth in Afghanistan, Afghānī was probably of Iranian Shīʿite origin. See Keddie, *Islamic Response to Imperialism*, 4–9.
4. Riḍā, *Tārīkh*, 303. My translation here loosely follows that of Hourani in *Arabic Thought in the Liberal Age*, 226.
5. Badawi, *Reformers of Egypt*, 97.
6. See Shahin, "Salafīyah," 30–34. Bannā was so impressed by *al-Manār* that he briefly attempted to continue it after Riḍā's death (see Hourani, *Arabic Thought in the Liberal Age*, 360). The liberalist legacy of Afghānī and ʿAbduh lived on, not with Riḍā and Bannā but with figures such as the Egyptian jurist ʿAlī ʿAbd al-Rāziq (d. 1966), who favored the abolition of the caliphate.

7. Some maintain that the final Qur'anic verse treated in Riḍā's *al-Manār* was in fact 12:25 or 12:52. According to Aḥmad al-Sharabāṣī (d. 1980), however, Riḍā's involvement ceased at Q. 12:101. See Sharabāṣī, *Riḍā*, 157–159.
8. See Riḍā, *Tafsīr*, 1:14; 5:441, 476. ʿAbduh also published his own brief commentary on sura 103 ("al-ʿAṣr") in 1903 (see *ʿAṣr*) and, the following year, the last thirtieth part of the Qur'an (suras 78–114) (see *ʿAmma*).
9. Riḍā, *Tafsīr*, 2:498.
10. See Jansen's discussion of the nature and popularity of ʿAbduh and Riḍā's commentary in *Interpretation of the Koran in Modern Egypt*, 18–34. On the widespread impact of *al-Manār* on early twentieth-century Muslim societies, see Dudoignon, Komatsu, and Kosugi, *Intellectuals in the Modern Islamic World*, part 1.
11. Sachedina, "Qur'ān and Other Religions," 308n10.
12. Esack, *Qur'ān, Liberation and Pluralism*, 165–166.
13. Ibid., 171.
14. Winter, "Last Trump Card," 135.
15. McAuliffe, *Qur'ānic Christians*, 179.
16. See Riḍā, *Tafsīr*, 1:333–336. Cf. Esack's discussion of this in *Qur'ān, Liberation and Pluralism*, 165, 167–168.
17. Riḍā, *Tafsīr*, 1:336–338. See also ibid., 1:428–430, 496.
18. Ibid., 5:431–434, 6:479.
19. Ibid., 3:257–260. Cf. Esack's related remarks in *Qur'ān, Liberation and Pluralism*, 127–128, 130. In Riḍā's discussion of Q. 2:167, he warns that the reference therein to damned unbelievers could include those who merely call themselves Muslim (*Tafsīr*, 2:81ff.).
20. Riḍā, *Tafsīr*, 6:412ff. Cf. Esack's related remarks in *Qur'ān, Liberation and Pluralism*, 167.
21. This verse (Q. 5:49) reads as follows: "So [Prophet] judge between them according to what God has sent down. Do not follow their whims, and take good care that they do not tempt you away from any of what God has sent down to you. If they turn away, remember that God intends to punish them for some of the sins they have committed: a great many people are wrongdoers."
22. Riḍā, *Tafsīr*, 6:410–422. See ibid., 10:279–411, where Riḍā develops this point in his lengthy discussion of Q. 9:29–35. Affirmations of Islamic superiority also appear in ʿAbduh's own writings. In his book *al-Islām wa-l-Naṣrāniyya maʿa al-ʿilm wa-l-madaniyya* (Islam and Christianity in relation to science and civilization), for example, we read that, in contrast to Christianity, Islam is "the religion of refinement and true perfection" (9).
23. Riḍā, *Tafsīr*, 6:476.
24. Ibid., 10:340. See ibid., 6:86–95, 307–310; 10:329–340.
25. Ibid., 3:258–259. The Arians reportedly held that Jesus was the created Son of God—a position that is ostensibly less problematic according to Islamic thought than the council's pronouncement that Jesus was "begotten, not made," and

of the same substance as and coeternal with God the Father. For a thorough study of Riḍā's polemics on Christianity, which were often produced in response to the writings of missionaries, see Ryad, *Islamic Reformism and Christianity*. See also Riḍā, *Tafsīr*, 1:338, where Riḍā describes Christians as having become "the most insolent community in the world."

26. Riḍā, *Waḥy*, 26. Riḍā makes similar pronouncements elsewhere, as in the *Tafsīr*, 10:361–362, and *al-Manār* 33, no. 2 (April 1933): 104–105.
27. Riḍā, *Tafsīr*, 4:315–318.
28. Ibid., 6:276. See also ibid., 6:7–10. Riḍā maintains that although most people—including most unbelievers—accept the existence of a creator and designer, the most common form of unbelief in his day is unbelief in all prophets and the divine origins of their revelations. On this point, see ibid., 6:8, 8:274. See also ibid., 10:352, where Riḍā claims that while only a minority of modern European intellectuals are atheists, only a minority believe in a retributive afterlife.
29. See McAuliffe's translation of Riḍā, *Tafsīr* (4:317–318), in *Qur'ānic Christians*, 173, 176. My insertion of "certain self-absorbed, stubborn People of the Book" is based on Riḍā's clarification in the *Tafsīr*, 4:318.
30. Riḍā, *Tafsīr*, 1:337–338. Here ʿAbduh also reportedly cited Q. 4:165, which states that messengers were sent "so that people would have no excuse before God."
31. Riḍā, *Tafsīr*, 1:338. Cf. Q. 28:59, where this phrase (*mā kunnā*) is used in reference to the destruction of "towns": "Your Lord would never [*mā kāna*] destroy towns without first raising a messenger in their midst to recite Our messages to them, nor would We [*mā kunnā*] destroy towns unless their inhabitants were evildoers." No similar restriction to towns appears in Q. 17:15. Assuming that the statement "We do not punish until We have sent a messenger" stands as a general principle applicable both to this life and to the next, it is interesting that the preceding verse (17:14) concerns Judgment Day, while the succeeding verse (17:16) turns our attention to the destruction of "towns." Cf. a related discussion in Riḍā, *Tafsīr*, 6:72–73.
32. Riḍā, *Tafsīr*, 6:73.
33. Ibid., 1:338–339.
34. Ibid. My reading of this passage differs markedly from that of Jane McAuliffe, who takes Riḍā here to be referring to the people of the gap "living on the American continent in the period between Jesus and Muḥammad" (*Qur'ānic Christians*, 114). To my mind, both Riḍā's wording and his reference to Ghazālī's post-Muḥammadan criterion are difficult to harmonize with McAuliffe's interpretation.
35. Riḍā, *Tafsīr*, 1:339. See Riḍā's related remarks in ibid., 6:72–75. Before Riḍā, the Indian modernist reformer Sir Sayyid Aḥmad Khān (d. 1898), in his *al-Naẓar fī baʿḍ masā'il al-imām Abī Ḥāmid Muḥammad al-Ghazālī* (Reflections on some of the matters pertaining to the imam Abū Ḥāmid Muḥammad al-Ghazālī), critiques Ghazālī's criterion under the assumption that it allows for the salvation

of polytheists, who, according to Khān, are guilty of *shirk*, regardless of whether they had been exposed to the message. By the same token, Khān held that non-Muslim monotheists could be saved. See Christian Troll's brief discussion of this in "Salvation of Non-Muslims," 183–186.

36. *Al-Manār* 7, no. 13 (September 1904): 496.
37. *Al-Manār* 20, no. 10 (October 1918): 448; *al-Manār* 33, no. 9 (February 1933): 674–675.
38. See Riḍā, *Tafsīr*, 8:431–435.
39. Ibid., 1:337.
40. *Al-Manār* 4, no. 12 (August 1901): 448–451. On this point, see Ryad, *Islamic Reformism and Christianity*, 186ff. See also Riḍā, *Tafsīr*, 4:316, where Riḍā conveys ʿAbduh's teaching that the current scriptures used by the People of the Book are sources of delusion and misguidance.
41. Riḍā, *Tafsīr*, 1:337–338. See *al-Manār* 25, no. 3 (March 1924): 227, where Riḍā opines that religions like Buddhism and Zoroastrianism were divinely inspired; however, he notes, their revelations have become so corrupted that the truth of their divine message is now obscured.
42. *Al-Manār* 6, no. 2 (April 1903): 47–54.
43. Cf. *al-Manār* 4, no. 13 (September 1901): 497, where Riḍā briefly remarks that the unreached are excused, while making no reference to the reached.
44. *Al-Manār* 6, no. 7 (June 1903): 267–268. See Riḍā, *Tafsīr*, 5:410, where Riḍā, referencing ʿAbduh, indicates that the majority view among Ashʿarites is that God will excuse the sincere truth-seekers among the reached.
45. *Al-Manār* 7, no. 7 (June 1904): 258–259.
46. Ibid. This exact quote also appears in fatwas published in *al-Manār* 4, no. 13 (September 1901): 497, and *al-Manār* 7, no. 13 (September 1904): 496. In both cases, Riḍā addresses questions concerning the status of unreached non-Muslims.
47. See Jackson's translation of Ghazālī, *Fayṣal*, in *On the Boundaries of Theological Tolerance in Islam*, 126; Ghazālī, *Fayṣal*, 84.
48. See *al-Manār* 13, no. 8 (September 1910): 572–576. See also *al-Manār* 4, no. 13 (September 1901): 497, where Riḍā indicates that the proper method of calling people to Islam (*daʿwa*) in modern times is unlike that of the Prophet's era; and *al-Manār* 3, no. 21 (September 1900): 481–490 (especially 485), where Riḍā advises his fellow Muslims to call Others to Islam in a manner that prompts investigation.
49. *Al-Manār* 13, no. 8 (September 1910): 574–575.
50. See ibid., 572–576. In a relatively brief fatwa published several years earlier, Riḍā explicitly indicates that these are the only two groups of unexcused non-Muslims. Riḍā issued this particular fatwa in response to a letter by a certain Maḥmūd of Sudan, a railroad employee who had inquired as to the status of the unreached. See *al-Manār* 7, no. 13 (September 1904): 495–496.
51. See *al-Manār* 13, no. 8 (September 1910): 574–575.

52. See, for instance, Ṭabarī, *Jāmiʿ*, 4:2540; Zamakhsharī, *Kashshāf*, 1:599; Qurṭubī, *Jāmiʿ*, 7:130–131.
53. See *al-Manār* 15, no. 3 (March 1912): 168–176.
54. Riḍā, *Tafsīr*, 5:410.
55. Ibid.
56. See ibid., 5:410–412.
57. Ibid., 5:410.
58. Ibid.
59. Ibid., 5:416.
60. Here Riḍā uses the term *kuffār* (sing. *kāfir*). Although this term is typically used in the Qur'an to connote "unbelievers" worthy of Hell, it is often employed in Islamic discourse to mean anyone who is not legally a Muslim. (See my discussion of this in chapter 1.) Here Riḍā must be using this term to mean simply "non-Muslims," as he is referring to the unreached.
61. Riḍā, *Tafsīr*, 5:412–413.
62. Ibid., 5:414.
63. Ibid., 5:418. Riḍā makes this statement at the beginning of his commentary on the next verse (Q. 4:116).
64. Riḍā, *Tafsīr*, 5:414–415.
65. *Al-Manār* 13, no. 8 (September 1910): 575–576. Cf. *al-Manār* 33, no. 2 (April 1933): 106, where Riḍā laments the general failure of the Muslim world to convey the message of Islam in a manner that would prompt investigation. Here Riḍā seems to imply that a revival of the caliphate, which was permanently abolished in 1924, would resolve this problem.
66. *Al-Manār* 33, no. 2 (April 1933): 106.
67. Riḍā, *Tafsīr*, 5:413.
68. Ibid. See Riḍā's related remarks in ibid., 10:345–363.
69. See Riḍā's related remarks in ibid., 12:220–222, 246; *al-Manār* 13, no. 11 (December 1910): 868–870.
70. Riḍā, *Tafsīr*, 12:52–53.
71. Ibid., 4:65–66.
72. See Jackson's translation of Ghazālī, *Fayṣal*, in *On the Boundaries of Theological Tolerance in Islam*, 126; Ghazālī, *Fayṣal*, 84.
73. Riḍā, *Tafsīr*, 12:162.
74. *Al-Manār* 8, no. 4 (April 1905): 154–155. Here Riḍā writes that those who are most developed intellectually and spiritually are "the perfect believers" (*al-muʾminūn al-kāmilūn*), and they are "small" in number. Between them and the worst of humanity, the rejecters of revelation, are various classes of people, including the truly unreached and those who accept the message but fail to "uphold its rights."
75. Notice that when describing Ghazālī's first category of non-Muslims, Riḍā provides a medieval example: the inhabitants of America during Ghazālī's time. The fact that it was becoming increasingly difficult to identify modern

non-Muslims who had never heard of the Prophet may have something to do with Riḍā's insistence that the distinction between Ghazālī's first and third categories is superfluous.

76. See, for instance, Riḍā, *Tafsīr*, 10:346, 354–355.
77. See *al-Manār* 11, no. 8 (September 1908): 615, where Riḍā asserts that the Muslim scholars of his age had failed to present Islam in a manner that would prompt investigation, that is, until ʿAbduh produced his modernist treatise *Risālat al-tawḥīd* (*The Theology of Unity*). See *al-Manār* 33, no. 2 (April 1933): 106, where Riḍā expresses his hope that his own work would similarly lead sincere non-Muslims, including European scholars, to contemplate Islam.
78. See Riḍā, *Tafsīr*, 10:355, 362, 384–392.
79. Ryad demonstrates this in *Islamic Reformism and Christianity*.
80. See, in particular, Riḍā, *Tafsīr*, 1:492–496.
81. The only instance after the 1910 fatwa in which Riḍā makes any explicit reference to Ghazālī's *Fayṣal*, the treatise in which Ghazālī presents his criterion for salvation, is in *al-Manār* in April 1935—just four months before his death. Rather than offering a critique of the *Fayṣal*, Riḍā honors the Saudi monarch Abdul Aziz Al Saud (d. 1953) by calling him the full title of the *Fayṣal* (*Fayṣal al-tafriqa bayna al-Islām wa-l-zandaqa*). See *al-Manār* 34, no. 9 (April 1935): 700. Needless to say, it would be a stretch to deduce from this either an affirmation or a negation of the kind of interreligious inclusivism Riḍā had expounded in his earlier works.
82. Riḍā, *Tafsīr*, 2:53.
83. Ibid., 2:54.
84. For the original printing, see *al-Manār* 7, no. 7 (June 1904): 252–253. This issue also contains the aforementioned query by Muḥammad, the prison clerk, who asks, "Is it true that the unbeliever and the Christian will remain in Hell?" In his response, Riḍā comments that the "established" view among rationalist theologians (*mutakallimūn*) is that true unbelievers (and not simply non-Muslims) "will remain in the abode that God the Exalted prepared for [them]." Here Riḍā gives no indication that he would qualify or emend this doctrine. See ibid., 258–259.
85. See *al-Manār* 22, no. 1 (December 1920): 13–33; *al-Manār* 22, no. 2 (January 1921): 81–92.
86. Riḍā, *Tafsīr*, 8:68.
87. Ibid., 8:69. The Prophet is said to have spoken these words after reciting Q. 11:106–107. See Riḍā, *Tafsīr*, 8:69–70, where Riḍā proceeds to list competing interpretations of the exception in Q. 11:107 (and, by extension, that in 6:128): it applies to all Qur'anic threats; it has been abrogated by Medinan passages that affirm everlasting damnation; it pertains only to sinning believers who will be saved through intercession; it affirms God's will to command the Fire to consume its inhabitants; and it signifies either prolongation or reduction of punishment. Riḍā informs us that his source here is the premodern Egyptian scholar Jalāl al-Dīn al-Suyūṭī's commentary on Q. 11:106–107 in his *al-Durr al-manthūr fī al-tafsīr al-maʾthūr*. Cf. Riḍā's related remarks in the *Tafsīr*, 12:160–161.

88. Riḍā, *Tafsīr*, 8:70.
89. See ibid., 8:70–98.
90. Ibid., 8:99.
91. Ibn Qayyim, *Shifā'*, 2:228.
92. Ibn Qayyim, *Ṣawā'iq*, 2:663, translated by Hoover in "Islamic Universalism," 196.
93. See *al-Manār* 19, no. 1 (June 1916): 56, where Riḍā includes the *Ṣawā'iq* in a list of works by Ibn Qayyim without commenting on its content. As I noted earlier, it is only the abridgment of the *Ṣawā'iq* that preserves Ibn Qayyim's case for universalism. This abridgment was published by the Meccan company al-Maṭba'a al-Salafiyya in 1929, over five years before Riḍā passed away. It is, therefore, possible that Riḍā encountered it without ever writing about it or that he read it but somehow missed Ibn Qayyim's change of approach.
94. *Al-Manār* 12, no. 10 (November 1909): 786. Ibn Qayyim's *Shifā'*—but not the universalist discourse therein—is occasionally referenced in *al-Manār* (as in vol. 9, no. 2 [March 1906]: 105, 107–108).
95. Riḍā, *Tafsīr*, 8:99. See ibid., 8:98–99.
96. Ibid., 8:99.
97. *Al-Manār* 22, no. 4 (March 1921): 315–320.
98. Ibid., 320.
99. Riḍā published two rejoinders. According to the first, by a certain Ibrāhīm, it is unthinkable that God would accept the repentance of associationists (*mushrikūn*) in Hell and that the damned, and indeed all of humanity, would dwell in Paradise. The second rejoinder, by a certain 'Abd al-Ẓāhir, attempts to undermine the reliability of the evidence marshaled by Ibn Qayyim, particularly the ostensibly universalist reports ascribed to the Prophet's Companions. Here Riḍā explicitly states that his intention is not to engage in debate, thus leaving the reader to suspect that Riḍā is unconvinced. See *al-Manār* 22, no. 5 (April 1921): 379–389. Two issues later, Riḍā published another rejoinder by the same 'Abd al-Ẓāhir. Here 'Abd al-Ẓāhir challenges Riḍā's reading of scripture and his understanding of the terms used in reference to the duration of Hell, such as *khulūd* and *abadan*. Once again unconvinced, Riḍā responds in endnotes inserted at specific points in the text. See *al-Manār* 22, no. 7 (August 1921): 553–560.
100. *Al-Manār* 22, no. 4 (March 1921): 315.
101. Riḍā, *Tafsīr*, 8:68.
102. *Al-Manār* 8, no. 4 (April 1905): 155.
103. See, for instance, *al-Manār* 4, no. 13 (September 1901): 497.
104. See, for example, Q. 2:261; 4:40, 173; 24:38; 35:30. Prophetic reports of multiplied reward appear, among other places, in the *Ṣaḥīḥ al-Bukhārī* hadith collection (in "Kitāb al-īmān").
105. Riḍā, *Tafsīr*, 12:161–162. Cf. related remarks in ibid., 12:214, 216.

106. Ibid., 12:215–216. Cf. chapter 3, note 147.
107. Riḍā, *Tafsīr*, 12:216.
108. Ibid.
109. See Shawkānī, *Fatḥ*, 5:366. See also chapter 3, note 106. I should mention that Shawkānī's commentary on Q. 11:106–108, taken in isolation, might give the impression that he was at least open to the possibility of universal salvation. He cites the familiar, ostensibly universalist reports ascribed to the Prophet's Companions; however, he does so primarily to reject the claim that sinning believers will be forever damned. See Shawkānī, *Fatḥ*, 2:525–528.
110. See Khān, *Yaqẓat*, 15–18 (especially 16–17), 122–126. See also chapter 3, note 102.
111. See Qaradawi, *Fatāwā*, 3:154–156; Shaltout, *Tafsīr*, 228–229 (on Q. 4:115). According to Shaltout, Q. 4:116, which condemns *shirk*, might be an indication that God generally condemns nonmonotheists, as His existence and oneness are self-evident (*Tafsīr*, 230).
112. See Qutb, *Ẓilāl*, 1:75–76.
113. Ibid., 1:377.
114. Ibid., 4:2217, 2:759.
115. Ibid., 2:809–814.
116. See ibid., 3:1293.
117. Ibid., 6:3947–3952.
118. See Qutb, *Maʿālim*, chap. 9.
119. Qutb, *Ẓilāl*, 3:1207.
120. Ibid., 4:1929.
121. Ibid., 6:3807.
122. Ibid., 2:813.
123. Ibid., 5:2882–2883.
124. See, for example, ibid., 3:1638–1639, where Qutb approvingly quotes a significant portion of Riḍā's discourse on the trinity. As for Ibn Qayyim, it is widely known that in the *Maʿālim* Qutb invokes him throughout the chapter on jihad and cites his fairly lengthy discussion of the Prophet's evolving relationship with non-Muslims (see *Maʿālim*, chap. 4).
125. See, for example, Maududi, *Ḥaqīqat*, 64, where Maududi writes that an Islamic state should expand its borders in order to spread the religion of Islam, which, he notes in passing and without qualification, is the only path to salvation. Additionally, Qutb's treatment of certain aforementioned Qur'anic passages often parallels Maududi's (originally Urdu) commentary on the Qur'an—a three-decade-long project that began in the early 1940s. See, for instance, Maududi, *Tafhīm*, 1:74n80 (on Q. 2:62), 4:32n34 (on Q. 7:46–49), 5:112n108 (on Q. 11:106–107). In his commentary on Q. 78:23, Maududi explicitly affirms damnationism. Despite all this, he occasionally withholds judgment, as in his discussion of Q. 17:15. Here Maududi states that Muslims should not concern themselves with the question of whether

certain non-Muslims will be saved, for only God knows the answer (*Tafhīm*, 6:131n17).

126. See Naik, "Will Humans Born in Non Muslim Family Be Punished by GOD?"
127. See Naik, "Will the Righteous Non Muslims Go to Heaven or Hell?"
128. Esack, *Qur'ān, Liberation and Pluralism*, 14.
129. Ibid., 162.
130. Ibid., 158–159. See also Q. 2:113, 120, 135; 5:18.
131. Esack, *Qur'ān, Liberation and Pluralism*, 169, 173–174.
132. Ibid., 139.
133. Ibid. See also ibid., 134–144.
134. Ibid., 174.
135. Ibid.
136. Ibid., 167–171.
137. Ibid., 126–134, 166–172. Sounding much like Riḍā, Esack describes this *dīn* as "an active response to the will of God rather than ethno-social membership of a particular group" (ibid., 133). See also ibid., 126–134, 166–172.
138. Ibid., 174.
139. Ibid., 136.
140. Ibid., 260–261.
141. Ibid., 175.
142. Ibid., 154–155.
143. Ibid., 104. Rather than providing specific examples of what would constitute *shirk* today, Esack calls for a thorough reassessment of the boundaries of exclusion and inclusion (ibid., 260–261).
144. Ibid., 156.
145. Ibid.
146. See Sachedina, "Qur'ān and Other Religions," 298. See also Sachedina, *Islamic Roots of Democratic Pluralism*; Sachedina, "Is Islamic Revelation an Abrogation of Judeo-Christian Revelation?" For additional examples of the pluralist emphasis on good works, as opposed to theological doctrines, see Engineer, *Rethinking Issues in Islam*, 14–15, 60ff.; Engineer, "Islam and Pluralism"; Afsaruddin, "Hermeneutics of Inter-faith Relations."
147. Sachedina, "Qur'ān and Other Religions," 300.
148. Ibid., 304–306. Cf. Rizvi, "Primordial *e pluribus unum*?" 30, where Sajjad Rizvi critiques Sachedina's use of Q. 2:213 and his reading of Ṭabāṭabā'ī.
149. Sachedina, "Qur'ān and Other Religions," 306. Cf. Asani, "So That You May Know One Another," 44–45, where Ali Asani suggests that "while not all Muslims were comfortable with the broadening of the term 'People of the Book' to include religious scriptures and traditions not mentioned specifically by name in the Quran," the "pluralistic nature of the Quranic worldview" allows for precisely this.
150. Ayoub, "Nearest in Amity," 148.

151. Ibid., 162.
152. Ibid., 158.
153. Rahman, *Major Themes of the Qur'an*, 165–166.
154. Ibid., 164. Cf. ibid., 168–169, where Rahman discusses the Qur'anic rejection of the Christian doctrines of the trinity and the incarnation.
155. Representative works by Nasr include (but are not limited to) *Knowledge and the Sacred*, *Sufi Essays*, "Religion and Religions," and his various "Replies" (for example, "Reply to Sally B. King") in *The Philosophy of Seyyed Hossein Nasr*. See Nasr, *Heart of Islam*, 21–22, where Nasr states that, with the coming of Muḥammad, "the earlier prophets lose none of their spiritual significance. Rather, they appear in the Islamic firmament as stars, while the Prophet is like the moon in that Islamic sky"—an alternative to Ibn ʿArabī's Islam-as-sunlight metaphor.
156. Other prominent perennialists—not all of whom label themselves as Muslim—include Ananda Coomaraswamy (d. 1947), Titus Burckhardt (d. 1984), Frithjof Schuon (d. 1998), Martin Lings (d. 2005), Charles Le Gai Eaton (d. 2010), Huston Smith, and William Chittick. For a representative example of a perennialist philosophical work, see Schuon, *Transcendent Unity of Religions*.
157. Shah-Kazemi, *Other in the Light of the One*, xxiv. Cf. Hick, *Metaphor of God Incarnate*, 146, where Hick describes religious experience as a "cognitive response to the universal presence of the ultimate divine Reality that, in itself, exceeds human conceptuality." Accordingly, Hick states that the major religious traditions are partly "human creations." See Aslan, *Religious Pluralism in Christian and Islamic Philosophy*, where Adnan Aslan compares and contrasts Hick and the perennialist Nasr. An example of a Hick-inspired scholar of Muslim heritage is the Indian thinker Hasan Askari (d. 1978). See, for example, Askari, "Within and Beyond the Experience of Religious Diversity."
158. Shah-Kazemi, *Other in the Light of the One*, xxiv. Shah-Kazemi's definition and understanding of "pluralism" can be traced back to the work of Alan Race (see *Christians and Religious Pluralism*) and Gavin D'Costa (see *Theology and Religious Pluralism*). Nevertheless, as Shah-Kazemi observes, Diana Eck's understanding of pluralism (see Eck, *Encountering God*) is closer to his "universalism" (Shah-Kazemi, *Other in the Light of the One*, 249n66).
159. Shah-Kazemi, *Other in the Light of the One*, xxiv–xxv. See ibid., 249–266, where Shah-Kazemi elaborates on the distinction between "universalism" and Hick's pluralism. According to Shah-Kazemi, a problem with Esack's case for pluralism is that "it goes too far in the direction of excluding the exclusivists." This runs counter to Shah-Kazemi's "inclusive Sufi approach," which assumes that all orientations, including the exclusivist, are divinely sanctioned (ibid., 24n45).
160. Ibid., 233. On this point, see Schuon, *Transcendent Unity of Religions*, 36, where Schuon discusses the "contingent superiority" of each divinely inspired religion.

Vincent Cornell adopts a somewhat similar Sufi-inspired pluralist approach in "Practical Sufism."

161. See Qaradawi, *Fatāwā*, 3:151–156.
162. See D'Costa, "John Hick's Transcendental Agnosticism"; Winter, "Last Trump Card," 135–136. Cf. Rizvi, "Primordial *e pluribus unum*?" 34–35, where Rizvi dismisses the pluralist attempt to reconcile competing Buddhist, Muslim, and Christian conceptions of reality and warns of the moral relativism that follows. As Muhammad Legenhausen notes, this reconciliation can lead to "intolerance" of traditional theologies (*Islam and Religious Pluralism*, 81). (This is the problem that Shah-Kazemi in particular attempts to address.) Cf. Soroush, *Ṣirāṭhā*, where Iranian thinker Abdolkarim Soroush asserts that it would be problematic to maintain that one religion must be true and another false because of ostensibly conflicting truth claims concerning, for instance, Jesus' divinity. Instead, Soroush argues, one must consider each religious tradition on its own terms and as a whole. In this light, the various religious systems appear more congruous and may be said to represent different schools of thought, as they reflect different aspects of the same reality. As such, the debate over pluralism should not be confined to an Islamic (or Christian, Jewish, etc.) framework.
163. Winter, "Last Trump Card," 136. See a similar remark in Winter, "Pluralism from a Muslim Perspective," 203. Cf. Rizvi, "Primordial *e pluribus unum*?" 32, where Rizvi makes an analogous criticism of Esack, stating that a "certain ambivalence towards tradition emerges in his approach: an attempt at co-opting it and yet using tradition against itself." Here Rizvi also observes that Esack's pluralism was inspired by a unique apartheid context.
164. Winter, "Last Trump Card," 135. Cf. Winter's more pointed critique of Esack in his online "Book Review of Farid Esack's Qur'an, Liberation and Pluralism."
165. Winter, "Last Trump Card," 144–145. See similar remarks in Winter, "Pluralism from a Muslim Perspective," 207–209.
166. Winter, "Last Trump Card," 137–139, 147–152. See similar remarks in Winter, "Pluralism from a Muslim Perspective," 209ff.
167. Winter, "Last Trump Card," 149–151; Winter, "Pluralism from a Muslim Perspective," 209–210.
168. Winter, "Last Trump Card," 151–152. See Winter's related remarks in ibid., 148–150; Winter, "Pluralism from a Muslim Perspective," 209–211.
169. Winter, "Last Trump Card," 152. This notion of anonymous Christians was popularized during the Second Vatican Council (1962–1965) but remains a point of controversy among Catholics.
170. Winter, "Last Trump Card," 152. See similar remarks in Winter, "Pluralism from a Muslim Perspective," 211.
171. See Legenhausen, "Islam and Religious Pluralism." For further expositions of Legenhausen's "non-reductive pluralism," see his *Islam and Religious Pluralism*,

"A Muslim's Non-Reductive Religious Pluralism," "A Muslim's Proposal," and "On the Plurality of Religious Pluralisms."

172. Legenhausen, "Islam and Religious Pluralism," 132–134.
173. Cf. Muhammad Asad's alternative translation of this passage: "Verily, those who deny God and His apostles by endeavouring to make a distinction between [belief in] God and [belief in] His apostles, and who say, 'We believe in the one but we deny the other,' and want to pursue a path in-between—it is they, they who are truly denying the truth: and for those who deny the truth We have readied shameful suffering" (*Message of the Qur'ān*, 152).
174. See, for instance, Motahhari, *'Adl*, 287–381.
175. Cf. a similar argument in Aslan, "Islam and Religious Pluralism."
176. Legenhausen, "Islam and Religious Pluralism," 141–148. Dara Shikoh (d. 1069/1659) of India, a Moghul prince, claimed that the Upanishads are what the Qur'an (56:77–80) refers to as the "hidden scripture" or "protected record" (*kitāb maknūn*) (see Asani, "So That You May Know One Another," 44). As A. Yusuf Ali would have it, the term *Sabians* in Q. 2:62 "can be extended by analogy to cover earnest followers of Zoroaster, the Vedas, Buddha, Confucius and other Teachers of the moral law" (*Holy Qur'ān*, 33n76). Syed Ashraf Ali seems to support this claim (see "Tolerance and Pluralism in Islam," 62). He also subscribes to the opinion that the fig mentioned in Q. 95:1 ("By the fig, by the olive") is a reference to the Bodhi tree (a fig tree) under which the Buddha attained Nirvana (Ali, "Tolerance and Pluralism in Islam," 65–66). Yusuf Ali cites this opinion but does not seem to find it entirely convincing (*Holy Qur'ān*, 1758n6198). The question of whether the Buddha could have been a prophet and messenger is taken up in Shah-Kazemi, *Common Ground between Islam and Buddhism*, 14–19; and Yusuf, "Buddha in the Qur'ān?"
177. Legenhausen, "Islam and Religious Pluralism," 148.
178. See my brief discussion of the direction and significance of the pluralist-inclusivist debate in Khalil, "Salvation and the 'Other' in Islamic Thought."

Bibliography

Abdel Haleem, M. A. S. *The Qur'an: A New Translation*. Oxford: Oxford University Press, 2008.

ʿAbduh, Muḥammad. *al-Islām wa-l-Naṣrāniyya maʿa al-ʿilm wa-l-madaniyya*. Giza: Maktabat al-Nāfidha, 2006.

———. *Risālat al-tawḥīd*. Cairo: Dār al-Maʿārif, 1966.

———. *Tafsīr Juzʾ ʿAmma*. [Cairo]: M. ʿA. Ṣubayḥ, 1967.

———. *Tafsīr Sūrat al-ʿAṣr*. [Beirut]: Dār al-Kitāb al-Jadīd, 1968.

Abrahamov, Binyamin. "The Creation and Duration of Paradise and Hell in Islamic Theology." *Der Islam* 79 (2002): 87–102.

———. "Ibn Taymiyya on the Agreement of Reason with Tradition." *The Muslim World* 82 (1992): 256–273.

Abu Rumaysah. "Reply to Accusations against Shaykh ul-Islâm ibn Taymiyyah." SunnahOnline.com. Accessed October 3, 2011, http://www.sunnahonline.com/ilm/seerah/0048.htm.

Abul Quasem, Muhammad. *Salvation of the Soul and Islamic Devotions*. London: Kegan Paul, 1983.

Addas, Claude. *Quest for the Red Sulphur: The Life of Ibn ʿArabī*. Translated by P. Kingsley. Cambridge: Islamic Texts Society, 1993.

Afsaruddin, Asma. "The Hermeneutics of Inter-faith Relations: Retrieving Moderation and Pluralism as Universal Principles in Qur'anic Exegeses." *Journal of Religious Ethics* 37 (2009): 331–354.

Albanese, Catherine L. *A Republic of Mind and Spirit: A Cultural History of American Metaphysical Religion*. New Haven, CT: Yale University Press, 2007.

Ali, A. Yusuf. *The Holy Qur'ān: Text, Translation and Commentary*. Brentwood, MD: Amana, 1983.

Ali, Maulana Muhammad. *The Holy Quran: Arabic Text with English Translation, Commentary and Comprehensive Introduction*. Lahore, Pakistan: Ahmadiyya

Movement, 2002. Accessed October 3, 2011, http://www.muslim.org/english-quran/quran.htm.

———. *The Religion of Islam: A Comprehensive Discussion of the Sources, Principles and Practices of Islam*. Cairo: National Publication and Printing House, 1967.

———. *Translation of the Holy Quran (without Arabic Text)*. Lahore, Pakistan: Ahmadiyya Anjuman-i-Ishāʿat-i-Islām, 1934.

Ali, Syed Ashraf. "Tolerance and Pluralism in Islam." *Asian Affairs* 25 (2003): 57–66.

al-Āmidī, Sayf al-Dīn. *Akbār al-afkār fī uṣūl al-dīn*. Edited by A. M. al-Mahdī. 5 vols. Cairo: Maṭbaʿat Dār al-Kutub wa-l-Wathāʾiq al-Qawmiyya, 2002–2004.

Andrae, Tor. *In the Gardens of Myrtles: Studies in Early Islamic Mysticism*. Translated by B. Sharpe. Albany: State University of New York Press, 1987.

———. *Mohammed: The Man and His Faith*. Translated by T. Menzel. New York: Harper and Row, 1960.

al-ʿAqqād, ʿAbbās M. *al-Falsafa al-qurʾāniyya*. Cairo: n.d.

Arberry, A. J. *Revelation and Reason in Islam*. London: George Allen and Unwin, 1957.

Asad, Muhammad. *The Message of the Qurʾān: The Full Account of the Revealed Arabic Text Accompanied by Parallel Transliteration*. Bristol, UK: Book Foundation, 2003.

Asani, Ali S. "'So That You May Know One Another': A Muslim American Reflects on Pluralism and Islam." *Annals of the American Academy of Political and Social Sciences* 588 (2003): 40–51.

al-Ashqar, ʿUmar. *al-Janna wa-l-nār*. Cairo: Dār al-Salām, 2005.

Askari, Hasan. "Within and Beyond the Experience of Religious Diversity." In *The Experience of Religious Diversity*, edited by J. Hick and H. Askari, 191–218. Aldershot, UK: Gower Press, 1985.

Aslan, Adnan. "Islam and Religious Pluralism." *Islamic Quarterly* 40 (1996): 172–187.

———. *Religious Pluralism in Christian and Islamic Philosophy: The Thought of John Hick and Seyyed Hossein Nasr*. Richmond, VA: Curzon Press, 1998.

Aslan, Reza. *No god but God: The Origins, Evolution, and Future of Islam*. New York: Random House, 2006.

Awn, Peter. *Satan's Tragedy and Redemption: Iblīs in Sufi Psychology*. Leiden: Brill, 1983.

Aydin, Mahmut. "Religious Pluralism: A Challenge for Muslims—A Theological Evaluation." *Journal of Ecumenical Studies* 38 (2001): 330–352.

Ayoub, Mahmoud. "Nearest in Amity: Christians in the Qurʾān and Contemporary Exegetical Tradition." *Islam and Christian–Muslim Relations* 8 (1997): 145–164.

———. *The Qur'an and Its Interpreters*, vol. 1. Albany: State University of New York Press, 1984.

Badawi, Muhammad Zaki. *The Reformers of Egypt: A Critique of Al-Afghani, Abduh and Ridha*. London: Croom Helm, 1978.

al-Baghdādī, ʿAbd al-Qāhir. *Uṣūl al-dīn*. Istanbul: Dār al-Funūn al-Turkiyya, 1928.

Baljon, J. M. S. *Modern Muslim Koran Interpretation (1880–1960)*. Leiden: Brill, 1961.

Bamyeh, Mohammad A. *The Social Origins of Islam: Mind, Economy, Discourse*. Minneapolis: University of Minnesota Press, 1999.

Bell, Joseph N. *Love Theory in Later Ḥanbalite Islam*. Albany: State University of New York Press, 1979.

Bouman, Johan. *Gott und Mensch im Koran: Eine Strukturform religiöser Anthropologie anhand des Beispiels Allah und Muhammad*. Darmstadt, Germany: Wissenschaftliche Buchgesellschaft, 1977.

Bouyges, Maurice. *Essai de chronologie des œuvres de al-Ghazali (Algazel)*. Edited by M. Allard. Beirut: Imprimerie Catholique, 1959.

Calder, Norman. "The Limits of Islamic Orthodoxy." In *Defining Islam: A Reader*, edited by A. Rippin, 222–236. London: Equinox, 2007.

Cantwell-Smith, Wilfred. *The Meaning and End of Religion*. New York: Mentor Books, 1991.

Chittick, William C. "Ibn al-ʿArabī's Hermeneutics of Mercy." In *Mysticism and Sacred Scripture*, edited by S. T. Katz, 153–168. New York: Oxford University Press, 2000.

———. *Ibn 'Arabi: Heir to the Prophets*. Oxford: Oneworld, 2005.

———. *Imaginal Worlds: Ibn al-ʿArabī and the Problem of Religious Diversity*. Albany: State University of New York Press, 1994.

———. *The Self-Disclosure of God: Principles of Ibn al-ʿArabī's Cosmology*. Albany: State University of New York Press, 1998.

———. *The Sufi Path of Knowledge: Ibn al-ʿArabī's Metaphysics of Imagination*. Albany: State University of New York Press, 1989.

Chodkiewicz, Michel. *An Ocean without Shore: Ibn Arabi, the Book, and the Law*. Translated by D. Streight. Albany: State University of New York Press, 1993.

———. *Seal of the Saints: Prophethood and Sainthood in the Doctrine of Ibn ʿArabī*. Translated by L. Sherrard. Cambridge: Islamic Texts Society, 1993.

Clark, Elizabeth A. *The Origenist Controversy: The Cultural Construction of an Early Christian Debate*. Princeton, NJ: Princeton University Press, 1992.

Cook, David. *Studies in Muslim Apocalyptic*. Princeton, NJ: Darwin Press, 2002.

Cornell, Vincent. "Fruit of the Tree of Knowledge: The Relationship between Faith and Practice in Islam." In *The Oxford History of Islam*, edited by John L. Esposito, 63–105. New York: Oxford University Press, 1999.

———. "Practical Sufism: An Akbarian Basis for a Liberal Theology of Difference." *Journal of the Muhyiddin Ibn Arabi Society* 36 (2004): 59–84.

Cragg, Kenneth. *Jesus and the Muslim: An Exploration*. Oxford: Oneworld, 1999.

Craig, William Lane. *The Kalām Cosmological Argument*. Eugene, OR: Wipf and Stock, 2000.

Crone, Patricia. *God's Rule: Government and Islam*. New York: Columbia University Press, 2004.

Curtis, Edward E., IV. *Black Muslim Religion in the Nation of Islam, 1960–1975*. Chapel Hill: University of North Carolina Press, 2006.

al-Dānī, Abū ʿAmr. *al-Risāla al-wāfiya li-madhhab ahl al-sunna fī al-iʿtiqādāt wa-uṣūl al-diyānāt*. Edited by A. A. al-Rashīdī. Alexandria, Egypt: Dār al-Baṣīra, 2005.

D'Costa, Gavin. "John Hick's Transcendental Agnosticism." In *John Hick's Philosophy of Religion*, edited by H. Hewitt, 102–116. London: Macmillan, 1991.

———. *Theology and Religious Pluralism*. Oxford: Blackwell, 1986.

Delong-Bas, Natana J. *Wahhabi Islam: From Revival and Reform to Global Jihad*. Oxford: Oxford University Press, 2004.

Donner, Fred M. "From Believers to Muslims: Confessional Self-Identity in the Early Islamic Community." *Al-Abhath* 50–51 (2002–2003): 9–53.

———. *Muhammad and the Believers: At the Origins of Islam*. Cambridge, MA: Harvard University Press, 2010.

Dudoignon, Stéphane A., Hisao Komatsu, and Yasushi Kosugi, eds. *Intellectuals in the Modern Islamic World: Transmission, Transformation, Communication*. Abingdon, UK, and New York: Routledge, 2006.

Ebied, Rifaat, and David Thomas, eds. *Muslim–Christian Polemic during the Crusades: The Letter from the People of Cyprus and Ibn Abī Ṭālib al-Dimashqī's Response*. Leiden: Brill, 2005.

Eck, Diana L. *Encountering God: A Spiritual Journey from Bozeman to Banares*. Boston: Beacon Press, 1993.

Eklund, Ragnar. *Life between Death and Resurrection According to Islam*. Uppsala, Sweden: Almqvist and Wiksells, 1941.

El-Saleh, Soubhi. *La vie future selon le Coran*. Paris: J. Vrin, 1971.

Engineer, Asghar Ali. "Islam and Pluralism." In *The Myth of Religious Superiority: A Multifaith Exploration*, edited by P. Knitter, 211–219. Maryknoll, NY: Orbis, 2005.

———. *Rethinking Issues in Islam*. Mumbai: Orient Longman, 1998.

Esack, Farid. *Qur'ān, Liberation and Pluralism: An Islamic Perspective of Interreligious Solidarity against Oppression*. Oxford: Oneworld, 1997.

Esposito, John L. *Islam: The Straight Path*. 4th ed. New York: Oxford University Press, 2011.

———. *Unholy War: Terror in the Name of Islam*. New York: Oxford University Press, 2002.

———. *What Everyone Needs to Know about Islam*. New York: Oxford University Press, 2002.

Fakhry, Majid. *A History of Islamic Philosophy*. 3rd ed. New York: Columbia University Press, 2004.

———. "Philosophy and Theology: From the Eighth Century C.E. to the Present." In *The Oxford History of Islam*, edited by John L. Esposito, 269–303. New York: Oxford University Press, 1999.

"Fanā' al-nār 'ind Ibn Taymiyya wa-Ibn al-Qayyim." Fatwa 64739, July 16, 2005. Accessed October 3, 2011, http://www.islamweb.net/ver2/Fatwa/ShowFatwa.php?lang=A&Id=64739&Option=FatwaId.

Firestone, Reuven. *Children of Abraham: An Introduction to Judaism for Muslims*. New York: Ktav, 2001.

Friedmann, Yohanan. "Aḥmadīyah." In *The Oxford Encyclopedia of the Modern Islamic World*, vol. 1, edited by John L. Esposito, 81–85. New York: Oxford University Press, 2009.

———. *Prophecy Continuous: Aspects of Aḥmadī Religious Thought and Its Medieval Background*. Berkeley: University of California Press, 1989.

———. *Tolerance and Coercion in Islam: Interfaith Relations in the Muslim Tradition*. Cambridge: Cambridge University Press, 2003.

Fyzee, Asaf, trans. *A Shiite Creed*. London: Oxford University Press, 1942.

al-Ghazālī, Abū Ḥāmid. *Fayṣal al-tafriqa bayna al-Islām wa-l-zandaqa*. Edited by M. Bījū. Damascus: M. Bījū, 1993.

———. *Deliverance from Error: Five Key Texts Including His Spiritual Autobiography, al-Munqidh min al-Dalal*. Translated by R. McCarthy. Louisville, KY: Fons Vitae, 2000.

———. *Faḍā'il al-anām min rasā'il ḥujjat al-Islām*. Edited by N. al-Dīn. Tunis: al-Dār al-Tūnisiyya li-l-Nashr, 1972.

———. *Iḥyā' 'ulūm al-dīn*. 5 vols. Cairo: Dār al-Bayān al-'Arabī, [1990].

———. *al-Iqtiṣād fī al-i'tiqād*. Edited by M. M. Abū al-'Ilā. Cairo: Maktabat al-Jundī, 1972.

———. *Kīmiyā-yi sa'ādat*. Edited by M. 'Abbāsī. [Tehran]: Ṭulū' va Zarrīn, [1982].

———. *Kīmiyā-yi sa'ādat*. Translated by C. Field as *The Alchemy of Happiness*. London: J. Murray, 1909.

———. *Kitāb al-arba'īn fī uṣūl al-dīn*. Edited by 'A. 'Arwānī. Damascus: Dār al-Qalam, 2003.

———. *al-Maqṣad al-asnā fī sharḥ asmā' Allāh al-ḥusnā*. Translated by D. B. Burrell and N. Daher as *The Ninety-nine Beautiful Names of God*. Cambridge: Islamic Texts Society, 1995.

———. *al-Maqṣad al-asnā fī sharḥ ma'ānī asmā' Allāh al-ḥusnā*. Edited by F. Shehadi. Beirut: Dār al-Mashriq, 1971.

———. *Mishkāt al-anwār*. Edited by A. 'Afīfī. Cairo: al-Dār al-Qawmiyya li-l-Ṭibā'a wa-l-Nashr, 1964.

———. *Mishkāt al-anwār*. Translated by D. Buchman as *The Niche of Lights*. Provo, UT: Brigham Young University Press, 1998.

———. *Mishkāt al-anwār*. Translated by W. H. T. Gairdner as *Al-Ghazzali's Mishkat al-Anwar ("The Niche for Lights")*. Lahore, Pakistan: Sh. Muhammad Ashraf, 1952.

———. *al-Munqidh min al-ḍalāl*. Edited by M. Bījū. Damascus: Dār al-Taqwā, 1992.

———. *al-Mustaṣfā min 'ilm al-uṣūl*. Edited by M. S. al-Ashqar. 2 vols. Beirut: Mu'assasat al-Risāla, 1997.

———. *Tahāfut al-falāsifa*. Edited by M. Bouyges. Beirut: Imprimerie Catholique, 1927.

Gianotti, Timothy J. *Al-Ghazālī's Unspeakable Doctrine of the Soul: Unveiling the Esoteric Psychology and Eschatology of the Iḥyā'*. Leiden: Brill, 2001.

Griffel, Frank. *Apostasie und Toleranz im Islam: Die Entwicklung zu al-Gazalis Urteil gegen die Philosophie und die Reaktionen der Philosophen*. Leiden: Brill, 2000.

———. "Divine Actions, Creation, and the Human Fate after Death in 9th/15th-Century Imāmī Shi'ite Theology." *Journal of the American Oriental Society* 125 (2005): 67–78.

———. *Al-Ghazālī's Philosophical Theology*. New York: Oxford University Press, 2009.

Griffith, R. Marie. *Born Again Bodies: Flesh and Spirit in American Christianity*. Berkeley: University of California Press, 2004.

Gutas, Dimitri. *Greek Thought, Arabic Culture: The Graeco-Arabic Translation Movement in Baghdad and Early 'Abbāsid Society*. London: Routledge, 1998.

al-Ḥabashī, 'Abd Allāh. *al-Maqālāt al-sunniyya fī kashf ḍalālāt Aḥmad ibn Taymiyya*. Beirut: Dār al-Mashārī', 2004.

Haim, Sylvia, ed. *Arab Nationalism: An Anthology*. Berkeley: University of California Press, 1962.

Hallaq, Wael B. "Ibn Taymiyya on the Existence of God." *Acta Orientalia* 52 (1991): 49–69.

al-Ḥamawī, Yāqūt. *Kitāb mu'jam al-buldān*. 5 vols. Beirut: Dār Ṣādir, [1955–1957].

Hamza, Feras. *To Hell and Back: The Making of Temporary Hellfire in Early Muslim Exegesis*. Leiden: Brill, forthcoming.

al-Ḥarbī, 'Alī. *Kashf al-astār li-ibṭāl iddi'ā' fanā' al-nār: al-Mansūb li-shaykh al-Islām Ibn Taymiyya wa-tilmīdhihi Ibn Qayyim al-Jawziyya*. Mecca: Dār Ṭayba, 1990.

Harris, Sam. *The End of Faith: Religion, Terror, and the Future of Reason*. New York: W. W. Norton, 2005.

al-Hāshimī, 'Abd al-Mun'im. *Ibn Taymiyya: al-'Ālim al-jarī'*. Damascus: Dār Ibn Kathīr, 1993.

Heck, Paul L. "*Jihad* Revisited." *Journal of Religious Ethics* 32 (2004): 95–128.

Hermansen, Marcia K. "Shāh Walī Allāh of Delhi's *Ḥujjat Allāh Al-Bāligha*: Tensions between the Universal and the Particular in an Eighteenth-Century Islamic Theory of Religious Revelation." *Studia Islamica* 63 (1986): 143–157.

Hick, John. *The Metaphor of God Incarnate: Christology in a Pluralistic Age*. Louisville, KY: Westminster John Knox Press, 2006.

al-Ḥiṣnī, Taqī al-Dīn Abū Bakr. *Daf' shubah man shabbaha wa-tamarrada wa-nasaba dhālika ilā al-sayyid al-jalīl al-imām Aḥmad*. Edited by 'A. Muṣṭafā. Amman: Dār al-Rāzī, 2003.

Hoover, Jon. "Against Islamic Universalism: 'Alī al-Ḥarbī's 1990 Attempt to Prove that Ibn Taymiyya and Ibn Qayyim al-Jawziyya Affirm the Eternity of Hell-Fire." In *Neo-Hanbalism Reconsidered: The Impact of Ibn Taymiyya and Ibn Qayyim al-Jawziyya*, edited by G. Tamer and B. Krawietz. Berlin: de Gruyter, forthcoming.

———. *Ibn Taymiyya's Theodicy of Perpetual Optimism*. Leiden: Brill, 2007.

———. "Islamic Universalism: Ibn Qayyim al-Jawziyya's Salafī Deliberations on the Duration of Hell-Fire." *The Muslim World* 99 (2009): 181–201.

Hourani, Albert. *Arabic Thought in the Liberal Age, 1798–1939*. Cambridge: Cambridge University Press, 1983.

———. *A History of the Arab Peoples*. Cambridge, MA: Harvard University Press, 1991.

Hourani, George F. "A Revised Chronology of Ghazālī's Writings." *Journal of the American Oriental Society* 104 (1984): 289–302.

Huda, Qamar-ul. "Knowledge of Allah and the Islamic View of Other Religions." *Theological Studies* 64 (2003): 278–305.

al-Ḥumayd, ʿAbd al-Karīm ibn Ṣāliḥ. *al-Inkār ʿalā man lam yaʿtaqid khulūd wa-taʾbīd al-kuffār fī al-nār*. Buraydah, Saudi Arabia: Markaz al-Najīdī, 2001.

Ibn Abī al-ʿIzz al-Ḥanafī [or al-Dimashqī]. *Sharḥ al-ʿaqīda al-ṭaḥāwiyya*. Edited by M. Ḥ. al-Najdī. Riyadh: Aḍwāʾ al-Salaf, 2002.

Ibn al-ʿArabī, Muḥyī al-Dīn. *Fuṣūṣ al-ḥikam*. Edited by A. ʿAfīfī. Beirut: Dār al-Kutub al-ʿArabī, 1946.

———. *al-Futūḥāt al-makkiyya*. 4 vols. Beirut: Dār Ṣādir, [1968].

———. *Muḥāḍarat al-abrār wa-musāmarat al-akhyār fī al-adabīyyāt wa-l-nawādir wa-l-akhbār*. 2 vols. [Cairo]: Maṭbaʿat al-Saʿāda, 1906.

———. *Tadhkirat al-khawāṣṣ wa-ʿaqīdat ahl al-ikhtiṣāṣ*. Translated by R. Deladrière as *Ibn ʿArabî: La profession de foi*. Paris: Michel Allard, 1978.

———. *Tarjumān al-ashwāq*. Translated by R. A. Nicholson as *The Tarjumán Al-Ashwáq: A Collection of Mystical Odes*. London: Royal Asiatic Society, 1911.

Ibn ʿAṭiyya al-Andalusī. *al-Muḥarrar al-wajīz fī tafsīr al-kitāb al-ʿazīz*. Edited by ʿA. Muḥammad. 5 vols. Beirut: Dār al-Kutub al-ʿIlmiyya, 1993.

Ibn Ḥajar al-ʿAsqalānī. *al-Durar al-kāmina fī aʿyān al-miʾa al-thāmina*. Edited by M. S. J. al-Ḥaqq. 5 vols. Cairo: Dār al-Kutub al-Ḥadītha, 1966.

Ibn Ḥazm, ʿAlī ibn Aḥmad. *al-Iḥkām fī uṣūl al-aḥkām*. Edited by I. ʿAbbās. 8 vols. Beirut: Dār al-Āfāq al-Jadīda, 1980.

———. *Marātib al-ijmāʿ fī al-ʿibādāt wa-l-muʿāmalāt wa-l-iʿtiqādāt*. [Cairo]: Dār Zāhid al-Qudsī, [1983].

Ibn Kathīr, Ismāʿīl. *Tafsīr al-Qurʾān al-ʿaẓīm*. 7 vols. Beirut: Dār al-Andalus, 1966.

Ibn Qayyim al-Jawziyya, Shams al-Dīn Abū Bakr. *Asmāʾ Allāh al-ḥusnā*. Edited by Y. Bidīwī and A. al-Shawwā. Damascus: Dār Ibn Kathīr; and Beirut: Dār al-Kalim al-Ṭayyib, 1997.

———. *al-Dāʾ wa-l-dawāʾ*. Edited by ʿA. Ḥ. al-Ḥalabī al-Atharī. Riyadh: Dār Ibn al-Jawzī, 1996.

———. *al-Ḍawʾ al-munīr ʿalā al-tafsīr*. Edited by ʿA. Ḥ. al-Ṣāliḥī. 6 vols. Dakhnah, Saudi Arabia: Muʾassasat al-Nūr li-l-Ṭibāʿa wa-l-Tajlīd, 1995–1999.

———. *Ḥādī al-arwāḥ ilā bilād al-afrāḥ*. Edited by M. I. al-Zaghlī. Dammam, Saudi Arabia: Ramādī li-l-Nashr, 1997.

———. *Hidāyat al-ḥayārā fī ajwibat al-Yahūd wa-l-Naṣārā*. Edited by M. A. al-Ḥājj. Damascus: Dār al-Qalam, 1996.

———. *Ighāthat al-lahfān min maṣāyid al-Shayṭān*. Edited by M. S. Kīlānī. Cairo: Muṣṭafā al-Bābī al-Ḥalabī, 1961.

———. *Mukhtaṣar al-ṣawāʿiq al-mursala ʿalā al-Jahmiyya wa-l-Muʿaṭṭilla*. Abridgment by Muḥammad ibn al-Mawṣilī. Edited by Ḥ. ʿAbd al-Raḥmān al-ʿAlawī. 4 vols. Riyadh: Aḍwāʾ al-Salaf, 2004.

———. *Shifāʾ al-ʿalīl*. Edited by M. al-Shalabī. 2 vols. Jeddah: Maktabat al-Sawādī li-l-Tawzīʿ, 1991.

———. *Ṭarīq al-hijratayn wa-bāb al-saʿādatayn*. Edited by S. Ibrāhīm. Cairo: Dār al-Ḥadīth, 1991.

———. *al-Wābil al-ṣayyib min al-kalim al-ṭayyib*. Edited by S. Ibrāhīm. Cairo: Dār al-Ḥadīth, 1991.

———. *Zād al-maʿād fī hady khayr al-ʿibād*. Edited by S. al-Arnaʾūṭ and ʿA. al-Arnaʾūṭ. 6 vols. Beirut: Muʾassasat al-Risāla, 1994.

Ibn Rajab, ʿAbd al-Raḥmān. *al-Dhayl ʿalā Ṭabaqāt al-Ḥanābila*. Edited by M. Ḥ. al-Fiqī. 2 vols. Cairo: Maṭbaʿat al-Sunna al-Muḥammadiyya, 1952–1953.

Ibn Rushayyiq al-Maghribī. "Asmāʾ muʾallafāt Ibn Taymiyya." In *al-Jāmiʿ li-sīrat shaykh al-Islām Ibn Taymiyya (661–728) khilāl sabʿat qurūn*, edited by M. ʿU. Shams and ʿA. M. al-ʿImrān, 220–249. Mecca: Dār ʿĀlam al-Fawāʾid, 1999.

Ibn Taymiyya, Taqī al-Dīn Aḥmad. *Bayān talbīs al-Jahmiyya fī taʾsīs bidaʿihim al-kalāmiyya*. Edited by M. ʿA. Ibn Qāsim. 2 vols. Riyadh: Dār al-Qāsim, [2000].

———. *al-Fatwā al-ḥamawiyya al-kubrā*. Cairo: al-Maṭbaʿa al-Salafiyya, 1967.

———. *Iqtiḍāʾ al-ṣirāṭ al-mustaqīm mukhālafat aṣḥāb al-jaḥīm*. Edited by M. Ḥ. al-Fiqī. Cairo: Maṭbaʿat al-Sunna al-Muḥammadiyya, 1950.

———. *al-Jawāb al-ṣaḥīḥ li-man baddala dīn al-Masīḥ*. Edited by M. Ḥ. Ismāʿīl. 2 vols. Beirut: al-Maktaba al-ʿIlmiyya, 2003.

———. *al-Jawāb al-ṣaḥīḥ li-man baddala dīn al-Masīḥ*. Translated and edited by T. F. Michel as *A Muslim Theologian's Response to Christianity: Ibn Taymiyya's Al-Jawab Al-Sahih*. Delmar, NY: Caravan Books, 1984.

———. *Majmūʿ fatāwā shaykh al-Islām Aḥmad ibn Taymiyya*. 37 vols. Cairo: al-Shurafāʾ li-l-Ṭibāʿa wa-Taṣwīr al-Mustanadāt, 1979.

———. *Mardin: Hégire, fuite du péché et "demeure de l'Islam."* Translated by Yahya Michot. Beirut: Dar Al-Bouraq, 2004.

———. *Naqd Marātib al-ijmāʿ*. Beirut: 1978.

———. *al-Nubuwwāt*. Cairo: al-Maṭbaʿa al-Salafiyya, 1966.

———. *al-Radd ʿalā man qāla bi-fanāʾ al-janna wa-l-nār*. Edited by M. ʿA. al-Samharī. Riyadh: Dār al-Balansiyya, 1995.

———. *Sharḥ al-ʿaqīda al-aṣfahāniyya*. Edited by A. S. Aḥmad. Cairo: Dār al-Kutub al-Ḥadītha, 1966.

Ibn al-Wazīr, Abū ʿAbd Allāh. *Īthār al-ḥaqq ʿalā al-khalq: Fī radd al-khilāfāt ilā al-madhhab al-ḥaqq min uṣūl al-tawḥīd*. Cairo: Sharikat Ṭabʿ al-Kutub al-ʿArabiyya, [1900].

al-Ījī, ʿAḍud al-Dīn. *Kitāb al-mawāqif*. Commentary by al-Jurjānī. 3 vols. Beirut: Dār al-Jīl, 1997.

Iqbal, Sir Muhammad. *Islam and Ahmadism*. Lucknow, India: Academy of Islamic Research and Publications, 1974.

———. *The Reconstruction of Religious Thought*. Lahore, Pakistan: Shaikh Muhammad Ashraf, 1944.

Izutsu, Toshihiko. *The Concept of Belief in Islamic Theology: A Semantic Analysis of Îmân and Islâm*. New York: Books for Libraries, 1980.

———. *Ethico-religious Concepts in the Qur'ān*. Montreal: McGill University Press, 1966.

Jackson, Sherman A. "The Alchemy of Domination? Some Ash'arite Responses to Mu'tazilite Ethics." *International Journal of Middle East Studies* 31 (1999): 185–201.

———. "Domestic Terrorism in the Islamic Legal Tradition." *The Muslim World* 91 (2001): 293–310.

———. "Ibn Taymiyyah on Trial in Damascus." *Journal of Semitic Studies* 39 (1994): 41–85.

———. "Jihad and the Modern World." *Journal of Islamic Law and Culture* 7 (2002): 1–26.

———. *On the Boundaries of Theological Tolerance in Islam: Abū Ḥāmid al-Ghazālī's Fayṣal al-Tafriqa*. Karachi, Pakistan: Oxford University Press, 2002.

Jalal, Ayesha. *Partisans of Allah: Jihad in South Asia*. Cambridge, MA: Harvard University Press, 2008.

Jansen, J. J. G. "Ibn Taymiyyah and the Thirteenth Century: A Formative Period of Modern Muslim Radicalism." *Quaderni di Studi Arabi* 5–6 (1987–1988): 391–396.

———. *The Interpretation of the Koran in Modern Egypt*. Leiden: Brill, 1974.

al-Juwaynī, Imām al-Ḥaramayn. *Kitāb al-irshād ilā qawāṭiʿ al-adilla fī uṣūl al-iʿtiqād*. Edited by M. Y. Mūsā and ʿA. ʿAbd al-Ḥamīd. Cairo: Maktabat al-Khanjī, 1950.

al-Karmī, Marʿī ibn Yūsuf. *Tawqīf al-farīqayn ʿalā khulūd ahl al-dārayn*. Edited by K. al-Sabīʿī, with an introduction by ʿA. Ibn Jibrīn. Beirut: Dār Ibn Ḥazm, 1998.

al-Kāshānī, ʿAbd al-Razzāq (pseudo–Ibn ʿArabī). *Tafsīr al-Qur'ān al-karīm*. 2 vols. Beirut: Dār al-Yaqaẓa al-ʿArabiyya, 1968.

Keddie, Nikki R. *An Islamic Response to Imperialism: Political and Religious Writings of Sayyid Jamal ad-Din "al-Afghani."* Berkeley: University of California Press, 1968.

Khalidi, Tarif, ed. and trans. *The Muslim Jesus: Sayings and Stories in Islamic Literature*. Cambridge, MA: Harvard University Press, 2001.

Khalil, Mohammad Hassan. "Salvation and the 'Other' in Islamic Thought: The Contemporary Pluralism Debate (in English)." *Religion Compass* 5 (2011): 511–519.

Khan, Hafiz A. Ghaffar. "Shah Wali Allah." In *Routledge Encyclopedia of Philosophy*, vol. 8, edited by E. Craig, 732–735. London: Routledge, 1998.

Khān, Ḥasan Ṣiddīq. *Yaqẓat ūlī al-iʿtibār mimmā warada fī dhikr al-nār wa-aṣḥāb al-nār*. Edited by Z. Yūsuf. Cairo: Maṭbaʿat al-Imām, [1964].

Knietschke, W. "The Koran Doctrine of Redemption." *The Moslem World* 2 (1912): 60–65.

Knysh, Alexander D. *Ibn ʿArabi in the Later Islamic Tradition: The Making of a Polemical Image in Medieval Islam*. Albany: State University of New York Press, 1999.

———. "The Realms of Responsibility in Ibn 'Arabi's *al-Futuhat al-makkiya*." *Journal of the Muhyiddin Ibn Arabi Society* 31 (2002): 87–99.

Landolt, Hermann. "Ghazālī and 'Religionswissenschaft': Some Notes on the *Mishkāt al-Anwār*." *Asiatische Studien* 45 (1991): 19–72.

Lange, Christian. *Justice, Punishment, and the Medieval Muslim Imagination.* Cambridge: Cambridge University Press, 2008.

Laoust, Henri. "Ḥanābila." In *The Encyclopaedia of Islam,* 2nd ed., edited by P. Bearman et al. Leiden: Brill (Brill Online), 2011.

———. "Ibn Ḳayyim al-Djawziyya." In *The Encyclopaedia of Islam,* 2nd ed., edited by P. Bearman et al. Leiden: Brill (Brill Online), 2011.

———. "Ibn Taymiyya." In *The Encyclopaedia of Islam,* 2nd ed., edited by P. Bearman et al. Leiden: Brill (Brill Online), 2011.

Lari, Sayyid Mujtaba Musavi. *Resurrection Judgement and the Hereafter: Lessons on Islamic Doctrine (Book 3).* Translated by H. Algar. Qom, Iran: Foundation of Islamic Cultural Propagation in the World, 1992.

Legenhausen, Muhammad (Gary). "Islam and Religious Pluralism." *Al-Tawhid: A Quarterly Journal of Islamic Thought and Culture* 14 (1997): 115–154.

———. *Islam and Religious Pluralism.* London: Al-Hoda, 1999.

———. "A Muslim's Non-Reductive Religious Pluralism." In *Islam and Global Dialogue: Religious Pluralism and the Pursuit of Peace,* edited by Roger Boase, 51–73. Aldershot, UK: Ashgate, 2005.

———. "A Muslim's Proposal: Non-Reductive Religious Pluralism." Universität Innsbruck: Der Innsbrucker Theologische Leseraum, January 25, 2006. Accessed October 3, 2011, http://www.uibk.ac.at/theol/leseraum/texte/626.html.

———. "On the Plurality of Religious Pluralisms." *International Journal of Hekmat* 1 (Autumn 2009): 5–42.

Little, Donald P. "Did Ibn Taymiyya Have a Screw Loose?" *Studia Islamica* 41 (1975): 93–111.

———. "The Historical and Historiographical Significance of the Detention of Ibn Taymiyya." *International Journal of Middle East Studies* 4 (1973): 311–327.

Lory, Pierre. *Les commentaires ésotériques du Coran d'après ʿAbd al-Razzâq al-Qâshânî.* Paris: Les Deux Océans, 1980.

Madhany, al-Husein N. "Pooh-Poohing Pluralism: *Ijtihāding Ḥadīth* to Build a Theology of Exclusion." *The Muslim World* 98 (2008): 407–422.

al-Maḥallī, Jalāl al-Dīn, and Jalāl al-Dīn al-Suyūṭī. *Tafsīr al-Jalālayn.* Edited by Ṣ. al-Mubārakfūrī. Riyadh: Dār al-Salām, 2002.

al-Manāʿī, ʿĀʾisha bint Yūsuf. "ʿAqīdat fanāʾ al-nār: Bayna Ibn ʿArabī wa-Ibn Taymiyya wa-Ibn al-Qayyim." *Majallat markaz buḥūth al-sunna wa-l-sīra* 11 (2002): 86–141.

Manṣūr, Saʿīd Ḥ. *The World-View of al-Jāḥiẓ in Kitāb al-Ḥayawān.* Alexandria, Egypt: Dar al-Maaref, 1977.

Marshall, David. *God, Muhammad and the Unbelievers: A Qur'anic Study.* Surrey, UK: Curzon Press, 1999.

Martin, Richard C., and Mark R. Woodward. *Defenders of Reason in Islam: Muʿtazilism from Medieval School to Modern Symbol.* Oxford: Oneworld Publications, 1997.

Maududi, Abul Ala. *Ḥaqīqat-i-jihād.* Lahore, Pakistan: Taj, 1964.

———. *Tafhīm al-Qur'ān*. Translated by M. Akbar as *The Meaning of the Quran*. Edited by A. Kamal. 16 vols. Lahore, Pakistan: Islamic Publications, 1967–1988.

McAuliffe, Jane. "Exegetical Identification of the Ṣābi'ūn." *The Muslim World* 72 (1982): 95–106.

———. *Qur'ānic Christians: An Analysis of Classical and Modern Exegesis*. Cambridge: Cambridge University Press, 1991.

Moosa, Ebrahim. *Ghazālī and the Poetics of Imagination*. Chapel Hill: University of North Carolina Press, 2005.

Morris, James W. "Ibn 'Arabī and His Interpreters." *Journal of the American Oriental Society* 106 (1986): 539–551, 733–756; 107 (1987): 101–119.

Motahhari, Morteza. *'Adl ilāhī*. Qom, Iran: Ṣadrā, 1978.

Mourad, Suleiman Ali. *Early Islam between Myth and History: Al-Ḥasan al-Baṣrī (d. 110H/728CE) and the Formation of His Legacy in Classical Islamic Scholarship*. Leiden: Brill, 2006.

Muhammad, Elijah. *The Supreme Wisdom: Solution to the So-Called Negroes's Problem*. Atlanta: Messenger Elijah Muhammad Propagation Society, n.d.

———. *The Supreme Wisdom: Vol. 2*. Phoenix: Secretarius, 2006.

Murata, Sachiko, and William C. Chittick. *The Vision of Islam*. New York: Paragon House, 1994.

Mullā Ṣadrā. *al-Ḥikma al-muta'āliya fī al-Asfār al-'aqliyya al-arba'a*. Edited by R. Luṭfī, I. Amīnī, and F. A. Ummīd. 9 vols. Beirut: Dār Iḥyā' al-Turāth al-'Arabī, 1981.

———. *al-Ḥikma al-'arshiyya*. Translated by James Morris as *The Wisdom of the Throne: An Introduction to the Philosophy of Mulla Sadra*. Princeton, NJ: Princeton University Press, 1981.

———. *Tafsīr al-Qur'ān al-karīm*. Edited by M. Khwājawī. 7 vols. Qom, Iran: Intishārāt-i Bīdār, 1987–1990.

Naik, Zakir. "Will Humans Born in Non Muslim Family Be Punished by GOD? Dr Zakir Naik." Accessed October 3, 2011, http://www.youtube.com/watch?v=AuTdaxxUJlg.

———. "Will the Righteous Non Muslims Go to Heaven or Hell? Dr Zakir Naik." Accessed October 3, 2011, http://www.youtube.com/watch?v=HbSUkq5ePew.

Nasr, Seyyed Hossein. *The Garden of Truth: The Vision and Promise of Sufism, Islam's Mystical Tradition*. New York: HarperCollins, 2007.

———. *The Heart of Islam: Enduring Values for Humanity*. San Francisco: HarperCollins, 2004.

———. *Islamic Life and Thought*. Albany: State University of New York Press, 1981.

———. *Knowledge and the Sacred*. Albany: State University of New York Press, 1989.

———. "Mullā Ṣadrā and the Doctrine of the Unity of Being." *Philosophical Forum* 9 (1973): 153–161.

———. "Religion and Religions." In *The Religious Other: Towards a Muslim Theology of Other Religions in a Post-Prophetic Age*, edited by M. S. Umar, 59–81. Lahore, Pakistan: Iqbal Academy, 2008.

———. "Reply to Sally B. King." In *The Philosophy of Seyyed Hossein Nasr*, edited by L. E. Hahn, R. E. Auxier, and L. W. Stone Jr., 221–231. Chicago: Open Court, 2001.

———. *Sufi Essays*. London: George Allen and Unwin, 1972.

al-Nawawī, Yaḥyā ibn Sharaf. *al-Minhāj fī sharḥ Ṣaḥīḥ Muslim ibn al-Ḥajjāj*. 19 vols. Damascus: Dār al-Khayr, 1998.

———. *Rawḍat al-ṭālibīn*. 12 vols. Beirut: al-Maktab al-Islāmī, 1991.

Ormsby, Eric. "The Faith of Pharaoh: A Disputed Question in Islamic Theology." In *Reason and Inspiration in Islam: Theology, Philosophy and Mysticism in Muslim Thought*, edited by T. Lawson, 471–489. London: I. B. Taurus in association with the Institute of Ismaili Studies, 2005.

———. *Ghazali: The Revival of Islam*. Oxford: Oneworld, 2008.

———. *Theodicy in Islamic Thought: The Dispute over al-Ghazālī's "Best of All Possible Worlds."* Princeton, NJ: Princeton University Press, 1984.

O'Shaughnessy, Thomas. *Muhammad's Thoughts on Death: A Thematic Study of the Qur'anic Data*. Leiden: Brill, 1969.

———. "The Seven Names for Hell in the Koran." *Bulletin of the School of Oriental and African Studies* 24 (1961): 444–465.

al-Qaradawi, Yusuf. "Allāh lam yakhluq al-insān li-yuʿadhdhibahu wa-lan takhlud al-nufūs fī al-nār." *al-Ahrām al-ʿarabī*, July 19, 2002: 36–37.

———. *Fatāwā muʿāṣira*. 3 vols. Beirut: al-Maktab al-Islāmī, 2003.

al-Qurṭubī, Muḥammad ibn Aḥmad. *al-Jāmiʿ li-aḥkām al-Qurʾān*. Edited by ʿA. al-Turkī. 24 vols. Beirut: Muʾassasat al-Risāla, 2006.

———. *al-Tadhkira fī aḥwāl al-mawtā wa-umūr al-ākhira*. Edited by A. M. al-Basṭawīsī. 2 vols. Medina: Dār al-Bukhārī li-l-Nashr wa-l-Tawzīʿ, 1997.

Qutb, Sayyid. *Fī ẓilāl al-Qurʾān*. 6 vols. Beirut: Dār al-Shurūq, 1973–1974.

———. *Maʿālim fī al-ṭarīq*. Cairo: Dār al-Shurūq, [1970].

Race, Alan. *Christians and Religious Pluralism: Patterns in the Christian Theology of Religions*. Maryknoll, NY: Orbis Books, 1983.

Rahbar, Daud. *God of Justice: A Study in the Ethical Doctrine of the Qurʾān*. Leiden: Brill, 1960.

Rahman, Fazlur. *Major Themes of the Qur'an*. 2nd ed. Minneapolis: Bibliotheca Islamica, 1994.

Ramadan, Tariq. *The Quest for Meaning: Developing a Philosophy of Pluralism*. London: Allen Lane, 2010.

al-Rāzī, Fakhr al-Dīn. *Muḥaṣṣal afkār al-mutaqaddimīn wa-l-mutaʾakhkhirīn min al-ʿulamāʾ wa-l-ḥukamāʾ wa-l-mutakallimīn*. Edited by Ṭ. ʿA. Saʿd. Cairo: Maktabat al-Kulliyyāt al-Azhariyya, [1978].

———. *al-Tafsīr al-kabīr aw mafātīḥ al-ghayb*. 33 vols. Beirut: Dār al-Kutub al-ʿIlmiyya, 2004.

Reinhart, A. Kevin. *Before Revelation: The Boundaries of Muslim Moral Thought*. Albany: State University of New York Press, 1995.

Riḍā, Muḥammad Rashīd. *Tafsīr al-Qur'ān al-ḥakīm al-shahīr bi-tafsīr al-Manār*. 12 vols. Beirut: Dār al-Ma'rifa, 1970.

———. *Tārīkh al-ustādh al-imām al-shaykh Muḥammad 'Abduh*. 3 vols. Cairo: Maṭba'at al-Manār, 1906–1931.

———. *al-Waḥy al-muḥammadī*. Cairo: al-Majlis al-A'lā li-l-Shu'ūn al-Islāmiyya, 2000.

———, ed. *al-Manār*, 1898–1935. Cairo: Idārat Majallat al-Manār.

Rizvi, Sajjad H. *Mullā Ṣadrā Shīrāzī: His Life and Works and the Sources for Safavid Philosophy*. Oxford: Oxford University Press, 2007.

———. "A Primordial *e pluribus unum*? Exegeses on Q. 2:213 and Contemporary Muslim Discourses on Religious Pluralism." *Journal of Qur'anic Studies* 6 (2004): 21–42.

Robson, James. "Is the Moslem Hell Eternal?" *The Moslem World* 28 (1938): 386–396.

Rūmī, Jalāl al-Dīn. *Discourses of Rumi*. Translated by A. J. Arberry. London: John Murray, 1961.

———. *Rūmī: Poet and Mystic (1207–1273)*. Translated by R. A. Nicholson. London: George Allen and Unwin, 1964.

Rustom, Mohammed. "Is Ibn al-'Arabī's Ontology Pantheistic?" *Journal of Islamic Philosophy* 2 (2006): 53–67.

———. "The Nature and Significance of Mullā Ṣadrā's Qur'ānic Writings." *Journal of Islamic Philosophy* 6 (2010): 109–130.

———. *The Triumph of Mercy: Philosophy and Scripture in Mullā Ṣadrā*. Albany: State University of New York Press, forthcoming.

Rustomji, Nerina. *The Garden and the Fire: Heaven and Hell in Islamic Culture*. New York: Columbia University Press, 2008.

Ruthven, Malise. "Introduction." In *Islamic Interpretations of Christianity*, edited by L. Ridgeon, xi–xx. New York: St. Martin's Press, 2001.

Ryad, Umar. *Islamic Reformism and Christianity: A Critical Reading of the Works of Muḥammad Rashīd Riḍā and His Associates (1898–1935)*. Leiden: Brill, 2009.

Saab, Hassan. "Communication between Christianity and Islam." *Middle East Journal* 18 (1964): 41–62.

Sachedina, Abdulaziz. "Is Islamic Revelation an Abrogation of Judeo-Christian Revelation?" *Concilium: International Review of Theology* 3 (1994): 94–102.

———. *The Islamic Roots of Democratic Pluralism*. Oxford: Oxford University Press, 2001.

———. "The Qur'ān and Other Religions." In *The Cambridge Companion to the Qur'ān*, edited by J. McAuliffe, 291–309. Cambridge: Cambridge University Press, 2006.

al-Ṣafadī, Ṣalāḥ al-Dīn. *A'yān al-'aṣr wa-a'wān al-naṣr*. Edited by 'A. Abū Zayd. 6 vols. Beirut: Dār al-Fikr al-Mu'āṣir, 1998.

Salvatore, Armando. "Beyond Orientalism? Max Weber and the Displacements of 'Essentialism' in the Study of Islam." In *Defining Islam: A Reader*, edited by A. Rippin, 148–172. London: Equinox, 2007.

al-Ṣanʿānī, Muḥammad ibn Ismāʿīl. *Rafʿ al-astār li-ibṭāl adillat al-qāʾilīn bi-fanāʾ al-nār*. Edited by M. N. al-Albānī. Beirut: al-Maktab al-Islāmī, 1984.

Schacht, Joseph. "Al-Subkī." In *The Encyclopaedia of Islam*, 2nd ed., edited by P. Bearman et al. Leiden: Brill (Brill Online), 2011.

Schuon, Frithjof. *The Transcendent Unity of Religions*. 2nd ed. Translated by P. Townsend. Wheaton, IL: Theosophical Publishing House, 1993.

Sells, Michael. *Approaching the Qurʾán: The Early Revelations*. Ashland, OR: White Cloud Press, 1999.

Sezgin, Fuat. *Geschichte des arabischen Schrifttums*, vol. 1. Leiden: Brill, 1967.

Shah-Kazemi, Reza. *Common Ground between Islam and Buddhism*. Louisville, KY: Fons Vitae, 2010.

———. *The Other in the Light of the One: The Universality of the Qurʾān and Interfaith Dialogue*. Cambridge: Islamic Texts Society, 2006.

Shahin, Emad Eldin. "Rashīd Riḍā, Muḥammad." In *The Oxford Encyclopedia of the Modern Islamic World*, vol. 4, edited by John L. Esposito, 508–510. New York: Oxford University Press, 2009.

———. "Salafīyah." In *The Oxford Encyclopedia of the Modern Islamic World*, vol. 5, edited by John L. Esposito, 28–35. New York: Oxford University Press, 2009.

al-Shahrastānī, Muḥammad ibn ʿAbd al-Karīm. *al-Milal wa-l-niḥal*. Edited by ʿA. al-Wakīl. Beirut: Dār al-Fikr, n.d.

Shahrur, Muhammad. *al-Kitāb wa-l-Qurʾān: Qirāʾa muʿāṣira*. Damascus: Dār al-Ahālī, 1990.

Shaltout, Mahmoud. *al-Islām ʿaqīda wa-sharīʿa*. Cairo: Dār al-Shurūq, 1990.

———. *Tafsīr al-Qurʾān al-karīm*. Cairo: Dār al-Qalam, 1966.

al-Sharabāṣī, Aḥmad. *Rashīd Riḍā al-ṣiḥāfī al-mufassir al-shāʿir al-lughawī*. Cairo: al-Hayʾa al-ʿĀmma li-Shuʾūn al-Maṭābiʿ al-Amīriyya, 1977.

al-Shawkānī, Muḥammad. *Fatḥ al-qadīr*. 5 vols. Cairo: Muṣṭafā al-Bābī al-Ḥalabī, 1964.

al-Shinqīṭī, Muḥammad. *Dafʿ īhām al-iḍṭirāb ʿan āyāt al-kitāb*. Cairo: Maṭbaʿat al-Madanī, [1970].

Sivan, Emmanuel. "Ibn Taymiyya: Father of the Islamic Revolution: Medieval Theology and Modern Politics." *Encounter* 60, no. 5 (1983): 41–50.

Smith, Jane. *A Historical and Semantic Study of the Term "Islām" as Seen in a Sequence of Qurʾān Commentaries*. Missoula, MT: Scholars Press, 1975.

———. "Old French Travel Accounts of Muslim Beliefs Concerning the Afterlife." In *Christian-Muslim Encounters*, edited by Y. Haddad and W. Haddad, 221–241. Gainesville: University Press of Florida, 1995.

Smith, Jane, and Yvonne Haddad. *The Islamic Understanding of Death and Resurrection*. Oxford: Oxford University Press, 2002.

Soroush, Abdolkarim. *Reason, Freedom, and Democracy in Islam*. New York: Oxford University Press, 2002.

———. *Ṣirāṭhā-yi mostaqīm*. Tehran: Serat, 1998.

St. Clair-Tisdall, W. *The Sources of Islam: A Persian Treatise*. Translated and edited by W. Muir. Edinburgh: T. and T. Clark, 1901.

Stewart, Devin. "Notes on Medieval and Modern Emendations of the Qur'ān." In *The Qur'ān in Its Historical Context*, edited by G. S. Reynolds, 225–248. London: Routledge, 2008.

Stöckle, Johannes. *The Doctrine of Islam and Christian Belief: Common Ground and Differences*. Bonn: Verlag für Kultur und Wissenschaft, 1997.

al-Subkī, Taqī al-Dīn ʿAlī ibn ʿAbd al-Kāfī. *al-Rasāʾil al-subkiyya: Fī al-radd ʿalā Ibn Taymiyya wa-tilmīdhihi Ibn Qayyim al-Jawziyya*. Beirut: ʿĀlam al-Kutub, 1983.

———. *Shifāʾ al-saqām fī ziyārat khayr al-anām*. Hyderabad: [1897].

al-Ṭabarī, Muḥammad ibn Jarīr. *Jāmiʿ al-bayān ʿan taʾwīl āy al-Qurʾān*. Edited by A. al-Bakrī, M. Muḥammad, M. Khalaf, and M. ʿAbd al-Ḥamīd. 10 vols. Cairo: Dār al-Salām, 2007.

al-Taftāzānī, Saʿd al-Dīn. *Sharḥ al-ʿaqāʾid al-nasafiyya*. Edited by K. Salāma. Damascus: Wizārat al-Thaqāfa wa-l-Irshād al-Qawmī, 1974.

Thomassen, Einar. "Islamic Hell." *Numen* 56 (2009): 401–416.

Treiger, Alexander. "Monism and Monotheism in al-Ghazālī's *Mishkāt al-anwār*." *Journal of Qur'anic Studies* 9 (2007): 1–27.

Troll, Christian W. "The Salvation of Non-Muslims: Views of Some Eminent Muslim Religious Thinkers." In *Reason and Tradition in Islamic Thought*, edited by M. Haq, 175–190. Aligarh, India: Institute of Islamic Studies, Aligarh Muslim University, 1992.

al-ʿUthmān, ʿAbd al-Karīm. *Sīrat al-Ghazālī wa-aqwāl al-mutaqaddimīn fīh*. Damascus: Dār al-Fikr, [1960].

van Ess, Josef. "Das Begrenzte Paradies." In *Mélanges D'Islamologie: Volume dédié à la mémoire de Armand Abel par ses collègues, ses élèves et ses amis*, edited by P. Salmon, 108–127. Leiden: Brill, 1974.

Vasalou, Sophia. *Moral Agents and Their Deserts: The Character of Muʿtazilite Ethics*. Princeton, NJ: Princeton University Press, 2008.

Keller, Carl-A. "Perceptions of Other Religions in Sufism." In *Muslim Perceptions of Other Religions: A Historical Survey*, edited by Jean J. Waardenburg, 181–194. New York: Oxford University Press, 1999.

Walī Allāh, Shāh. *al-Budūr al-bāzigha*. Translated by J. M. S. Baljon as *Full Moon Appearing on the Horizon*. Lahore, Pakistan: Sh. Muhammad Ashraf, 1990.

———. *Fuyūḍ al-Ḥaramayn*. Karachi: Muḥammad Saʿīd, n.d.

———. *Ḥujjat Allāh al-bāligha*. Translated by Marcia Hermansen as *The Conclusive Argument from God: Shāh Walī Allāh of Delhi's Ḥujjat Allāh al-Bāligha*. Leiden: Brill, 1996.

———. *al-Khayr al-kathīr*. Cairo: Maktabat al-Qāhira, 1974.

———. *al-Tafhīmāt al-ilāhiyya*. 2 vols. Hyderabad: Shāh Walī Allāh Academy, 1973.

Watt, W. Montgomery. "The Christianity Criticized in the Qur'an." *The Muslim World* 57 (1967): 197–201.

———. "A Forgery in al-Ghazālī's *Mishkāt*?" *Journal of the Royal Asiatic Society* 81 (1949): 5–22.

———. *Islamic Philosophy and Theology*. Chicago: Aldine Transaction, 2008.

———. *Muslim Intellectual: A Study of al-Ghazali*. Edinburgh: Edinburgh University Press, 1963.

———. *What Is Islam?* London: Longman, 1979.

———, trans. *Islamic Creeds: A Selection*. Edinburgh: Edinburgh University Press, 1994.

Weber, Max. *The Sociology of Religion*. Translated by E. Fischoff. New York: Beacon Press, 1963.

Wensinck, A. J. *al-Muʿjam al-mufahras li-alfāẓ al-ḥadīth al-nabawī* (Concordance et indices de la tradition musulmane). 8 vols. Leiden: Brill, 1936–1988.

Winter, Michael. "A Polemical Treatise by ʿAbd al-Ġanī al-Nābulusī against a Turkish Scholar on the Religious Status of the Ḏimmīs." *Arabica* 35 (1988): 92–103.

Winter, T. J. (Abdal-Hakim Murad). "Book Review of Farid Esack's Qur'an, Liberation and Pluralism, Oxford: Oneworld, 1997." Accessed October 3, 2011, http://www.masud.co.uk/ISLAM/ahm/esack.htm.

———. "Ibn Kemāl (d. 940/1534) on Ibn ʿArabī's Hagiology." In *Sufism and Theology*, edited by A. Shihadeh, 137–157. Edinburgh: Edinburgh University Press, 2007.

———. "The Last Trump Card: Islam and the Supersession of Other Faiths." *Studies in Interreligious Dialogue* 9 (1999): 133–155.

———. "Pluralism from a Muslim Perspective." In *Abraham's Children: Jews, Christians and Muslims in Conversation*, edited by N. Soloman, R. Harries, and T. J. Winter, 202–211. Edinburgh: T and T Clark, 2006.

Yahia, Osman. *Histoire et classification de l'œuvre d'Ibn ʿArabi*. 2 vols. Damascus: Institut Français de Damas, 1964.

Yahya, Harun. *Basic Tenets of Islam*. Edited by D. Livingstone. New Delhi: Islamic Book Service, 2002.

Yusuf [Hanson], Hamza. "Buddha in the Qur'ān?" In Reza Shah-Kazemi, *Common Ground between Islam and Buddhism*, 113–136. Louisville, KY: Fons Vitae, 2010.

———. "Who Are the Disbelievers?" *Seasons: The Journal of Zaytuna Institute* 5 (Spring 2008): 31–50.

al-Zamakhsharī, Abū al-Qāsim. *al-Kashshāf ʿan ḥaqāʾiq al-tanzīl wa-ʿuyūn al-aqāwīl fī wujūh al-taʾwīl*. Edited by ʿA. al-Mahdī. 4 vols. Beirut: Dār Iḥyāʾ al-Turāth al-ʿArabī, 2001.

Zwemer, Samuel M. *A Moslem Seeker after God*. New York: Fleming H. Revell, 1920.

Index

abad/abadan (from ʾ-*b*-*d*), 15, 46, 95, 131, 193n147, 207n99
"for a long time", 82, 105–6, 127, 197n197
"forever", 89, 96, 98, 103, 106, 133, 190n115
meaning of, 15, 103, 130, 193n146
ʿAbduh, Muḥammad (d. 1905), 111–113, 116, 120–121, 125–126, 132, 153n31, 201n6, 202n8, 202n22, 203n30, 206n77
Abraham, 10, 30, 61, 66, 114, 152n24, 154n34, 163n29
Abrahamic (traditions), 138
Abrahamov, Binyamin, 16, 21, 196n184
abrogated
laws, 29, 58, 114, 137
message, 76, 142, 165n58
verses, 8, 138, 153n27, 187n72, 206n87
Abū Ḥanīfa (d. 150/767), 156n50
Abū al-Hudhayl (d. 226/840), 186n59
Abū Hurayra (d. 58/678), 83, 96, 127
Abū Jahl, 91
Abū al-Khaṭṭāb (d. 410/1116), 78
Abū Lahab, 6, 15, 77, 107, 130
Abū Ṭālib, 77
Abul Quasem, Muhammad, 12
accident(al), nature of sin, 72
accidents (philosophical sense), 63–65, 81, 156n49
acts, of God, 84, 98
acts. *See* deeds
Adam, 40, 54, 152n21, 174n12, 200n215
Children of, 27, 60, 151n16
descendants of, 5
ʿ*adhāb* (from ʿ-*dh*-*b*), 63, 66, 71. *See also* punishment/chastisement
al-Afghānī, Jamāl al-Dīn (d. 1897), 111, 201n3
afterlife. *See* hereafter/afterlife
ages (*aḥqāb/aḥqāban*), 15, 83, 101, 103, 123, 131, 133, 186n70, 187n71, 187n72, 190n119, 193n145, 197n198
meaning/duration of, 83, 90, 97, 106
agnosticism, 141
agnostics, 6, 38, 52, 137
Aḥmad, Mirzā Ghulām (d. 1908), 102
Ahmadiyya, 102, 104, 106, 200n213
al-Albānī, Muḥammad Nāṣir al-Dīn (d. 1999), 87, 188n94, 194n165, 195n175, 196n180
Ali, A. Yusuf (d. 1953), 105, 195n166, 198n210, 212n176
ʿAlī ibn Abī Ṭālib (d. 40/661), 99

Index of Qur'anic Verses